THE HEALTH CARE SYSTEM

ISSN 1543-2556

THE HEALTH CARE SYSTEM

Barbara Wexler

INFORMATION PLUS® REFERENCE SERIES
Formerly published by Information Plus, Wylie, Texas

THOMSON

GALE

Detroit • New York • San Francisco • San Diego • New Haven, Conn. • Waterville, Maine • London • Munich

THOMSON

GALE

The Health Care System

Barbara Wexler

Paula Kepos, Series Editor

Project Editor
John McCoy

Permissions
Margaret Abendroth, Edna Hedblad, Emma Hull

Composition and Electronic Prepress
Evi Seoud

Manufacturing
Drew Kalasky

LIBRARY OF CONGRESS CATALOGING-IN-PUBLICATION DATA

ISBN 0-7876-5103-6 (set)
ISBN 0-7876-9077-5
ISSN 1543-2556

Printed in the United States of America
10 9 8 7 6 5 4 3 2 1

TABLE OF CONTENTS

The health of the nation depends on access to and availability of health care. This chapter describes the components of the health care system in the United States and the characteristics of both people who receive regular medical care and those who do not have access to it.

Modern health care treatment requires that its practitioners have a great deal of training and skill. This chapter examines the training, working conditions, and earnings of health care practitioners, along with physician-patient communication.

Many different types of health care institutions exist in the United States, including hospitals, hospices, nursing homes, home health care, and mental health facilities; each is profiled here. Among the issues discussed are the plight of public hospitals and the rapid rise of home health care agencies.

There are a variety of measures of health care quality; the professional, government, and voluntary organizations and agencies charged with evaluating quality are described in this chapter. Included are examples and descriptions of the fraud, abuse, and mistakes that compromise quality care. Also considered are efforts to standardize and regulate the quality of medical care, including medical practice guidelines, professional licensure, institutional accreditation, and peer review.

Americans are spending an increasing amount of money on health care, with the money coming from both private and public funds. This chapter explores the types of services that Americans pay for, the reasons for cost increases, and what can be done about controlling sky-

rocketing costs. Programs such as Medicare, Medicaid, and long-term health care are also discussed.

Many factors affect the availability of health insurance, including employment, income, and age. Sources of health insurance—for those who can afford it or are eligible to receive it—are private insurance, Medicare, and Medicaid. Although many Americans, including millions of children, are uninsured, government programs and legislation have been designed to reverse this strain on American society.

This chapter begins with a comparison of expenditures for health care. It contains a comparison of key health care quality indicators and concludes with overviews of the health care systems in the United States, Germany, Canada, United Kingdom, France, and Japan.

The delivery of health care services has changed dramatically since the 1950s. The Internet and advancing technology have produced new methods of health care delivery such as telemedicine and online pharmaceutical services. This chapter describes challenges faced by the U.S. health care system, recent innovations, and efforts to improve quality in health service delivery.

Consumer satisfaction or dissatisfaction with health care has an impact on utilization, reimbursement, and even health outcomes—how well patients fare after treatment. This chapter looks at how consumers assess quality and the evaluative measures that providers and payers use to monitor consumer satisfaction with care and treatment.

PREFACE

The Health Care System is part of the *Information Plus Reference Series*. The purpose of each volume of the series is to present the latest facts on a topic of pressing concern in modern American life. These topics include today's most controversial and most studied social issues: abortion, capital punishment, care for the elderly, crime, health care, the environment, immigration, minorities, social welfare, women, youth, and many more. Although written especially for the high school and undergraduate student, this series is an excellent resource for anyone in need of factual information on current affairs.

By presenting the facts, it is Thomson Gale's intention to provide its readers with everything they need to reach an informed opinion on current issues. To that end, there is a particular emphasis in this series on the presentation of scientific studies, surveys, and statistics. These data are generally presented in the form of tables, charts, and other graphics placed within the text of each book. Every graphic is directly referred to and carefully explained in the text. The source of each graphic is presented within the graphic itself. The data used in these graphics are drawn from the most reputable and reliable sources, in particular from the various branches of the U.S. government and from major independent polling organizations. Every effort has been made to secure the most recent information available. The reader should bear in mind that many major studies take years to conduct, and that additional years often pass before the data from these studies are made available to the public. Therefore, in many cases the most recent information available in 2005 dated from 2002 or 2003. Older statistics are sometimes presented as well, if they are of particular interest and no more recent information exists.

Although statistics are a major focus of the *Information Plus Reference Series*, they are by no means its only content. Each book also presents the widely held positions and important ideas that shape how the book's subject is discussed in the United States. These positions are explained in detail and, where possible, in the words of their proponents. Some of the other material to be found in these books includes: historical background; descriptions of major events related to the subject; relevant laws and court cases; and examples of how these issues play out in American life. Some books also feature primary documents, or have pro and con debate sections giving the words and opinions of prominent Americans on both sides of a controversial topic. All material is presented in an even-handed and unbiased manner; the reader will never be encouraged to accept one view of an issue over another.

HOW TO USE THIS BOOK

The U.S. health care system is a multi-faceted establishment consisting of health care providers, patients, and treatment facilities, just to name a few components. This book examines the state of the nation's health care system, the education and training of health care providers, and the various types of health care institutions. The ever-increasing cost of health care, prevalence of insurance, and a comparison of health care throughout the world are also covered.

The Health Care System consists of nine chapters and three appendices. Each of the chapters is devoted to a particular aspect of the health care system in the United States. For a summary of the information covered in each chapter, please see the synopses provided in the Table of Contents at the front of the book. Chapters generally begin with an overview of the basic facts and background information on the chapter's topic, then proceed to examine subtopics of particular interest. For example, Chapter 3: Health Care Institutions begins with a brief history of hospitals in the United States and describes the different types of hospitals and the patients they serve. Explored next are other health care facilities commonly utilized, including surgical centers and urgent care facilities; long-term care facilities such as nursing homes; mental health facilities; home health care; and hospice. The chapter concludes with a discussion of managed care organizations, highlighting health maintenance organizations (HMOs) and preferred provider organizations (PPOs). Readers can find their way through a chapter by looking for the section and subsection headings, which are clearly set off from the text. Or, they can refer to the book's extensive index if they already know what they are looking for.

Statistical Information

The tables and figures featured throughout *The Health Care System* will be of particular use to the reader in learning about this issue. These tables and figures represent an extensive collection of the most recent and important statistics on the health care system, as well as related issues—for example, graphics in the book cover the rate of home health care usage; number of emergency department visits; national health expenditure amounts; percent of people without health insurance; and public opinion on the state of the health care system. Thomson Gale believes that making this information available to the reader is the most important way in which we fulfill the goal of this book: to help readers understand the issues and controversies surrounding the health care system in the United States and reach their own conclusions.

Each table or figure has a unique identifier appearing above it, for ease of identification and reference. Titles for the tables and figures explain their purpose. At the end of each table or figure, the original source of the data is provided.

In order to help readers understand these often complicated statistics, all tables and figures are explained in the text. References in the text direct the reader to the relevant statistics. Furthermore, the contents of all tables and figures are fully indexed. Please see the opening section of the index at the back of this volume for a description of how to find tables and figures within it.

Appendices

In addition to the main body text and images, *The Health Care System* has three appendices. The first is the Important Names and Addresses directory. Here the reader will find contact information for a number of government and private organizations that can provide further information on aspects of the health care system. The second appendix is the Resources section, which can also assist the reader in conducting his or her own research. In this section, the author and editors of *The Health Care System* describe some of the sources that were most useful during the compilation of this book. The final appendix is the index. It has been greatly expanded from previous editions, and should make it even easier to find specific topics in this book.

ADVISORY BOARD CONTRIBUTIONS

The staff of Information Plus would like to extend their heartfelt appreciation to the Information Plus Advisory Board. This dedicated group of media professionals provides feedback on the series on an ongoing basis. Their comments allow the editorial staff who work on the project to make the series better and more user-friendly. Our top priorities are to produce the highest-quality and most useful books possible, and the Advisory Board's contributions to this process are invaluable.

The members of the Information Plus Advisory Board are:

- Kathleen R. Bonn, Librarian, Newbury Park High School, Newbury Park, California

- Madelyn Garner, Librarian, San Jacinto College— North Campus, Houston, Texas

- Anne Oxenrider, Media Specialist, Dundee High School, Dundee, Michigan

- Charles R. Rodgers, Director of Libraries, Pasco-Hernando Community College, Dade City, Florida

- James N. Zitzelsberger, Library Media Department Chairman, Oshkosh West High School, Oshkosh, Wisconsin

COMMENTS AND SUGGESTIONS

The editors of the *Information Plus Reference Series* welcome your feedback on *The Health Care System* Please direct all correspondence to:

Editors
Information Plus Reference Series
27500 Drake Rd.
Farmington Hills, MI 48331-3535

CHAPTER 1

THE NATION'S HEALTH CARE SYSTEM

When asked to describe the U.S. health care system, most Americans would probably offer a description of just a single facet of a huge, complex interaction of people, institutions, and technology. Like snapshots, each account offers an image, frozen in time, of one of the many health care providers and the settings in which medical care is delivered. Examples of these include the following:

• Physician offices: For many Americans health care may be described as the interaction between a primary care physician and patient to address minor and urgent medical problems such as colds, flu, or back pain. A primary care physician (usually a general practitioner, family practitioner, internist, or pediatrician) is the "frontline" caregiver—the first practitioner to evaluate and treat the patient. Routine physical examinations, prevention such as immunization and health screening to detect disease, and treatment of acute and chronic diseases commonly take place in physicians' offices.

• Medical clinics: These settings provide primary care services comparable to those provided in physicians' offices and may be organized to deliver specialized support such as prenatal care for expectant mothers, well-baby care for infants, or treatment for specific medical conditions such as hypertension (high blood pressure), diabetes, or asthma.

• Hospitals: These institutions contain laboratories, imaging centers (also known as radiology departments, where X-rays and other imaging studies are performed), and other equipment for diagnosis and treatment, as well as emergency departments, operating rooms, and highly trained personnel.

Medical care is provided through many other avenues, including outpatient surgical centers, school health programs, pharmacies, worksite clinics, and voluntary health agencies such as Planned Parenthood, the American Red Cross, and the American Lung Association.

IS THE U.S. HEALTH CARE SYSTEM AILING?

While medical care in the United States is often considered the best available, some observers feel the system that delivers it is fragmented and in serious disarray. A report from the Institute of Medicine (IOM) of the National Academies, *Crossing the Quality Chasm: A New Health System for the 21st Century* (Washington, DC: Committee on Quality of Health Care in America, Institute of Medicine, 2001), described the nation's health care system as disjointed, inefficient, and in need of a major overhaul.

Dr. John P. Geyman, a retired physician and professor emeritus at the University of Washington in Seattle, believes that U.S. health care does not compare favorably with services provided in other industrialized Western nations. In *Health Care in America: Can Our Ailing System Be Healed?* (Boston, MA: Butterworth-Heinemann, 2002), Dr. Geyman contends that escalating costs and wide variations in access and quality are symptoms of our diseased health care delivery system.

Dr. Geyman cited the nearly forty-three million uninsured Americans (15% of the total 288 million people estimated by the U.S. Census Bureau to be living in the United States in 2002) and the fact that the United States has the highest health care expenditures of any of the world's other twenty-eight industrialized countries as indicators of serious systemic problems. By 2004 the Census Bureau estimated the number of uninsured Americans had exceeded 44 million. Dr. Geyman also noted that for eleven key indicators of health care quality (including measures of life expectancy at different ages) the United States earned tenth place or lower when ranked among thirteen industrialized nations. Dr. Geyman also observed that among comparable Western industrialized countries, the U.S. population is the only one without universal health insurance.

Dr. Geyman contends that the traditional approaches to solving health care delivery problems have been ineffective because they are incremental—shortsighted and piecemeal—rather than broad changes intended to provide optimal health care services to the greatest number of people. Global reform of health care financing is one solution Dr. Geyman offers to improve the system. He advocates a single-payer system, under which the government would pay for universal coverage but leave delivery under private control, intervening only as needed to improve access, affordability, and quality.

Other physicians, including Dr. Rudolph Mueller, a specialist in internal medicine just beginning his medical career, agree with Dr. Geyman's assessment. In *As Sick as It Gets: The Shocking Reality of America's Healthcare, A Diagnosis and Treatment Plan* (Dunkirk, NY: Olin Frederick, 2001), Dr. Mueller cited statistics to support the premise that the American health care system spends more money than other countries to deliver poorer results. Dr. Robert Lebow, a family practice physician who dedicated his career to serving indigent patients, offered still another scathing indictment of the health care system in *Health Care Meltdown: Confronting the Myths and Fixing Our Failing System* (Chambersburg, PA: Alan C. Hood & Co, 2003). Like Dr. Geyman, Dr. Lebow calls for a single-payer system to correct inefficiencies and equitably distribute health care resources to uninsured and underinsured Americans.

THE COMPONENTS OF THE HEALTH CARE SYSTEM

The health care system consists of all personal medical care services—prevention, diagnosis, treatment, and rehabilitation (services to restore function and independence)—plus the institutions and personnel that provide these services and the government, public, and private organizations and agencies that finance service delivery.

The health care system may be viewed as a complex made up of three interrelated components: people in need of health care services, called health care consumers; people who deliver health care services—the professionals and practitioners called health care providers; and the systematic arrangements for delivering health care—the public and private agencies that organize, plan, regulate, finance, and coordinate services—called the institutions or organizations of the health care system. The institutional component includes hospitals, clinics, and home-health agencies; the insurance companies and programs that pay for services like Blue Cross/Blue Shield, managed-care plans such as health maintenance organizations (HMOs), and preferred provider organizations (PPOs); and entitlement programs like Medicare and Medicaid (federal and state government public assistance programs). Other institutions are the professional schools that train students for careers in medical, public health, dental, and allied health professions, such as nursing. Also included are agencies and associations that research and monitor the quality of health care services; license and accreditation providers and institutions; local, state, and national professional societies; and the companies that produce medical technology, equipment, and pharmaceuticals.

Much of the interaction among the three components of the health care system occurs directly between individual health care consumers and providers. Other interactions are indirect and impersonal such as immunization programs or screening to detect disease, performed by public health agencies for whole populations. All health care delivery does, however, depend on interactions among all three components. The ability to benefit from health care depends on an individual's or group's ability to gain entry to the health care system. The process of gaining entry to the health care system is referred to as access, and many factors can affect access to health care. This chapter provides an overview of how Americans access the health care system.

ACCESS TO THE HEALTH CARE SYSTEM

Today, access to health care services is a key measure of the overall health and prosperity of a nation or a population, but access and availability were not always linked to health status. In fact, many medical historians assert that until the beginning of the twentieth century, a visit with a physician was as likely to be harmful as it was to be helpful. It is only relatively recently—since the early twentieth century—that medical care has been considered to have a positive influence on health and longevity.

There are three aspects of accessibility: consumer access, comprehensive availability of services, and supply of services adequate to meet community demand. Quality health care services must be accessible to health care consumers when and where they are needed. The health care provider must have access to a full range of facilities, equipment, drugs, and services provided by other practitioners. The institutional component of health care delivery—the hospitals, clinics, and payers—must have access to information to enable them to plan an adequate supply of appropriate services for their communities.

Consumer Access to Care

Access to health care services is influenced by a variety of factors. Characteristics of health care consumers strongly affect when, where, and how they access services. Differences in age, educational level achieved, economic status, race, ethnicity, cultural heritage, and geographic location determine when consumers seek health care services, where they go to receive them, their expectations of care and treatment, and the extent to which they wish to participate in decisions about their own medical care.

People have different reasons for seeking access to health care services. Their personal beliefs about health and illness, motivations to obtain care, expectations of the care they will receive, and knowledge about how and where to receive care vary. For an individual to have access to quality care, there must be appropriately defined points of entry into the health care system. For many consumers a primary care physician is the portal to the health care system. In addition to evaluating the patient's presenting problem (health care need), the primary care physician also directs the consumer to other providers of care such as physician specialists or mental health professionals.

Some consumers access the health care system by seeking care from a clinic or hospital outpatient department where teams of health professionals are available at one location. Others gain entry via a public health nurse, school nurse, social worker, pharmacist, or member of the clergy who can refer them to an appropriate source, site, or health care practitioner.

Comprehensive Availability of Health Care Services

Historically, the physician was the exclusive provider of all medical services. Until the twentieth century, the family doctor served as physician, surgeon, pharmacist, therapist, advisor, and dentist. He carried all of the tools of his trade in a small bag and could easily offer state-of-the-art medical care in his patient's home, since hospitals had little more to offer in the way of equipment or facilities. Today it is neither practical nor desirable to ask one practitioner to serve in all of these roles. It would be impossible for one professional to perform the full range of health care services, from primary prevention of disease and diagnosis to treatment and rehabilitation. Modern physicians and other health care practitioners must have access to a comprehensive array of trained personnel, facilities, and equipment so that they can, in turn, make them accessible to their patients.

While many medical problems are effectively treated in a single office visit with a physician, even simple diagnosis and treatment relies on a variety of ancillary (supplementary) services and personnel. To make the diagnosis, the physician may order an imaging study such as an X-ray that is performed by a radiology technician and interpreted by a radiologist (physician specialist in imaging techniques). Laboratory tests may be performed by technicians and analyzed by pathologists (physicians who specialize in microscopic analysis and diagnosis). More complicated medical problems involve teams of surgeons and high-tech surgical suites equipped with robotic assistants, and rehabilitation programs where highly trained physical and occupational therapists skillfully assist patients to regain function and independence.

Some health care services are more effectively, efficiently, and economically provided to groups rather than individuals. Immunization to prevent communicable diseases and screening to detect diseases in their earliest and most treatable stages are examples of preventive services best performed as cooperative efforts of voluntary health organizations, medical and other professional societies, hospitals, and public health departments.

Access Requires Enough Health Care Services to Meet Community Needs

For all members of a community to have access to the full range of health care services, careful planning is required to ensure both the adequate supply and distribution of needed services. To evaluate community needs and effectively allocate health care resources, communities must gather demographic data and information about social and economic characteristics of the population. They also must monitor the spread of disease and the frequency of specific medical conditions over time. All these population data must be considered in relation to available resources, including health care personnel, the distribution of facilities, equipment, and human resources (the available health care workforce), and advances in medicine and technology.

For example, a predicted shortage of nurses may prompt increased spending on nursing education; reviews of nurses' salary, benefits, and working conditions; and the cultivation of non-nursing personnel to perform specific responsibilities previously assigned to nurses. Similarly, when ongoing surveillance anticipates an especially virulent influenza (flu) season, public health officials, agencies, and practitioners intensify efforts to provide timely immunization to vulnerable populations such as older adults. Government agencies such as the Centers for Disease Control and Prevention, National Institutes of Health, state and local health departments, professional societies, voluntary health agencies, and universities work together to research, analyze, and forecast health care needs. Their recommendations allow health care planners, policymakers, and legislators to allocate resources so that supply keeps pace with demand and to ensure that new services and strategies are developed to address existing and emerging health care concerns.

A REGULAR SOURCE OF HEALTH CARE IMPROVES ACCESS

According to the Centers for Disease Control and Prevention, the determination of whether an individual has a regular source—a regular provider or site—of health care is a powerful predictor of access to health care services. Generally persons without regular sources have less access or access to fewer services, including key preventive medicine services such as prenatal care, routine immunization, and health screening. Many factors have been found to contribute to keeping individuals from having regular sources of medical care, with income level being the best predictor of unmet medical needs or problems gaining access to health care services.

FIGURE 1.1

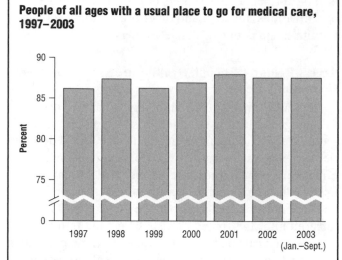

People of all ages with a usual place to go for medical care, 1997–2003

Note: The usual place to go for medical care does not include a hospital emergency room. The analyses excluded persons with unknown usual place to go for medical care (about 0.6% of respondents each year).

SOURCE: Zakia Coriaty-Nelson, Jeannine S. Schiller, Robin A. Cohen, Patricia M. Barnes, "Figure 2.1. Percent of Persons of All Ages with a Usual Place to Go for Medical Care: United States, 1997–2003," in *Early Release of Selected Estimates Based on Data from the 2003 National Health Interview Survey,* National Center for Health Statistics, June 2004, http://www.cdc.gov/nchs/data/nhis/earlyrelease/200406_02.pdf (accessed September 8, 2004)

FIGURE 1.2

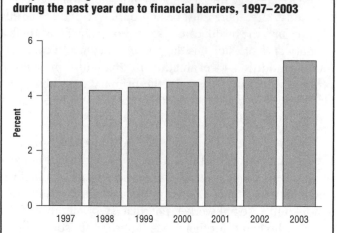

People of all ages who failed to obtain needed medical care during the past year due to financial barriers, 1997–2003

Notes: The analyses excluded persons with unknown success in obtaining needed medical care (about 0.5% of respondents each year).

SOURCE: Zakia Coriaty-Nelson, Jeannine S. Schiller, Robin A. Cohen, Patricia M. Barnes, "Figure 3.1. Percent of Persons of All Ages Who Failed to Obtain Needed Medical Care at Some Time during the Past 12 Months Due to Financial Barriers: United States, 1997–2003," in *Early Release of Selected Estimates Based on Data from the 2003 National Health Interview Survey,* National Center for Health Statistics, June 2004, http://www.cdc.gov/nchs/data/nhis/earlyrelease/200406_03.pdf (accessed September 8, 2004)

The National Health Interview Survey (NHIS is an annual nationwide survey of about thirty-six thousand households in the United States conducted by the National Center for Health Statistics, one of the Centers for Disease Control and Prevention) found that from 1997 through 2003 the percentage of persons of all ages with a usual source of medical care did not substantially vary—ranging from a low of 86.2% in 1997 to a high of 88% in 2001, where it remained through 2003. (See Figure 1.1.)

Still, from 1998 through 2003 the percentage of persons who needed medical care but did not obtain it because of financial barriers to access increased each year. The annual percentage of persons who experienced this lack of access to medical care rose from 4.2% in 1998 to 5.2% through September 2003. (See Figure 1.2.)

The 2003 NHIS revealed that people ages eighteen to twenty-four were least likely to have a regular source of care, but the likelihood of having a regular source of medical care increased with age among persons aged eighteen years and older. Children under age eighteen were more likely than adults aged eighteen to sixty-four to have a usual place to go for medical care. Among adults (aged eighteen to sixty-four), women were more likely than men to have a usual place to seek medical care. (See Figure 1.3.) The NHIS data indicate that not having a regular health care provider is a greater predictor of delay in seeking care than insurance status. Health care consumers with a regular physician or source of health care services are less likely to use the hospital emergency room to obtain routine nonemergency medical care, and are less likely to be hospitalized for preventable illnesses.

The National Association of Community Health Centers (NACHC) is a nonprofit organization that represents the interests of federally supported and other federally qualified health centers and serves as an information source about health care for poor and medically underserved populations in the United States. A report from NACHC found that thirty-six million Americans lacked access to basic health care and described low-income families and minorities, populations traditionally characterized as "medically underserved," as the hardest hit (Dan Hawkins and Michelle Proser, *A Nation's Health at Risk,* Washington, DC: National Association of Community Health Centers, 2004). Almost half of those without access to medical care—"medically unserved"—are from low-income families, and nearly two in five are members of minority groups. Hispanic adults have the highest concentration (28%) of medically unserved, followed by Asian Pacific Islander adults (16%) and African-Americans adults (12%).

The NACHC report asserts that the one in eight Americans (12% of the U.S. population) with no access to health care—the medically unserved—have been overlooked while the attention of policymakers has been focused on the 43 million Americans who lack health insurance. Although uninsured Americans often face barriers to access, nearly half of the 36 million Americans

FIGURE 1.3

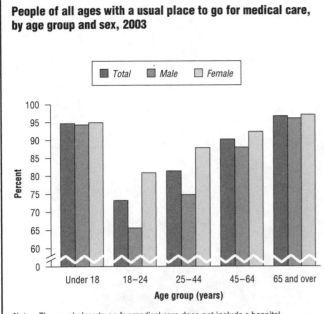

People of all ages with a usual place to go for medical care, by age group and sex, 2003

Notes: The usual place to go for medical care does not include a hospital emergency room. The analyses excluded 229 persons (0.5%) with unknown usual place to go for medical care.

SOURCE: Zakia Coriaty-Nelson, Jeannine S. Schiller, Robin A. Cohen, Patricia M. Barnes, "Figure 2.2. Percent of Persons of All Ages with a Usual Place to Go for Medical Care, by Age Group and Sex: United States, 2003," in *Early Release of Selected Estimates Based on Data from the 2003 National Health Interview Survey*, National Center for Health Statistics, June 2004, http://www.cdc.gov/nchs/data/nhis/earlyrelease/200406_02.pdf (accessed September 8, 2004)

without access to basic medical care have health insurance but encounter barriers in having their medical needs met too. Some of these barriers to access include scarcity of health care resources, geographically inaccessible services, and health care that is not culturally sensitive or is otherwise unacceptable to health care consumers.

There Are Americans without Access to Medical Care in Every State

According to the NACHC, there are medically unserved Americans in every state, with the highest concentrations in metropolitan areas with populations of less than one million. Figure 1.4 shows the percentage of the population in each state that was medically unserved in 2003. The NACHC reported that in thirteen states—Alabama, California, Florida, Georgia, Louisiana, Michigan, Missouri, New York, North Carolina, Ohio, Pennsylvania, Tennessee, and Texas—the medically unserved population exceeds one million persons, and these thirteen states account for about two-thirds (63%) of Americans who lack a regular source of health care.

In 2003 Texas was the state with the highest medically unserved population, followed by Florida, Georgia, Louisiana, Michigan, Missouri, New York, North Carolina, Ohio, Pennsylvania, and Tennessee.

Race and Ethnicity Continue to Affect Access to Health Care

The 2003 NHIS found that Hispanic adults and children continued to be less likely to have a regular source for medical care than white non-Hispanic and African-American non-Hispanic persons. After adjusting for age and gender, 78.1% of Hispanic persons had a usual source of medical care, compared to 90.4% of non-Hispanic white persons and 86.4% of non-Hispanic African-American persons. Hispanic persons and non-Hispanic African-American persons were more likely than non-Hispanic white persons to suffer financial barriers to access. After adjusting for age and gender, 6.3% of Hispanic persons and 6.5% of non-Hispanic African-American persons were unable to obtain needed medical care due to financial barriers, compared to 4.8% of non-Hispanic white persons. (See Figure 1.5.) Health educators speculate that language barriers and lack of information about the availability of health care services may serve to widen this gap.

The U.S. Public Health Service's Agency for Healthcare Research and Quality (AHRQ) looks at ways to identify, address, and ultimately eliminate differences in access, availability, and the quality of health care services. Working with the National Institutes of Health (NIH) and national and local foundations, AHRQ seeks to develop plans and strategies to reduce and overcome disparities. One example of this collaborative effort is a program to improve access and quality of care for African-Americans suffering from chronic illnesses who primarily receive care from inner-city and rural health care providers. Another project aims to expand access to preventive medicine services among low-income, Medicaid-eligible populations. (Medicaid is a program run by state and federal governments to provide health insurance for persons younger than age sixty-five who cannot afford to pay for private health insurance.)

The AHRQ observes that income level and lack of health insurance are not the only barriers to access faced by members of racial or ethnic minority populations. The AHRQ asserts that having health insurance does not guarantee access and that even entering a health care provider's office does not ensure receipt of appropriate or quality health care services. AHRQ researchers described asthma care as an example of consistent variation in access to and use of medical care. Among children with asthma enrolled in Medicaid, African-American children were 70% more likely to visit an emergency department and 52% less likely to be cared for in an office visit with a health care practitioner. African-American children were similarly less likely to obtain routine well-child visits (check-ups) and prescriptions for medication.

Women Face Additional Obstacles

Research conducted by the Henry J. Kaiser Family Foundation, a nonprofit, private operating foundation

FIGURE 1.4

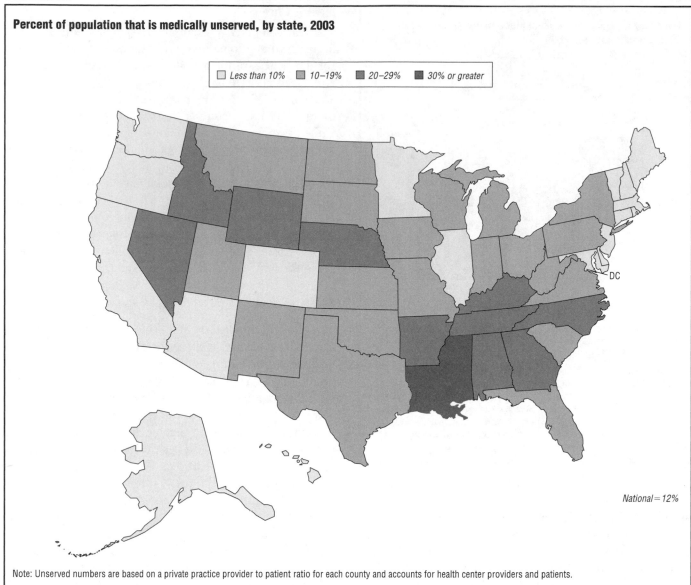

Percent of population that is medically unserved, by state, 2003

Less than 10%   10–19%   20–29%   30% or greater

DC

National = 12%

Note: Unserved numbers are based on a private practice provider to patient ratio for each county and accounts for health center providers and patients.

SOURCE: Dan Hawkins and Michelle Proser, "Map 1. Percent of State Population That Is Medically Unserved, 2003," in *A Nation's Health at Risk,* National Association of Community Health Centers, 2004, http://www.nachc.com/piforum/files/UnservedReportSTIB5.pdf (accessed September 8, 2004)

focusing on the major health care issues facing the nation, documented significant racial and ethnic differences in access to care. Analyzing data from the 2001 Kaiser Women's Health Survey, the investigators found that overall, Hispanic and African-American women fared worse than white women in terms of access to health care services (*Racial and Ethnic Disparities in Women's Health Coverage and Access to Care Findings from the 2001 Kaiser Women's Health Survey,* Menlo Park, CA, 2004).

According to the Kaiser survey, Hispanic women reported less access to care than their white counterparts. Almost one quarter of Hispanic women (24%) had not visited a physician in the year prior to the survey compared to 14% of African-American and 11% of white women. Just under one-third of Hispanic women and

African-American women said they had delayed or simply chose not to seek needed care, compared to one-quarter of white women.

Financial barriers—the costs of obtaining care and lack of insurance—were women's most frequently cited reason for delaying care and were reported by about one-third of Hispanic women. According to the Kaiser survey, more than three times as many Hispanic women (18%) and twice as many African-American women (10%) cited transportation problems as a barrier to access, compared to 5% of white women.

The 2003 NHIS also documented gender-based disparities in access. Women aged eighteen to sixty-four and those aged sixty-five and older were more likely than men to have failed to obtain needed medical care because of financial barriers to access. (See Figure 1.6.)

FIGURE 1.5

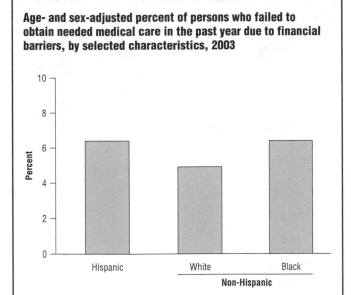

Age- and sex-adjusted percent of persons who failed to obtain needed medical care in the past year due to financial barriers, by selected characteristics, 2003

Notes: The analyses excluded 454 persons (0.5%) with unknown success in obtaining needed medical care. Estimates are age-sex-adjusted to the 2000 projected U.S. standard population using three age groups: under 18 years, 18–64 years, and 65 years and over.

SOURCE: Zakia Coriaty-Nelson, Jeannine S. Schiller, Robin A. Cohen, Patricia M. Barnes, "Figure 3.3. Age-Sex-Adjusted Percent of Persons Who Failed to Obtain Needed Medical Care at Some Time during the Past 12 Months Due to Financial Barriers, by Race/Ethnicity: United States, 2003," in *Early Release of Selected Estimates Based on Data from the 2003 National Health Interview Survey*, National Center for Health Statistics, June 2004, http://www.cdc.gov/nchs/data/nhis/earlyrelease/200406_03.pdf (accessed September 8, 2004)

FIGURE 1.6

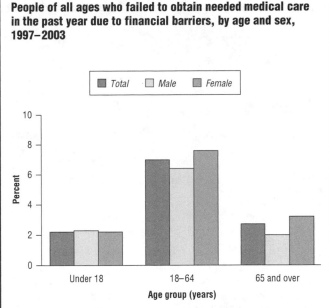

People of all ages who failed to obtain needed medical care in the past year due to financial barriers, by age and sex, 1997–2003

Note: The analyses excluded 454 persons (0.5%) with unknown success in obtaining needed medical care.

SOURCE: Zakia Coriaty-Nelson, Jeannine S. Schiller, Robin A. Cohen, Patricia M. Barnes, "Figure 3.2. Percent of Persons of All Ages Who Failed to Obtain Needed Medical Care at Some Time during the Past 12 Months Due to Financial Barriers, by Age and Sex: United States, 1997–2003," in *Early Release of Selected Estimates Based on Data from the 2003 National Health Interview Survey*, National Center for Health Statistics, June 2004, http://www.cdc.gov/nchs/data/nhis/earlyrelease/200406_03.pdf (accessed September 8, 2004)

Children Need Better Access to Health Care Too

Data from the more than 38,000 households included in the NHIS were analyzed to look at selected health measures, including children's access to care, and compiled in the report *Summary Health Statistics for U.S. Children in 2003.* Among other factors, the analysis focuses on the unmet health care needs of children seventeen years of age and under, poverty status, insurance coverage, usual place of medical care, and whether children's health needs were being met. The data from the NHIS reveal a relationship between family income and not having a usual source of medical care as well as having unmet medical needs. (See Table 1.1.) The likelihood of lacking a regular source of care or having unmet needs was higher among poor and near poor families of all races and ethnic groups. Having health insurance and the type of health insurance also predicted whether a child had a regular source of care and whether all of the child's medical needs were met. (See Table 1.2 and Table 1.1.)

In 2000, 6.4% of children in the United States (4.6 million) did not have a regular source of medical care. Hispanic children (12.7%) were least likely to have a regular source of care compared with 6.9% of non-Hispanic African-American children and 4.5% of non-Hispanic

white children. Twice as many Hispanic children (30%) as non-Hispanic white children (15%) received their usual health care in a clinic, and poor children were more than 2.5 times more likely to receive their usual care in a clinic than children who were not poor. (See Table 1.2.)

The survey also found that 25% more children with private health insurance (87%) received health care in a physician's office than children with public health insurance (62%). Children without health insurance were more likely to receive routine health care in an emergency room than were children with private or public health insurance.

Some 12% of U.S. children (8.8 million) had no health insurance coverage in 2000. More than one-fifth (21%) of children in families with incomes of less than $20,000 per year had no health insurance and the same proportion of children in families with incomes ranging from $20,000 to $34,999 were uninsured, compared with a scant 3% of children in households with incomes of $75,000 or more. Children from poor and near poor families were more likely to be uninsured, have unmet medical needs, delay seeking care because of financial barriers, have no usual place of health care, and visit hospital emergency rooms more frequently than children from families that were not poor. (See Table 1.1.) Health pro-

TABLE 1.1

Selected measures of health care access for children under 18, by selected characteristics, 2000

Selected characteristics	All children under 18 years	Selected measures of health care access[1]				
		Uninsured for health care[2]	Unmet medical need[3]	Delayed health care due to cost[4]	Had no usual place of health care[5]	2 or more visits to the emergency room in the past 12 months[6]
		Number in thousands[7]				
Total[8]	72,326	8,797	1,901	2,824	4,592	5,012
Sex						
Male	36,995	4,504	1,011	1,420	2,246	2,669
Female	35,331	4,293	890	1,404	2,346	2,343
Age						
0–4 years	19,609	2,246	437	608	782	1,991
5–17 years	52,717	6,551	1,464	2,216	3,810	3,021
5–11 years	28,958	3,550	706	1,121	1,596	1,616
12–17 years	23,759	3,001	758	1,095	2,215	1,405
Race						
1 race[9]	70,564	8,551	1,840	2,690	4,509	4,862
White	53,640	5,969	1,306	1,969	3,179	3,430
Black or African American	10,709	1,262	366	530	739	1,101
American Indian or Alaska Native	643	217	42	37	26	70
Asian	2,491	292	21	28	232	77
Native Hawaiian or other Pacific Islander	133	19	—	—	6	5
2 or more races[10]	1,762	246	61	135	84	150
Black or African American and white	500	64	14	22	13	59
American Indian or Alaska Native and white	318	83	28	68	34	30
Hispanic origin and race[11]						
Hispanic or Latino	11,803	3,061	378	466	1,494	820
Mexican or Mexican American	8,160	2,438	291	342	1,169	533
Not Hispanic or Latino	60,523	5,736	1,523	2,358	3,098	4,192
White, single race	45,428	3,779	1,053	1,645	2,053	2,841
Black or African American, single race	10,428	1,237	358	527	719	1,087
Family structure[12]						
Mother and father	52,422	5,721	950	1,617	2,958	2,974
Mother, no father	15,789	2,342	824	1,048	1,217	1,760
Father, no mother	2,126	318	30	73	193	131
Neither mother nor father	1,988	416	97	86	224	147
Parent's education[13]						
Less than high school diploma	9,510	2,568	440	520	1,362	981
High school diploma or GED[14]	16,788	2,592	592	845	1,222	1,432
More than high school	43,552	3,055	748	1,343	1,757	2,430
Family income[15]						
Less than $20,000	13,169	2,752	719	908	1,328	1,636
$20,000 or more	55,885	5,403	1,054	1,744	2,934	3,188
$20,000–$34,999	10,417	2,130	488	678	1,052	871
$35,000–$54,999	12,352	1,404	274	475	662	802
$55,000–$74,999	9,468	439	51	201	348	502
$75,000 or more	14,493	371	101	173	421	645
Poverty status[16]						
Poor	9,206	1,935	532	558	945	1,159
Near poor	12,528	2,620	546	844	1,227	1,059
Not poor	35,401	1,947	436	874	1,310	1,945
Health insurance coverage[17]						
Private	48,408	...	407	856	1,557	2,518
Medicaid/other public	13,288	...	385	549	512	1,734
Other	1,609	...	—	26	125	143
Uninsured	8,797	8,797	1,103	1,381	2,385	582
Place of residence[18]						
Large MSA	35,175	4,219	844	1,287	2,296	2,131
Small MSA	23,035	2,747	707	1,054	1,278	1,676
Not in MSA	14,116	1,831	350	483	1,019	1,205

fessionals are especially concerned about delayed or missed medical visits for children because well-child visits are not only opportunities for early detection of developmental problems and timely treatment of illnesses but also ensure that children receive the recommended schedule of immunizations.

According to the survey, there was significant geographic variation in insurance status, which was strongly linked to

TABLE 1.1

Selected measures of health care access for children under 18, by selected characteristics, 2000 [CONTINUED]

Selected characteristics	All children under 18 years	Selected measures of health care access[1]				
		Uninsured for health care[2]	Unmet medical need[3]	Delayed health care due to cost[4]	Had no usual place of health care[5]	2 or more visits to the emergency room in the past 12 months[6]
Region		Number in thousands[7]				
Northeast	13,448	897	237	370	320	837
Midwest	17,884	1,451	433	662	914	1,178
South	25,467	4,003	833	1,159	1,958	2,161
West	15,527	2,446	398	634	1,401	836
Current health status						
Excellent/very good/good	70,975	8,621	1,762	2,641	4,502	4,623
Fair/poor	1,312	164	127	171	78	389
Sex and age						
Male:						
0–4 years	10,021	1,143	225	287	357	1,011
5–17 years	26,974	3,361	786	1,133	1,889	1,657
5–11 years	14,805	1,831	414	615	819	919
12–17 years	12,169	1,530	372	518	1,070	738
Female:						
0–4 years	9,588	1,103	213	321	425	979
5–17 years	25,743	3,190	677	1,083	1,921	1,364
5–11 years	14,153	1,718	292	505	776	697
12–17 years	11,591	1,472	386	578	1,145	667

— Quantity zero.

[1] In the 1997–1999 reports, this table was titled "Frequencies of selected health care risk factors, for children 17 years of age and under, by selected characteristics."

[2] Uninsured for health care is based on the following question in the family core section of the survey: "[Are you/Is anyone] covered by health insurance or some other kind of health care plan?"

[3] Unmet medical need is based on the following question in the family core section of the survey: "DURING THE PAST 12 MONTHS, was there any time when [you/someone in the family] needed medical care, but did not get it because [you/the family] couldn't afford it?"

[4] Delayed health care due to cost is based on the following question in the family core section of the survey: "DURING THE PAST 12 MONTHS" [have/has] [you/anyone in the family] delayed seeking medical care because of worry about the cost?"

[5] Had no usual place of health care is based on the following question in the sample child core section of the survey: "Is there a place that [child's name] USUALLY goes when [he/she] is sick or you need advice about [his/her] health?"

[6] Two or more visits to the emergency room in the past 12 months is based on the following question in the sample child core section of the survey: "DURING THE PAST 12 MONTHS, how many times has [child's name] gone to the hospital emergency room about [his/her] health? (This includes emergency room visits that resulted in a hospital admission.)"

[7] Unknowns for the column variables are not included in the frequencies but they are included in the "All children under 18 years" column.

[8] Total includes other races not shown separately and children with unknown family structure, parent's education, family income, poverty status, health insurance, or current health status. Additionally, numbers within selected characteristics may not add to totals because of rounding.

[9] In accordance with the 1997 Standards for Federal data on race and Hispanic or Latino origin the category "1 race" refers to persons who indicated only a single race group. Persons who indicated a single race other than the groups shown are included in the total for "1 race" but are not shown separately due to small sample sizes. Therefore, the frequencies for the category "1 race" will be greater than the sum of the frequencies for the specific groups shown separately. Persons of Hispanic or Latino origin may be of any race or combination of races.

[10] The category "2 or more races" refers to all persons who indicated more than one race group. Only two combinations of multiple race groups are shown due to small sample sizes for other combinations. Persons of Hispanic or Latino origin may be of any race or combination of races.

[11] Persons of Hispanic or Latino origin may be of any race or combination of races. Similarly, the category "Not Hispanic or Latino" refers to all persons who are not of Hispanic or Latino origin, regardless of race. The tables in this report use the complete new OMB race and Hispanic origin terms, and the text uses shorter versions of these terms for conciseness. For example, the category "Not Hispanic or Latino black or African American, single race" in the tables is referred to as "non-Hispanic black" in the text.

[12] Family structure refers to parents living in the household. "Mother and father" can include biological, adoptive, step, in-law, or foster relationships. Legal guardians are classified in "Neither mother nor father."

[13] Parent's education is the education level of the parent with the higher level of education, regardless of that parent's age.

[14] GED is General Educational Development high school equivalency diploma.

[15] The categories "Less than $20,000" and "$20,000 or more" include both persons reporting dollar amounts and persons reporting only that their incomes were within one of these two categories. The indented categories include only those persons who reported dollar amounts.

[16] Poverty status is based on family income and family size using the Census Bureau's poverty thresholds for the previous calendar year. "Poor" persons are defined as below the poverty threshold. "Near poor" persons have incomes of 100% to less than 200% of the poverty threshold. "Not poor" persons have incomes that are 200% of the poverty threshold or greater.

[17] Classification of health insurance coverage is based on a hierarchy of mutually exclusive categories. Persons with more than one type of health insurance were assigned to the first appropriate category in the hierarchy. The category "Uninsured" includes persons who had no coverage as well as those who had only Indian Health Service coverage or had only a private plan that paid for one type of service such as accidents or dental care.

[18] MSA is metropolitan statistical area. Large MSAs have a population size of 1,000,000 or more; small MSAs have a population size of less than 1,000,000. "Not in MSA" consists of persons not living in a metropolitan statistical area.

SOURCE: Debra L. Blackwell, Jackline L. Vickerie, and Ethiopia A. Wondimu, "Table 15. Frequencies of Selected Measures of Health Care Access, for Children under 18 Years of Age, by Selected Characteristics: United States, 2000," in *Summary Health Statistics for U.S. Children: National Health Interview Survey, 2000,* National Center for Health Statistics, Vital Health Statistics, vol. 10, no. 213, 2003, http://www.cdc.gov/nchs/data/series/sr_10/sr10_213.pdf (accessed June 1, 2004)

children's access to health care services. The percentage of children in the West and South (16% in each region) who were uninsured was twice the percentage of uninsured children in the Midwest (8%) or the Northeast (7%).

Do Americans Underestimate Access Problems?

A Kaiser Health Poll Survey from 2000–01 found Americans' knowledge about barriers to access was uneven. While almost three-quarters of survey respondents

TABLE 1.2

Usual place of health care for children under 18 with a usual place of health care, by selected characteristics, 2000

Selected characteristics	All children under 18 years	Has no usual place of health care[1]	Has usual place of health care[1]	Usual place of health care[2]					
				Clinic	Doctor's office	Emergency room	Hospital outpatient	Some other place	Does not go to 1 place most often
				Number in thousands[3]					
Total[4]	72,326	4,592	67,584	12,875	53,033	435	823	140	182
Sex									
Male	36,995	2,246	34,700	6,514	27,409	178	397	62	84
Female	35,331	2,346	32,884	6,361	25,624	258	426	78	98
Age									
0–4 years	19,609	782	18,809	3,919	14,484	98	230	19	16
5–17 years	52,717	3,810	48,775	8,956	38,549	337	594	121	166
5–11 years	28,958	1,596	27,309	5,016	21,669	191	287	47	65
12–17 years	23,759	2,215	21,466	3,941	16,880	147	307	74	101
Race									
1 race[5]	70,564	4,509	65,906	12,486	51,785	426	796	137	182
White	53,640	3,179	50,354	8,222	41,191	193	423	124	125
Black or African American	10,709	739	9,940	2,601	6,842	153	278	7	42
American Indian or Alaska Native	643	26	617	289	302	8	14	3	—
Asian	2,491	232	2,249	425	1,746	38	26	3	8
Native Hawaiian or other Pacific Islander	133	6	127	10	116	—	—	—	—
2 or more races[6]	1,762	84	1,678	390	1,248	10	28	3	—
Black or African American and white	500	13	487	91	391	—	5	—	—
American Indian or Alaska Native and white	318	34	284	82	198	—	5	—	—
Hispanic origin and race[7]									
Hispanic or Latino	11,803	1,494	10,292	3,050	6,860	129	160	9	48
Mexican or Mexican American	8,160	1,169	6,980	2,114	4,609	90	84	9	39
Not Hispanic or Latino	60,523	3,098	57,293	9,825	46,174	307	663	131	134
White, single race	45,428	2,053	43,282	6,267	36,350	97	329	115	83
Black or African American, single race	10,428	719	9,680	2,537	6,655	153	270	7	42
Family structure[8]									
Mother and father	52,422	2,958	49,420	8,277	40,140	233	472	117	115
Mother, no father	15,789	1,217	14,507	3,624	10,403	137	263	19	39
Father, no mother	2,126	193	1,906	433	1,349	45	47	4	25
Neither mother nor father	1,988	224	1,749	539	1,140	20	41	—	4
Parent's education[9]									
Less than high school diploma	9,510	1,362	8,131	2,994	4,716	165	134	14	62
High school diploma or GED[10]	16,788	1,222	15,536	3,343	11,799	133	204	20	30
More than high school	43,552	1,757	41,711	5,915	35,020	117	444	105	86
Family income[11]									
Less than $20,000	13,169	1,328	11,796	3,892	7,398	193	252	14	44
$20,000 or more	55,885	2,934	52,858	8,297	43,459	235	560	121	131
$20,000–$34,999	10,417	1,052	9,336	2,401	6,584	109	156	26	46
$35,000–$54,999	12,352	662	11,662	1,997	9,380	68	161	29	25
$55,000–$74,999	9,468	348	9,119	1,175	7,826	9	77	6	25
$75,000 or more	14,493	421	14,069	1,522	12,352	36	95	55	10
Poverty status[12]									
Poor	9,206	945	8,252	2,895	4,974	168	160	24	31
Near poor	12,528	1,227	11,259	2,832	8,044	146	171	18	46
Not poor	35,401	1,310	34,060	4,493	28,985	84	333	87	63
Health insurance coverage[13]									
Private	48,408	1,557	46,774	5,616	40,649	87	187	83	104
Medicaid/other public	13,288	512	12,755	4,319	7,936	128	298	9	28
Other	1,609	125	1,483	638	618	—	198	24	5
Uninsured	8,797	2,385	6,369	2,273	3,686	218	125	22	37
Place of residence[14]									
Large MSA	35,175	2,296	32,824	5,613	26,203	263	524	48	117
Small MSA	23,035	1,278	21,692	4,084	17,107	139	281	28	24
Not in MSA	14,116	1,019	13,068	3,179	9,724	33	19	64	41

knew that persons without insurance were less likely to have had a recent physician visit or a regular source of medical care, more than half (52%) were unaware that uninsured persons are more likely to have hospital and emergency room visits that could have been avoided if they had a regular source of medical care. (See Figure 1.7.)

The poll also revealed that about two-thirds of Americans (65%) acknowledged that the uninsured would be more likely to put off seeking needed medical care, and 62% thought the uninsured would be less likely to obtain preventive care. However, more than half (55%) said they thought that most uninsured per-

TABLE 1.2

Usual place of health care for children under 18 with a usual place of health care, by selected characteristics, 2000 [CONTINUED]

Selected characteristics	All children under 18 years	Has no usual place of health care[1]	Has usual place of health care[1]	Usual place of health care[2]					
				Clinic	Doctor's office	Emergency room	Hospital outpatient	Some other place	Does not go to 1 place most often
				Number in thousands[3]					
Region									
Northeast	13,448	320	13,106	1,767	11,008	101	188	10	26
Midwest	17,884	914	16,965	4,139	12,488	68	170	39	39
South	25,467	1,958	23,436	3,895	18,996	190	211	44	86
West	15,527	1,401	14,078	3,074	10,542	77	255	46	30
Current health status									
Excellent/very good/good	70,975	4,502	66,323	12,584	52,155	402	772	133	182
Fair/poor	1,312	78	1,234	289	854	34	51	6	—
Sex and age									
Male:									
0–4 years	10,021	357	9,656	1,998	7,413	44	138	19	10
5–17 years	26,974	1,889	25,044	4,516	19,996	133	259	42	74
5–11 years	14,805	819	13,953	2,613	11,107	60	111	19	30
12–17 years	12,169	1,070	11,091	1,903	8,889	73	148	23	44
Female:									
0–4 years	9,588	425	9,154	1,921	7,071	54	92	—	6
5–17 years	25,743	1,921	23,731	4,440	18,553	204	335	78	92
5–11 years	14,153	776	13,356	2,403	10,562	131	176	28	35
12–17 years	11,591	1,145	10,375	2,038	7,991	73	159	51	57

— Quantity zero.

[1]Having (or not having) a usual place of health care is based on the question, "Is there a place that [child's name] USUALLY goes when [he/she] is sick or you need advice about [his/her] health?"

[2]Usual place of health care is based on the question, "What kind of place is it—clinic or health center, doctor's office or HMO, hospital emergency room, hospital emergency room, hospital outpatient department or some that place?"

[3]Unknowns for the column variables are not included in the denominators when calculating percents.

[4]Total includes other races not shown separately and children with unknown family structure, parent's education, family income, poverty status, health insurance, or current health status. Additionally, numbers within selected characteristics may not add to totals because of rounding.

[5]In accordance with the 1997 Standards for Federal data on race and Hispanic or Latino origin the category "1 race" refers to persons who indicated only a single race group. Persons who indicated a single race other than the groups shown are included in the total for "1 race" but are not shown separately due to small sample sizes. Therefore, the frequencies for the category "1 race" will be greater than the sum of the frequencies for the specific groups shown separately. Persons of Hispanic or Latino origin may be of any race or combination of races.

[6]The category "2 or more races" refers to all persons who indicated more than one race group. Only two combinations of multiple race groups are shown due to small sample sizes for other combinations. Persons of Hispanic or Latino origin may be of any race or combination of races.

[7]Persons of Hispanic or Latino origin may be of any race or combination of races. Similarly, the category "Not Hispanic or Latino" refers to all persons who are not of Hispanic or Latino origin, regardless of race.

[8]Family structure refers to parents living in the household. "Mother and father" can include biological, adoptive, step, in-law, or foster relationships. Legal guardians are classified in "Neither mother nor father."

[9]Parent's education is the education level of the parent with the higher level of education, regardless of that parent's age.

[10]GED is General Educational Development high school equivalency diploma.

[11]The categories "Less than $20,000" and "$20,000 or more" include both persons reporting dollar amounts and persons reporting only that their incomes were within one of these two categories. The indented categories include only those persons who reported dollar amounts.

[12]Poverty status is based on family income and family size using the Census Bureau's poverty thresholds for the previous calendar year. "Poor" persons are defined as below the poverty threshold. "Near poor" persons have incomes of 100% to less than 200% of the poverty threshold. "Not poor" persons have incomes that are 200% of the poverty threshold or greater.

[13]Classification of health insurance coverage is based on a hierarchy of mutually exclusive categories. Persons with more than one type of health insurance were assigned to the first appropriate category in the hierarchy. The category "Uninsured" includes persons who had no coverage as well as those who had only Indian Health Service coverage or had only a private plan that paid for one type of service such as accidents or dental care.

[14]MSA is metropolitan statistical area. Large MSAs have a population size of 1,000,000 or more; small MSAs have a population size of less than 1,000,000. "Not in MSA" consists of persons not living in a metropolitan statistical area.

SOURCE: Debra L. Blackwell, Jackline L. Vickerie, and Ethiopia A. Wondimu, "Table 11. Frequency Distributions of Having a Usual Place of Health Care, and Frequency Distributions of Usual Place of Health Care for Children with a Usual Place of Health Care, for Children under 18 Years of Age, by Selected Characteristics: United States, 2000," in *Summary Health Statistics for U.S. Children: National Health Interview Survey, 2000,* National Center for Health Statistics, Vital Health Statistics, vol. 10, no. 213, 2003, http://www.cdc.gov/nchs/data/series/sr_10/sr10_213.pdf (accessed June 1, 2004)

sons were able to obtain needed medical care. (See Figure 1.7.)

How to Reduce Disparities in Access to Care

Health services researchers think that many factors contribute to differences in access, including cultural perceptions and beliefs about health and illness, patient preferences, availability of services, and provider bias. They recommend special efforts to inform and educate minority health care consumers and increased understanding and sensitivity among practitioners and other providers of care. In addition to factual information, minority consumers must overcome the belief that they are at a disadvantage because of their race or ethnicity. Along with action to dispel barriers to access, educating practitioners, policymakers, and consumers can help to reduce the perception of disadvantage.

For decades, health care researchers have documented sharp differences in the ability of ethnic and racial groups

FIGURE 1.7

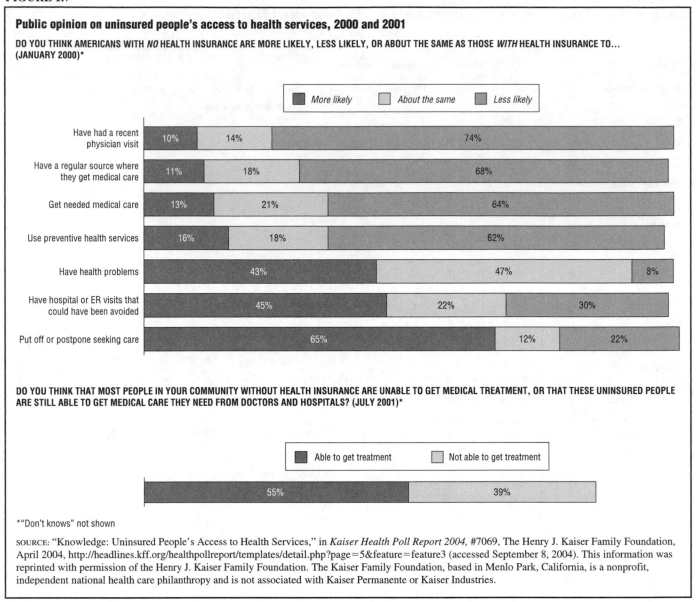

Public opinion on uninsured people's access to health services, 2000 and 2001

DO YOU THINK AMERICANS WITH *NO* HEALTH INSURANCE ARE MORE LIKELY, LESS LIKELY, OR ABOUT THE SAME AS THOSE *WITH* HEALTH INSURANCE TO... (JANUARY 2000)*

More likely / About the same / Less likely

	More likely	About the same	Less likely
Have had a recent physician visit	10%	14%	74%
Have a regular source where they get medical care	11%	18%	68%
Get needed medical care	13%	21%	64%
Use preventive health services	16%	18%	62%
Have health problems	43%	47%	8%
Have hospital or ER visits that could have been avoided	45%	22%	30%
Put off or postpone seeking care	65%	12%	22%

DO YOU THINK THAT MOST PEOPLE IN YOUR COMMUNITY WITHOUT HEALTH INSURANCE ARE UNABLE TO GET MEDICAL TREATMENT, OR THAT THESE UNINSURED PEOPLE ARE STILL ABLE TO GET MEDICAL CARE THEY NEED FROM DOCTORS AND HOSPITALS? (JULY 2001)*

Able to get treatment / Not able to get treatment

Able to get treatment	Not able to get treatment
55%	39%

*"Don't knows" not shown

SOURCE: "Knowledge: Uninsured People's Access to Health Services," in *Kaiser Health Poll Report 2004,* #7069, The Henry J. Kaiser Family Foundation, April 2004, http://headlines.kff.org/healthpollreport/templates/detail.php?page=5&feature=feature3 (accessed September 8, 2004). This information was reprinted with permission of the Henry J. Kaiser Family Foundation. The Kaiser Family Foundation, based in Menlo Park, California, is a nonprofit, independent national health care philanthropy and is not associated with Kaiser Permanente or Kaiser Industries.

to access medical services. The U.S. government has repeatedly called for an end to these disparities. Although some observers feel that universal health insurance coverage is an important first step in eliminating disparities, there is widespread concern that the challenge is more complicated and calls for additional analysis and action.

In an article in the June 2002 issue of the *Journal of General Internal Medicine* (vol. 17, no. 6), Harvard Medical School physician Dr. Judy Ann Bigby asserts that "eliminating racial disparities ... requires an understanding of the ecology of health, the interconnectedness of biologic, behavioral, physical, and socioenvironmental factors that determine health." Dr. Bigby believes that a multifaceted approach must be used to address the many issues involved in access, including improving the physical environment, overcoming economic and social barriers, ensuring the availability of effective health services, and acting to reduce personal behavioral risk factors such

as smoking, obesity, poor nutrition, substance abuse, and physical inactivity. Developing strategies to promote personal, institutional, and community change simultaneously may stimulate the sweeping reforms needed to reduce and ultimately eliminate disparities.

Managed care refers to a system of health payment or delivery in which the plan attempts to control or coordinate use of health services by its enrolled members in order to contain health expenditures, improve quality, or both. Research supported by the AHQR suggests that managed care, with its emphasis on preventive health services, may improve ethnic disparities in access for Hispanics and whites but not for African-Americans or Asians/Pacific Islanders. Jennifer S. Haas and her colleagues at the University of California, San Francisco, analyzed data about preventive health care use by persons enrolled in fee-for-service (FFS) and managed care plans from the AHRQ Medical Expenditure Panel Survey

(MEPS) of noninstitutionalized U.S. civilians ("Effect of Managed Care Insurance on the Use of Preventive Care for Specific Ethnic Groups in the United States," *Medical Care* vol. 40, no. 9, September 2002).

The investigators considered use of four preventive health screenings—mammography within the past two years for women aged fifty to seventy-five, breast examination within the past two years for women between forty and seventy-five, Pap smear (screening for cervical cancer) within the past two years for women between eighteen and sixty-five, and cholesterol screening within the past five years for men and women above age twenty. The analysis revealed that Hispanic and white women enrolled in managed care plans reported higher rates of mammography, breast exam, and Pap smear than Hispanic women with FFS insurance. There were no significant differences in access to preventive care for African-Americans or Asians/Pacific Islanders by type of insurance. The investigators theorize that managed care may improve access to a usual source of care for Hispanics, who are more likely to lack a usual source of care than whites.

REPORT DOCUMENTS DISPARITIES IN ACCESS AND SUGGESTS POSSIBLE SOLUTIONS. In July 2003 the AHRQ released a *National Healthcare Disparities Report* requested by Congress that documented racial health disparities including access to care. For example, the report cited the finding that African-American and low-income Americans have higher mortality rates for cancer than the general population because they are less likely to receive screening tests for certain forms of the disease and other preventive services. Although the report asserted that differential access may lead to disparities in quality and observed that opportunities to provide preventive care are often missed, it conceded that knowledge about why disparities exist is limited.

The report generated considerable controversy, and in January 2004 eight Democratic lawmakers wrote to Health and Human Services (HHS) Secretary Tommy Thompson, decrying its findings and conclusions as "watered down." The legislators wrote that the report, which had been released, edited, and re-released in December 2003, included revisions that "alter the original report's meaning, undermine efforts to address disparities and fit a pattern of the manipulation of science by the Bush administration." In response to this outcry, Thompson re-released the original report in February 2004.

The April 8, 2004, issue of the *New England Journal of Medicine* (vol. 350, no. 15) addressed the controversy surrounding the report, its re-release, and its findings. In "Disparities in Health Care—From Politics to Policy" Robert Steinbrook opined that "the controversy over the editing of the National Healthcare Disparities Report has focused attention yet again on problems with health care for racial and ethnic minorities in the United States. The dispute has

also focused attention on the risks of either overstating or understating the real problems related to disparities. Both overstatement and understatement can undermine the credibility of the federal government. Downplaying the magnitude of disparities may also make it less likely that Congress will provide sufficient funding for research and policy initiatives." Steinbrook also asserted, "Inequities in health care did not originate during the Bush administration and are likely to pose daunting challenges for future administrations, both Democratic and Republican."

In the same issue of the *New England Journal of Medicine* M. Gregg Bloche wrote that "Department of Health and Human Services (DHHS) Secretary Tommy Thompson has said that health disparities are a national priority, and congressional Democrats and Republicans are advocating competing remedies." ("Health Care Disparities—Science, Politics, and Race"). Bloche stated, "When Congress asks a federal research agency to examine an issue and report on it impartially, peer review must not be confounded by political spin management. Self-restraint in the executive branch should be enough to ensure this. But given the bitterly partisan mood that prevails in Washington today, legislation ought to require it."

In an April 10, 2004, letter to the editor of the New Orleans *Times-Picayune,* Senate Majority Leader Bill Frist, a Republican from Tennessee who is also a physician, exhorted legislators to take a comprehensive approach to eliminating health care disparities, focusing not only on race or ethnicity, but also on geographic and socioeconmonic factors. Frist opined that legislative efforts to reduce disparities won unanimous bipartisan support in 2000 in the U.S. Senate. He expressed optimism that the *Closing the Health Care Gap Act of 2004,* which he introduced with Senator Mary Landrieu, a Democrat from Louisiana, would garner comparable support and expand upon existing legislation.

Although the AHRQ report generated fiery debate in the health care community and among legislators and painted a rather bleak view of disparities, it did offer some hopeful findings that suggest that targeted improvement efforts could significantly reduce health care disparities. For example, it observed that "black patients are more likely to receive blood pressure monitoring without any disparity in blood pressure management. A greater perceived risk for significant cardiovascular disease among blacks may result in appropriately increased screening rates and treatment for risk factors. Directed public education campaigns about cardiac risk factors and the importance of an activated patient may play an important role in the lower observed rate of cardiac disparities among blacks." The report called for detailed data to support quality improvement initiatives and observed that "community-based participatory research has numerous examples of communities working to improve quality overall, while reducing healthcare disparities for vulnerable populations."

IS ACCESS A RIGHT OR A PRIVILEGE?

The AHRQ and other health care researchers and policymakers have observed that having health insurance does not necessarily ensure access to medical care. They contend that many other factors, including cost-containment measures put in place by private and public payers, have reduced access to care. Nonetheless, reduced access affects vulnerable populations—the poor, persons with disabilities and other special health care needs, and immigrants—more than others. These groups are disproportionately affected.

Health care is a resource that is rationed. In the United States and other countries without universal or national programs of health insurance, persons with greater incomes and assets are more likely than low-income families to have health insurance and as a result have greater access to health care services. According to the NHIS, in the United States in 2004, of 293 million Americans, more than forty-four million people, including more than nine million children, had no health insurance and either experienced sharply reduced access to the health care system or were excluded altogether.

A wide range of groups and organizations support the idea that health care is a fundamental human right, not a privilege. These organizations include Physicians for a National Health Program, the American Association of Retired Persons (AARP), National Health Care for the Homeless, Inc., and the Friends Committee on National Legislation, a Quaker public interest lobby. The American Medical Association's "Patient Bill of Rights" includes the "right to essential health care."

In April 2004 HHS secretary Tommy Thompson announced the creation of the Health Disparities Council, a new board charged with developing a plan to eliminate quality gaps in health care. Thompson maintained that the Bush administration's commitment to eliminating disparities in health care was evidenced by action to address racial disparities in health care. Specific actions include supporting research aimed at the health of minorities, providing more money for AIDS issues among minorities, and increasing the number of community health centers in racial and ethnic minority neighborhoods.

ACCESS DOES NOT NECESSARILY ENSURE QUALITY

Even insured Americans who live in metropolitan areas with an ample supply of available health care facilities and providers receive, on average, just half of the recommended screenings and other preventive health care services. A Rand Corporation study, funded by the Robert Wood Johnson Foundation and grants from the Veterans Affairs Health Services, found inadequate care in every one of the twelve metropolitan areas surveyed. Researchers Eve A. Kerr and her colleagues observed that "health care quality falls far short of its potential nationally" in "Profiling the Quality of Care in Twelve Communities: Results from the CQI Study" (*Health Affairs* vol. 23, no. 3, May/June 2004).

The investigators looked at interviews and medical records of 7,000 adults and analyzed them using 439 measures of quality for thirty medical conditions including asthma, diabetes, heart disease, and hypertension as well as preventive care. They found that just half of all heart attack patients receive timely treatment with two medications (aspirin and beta blockers) that have been proven to save lives. Of persons with chronic diseases, those with diabetes fared worst, failing to receive adequate treatment and counseling to prevent or delay the serious consequences of the disease. Some preventive services, such as immunizations and blood pressure screenings, were performed much more often than others, such as counseling about and screening for sexually transmitted diseases and counseling about substance abuse.

Although access problems are much greater for persons who are uninsured and those who live in rural or otherwise underserved areas, this research confirmed that ability to pay for needed medical care and availability of health services were necessary but not sufficient to guarantee access to quality care. The discrepancy between the health care that Americans should receive and the care that they actually receive is even more striking in view of the fact that the United states spends more on health care—an estimated $1.5 trillion each year—than any other nation in the world.

CHAPTER 2

PHYSICIANS, NURSES, DENTISTS,
AND OTHER HEALTH CARE PRACTITIONERS

*The art of medicine consists of amusing the patient
while nature cures the disease.*
—Voltaire (1694–1778)

*One of the first duties of the physician is to educate the
masses not to take medicine.*
—William Osler (1849–1919)

PHYSICIANS

Physicians routinely perform medical examinations,
provide preventive medicine services, diagnose illness, treat
patients suffering from injury or disease, and offer counsel
about how to achieve and maintain good health. There are
two types of physicians trained in traditional Western medicine: the MD (Doctor of Medicine) is schooled in allopathic
medicine and the DO (Doctor of Osteopathy) learns
osteopathy. Allopathy is the philosophy and system of curing disease by producing conditions that are incompatible
with disease, such as prescribing antibiotics to combat bacterial infection. The philosophy of osteopathy is different; it
is based on recognition of the body's capacity for self-healing and it emphasizes structural and manipulative therapies
such as postural education, manual treatment of the musculoskeletal system (osteopathic physicians are trained in
hands-on diagnosis and treatment), and preventive medicine. Osteopathy is also considered a "holistic" practice
because it considers the whole person, rather than simply
the diseased organ or system.

In modern medical practice, the philosophical differences may not be obvious to most health care consumers
since MDs and DOs use many comparable methods of
treatment, including prescribing medication and performing surgery. In fact, the American Osteopathic Association
(AOA), the national medical professional society that represents about fifty-two thousand DOs, admits that many
people who seek care from osteopathic physicians may be
entirely unaware of their physicians' training, which
emphasizes holistic interventions or special skills such as

manipulative techniques. Like MDs, DOs complete four
years of medical school and postgraduate residency training; may specialize in areas such as surgery, psychiatry, or
obstetrics; and must pass state licensing examinations in
order to practice.

Medical School, Postgraduate Training, and Qualifications

Modern medicine requires considerable skill and
extensive training. The road to gaining admission to medical school and becoming a physician is long, difficult,
and intensely competitive. Applicants to medical school
must earn excellent college grades while acquiring their
undergraduate degrees, achieve high scores on entrance
exams, and demonstrate emotional maturity and motiva-
tion to be admitted to medical school. Once admitted to
medical school, students spend the first two years primarily in laboratories and classrooms learning basic medical
sciences such as anatomy (detailed understanding of body
structure), physiology (biological processes and vital
functions), and biochemistry. They also learn how to take
medical histories, perform complete physical examinations, and recognize symptoms of diseases. During their
third and fourth years, the medical students work under
supervision at teaching hospitals and clinics where they
learn acute, chronic, preventive, and rehabilitative patient
care. By completing "clerkships"—spending time in different specialties such as internal medicine, obstetrics and
gynecology, pediatrics, psychiatry, and surgery—they
acquire the necessary skills and gain experience to diagnose and treat a wide variety of illnesses.

Following medical school, new physicians must complete a year of internship, also referred to as "postgraduate
year 1 (PGY1)" emphasizing either general medical practice or one of the specialties and providing clinical experience in various hospital services—inpatient care,
outpatient clinics, emergency rooms, and operating rooms.
In the past, many physicians entered practice after this first

year of postgraduate training. In the present era of specialization, most physicians choose to continue in residency training, which lasts an additional three to six years, depending on the specialty. Those who choose a subspecialty such as cardiology, infectious diseases, oncology, or plastic surgery must spend additional years in residency and may then choose to complete fellowship training. Immediately after residency, they are eligible to take an examination to earn board certification in their chosen specialty. Fellowship training involves a year or two of laboratory and clinical research work as well as opportunities to gain additional clinical and patient care expertise.

Conventional and Newer Medical Specialties

Rapid advances in science and medicine along with changing needs have resulted in a variety of new medical and surgical specialties, subspecialties, and concentrations. For example, geriatrics, the medical subspecialty concerned with the prevention and treatment of diseases in the elderly, has developed in response to the growing population of older adults in need of medical care. In 1909 Dr. Ignatz L. Nascher coined the term geriatrics from the Greek "geras" (old age) and "iatrikos" (physician). Geriatricians are physicians trained in internal medicine or family practice who obtain additional training and certification in the diagnosis and treatment of older adults. According to the American Geriatrics Society, the United States currently needs at least 20,000 geriatricians to care for its 36 million older adults. In 2004 board-certified geriatricians numbered only 9,500—still less than half of the estimated need.

Another relatively new medical specialty has resulted in physician "intensivists." Intensivists, as the name indicates, are trained to staff hospital intensive care units (ICUs, sometimes known as critical care units or CCUs), where the most critically ill patients are cared for using a comprehensive array of state-of-the-art technology and equipment. This specialty arose in response to both the increasing complexity of care provided in ICUs and the demonstrated benefits of immediate availability of highly trained physicians to care for critically ill patients.

More traditional medical specialties include:

- Anesthesiologist—administers anesthesia (partial or complete loss of sensation) and monitors patients in surgery

- Cardiologist—diagnoses and treats diseases of the heart and blood vessels

- Dermatologist—trained to diagnose and treat diseases of the skin, hair, and nails

- Family Practitioner—delivers primary care to persons of all ages and, when necessary, refers patients to other physician specialists

- Gastroenterologist—specializes in digestive system disorders

- Internist—provides diagnosis and nonsurgical treatment of a broad array of illnesses affecting adults

- Neurologist—specializes in the nervous system—diagnosis and treatment of brain, spinal cord, and nerve disorders

- Obstetrician-gynecologist—provides health care for women and their reproductive systems, as well as care for mother and baby before, during, and immediately following delivery

- Oncologist—dedicated to the diagnosis and treatment of cancer

- Otolaryngologist—skilled in the medical and surgical treatment of ear, nose, and throat disorders and related structures of the face, head, and neck

- Pathologist—uses skills in microscopic chemical analysis and diagnostics to direct detection of disease in the laboratory

- Psychiatrist—specializes in the prevention, diagnosis, and treatment of mental health and emotional disorders

- Pulmonologist—specializes in diseases of the lungs and respiratory system

- Urologist—provides diagnosis as well as medical and surgical treatment of the urinary tract in both men and women as well as male reproductive health services

High Costs, Long Hours, and Low Wages

According to the Association of American Medical Colleges (AAMC), in the 2003–04 school year median medical school costs were $14,544 for in-state residents at public schools and $32,028 for private school tuition and fees. (See Table 2.1.) Still, tuition and fees do not even completely cover the cost of educating prospective physicians—tuition is subsidized by other university teaching hospital activities as well as grants and endowments. According to other AAMC data, public medical school students graduating in 2003 had incurred a median debt comparable to a home mortgage—about $100,000—and private medical school students incurred a median debt of $135,000. More than one-fifth of students (21.4%) incurred a debt of more than $150,000. Medical school debt has increased more than 60% since 1993, when students owed an average of $60,000 at graduation. Although physicians' earning power is considerable, and many students are able to repay their debts during their first years of practice, some observers believe that the extent of their indebtedness may unduly influence medical students' career choices. They may train for higher paying specialties and subspecialties rather than following their natural interests or opting to practice in underrepresented specialties or underserved geographic areas. The high cost of

TABLE 2.1

Medical school tuition and student fees for first-year students, 2002–03 and 2003–04

	2003–2004 (n=75)			2002–2003 (n=74)		
	Range	**Median**	**Average**	**Range**	**Median**	**Average**
Public medical schools						
Tuition						
Resident	0–26,062	14,544	13,447	0–25,073	12,309	12,309
Non-resident	10,000–67,000	30,708	30,642	10,000–64,186	28,392	28,392
Fees						
Resident	50–16,332	1,523	2,701	40–11,100	1,436	2,268
Non-resident	50–28,472	1,536	2,984	40–24,947	1,389	2,532
Tuition & fees						
Resident	4,922–26,422	16,332	16,149	4,795–27,070	13,873	14,577
Non-resident	12,392–69,174	32,534	33,629	12,692–66,360	30,428	30,924
Private medical schools						
	2003–2004 (n=50)			2002–2003 (n=50)		
Tuition						
Resident	6,550–39,579	32,028	30,748	6,550–39,579	30,589	29,308
Non-resident	19,650–39,579	32,950	32,291	18,700–39,579	31,213	30,915
Fees						
Resident	0–6,750	1,594	1,740	0–5,300	1,593	1,652
Non-resident	0–6,750	1,594	1,775	0–5,300	1,593	1,686
Tuition & fees						
Resident	9,558–40,459	33,817	32,488	9,785–40,094	32,107	30,960
Non-resident	22,500–40,459	34,247	34,067	21,500–40,094	32,649	32,601

SOURCE: "Table 1. U.S. Medical Schools Tuition and Student Fees—First Year Students 2003–2004 and 2002–2003," in *Tuition and Student Fees Reports,* Association of American Medical Colleges, November 2003, http://services.aamc.org/tsf/TSF_Report/report_median.cfm?year_of_study=2004 (accessed June 2, 2004)

medical education also is believed to limit the number of minority applicants to medical school.

Historically, medical training has been difficult and involved long hours. Residents typically worked twenty-four- to thirty-six-hour shifts and more than eighty hours a week. Lack of sleep and low wages are a way of life for most medical students and residents, although the thirty-six hour shift has come under criticism as an unnecessary, and possibly dangerous, practice. In 1995 the state of New York limited most residents to twenty-four-hour shifts and eighty-hour weeks. The regulations were the first of their kind in the country. New York has almost 150 teaching hospitals and trains 16% of the nation's doctors.

In 2001 the Committee of Interns and Residents and the American Medical Student Association, which represents more than 30,000 physicians-in-training, were two of several groups to petition the U.S. Department of Labor's Occupational Safety and Health Administration (OSHA) to limit the number of hours medical residents must work. The petition observed that sleep deprivation among physicians in training, who may work as many as 130 hours a week with only one day off, increases their risk of automobile accidents, depression, and other ailments and poses risks to the patients they treat. The petition sought a limit of eighty hours per week, with a maximum of twenty-four hours in one shift and with ten hours between shifts. For emergency medicine residents, the maximum allowable hours of work per day would be twelve.

By 2002, several states and many professional associations including the AOA approved an eighty-hour work-week for all interns and residents. The AOA ruled that interns and residents may not work more than twenty-four consecutive hours. To reduce the possibility of diagnostic and treatment errors, residents are forbidden to assume responsibility for new patients after they have worked twenty-four hours. The AOA mandated that its training programs comply with this measure by November 1, 2002, in order to retain their accreditation. On July 20, 2002, in a published statement, Dr. James E. Zini, the 2001–02 president of the AOA, said: "Patient safety is our number one priority, and that is the main reason the osteopathic profession will implement these changes this fall."

In July 2003 the Accreditation Council for Graduate Medical Education, which oversees more than seventy-eight hundred residency programs, adopted guidelines that limited duty hours to eighty hours a week (surgical programs were permitted to have residents work eighty-eight hours per week) for the nation's one hundred thousand physicians-in-training. By July 2004, a study performed by the accreditation council found that most medical residency programs were adhering to the new guidelines. The council's review of 2,019 medical resi-

TABLE 2.2

Medical school applicants, accepted applicants, and matriculants, by gender, 1992–2003

								Year							Change 2002–2003
1992–2003		1992	1993	1994	1995	1996	1997	1998	1999	2000	2001	2002	2003	2002–2003
Applicants by gender														
Women	N	15,618	17,957	18,967	19,776	20,028	18,271	17,785	17,395	17,273	16,718	16,556	17,672	6.7%
	%	41.8	41.9	41.8	42.5	42.6	42.5	43.4	45.2	46.6	48.0	49.2	50.8	1.6
Men	N	21,784	24,849	26,393	26,810	26,937	24,745	23,211	21,048	19,816	18,142	17,069	17,114	0.3%
	%	58.2	58.1	58.2	57.5	57.4	57.5	56.6	54.8	53.4	52.0	50.8	49.2	−1.6
Applicants total		**37,402**	**42,806**	**45,360**	**46,586**	**46,965**	**43,016**	**40,996**	**38,443**	**37,089**	**34,860**	**33,625**	**34,786**	**3.5%**
First-time applicants by gender														
Women	N	12,171	13,369	13,644	13,980	13,779	12,698	12,493	12,469	12,480	12,357	12,649	13,730	8.5%
	%	42.3	42.6	42.8	44.1	43.9	44.4	45.4	47.7	48.4	49.6	50.8	52.5	1.7
Men	N	16,596	18,020	18,259	17,718	17,598	15,929	15,042	13,658	13,279	12,557	12,238	12,430	1.6%
	%	57.7	57.4	57.2	55.9	56.1	55.6	54.6	52.3	51.6	50.4	49.2	47.5	−1.7
First-time applicants total		**28,767**	**31,389**	**31,903**	**31,698**	**31,377**	**28,627**	**27,535**	**26,127**	**25,759**	**24,914**	**24,887**	**26,160**	**5.1%**
Acceptees by gender														
Women	N	7,257	7,288	7,255	7,437	7,439	7,485	7,685	7,966	8,027	8,294	8,631	8,732	1.2%
	%	41.6	42.0	41.9	42.8	42.8	43.2	44.2	45.7	45.8	47.5	49.1	49.8	0.7
Men	N	10,208	10,073	10,063	9,920	9,946	9,828	9,688	9,455	9,509	9,160	8,962	8,807	−1.7%
	%	58.4	58.0	58.1	57.2	57.2	56.8	55.8	54.3	54.2	52.5	50.9	50.2	−0.7
Acceptees total		**17,465**	**17,361**	**17,318**	**17,357**	**17,385**	**17,313**	**17,373**	**17,421**	**17,536**	**17,454**	**17,593**	**17,539**	**−0.3%**
Matriculants by gender														
Women	N	6,772	6,851	6,819	6,941	6,918	6,995	7,162	7,412	7,472	7,784	8,113	8,212	1.2%
	%	41.6	42.0	41.9	42.7	42.7	43.3	44.3	45.7	45.8	47.6	49.2	49.7	0.5
Men	N	9,517	9,456	9,468	9,312	9,283	9,170	9,008	8,809	8,829	8,581	8,375	8,326	0.6%
	%	58.4	58.0	58.1	57.3	57.3	56.7	55.7	54.3	54.2	52.4	50.8	50.3	−0.5
Matriculants total		**16,289**	**16,307**	**16,287**	**16,253**	**16,201**	**16,165**	**16,170**	**16,221**	**16,301**	**16,365**	**16,488**	**16,538**	**0.3%**

SOURCE: "Applicants, Accepted Applicants, and Matriculants by Gender, 1992–2003," in *FACTS—Applicants, Matriculants and Graduates,* Association of American Medical Colleges, November 2003, http://www.aamc.org/data/facts/2003/2003summary.htm (accessed June 2, 2004)

dency training programs found that just 5% of programs did not comply with the new standards ("New Doctors Work Less but Problems Persist," Associated Press, CNN.com, July 28, 2004).

Applying to Medical School

The average premedical student applies to twelve medical schools. There is an average of 2.6 applicants for every available opening. The ratio, however, jumps as high as seventy to one for small, selective schools such as the Mayo Medical School in Rochester, Minnesota, or the Yale College of Medicine in New Haven, Connecticut. After a six-year decline, the number of applicants to U.S. medical schools is on the rise, according to a survey by the Association of American Medical Colleges published in 2003. There were nearly thirty-five thousand applicants in the 2003–04 school year, a 3.4% increase over the prior year's applicant pool of 33,625. The increase was driven by the number of women applicants—17,672—an almost 7% rise over the prior year's total. For the first time ever, women made up the majority of medical school applicants. Despite this increase the number of applicants was still well below the all-time high of 46,965 in 1996. (See Table 2.2.) These applicants were vying for 16,500 available places.

There are several explanations for the six-year (1996–2002) decline in medical school applications. With the exponential growth in the cost of medical school, some prospective students may no longer be willing or able to incur such significant debt. Another factor may be physician concern about the growing health care system bureaucracy and unavoidable paperwork, including requirements to seek approval from insurers for many diagnostic tests, surgical procedures, and admission of patients to hospitals. Intrusion into medical practice from government and private payers, fear of malpractice suits, and increasing consumer demand for greater equality in physician-patient relationships may have combined to diminish some of the professional satisfaction and prestige associated with the medical practice.

Still, despite mounting costs for medical education and growing constraints on physicians' practices, a medical degree still offers continuing employment, economic security, and a measurable way to help people. Many potential physicians consider medicine a rewarding and relatively "recession-proof" way to earn a living.

APPLICANTS AND STUDENTS BECOMING OLDER AND MORE DIVERSE. Data from the AAMC also indicate that class-

TABLE 2.3

Primary care physicians by specialty in the United States and outlying U.S. areas, selected years 1949–2001

[Data are based on reporting by physicians]

Specialty	1949[1]	1960[1]	1970	1980	1990	1995	1997	1998	1999	2000	2001
						Number					
Total doctors of medicine[2]	201,277	260,484	334,028	467,679	615,421	720,325	766,710	777,859	797,634	813,770	836,156
Active doctors of medicine[3]	191,577	247,257	310,845	414,916	547,310	625,443	664,556	667,000	669,949	692,368	713,375
Primary care generalists	113,222	125,359	115,822	146,093	183,294	207,810	216,598	218,421	221,206	227,992	246,714
General/family practice	95,980	88,023	57,948	60,049	70,480	75,976	78,258	79,769	81,487	83,165	88,597
Internal medicine	12,453	26,209	39,924	58,462	76,295	88,240	93,797	93,227	92,976	96,469	105,229
Pediatrics	4,789	11,127	17,950	27,582	36,519	43,594	44,543	45,425	46,743	48,358	52,888
Primary care specialists	—	—	2,817	14,949	27,434	35,290	32,918	34,299	37,424	40,675	51,134
Internal medicine	—	—	1,948	13,069	22,054	26,928	24,582	25,365	24,140	29,382	37,558
Pediatrics	—	—	869	1,880	5,380	8,362	8,336	8,934	10,284	11,293	13,576
					Percent of active doctors of medicine						
Primary care generalists	59.1	50.7	37.3	35.2	33.5	33.2	32.6	32.7	33.0	32.9	34.6
General/family practice	50.1	35.6	18.6	14.5	12.9	12.1	11.8	12.0	12.2	12.0	12.4
Internal medicine	6.5	10.6	12.8	14.1	13.9	14.1	14.1	14.0	13.9	13.9	14.8
Pediatrics	2.5	4.5	5.8	6.6	6.7	7.0	6.7	6.8	7.0	7.0	7.4
Primary care specialists	—	—	0.9	3.6	5.0	5.6	5.0	5.1	5.6	5.9	7.2
Internal medicine	—	—	0.6	3.1	4.0	4.3	3.7	3.8	4.1	4.2	5.3
Pediatrics	—	—	0.3	0.5	1.0	1.3	1.3	1.3	1.5	1.6	1.9

Note: Data are as of December 31 except for 1990–94 data, which are as of January 1, and 1949 data, which are as of midyear. Outlying areas include Puerto Rico, Virgin Islands, and the Pacific Islands of Canton, Caroline, Guam, Mariana, Marshall, American Samoa, and Wake.
— Data not available.
[1]Estimated by the Bureau of Health Professions, Health Resources Administration. Active doctors of medicine (M.D.'s) include those with address unknown and primary specialty not classified.
[2]Includes M.D.'s engaged in federal and non-federal patient care (office-based or hospital-based) and other professional activities.
[3]Beginning in 1970, M.D.'s who are inactive, have unknown address, or primary specialty not classified are excluded.

SOURCE: "Table 101. Doctors of Medicine in Primary Care, according to Specialty: United States and Outlying U.S. Areas, Selected Years 1949–2001," in *Health, United States, 2003*, National Center for Health Statistics, 2003, http://www.cdc.gov/nchs/data/hus/tables/2003/03hus101.pdf (accessed June 2, 2004)

es in American medical schools more closely resemble the American population in gender and ethnic background than they did two decades ago. However, minority enrollment has declined in recent years from its peak in the early and mid-1990s. For the 2003–04 school year, the number of African-American applicants rose almost 5% to 2,736 (1,904 of the 2,736 were African-American female applicants), but the number of African-Americans who entered medical school declined by 6% to 1,056 from the prior year. Hispanic applicants increased by less than 2% to 2,483, while the number who entered medical school declined by almost 4% to 1,089.

Medical students are also older than they used to be. In the past, almost all students entered medical school directly from undergraduate college. While the majority of students in the late 1990s were still fresh from college, in recent years older applicants have gained admission, and many medical schools have come to value the maturity and experience of older students.

Number of Physicians in Practice Is Increasing

In 2001 an estimated 713,375 physicians practiced medicine in the United States, about 23% more than the 547,310 practicing in 1990. (See Table 2.3.) The proportion of physicians in patient care (as opposed to researchers, educators, or retired) has increased dramatically—from 13.5 per ten thousand civilian population in 1975, to 21.3 in 1995, to 22.6 in 2001. (See Table 2.4.)

Table 2.4 reveals that in 2001, New England and the Middle Atlantic states had the highest ratio (31.2 and 29.4

per ten thousand respectively) of physicians practicing in patient care to civilian population. Idaho and Oklahoma were the states with the fewest physicians active in patient care (14.8 and 15 per ten thousand) and the Mountain region—including Montana, Idaho, Wyoming, Colorado, New Mexico, Arizona, Utah, and Nevada—was the region with the fewest practicing physicians (18.4 per ten thousand).

Many Are Specialists

Most doctors are specialists rather than primary care generalists. Primary care physicians are the "frontline" of the health care system—the first health professionals most people see for medical problems or routine care. Family practitioners, internists, pediatricians, and general practitioners are considered to be primary care practitioners. Primary care physicians tend to see the same patients regularly and develop relationships with patients over time as they offer preventive services, scheduled visits, follow-up, and urgent medical care. When necessary, they refer patients for consultation with, and care from, physician specialists. In 2001, 34.6% of active physicians were primary care generalists. Of this group, 12.4% were in general and family practice, 14.8% were in internal medicine, and 7.4% were in pediatrics. (See Table 2.3.)

Working Conditions

Many physicians work long, irregular hours. The U.S. Department of Labor Bureau of Labor Statistics (BLS) reported that in 2002 about one-third of physicians worked sixty hours or more a week in 2002, performing patient care and administrative duties such as office management.

TABLE 2.4

Active non-federal physicians in patient care, by geographic region and state, 1975, 1985, 1995, and 2001

[Data are based on reporting by physicians]

Geographic division and state	Total physicians[1]				Doctors of medicine in patient care[2]			
	1975	1985	1995[3]	2001[4]	1975	1985	1995	2001
	Number per 10,000 civilian population							
United States	15.3	20.7	24.2	25.5	13.5	18.0	21.3	22.6
New England	19.1	26.7	32.5	35.0	16.9	22.9	28.8	31.2
Maine	12.8	18.7	22.3	27.3	10.7	15.6	18.2	22.4
New Hampshire	14.3	18.1	21.5	24.7	13.1	16.7	19.8	22.6
Vermont	18.2	23.8	26.9	33.2	15.5	20.3	24.2	30.1
Massachusetts	20.8	30.2	37.5	39.3	18.3	25.4	33.2	35.2
Rhode Island	17.8	23.3	30.4	33.4	16.1	20.2	26.7	29.8
Connecticut	19.8	27.6	32.8	34.4	17.7	24.3	29.5	31.0
Middle Atlantic	19.5	26.1	32.4	34.0	17.0	22.2	28.0	29.4
New York	22.7	29.0	35.3	36.7	20.2	25.2	31.6	32.9
New Jersey	16.2	23.4	29.3	31.4	14.0	19.8	24.9	26.9
Pennsylvania	16.6	23.6	30.1	31.6	13.9	19.2	24.6	25.8
East North Central	13.9	19.3	23.3	25.0	12.0	16.4	19.8	21.5
Ohio	14.1	19.9	23.8	25.8	12.2	16.8	20.0	21.9
Indiana	10.6	14.7	18.4	20.6	9.6	13.2	16.6	18.7
Illinois	14.5	20.5	24.8	26.2	13.0	18.2	22.1	23.3
Michigan	15.4	20.8	24.8	26.2	12.0	16.0	19.0	20.6
Wisconsin	12.5	17.7	21.5	23.6	11.4	15.9	19.6	21.5
West North Central	13.3	18.3	21.8	23.5	11.4	15.6	18.9	20.4
Minnesota	14.9	20.5	23.4	25.7	13.7	18.5	21.5	23.7
Iowa	11.4	15.6	19.2	20.0	9.4	12.4	15.1	15.8
Missouri	15.0	20.5	23.9	24.9	11.6	16.3	19.7	20.8
North Dakota	9.7	15.8	20.5	22.1	9.2	14.9	18.9	20.4
South Dakota	8.2	13.4	16.7	19.8	7.7	12.3	15.7	18.3
Nebraska	12.1	15.7	19.8	22.4	10.9	14.4	18.3	20.8
Kansas	12.8	17.3	20.8	21.9	11.2	15.1	18.0	19.0
South Atlantic	14.0	19.7	23.4	24.8	12.6	17.6	21.0	22.3
Delaware	14.3	19.7	23.4	25.1	12.7	17.1	19.7	21.7
Maryland	18.6	30.4	34.1	35.9	16.5	24.9	29.9	31.7
District of Columbia	39.6	55.3	63.6	62.5	34.6	45.6	53.6	54.6
Virginia	12.9	19.5	22.5	24.4	11.9	17.8	20.8	22.5
West Virginia	11.0	16.3	21.0	23.7	10.0	14.6	17.9	20.0
North Carolina	11.7	16.9	21.1	23.0	10.6	15.0	19.4	21.2
South Carolina	10.0	14.7	18.9	21.5	9.3	13.6	17.6	19.9
Georgia	11.5	16.2	19.7	20.4	10.6	14.7	18.0	18.8
Florida	15.2	20.2	22.9	24.0	13.4	17.8	20.3	21.3
East South Central	10.5	15.0	19.2	21.1	9.7	14.0	17.8	19.5
Kentucky	10.9	15.1	19.2	21.0	10.1	13.9	18.0	19.6
Tennessee	12.4	17.7	22.5	24.0	11.3	16.2	20.8	22.3
Alabama	9.2	14.2	18.4	20.0	8.6	13.1	17.0	18.4
Mississippi	8.4	11.8	13.9	17.1	8.0	11.1	13.0	15.6
West South Central	11.9	16.4	19.5	20.7	10.5	14.5	17.3	18.5
Arkansas	9.1	13.8	17.3	19.0	8.5	12.8	16.0	17.7
Louisiana	11.4	17.3	21.7	24.4	10.5	16.1	20.3	23.1
Oklahoma	11.6	16.1	18.8	19.2	9.4	12.9	14.7	15.0
Texas	12.5	16.8	19.4	20.4	11.0	14.7	17.3	18.2
Mountain	14.3	17.8	20.2	20.8	12.6	15.7	17.8	18.4
Montana	10.6	14.0	18.4	21.4	10.1	13.2	17.1	19.9
Idaho	9.5	12.1	13.9	16.1	8.9	11.4	13.1	14.8
Wyoming	9.5	12.9	15.3	18.0	8.9	12.0	13.9	16.5
Colorado	17.3	20.7	23.7	24.1	15.0	17.7	20.6	21.2
New Mexico	12.2	17.0	20.2	21.3	10.1	14.7	18.0	19.0
Arizona	16.7	20.2	21.4	20.7	14.1	17.1	18.2	17.7
Utah	14.1	17.2	19.2	19.9	13.0	15.5	17.6	18.0
Nevada	11.9	16.0	16.7	18.0	10.9	14.5	14.6	16.1

The BLS reported that physicians and surgeons held about 583,000 jobs in 2002, and one out of six was self-employed. Physicians in salaried positions, such as those employed by health maintenance organizations (HMOs), usually have shorter and more regular hours and enjoy more flexible work schedules than those in private practice. Instead of working as solo practitioners, growing numbers of physicians work in clinics, or are partners in group prac-

tices or other integrated health care systems. Medical group practices allow physicians to have more flexible schedules, realize purchasing economies of scale, pool their money to finance expensive medical equipment, and be better able to adapt to changes in the health care environment.

Data from the 2001 National Ambulatory Medical Care Survey (NAMCS) revealed that about one-third of office-based

TABLE 2.4

Active non-federal physicians in patient care, by geographic region and state, 1975, 1985, 1995, and 2001 [CONTINUED]

[Data are based on reporting by physicians]

Geographic division and state	Total physicians[1]				Doctors of medicine in patient care[2]			
	1975	1985	1995[3]	2001[4]	1975	1985	1995	2001
Pacific	17.9	22.5	23.3	24.1	16.3	20.5	21.2	21.9
Washington	15.3	20.2	22.5	24.4	13.6	17.9	20.2	22.0
Oregon	15.6	19.7	21.6	23.7	13.8	17.6	19.5	21.4
California	18.8	23.7	23.7	24.0	17.3	21.5	21.7	21.9
Alaska	8.4	13.0	15.7	19.3	7.8	12.1	14.2	17.0
Hawaii	16.2	21.5	24.8	27.4	14.7	19.8	22.8	25.0

Note: Data for doctors of medicine are as of December 31.
[1]Includes active non-federal doctors of medicine and active doctors of osteopathy.
[2]Excludes doctors of osteopathy (DO's); states with more than 2,500 active DO's are Pennsylvania, Michigan, Ohio, Florida, New York, and Texas. States with fewer than 100 active DO's are Wyoming, Vermont, North Dakota, South Dakota, Montana, Louisiana, Alaska, Nebraska, and District of Columbia. Excludes doctors of medicine in medical teaching, administration, research, and other nonpatient care activities.
[3]Data for doctors of osteopathy are as of July 1996.
[4]Data for doctors of osteopathy are as of June 2001.

SOURCE: "Table 99. Active Non-Federal Physicians and Doctors of Medicine in Patient Care, according to Geographic Division and State: United States, 1975, 1985, 1995, and 2001," in *Health, United States, 2003,* National Center for Health Statistics, 2003, http://www.cdc.gov/nchs/data/hus/tables/2003/03hus099.pdf (accessed June 2, 2004)

physicians were in solo practice, 40.8% were in a single-specialty group practice, and 25.9% were in multispecialty group practices. During 2001 the typical physician in an office-based practice saw about eighty patients in the office, provided sixteen telephone and 0.5 e-mail consultations, and made thirteen hospital visits and 0.9 house calls each week. Naturally, physicians' hours and the settings in which they provided care varied somewhat depending on their specialties. General and family practitioners and pediatricians spent far more time conducting office visits, while surgeons, obstetricians, and gynecologists spent more time at the hospital performing procedures. About 17.8% of physicians made house calls during a typical week, and primary care physicians were much more likely to make house calls than physician specialists. According to the American Academy of Family Physicians, in 2003 the average family physician saw about ninety patients per week in the office, 10.5 patients in the hospital, and supervised the care of 10.5 nursing home patients, 5.7 patients receiving home health care, and 1.5 hospice patients.

The number of office visits per week varied by geographic location. Rural family physicians saw more patients in their offices (93.9) per week than their urban counterpart (89.1). Family physicians in the West South Central region reported the highest number of office visits per week— 104.5—while family physicians in New England had the fewest office visits per week—75.1 (*American Academy of Family Physicians, Practice Profile Survey, May 2003*).

Physicians' Earnings and Opportunities

Physicians' earnings are among the highest of any profession. According to the Medical Group Management Association (MGMA) publication *Physician Compensation and Production Report, 2003,* the median total compensation for physicians in 2002 varied by specialty. The range of salaries varies widely and is often based on a

FIGURE 2.1

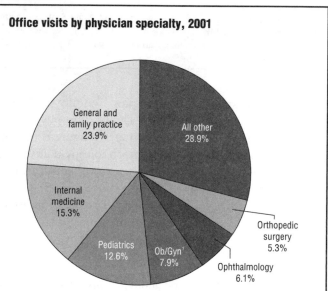

Office visits by physician specialty, 2001

General and family practice 23.9%
All other 28.9%
Internal medicine 15.3%
Orthopedic surgery 5.3%
Ophthalmology 6.1%
Pediatrics 12.6%
Ob/Gyn[1] 7.9%

[1]Ob/Gyn is obstetrics/gynecology.

SOURCE: Donald K. Cherry, Catherine W. Burt, and David A. Woodell, "Figure 1. Percent Distribution of Office Visits by Physician Specialty: United States, 2001," in "National Ambulatory Care Survey: 2001 Summary," in *Advance Data from Vital and Health Statistics,* no. 337, Centers for Disease Control and Prevention, National Center for Health Statistics, August 11, 2003, http://www.cdc.gov/nchs/data/ad/ad337.pdf (accessed July 2, 2004)

physician's specialty, the number of years in practice, hours worked, and geographic location. Anesthesiologists and general surgeons were among the top earners with median earnings of $306,964 and $255,438, respectively, while pediatricians and family practitioners earned the least, $152,690 and $150,267 a year, respectively.

Although the costs of running a medical practice have increased as a result of additional administrative requirements such as complicated billing and reimbursement for-

FIGURE 2.2

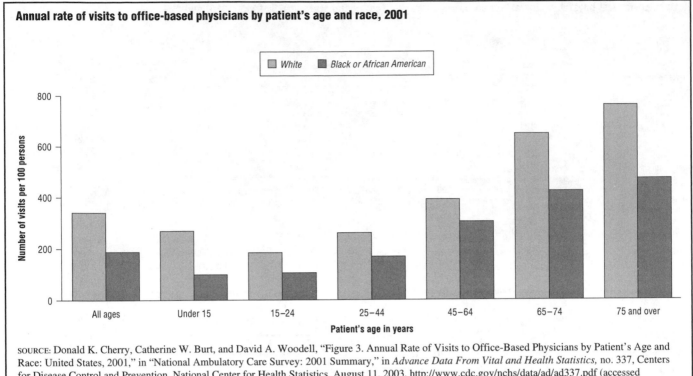

Annual rate of visits to office-based physicians by patient's age and race, 2001

Legend: ▢ White ▪ Black or African American

SOURCE: Donald K. Cherry, Catherine W. Burt, and David A. Woodell, "Figure 3. Annual Rate of Visits to Office-Based Physicians by Patient's Age and Race: United States, 2001," in "National Ambulatory Care Survey: 2001 Summary," in *Advance Data From Vital and Health Statistics,* no. 337, Centers for Disease Control and Prevention, National Center for Health Statistics, August 11, 2003, http://www.cdc.gov/nchs/data/ad/ad337.pdf (accessed July 2, 2004)

mulas, the prospects for physicians' employment and earnings continue to be excellent. Demand for physicians' services keeps pace with the growing and aging U.S. population, and rapidly evolving biotechnological advances promise to enable physicians to do more, and for more people. According to the U.S. Bureau of Labor Statistics, future opportunities for physicians will be plentiful, especially in rural and low-income communities.

Physician Visits

In 2001 Americans made about 3.1 physician office visits per person for a total of more than 880 million office visits to physicians, and half of these visits were to primary care physicians. (See Figure 2.1.) Women visited physicians more often than men, and, as expected, persons over seventy-five years of age saw doctors more than twice as often as most younger persons. African-Americans of all ages made fewer physician office visits than whites, about 1.9 times per year compared with 3.4 visits per year. (See Figure 2.2.)

According to the National Center for Health Statistics' *Health, United States, 2003,* people also visited physicians in other settings including hospital emergency departments and home visits, making the total of all ambulatory care visits to physician offices, hospital outpatient, and emergency departments more than one billion for the second consecutive year in 2001.

Understandably, older adults made more ambulatory care visits, with men over age seventy-five making the

most frequent visits to physicians' offices and hospital outpatient and emergency departments. In 2001 African-American older adults (aged seventy-five and older) made more than twice as many hospital outpatient visits (sixty-seven visits per one hundred persons) as white older adults (thirty-six visits per one hundred persons). Similarly African-American older adults were seen much more frequently by physicians in hospital emergency departments (ninety-one visits per one hundred persons) than white older adults (fifty-eight visits per one hundred persons), according to the National Center for Health Statistics.

Physician Satisfaction

Changes in the health care delivery system, particularly the shift from traditional fee-for-service practice to managed care, with its efforts to standardize medical practice—which reduces physicians' ability to manage their time, schedules, and professional relationships—have been named as factors contributing to physicians' dissatisfaction with their choice of career. Other changes, including decreasing reimbursement and an ever-increasing emphasis on documentation to satisfy government and private payers as well as administrative requirements that infringe on time physicians would rather spend caring for patients, have also fanned the flames of physician dissatisfaction.

Research conducted by Bruce Landon and his colleagues at Harvard Medical School and the Center for Studying Health System Change (HSC) found that while the majority of physicians were satisfied with their careers, there was significant geographic variation in physician satisfaction

TABLE 2.5

Active health personnel according to occupation, selected years 1980–2000

(Data are compiled by the Bureau of Health Professions)

Occupation	1980	1985[1]	1990	1995	1999	2000[2]
			Number of active health personnel			
Chiropractors	25,600	—	41,500	47,200	—	—
Dentists[3]	121,900	133,500	147,500	158,600	164,700	168,000
Nurses, registered	1,272,900	1,538,100	1,789,600	2,115,800	2,271,300	—
Associate and diploma	908,300	1,024,500	1,107,300	1,235,100	1,290,400	—
Baccalaureate	297,300	419,900	549,000	673,200	739,000	—
Masters and doctorate	67,300	93,700	133,300	207,500	241,900	—
Nutritionists/dieticians	32,000	—	67,000	—	—	97,000
Occupational therapists	25,000	—	34,000	—	—	55,000
Optometrists	22,330	23,900	26,000	28,900	—	29,500
Pharmacists	142,780	159,200	161,900	182,300	—	208,000
Physical therapists	50,000	—	92,000	—	—	144,000
Physicians	427,122	542,653	567,610	672,859	753,176	772,296
Federal	17,642	23,305	20,784	21,153	17,338	19,228
Doctors of medicine[4]	16,585	21,938	19,166	19,830	17,224	19,110
Doctors of osteopathy	1,057	1,367	1,618	1,323	114	118
Non-federal	409,480	519,348	546,826	651,706	735,838	753,068
Doctors of medicine[4]	393,407	497,473	520,450	617,362	693,345	708,463
Doctors of osteopathy	16,073	21,875	26,376	34,344	42,493	44,605
Podiatrists[5]	7,000	9,700	10,600	10,300	—	—
Speech therapists	50,000	—	65,000	—	—	97,000
			Number per 100,000 population			
Chiropractors	11.2	—	16.5	17.8	—	—
Dentists[3]	54.0	56.5	59.5	60.7	60.7	60.4
Nurses, registered	560.0	641.4	713.7	797.6	832.9	—
Associate and diploma	399.9	425.8	441.6	465.5	473.2	—
Baccalaureate	130.9	175.6	218.9	253.8	271.0	—
Masters and doctorate	29.6	39.9	53.2	78.2	88.7	—
Nutritionists/dieticians	14.0	—	26.7	—	—	35.2
Occupational therapists	10.9	—	13.5	—	—	20.0
Optometrists	9.8	9.9	10.4	10.9	—	11.1
Pharmacists	62.5	66.3	64.4	68.9	—	75.6
Physical therapists	21.8	—	36.6	—	—	52.3
Physicians	189.8	221.3	230.2	255.9	277.4	277.8
Federal	7.8	9.5	8.4	8.0	6.4	6.9
Doctors of medicine[4]	7.4	8.9	7.7	7.5	6.3	6.9
Doctors of osteopathy	0.5	0.6	0.7	0.5	0.1	0.0
Non-federal	182.0	211.8	221.8	247.9	271.0	270.9
Doctors of medicine[4]	174.9	202.9	211.1	234.8	255.4	254.9
Doctors of osteopathy	7.1	8.9	10.7	13.1	15.7	16.0
Podiatrists[5]	3.0	4.2	4.2	3.9	—	—
Speech therapists	21.8	—	25.9	—	—	36.4

Notes: Ratios for physicians and dentists are based on civilian population; ratios for all other health occupations are based on resident population.
— Data not available
[1]Osteopath data are for 1986 and podiatric data are for 1984.
[2]Data for optometrists and speech therapists are for 1996.
[3]Excludes dentists in military service, U.S. Public Health Service, and Department of Veterans Affairs.
[4]Excludes physicans with unknown addresses and those who do not practice or practice less than 20 hours per week. From 1989 to 1994 data for doctors of medicine are as of January 1; in other years these data are as of December 31.
[5]Podiatrists in patient care.

SOURCE: "Table 102. Active Health Personnel according to Occupation: United States, Selected Years 1980–2000," in *Health, United States, 2003,* National Center for Health Statistics,2003,http://www.cdc.gov/nchs/data/hus/tables/2003/03hus102.pdf (accessed June 2,2004.)

("Changes in Career Satisfaction among Primary Care and Specialist Physicians, 1997–2001," *Journal of the American Medical Association,* vol. 289, no. 4, January 22/29, 2003).

The researchers surveyed more than twelve thousand primary care and specialist physicians who spent at least twenty hours per week in patient care in 1997, 1999, and 2001. Each survey found that approximately 80% of primary care and specialist physicians were somewhat or very satisfied with their careers, and about 18% were somewhat or very dissatisfied with their careers. The study also examined physician career satisfaction in twelve market regions in an effort to identify some of the underlying reasons for satisfaction and dissatisfaction.

Although new state regulations and health plan mergers, as well as changes in hospital competition and practice ownership, may have contributed to the geographic variation physician dissatisfaction, the researchers found that physician independence—the freedom to make clinical decisions in the best interest of patients, being able to spend adequate time with patients, and maintaining ongoing relationships with patients—was more important than income in predicting changes in physician satisfaction. Physicians who felt they had the greatest degree of autonomy appear to be the most satisfied with their career choices.

REGISTERED NURSES

Registered nurses (RNs) are licensed by the state to care for the sick and to promote health. RNs supervise hospital care, administer medication and treatment as prescribed by physicians, monitor the progress of patients, and provide health education. Nurses work in a variety of settings, including hospitals, nursing homes, physicians' offices, clinics, and schools.

Education for Nurses

There are three types of education for registered nurses. These include associate degrees (two-year community college programs), baccalaureate programs (four years of college), and postgraduate (master's degree and doctorate) programs. The baccalaureate degree provides more knowledge of community health services, as well as the psychological and social aspects of caring for patients, than does the associate degree. Those who complete the four-year baccalaureate degree and the other advanced degrees are generally better prepared to eventually attain administrative or management positions and may have greater opportunities for upward mobility in related disciplines such as research, teaching, and public health.

Between 1980 and 1999, the number of registered nurses grew from 1.3 million to 2.3 million. Over the same period, the proportion of nurses per one hundred thousand population rose from 560 per one hundred thousand to 832.9 per one hundred thousand. (See Table 2.5.) The largest percentage increases occurred among those holding baccalaureate, master's, and doctorate degrees.

NEED FOR NURSES EXCEEDS SUPPLY. Although the number of registered nurses holding baccalaureate degrees increased sharply during the 1990s, there is still a shortage of nurses that is predicted to persist until 2020. Some health care experts believe that the shortage is intensifying because more lucrative fields are now open to women, the traditional nursing population. Nursing school enrollment has declined. In an article in the *Journal of Nursing Administration* (vol. 32, no. 2, February 2002), Marilyn Kettering Murray, MN, RN, reported that the nursing shortage has already sharply compromised hospital operations. Researchers have confirmed that since 2002 the nursing shortage has caused more than 25% of hospitals to redirect patients to alternative facilities for emergency treatment, reduce their available number of beds, and cancel scheduled surgeries.

Industry observers feel the shortage results from a combination of factors including an aging population, a sicker population of hospitalized patients requiring more labor-intensive care, and public perception that nursing is a thankless, unglamorous job involving grueling physical labor, long hours, and low pay. A 2002–03 survey found that nursing was rated the 143rd most desirable job out of 250 professions, down from 137th in 2001. Observers also note that the public, particularly high school students considering careers in health care, are unaware of the many new opportunities in nursing such as advance practice nursing, which offers additional independence and increased earning potential, and the technology-driven field of applied informatics (computer management of information).

ADVANCE PRACTICE NURSES AND PHYSICIAN ASSISTANTS

Much of the preventive medical care and treatment usually delivered by physicians may also be provided by mid-level practitioners—health professionals with less formal education and training than physicians. Advance practice nurses, a group that includes certified nurse midwives (CNMs), nurse practitioners (NPs), and clinical nurse specialists (CNS—registered nurses with advanced nursing degrees who specialize in areas such as mental health, gerontology, cardiac or cancer care, and community or neonatal health). Physician assistants (PAs) are mid-level practitioners who work under the auspices, supervision, or direction of physicians. They perform physical examinations, order and interpret laboratory and radiological studies, and prescribe medication. They even do procedures—flexible sigmoidoscopy, biopsy, suturing, casting, and administering anesthesia—once performed exclusively by physicians.

The origins of each profession are key to understanding the differences between them. Nursing has the longer history, and nurses are recognized members of the health care team. For this reason, NPs—registered nurses with advanced academic and clinical experience—initially were easily integrated into many practice settings.

Physician assistant is the newer of the two disciplines. PAs have been practicing in the United States since the early 1970s. The career originated as civilian employment for returning Vietnam War veterans who had worked as medics. The veterans needed immediate employment and few had the educational prerequisites, time, or resources to pursue the training necessary to become physicians. At the same time, the United States was projecting a dire shortage of primary care physicians, especially in rural and inner city practices. The use of PAs and NPs was seen as an ideal rapid response to the demand for additional medical services. They could be deployed quickly to serve remote communities or underserved populations for a fraction of the costs associated with physicians.

The numbers of physician assistants and nurse practitioners have increased dramatically since the beginning of the 1990s. In 2004 there were nearly 140,000 advanced practice nurses (48,237 nurse practitioners, seventy-four hundred certified nurse midwives, 58,185 clinical nurse specialists, and 25,238 certified registered nurse anesthetists) and more than fifty thousand practicing physician assistants in the United States. Together, mid-level practitioners are expected to outnumber primary care physicians in 2005. According to the American Academy of Physician Assistants (AAPA), at the start of the 2004 school year there were about ten thousand students enrolled in PA programs.

Training, Certification, and Practice

Advance practice nurses usually have considerable clinical nursing experience before completing certificate or master's degree nurse practitioner programs. Key components of NP programs are instruction in nursing theory and practice as well as a period of direct supervision by a physician or nurse practitioner. The American College of Nurse Practitioners states that NPs are prepared to practice "either independently or as part of a health care team," but NP scope of practice varies by state.

PA training programs are accredited by the Commission on Accreditation of Allied Health Education Programs. According to the AAPA, most students have an undergraduate degree and about 45 months of health care experience before they enter a two-year PA training program. Graduates sit for a national certifying examination and, once certified, must earn one hundred hours of continuing medical education every two years and pass a recertification exam every six years.

PA practice is always delegated by the physician and conducted with physician supervision. The extent and nature of physician supervision varies from state to state. For example, Connecticut permits a physician to supervise up to six PAs while California limits a supervising physician to two. Although PAs work interdependently with MDs, supervision is not necessarily direct and onsite; some PAs working in remote communities are supervised primarily by telephone.

PATIENTS ARE SATISFIED WITH CARE FROM MID-LEVEL PRACTITIONERS. Health care consumers bonded with NPs almost overnight. Their presence in neonatal and well-baby clinics, physicians' offices, school health, and busy pediatrics practices immediately improved access to, and availability of, primary health care services. Their focus on patient education, counseling, and preventive medicine generated measurable improvements in patient satisfaction.

During 2000, studies published in the *Journal of the American Medical Association* (JAMA) and *British Medical Journal* (BMJ) reported that patient satisfaction with NPs and clinical outcomes (the results of the care delivered) were indistinguishable from those achieved under physician care. Mary Mundinger, DrPH, RN, FAAN, and her colleagues conducted the first large-scale, randomized clinical trial of NPs and MDs in similar New York City practices. They found that physicians and NPs used comparable hospital and other services, and their patients, largely non-English speaking and medically underserved, fared equally well in terms of health outcomes.

Consumers seem receptive to care from advance practice nurses in a variety of settings. In other studies reported by *JAMA* and *BMJ* in 2000, researchers measured patient satisfaction with emergency services delivered by a family nurse practitioner in a rural hospital. They found "patients' perceptions of care provided by the NP were favorable." Physician response was equally approving— the physician group managing emergency services was so impressed with the competence of the first NP, they hired additional NPs to staff the department.

An editorial in the same issue of JAMA, written by a physician, was critical of Dr. Mundinger's research methods and conclusions. Harold Sox, MD, felt that the one-year follow-up was not long enough to assess outcomes or practitioner competence accurately. Dr. Sox argued that Dr. Mundinger's claim of comparable care was "far from convincing."

The BMJ study speculated that increased patient satisfaction with care from mid-level practitioners might be attributable to greater accessibility to NPs, such as the relative ease in obtaining same-day appointments and the extra time—in this study, an average of two additional minutes per visit—NPs spent with patients.

DENTISTS

Dentists diagnose and treat problems of the teeth, gums, and mouth, take X-rays, apply protective plastic sealant to children's teeth, fill cavities, straighten teeth, and treat gum disease. In 2003 there were about 152,000 professionally active (as opposed to retired or employed in other fields) dentists in the United States, almost twice as many as were practicing thirty years earlier.

Fluoridation of community water supplies and improved dental hygiene have dramatically improved the dental health of Americans. Dental caries (cavities) among all age groups have declined significantly. As a result, many dental services are shifting focus from young people to adults. Many adults today are choosing to have orthodontic services, such as straightening their teeth. In addition, the older adult population generally requires more complex dental procedures, such as endodontic (root canal) services, bridges, and dentures.

Most Dentists Have Their Own Practices

The overwhelming majority of dentists own solo dental practices, where only one dentist operates in each office. According to the American Dental Association (ADA), about two-thirds (66%) of the nation's private dentists work in solo practices and 33% work in group dental practices. Dentists work an average of 37.3 hours per week, supervise two full-time and two part-time staffers, such as dental technicians and hygienists, and schedule about eighty-four office visits per week. (Some of these patients are only seen by the hygienist.) According to the U.S. Bureau of Labor Statistics, self-employed dentists in general practice had an average net income (after taxes and expenses) of $158,080, and dental specialists netted about $240,580. In 2002 salaried dentists' median earnings were $123,210.

Dental Specialists

About 20% of all dentists practiced in one of the eight specialty areas recognized by the ADA. Orthodontists, who straighten teeth, make up the largest group of specialists. The next largest group, oral and maxillofacial surgeons, operate on the mouth and jaws. The rest of the specialists concentrate in pediatric dentistry (dentistry for children), periodontics (treating the gums), prosthodontics (making dentures and artificial teeth), endodontics (root canals), public health dentistry (community dental health), and oral pathology (diseases of the mouth). Cosmetic dentistry, including tooth whitening and restoration, is one of the newest and fastest-growing specialties.

As of 2004, seventeen states licensed or certified dentists who practice in a specialty area. Requirements vary by state and specialty and may include two to four years of postgraduate education and a passing score on a state-administered examination. Dentists who teach or conduct research generally spend an additional two to five years in advanced dental training in programs operated by dental schools or university-affiliated hospitals.

Training to Become a Dentist

Entry into dental schools requires two to four years of college-level pre-dental education—most dental students have earned excellent grades and have at least a bachelor's degree when they enter dental school. Dentists should have good visual memory, excellent judgment about space and shape, a high degree of manual dexterity, and scientific ability. Development and maintenance of a successful private practice requires business acumen, the ability to manage and organize people and materials, and strong interpersonal skills.

Dental schools require applicants to take the Dental Admissions Test (DAT). During the admission process, schools consider scores earned on the DAT, applicants' grade-point averages, and information gleaned from recommendations and interviews. Dental school usually lasts four academic years. A student begins by studying the basic sciences, including anatomy, microbiology, biochemistry, and physiology. During the last two years, students receive practical experience by treating patients, usually in dental clinics supervised by licensed dentists.

In 2003, 4,443 students graduated from the nation's fifty-six dental schools. Men outnumbered women graduates by almost two to one. Of the graduates, more than two-thirds were white and 5.4% were African-American, 5.9% were Hispanic, and 0.4% were Native American/Alaska Native (*2002/2003 Survey of Advanced Dental Education*, American Dental Association).

Visiting the Dentist

In 2001 more than two-thirds (65.6%) of Americans over two years of age had visited their dentists at least once in the past year. (See Table 2.6.) Children ages two to seventeen (73.3%) were more likely to have visited the dentist than any other age group, and women of all ages were somewhat more likely to see the dentist than men. Among adults aged eighteen to sixty-four, the proportion of non-Hispanic whites visiting dentists (66.6%) was considerably higher than the proportions of non-Hispanic African-Americans (55.8%) and Hispanics (49.2%). As anticipated, Table 2.6 shows that persons who were poor or near poor were much less likely to visit the dentist annually than those who were not poor.

SEVERE SHORTAGES OF DENTISTS IN SOME AREAS. The United States boasts the highest concentration of dentists of any country in the world. Nonetheless, health care planners caution that dentists' ranks will begin to decline during the coming decade as the number of dental school graduates, now about four thousand annually, falls below the number of dentists retiring from the work force. Even before this decline, residents of many states do not have adequate access to dental care, especially persons in rural communities and poor urban neighborhoods, where, arguably, the need is greatest.

The U.S. Department of Health and Human Services (HHS) reported that thirty-one million people live in shortage areas, with certain regions such as the Great Plains, southern Texas, much of Nevada, and northern Maine disproportionately affected. Health care planners estimate that 4,650 dentists are needed to restore access to dental care and deliver the appropriate level of service.

A September 20, 2003, CBS News report, "Where Have All the Dentists Gone?," described the plight of residents of Berlin, New Hampshire, one of 1,480 areas in the United States designated by federal authorities as suffering from a dentist shortage. Berlin has about 10,600 residents and just two dentists. In Berlin, even patients with private dental insurance often must wait months for an appointment, or travel long distances to visit a dentist. Uninsured and low-income families have even more difficulty gaining access to already overbooked dentists.

Dr. William Kassler, New Hampshire's state medical director, said nearly 20% of the state's 1.2 million residents live in communities with too few dentists. The dental problems resulting from the shortage are compounded by the fact that many towns, including Berlin, have unfluoridated water, causing higher cavity rates among local children who then lack ready access to treatment.

TABLE 2.6

Dental visits in the past year by selected characteristics, selected years 1997–2001

[Data are based on household interviews of a sample of the civilian noninstitutionalized population]

Characteristic	2 years of age and over[1]			2–17 years of age			18–64 years of age			65 years of age and over[2]		
	1997	1999	2001	1997	1999	2001	1997	1999	2001	1997	1999	2001
	Percent of persons with a dental visit in the past year[3]											
Total[4]	64.9	65.2	65.6	72.7	72.6	73.3	64.1	64.6	64.6	54.8	55.0	56.3
Sex												
Male	62.6	62.5	62.6	72.3	72.3	72.7	60.4	60.4	60.2	55.4	54.7	56.1
Female	67.2	67.8	68.5	73.0	72.8	73.9	67.7	68.5	68.9	54.4	55.2	56.5
Race[5]												
White only	66.5	67.2	67.4	74.0	74.5	74.9	65.7	66.6	66.6	56.8	56.8	58.5
Black or African American only	56.5	56.2	56.9	68.8	67.6	68.0	57.0	55.8	57.2	35.4	39.7	37.5
American Indian and Alaska Native only	51.5	56.2	53.9	66.8	58.2	72.9	49.9	55.2	47.7	*	*50.6	*50.7
Asian only	61.8	63.6	64.9	69.9	69.6	74.4	60.3	63.1	64.3	53.9	53.2	53.4
Native Hawaiian and other Pacific Islander only	—	*	*	—	*	*	—	*	*	—	*	*
2 or more races	—	58.6	56.3	—	73.0	69.3	—	57.8	57.1	—	*35.1	*34.5
Black or African American; White	—	63.7	52.7	—	68.7	57.6	—	58.8	55.5	—	*	*
American Indian and Alaska Native; White	—	55.8	58.7	—	70.3	79.2	—	53.5	53.6	—	*	*39.0
Hispanic origin and race[5]												
Hispanic or Latino	52.9	52.3	51.2	61.0	59.3	60.5	50.8	50.6	49.2	47.8	44.0	42.6
Not Hispanic or Latino	66.4	66.9	67.5	74.7	74.9	75.8	65.7	66.3	66.7	55.2	55.6	57.2
White only	68.2	68.9	69.6	76.4	77.0	77.8	67.5	68.3	68.7	57.2	57.3	59.4
Black or African American only	56.5	56.1	56.9	68.8	67.7	68.1	56.9	55.7	57.1	35.3	39.6	37.6
Poverty status[6]												
Poor	47.2	46.2	47.0	62.0	57.8	61.0	46.4	46.0	45.8	30.3	31.9	30.6
Near poor	48.9	48.5	49.7	61.6	61.6	63.2	46.4	46.1	46.9	39.6	38.9	40.0
Nonpoor	72.3	72.0	72.0	79.7	79.9	79.3	71.1	70.8	70.5	66.3	64.4	67.0
Hispanic origin and race and poverty status[5,6]												
Hispanic or Latino:												
Poor	41.9	41.5	38.7	56.8	49.6	54.2	39.0	39.7	35.1	33.0	32.1	29.8
Near poor	46.2	43.8	43.2	54.1	54.0	59.2	42.6	41.0	39.8	49.2	34.8	30.6
Nonpoor	65.1	63.8	64.4	74.8	72.0	71.1	62.5	62.0	62.8	56.5	58.9	60.8
Not Hispanic or Latino:												
White only:												
Poor	49.9	49.8	51.5	63.3	62.6	62.9	50.3	50.6	52.1	31.1	31.9	32.3
Near poor	51.0	50.2	52.9	64.8	63.2	64.4	48.2	48.0	51.0	41.2	39.6	42.1
Nonpoor	73.6	73.6	73.7	80.7	81.8	81.7	72.5	72.4	72.0	67.6	65.4	68.6
Black or African American only:												
Poor	46.7	44.9	45.1	66.7	61.0	63.2	44.5	42.1	42.9	26.2	33.5	25.2
Near poor	44.9	47.6	47.3	60.1	66.3	64.2	44.7	45.2	44.9	23.6	30.9	33.4
Nonpoor	65.4	64.2	64.1	75.5	72.7	72.4	66.2	64.7	65.4	48.9	51.5	46.1

Since New Hampshire is one of sixteen states with no dental school, it must actively recruit recent graduates or young dentists to serve needy towns or replace the many dentists now nearing retirement. Like many others states, New Hampshire is trying to attract dentists by offering to repay their student loans. Another state initiative pays the malpractice insurance and license fees of retired dentists willing to donate at least one hundred hours a year to treat underserved patients.

ALLIED HEALTH CARE PROVIDERS

Many health care services are provided by an interdisciplinary team of health professionals. The complete health care team may include physicians, nurses, mid-level practitioners, and dentists; physical and occupational therapists; audiologists and speech-language pathologists; licensed practical nurses, nurses' aides, and home health aides; and pharmacists, optometrists, podiatrists, dental hygienists, social workers, registered dieticians, and others. Table 2.7 describes some of these allied heath professions. Specific health care teams are assembled to meet the varying needs of patients. For example, the team involved in stroke rehabilitation might include a physician, nurse, physical and occupational therapists, a speech-language pathologist, and a social worker.

Physical and Occupational Therapists

Physical therapists (PTs) are licensed practitioners who work with patients to preserve and restore function, improve capabilities and mobility, and regain independence following illness or injury. They also aim to prevent or limit disability and slow the progress of debilitating diseases. Treatment involves exercise to improve range of motion, balance, coordination, flexibility, strength, and endurance. PTs may also use electrical stimulation to promote healing, hot and cold packs to relieve pain and inflammation (swelling), and therapeutic massage.

TABLE 2.6

Dental visits in the past year by selected characteristics, selected years 1997–2001 [CONTINUED]

[Data are based on household interviews of a sample of the civilian noninstitutionalized population]

Characteristic	2 years of age and over[1]			2–17 years of age			18–64 years of age			65 years of age and over[2]		
	1997	1999	2001	1997	1999	2001	1997	1999	2001	1997	1999	2001
	Percent of persons with a dental visit in the past year[3]											
Geographic region												
Northeast	69.6	70.9	72.2	77.5	78.5	79.6	69.6	71.5	72.2	55.5	54.3	59.6
Midwest	68.3	68.1	68.4	76.4	76.8	77.4	67.4	67.6	68.0	57.6	54.3	55.0
South	60.0	60.6	60.2	68.0	68.0	68.8	59.4	59.4	58.7	49.0	52.4	52.0
West	64.9	64.7	65.7	71.5	69.9	70.7	62.9	63.3	64.4	61.9	61.9	62.6
Location of residence												
Within MSA[7]	66.5	67.1	67.0	73.6	73.1	73.9	65.7	66.8	66.0	57.6	58.1	59.1
Outside MSA[7]	59.1	58.3	60.3	69.3	70.7	70.7	58.0	56.2	59.1	46.1	45.0	47.2

Note: In 1997 the National Health Interview Survey questionnaire was redesigned.

*Estimates are considered unreliable.

— Data not available.

[1]Estimates are age adjusted to the year 2000 standard using six age groups; 2–17 years, 18–44 years, 45–54 years, 55–64 years, 65–74 years, and 75 years and over.

[2]Estimates for the elderly are the percent of persons 65 years of age over with a dental visit in the past year. Data from the 1997–2001 National Health Interview Survey estimate that 28–30 percent of persons 65 years of age and over (elderly) were edentulous (having lost all their natural teeth). In 1997–2001 about 70 percent of elderly dentate persons compared with 17–20 percent of elderly edentate persons had a dental visit in the past year.

[3]Respondents were asked "About how long has it been since you last saw or talked to a dentist?"

[4]Includes all other races not shown separately and unknown poverty status.

[5]The race groups, white, black, American Indian and Alaska Native (AI/AN), Asian, Native Hawaiian and Other Pacific Islander, and 2 or more races, include persons of Hispanic and non-Hispanic origin. Persons of Hispanic origin may be of any race. Starting with data year 1999 race-specific estimates are tabulated according to 1997 Standards for Federal data on Race and Ethnicity and are not strictly comparable with estimates for earlier years. The five single race categories plus multiple race categories shown in the table conform to 1997 Standards. The 1999 race-specific estimates are for persons who reported only one racial group; the category "2 or more races" includes persons who reported more than on racial group. Prior to data year 1999, data were tabulated according to 1977 Standards with four racial groups and the category "Asian only" included Native Hawaiian and Other Pacific Islander. Estimates for single race categories prior to 1999 included persons who reported one race or, if they reported more than one race, identified one race as best representing their race. The effect of the 1997 Standard on the 1999 estimates can be seen by comparing 1999 data tabulated according to the two Standards: Age-adjusted estimates based on the 1977 Standard of the percent of persons with a recent dental visit are: 0.1 percentage points lower for white and black persons; identical for AI/AN persons; and 0.2 percentage points lower for Asian and Pacific Islander persons than estimates based on the 1997 Standards.

[6]Poor persons are defined as below the poverty threshold. Near poor persons have incomes of 100 percent to less than 200 percent of the poverty threshold. Nonpoor persons have incomes of 200 percent or greater than the poverty threshold. Poverty status was unknown for 20 percent of persons in the sample in 1997, 25 percent in 1998, 28 percent in 1999, 27 percent in 2000, and 28 percent in 2001.

[7]MSA is metropolitan statistical area.

SOURCE: "Table 78. Dental Visits in the Past Year according to Selected Characteristics: United States, Selected Years 1997–2001," in *Health, United States, 2003,* National Center for Health Statistics, 2003, http://www.cdc.gov/nchs/data/hus/tables/2003/03hus078.pdf (accessed June 2, 2004)

According to the U.S. Bureau of Labor Statistics, PTs worked at 137,000 jobs in 2002, but one in four were part-time jobs and some PTs held two or more jobs at the same time. Two-thirds of practicing PTs worked in hospitals and the remaining PTs were employed in physicians' offices, outpatient rehabilitation clinics, nursing homes, and home health agencies. Though most work in rehabilitation, PTs may specialize in areas such as sports medicine, pediatrics, or neurology. PTs often work as members of a health care team and may supervise physical therapy assistants or aides. Physical therapists' median annual earnings were $57,330 in 2002.

Occupational therapists (OTs) focus on helping people relearn and improve their abilities to perform the "activities of daily living," the tasks they perform during the course of their work and home lives. Examples of activities of daily living that OTs help patients to regain are dressing, bathing themselves, and meal preparation. For persons with long-term or permanent disabilities, OTs may assist them to find new ways to accomplish their responsibilities on the job, sometimes using adaptive equipment or by asking employers to accommodate workers with special needs such as persons in wheelchairs. OTs use computer programs and simulations to help patients restore fine motor skills and practice reasoning, decision making, and problem solving.

The U.S. Bureau of Labor Statistics reported that OTs filled eighty-two thousand jobs in 2002 with one in six holding more than one job at a time. The demand for OTs and PTs is expected to exceed the available supply through 2010. In addition to hospital and rehabilitation center jobs, it is anticipated that PTs and OTs will increasingly be involved in school program efforts to meet the needs of disabled and special education students.

Today, a bachelor's degree in occupational therapy is the minimum educational requirement; beginning in 2007, however, a master's degree or higher will be required. Median annual earnings of occupational therapists were $51,990 in 2002.

Pharmacists Provide Valuable Patient Care Services

Today pharmacists are involved in many more aspects of patient care than simply compounding and dispensing medication from behind the drugstore counter. According to the American Pharmaceutical Association (APhA), its more than 50,000 members (including practicing pharmacists, pharmaceutical scientists, students, and technicians) provide pharmaceutical care that not only improves patient adherence to prescribed drug treatment but also reduces

TABLE 2.7

Allied health care providers

Dental hygienists provide services for maintaining oral health. Their primary duty is to clean teeth.

Emergency Medical Technicians (EMTs) provide immediate care to critically ill or injured people in emergency situations.

Home health aides provide nursing, household, and personal care services to patients who are homebound or disabled.

Licensed practical nurses (LPNs) are trained and licensed to provide basic nursing care under the supervision of registered nurses and doctors.

Medical records personnel analyze patient records and keep them up-to-date, complete, accurate, and confidential.

Medical technologists perform laboratory tests to help diagnose diseases and to aid in identifying their causes and extent.

Nurses' Aides, Orderlies, and Attendants help nurses in hospitals, nursing homes and other facilities.

Occupational therapists help disabled persons adapt to their disabilities. This may include helping a patient relearn basic living skills or modifying the environment.

Optometrists measure vision for corrective lenses and prescribe glasses.

Pharmacists are trained and licensed to make up and dispense drugs in accordance with a physician's prescription.

Physician assistants (PAs) work under a doctor's supervision. Their duties include performing routine physical exams, prescribing certain drugs, and providing medical counseling.

Physical therapists work with disabled patients to help restore function, strength and mobility. PTs use exercise, heat, cold, water, and electricity to relieve pain and restore function.

Podiatrists diagnose and treat diseases, injuries, and abnormalities of the feet. They may use drugs and surgery to treat foot problems.

Psychologists are trained in human behavior and provide counseling and testing services related to mental health.

Radiation technicians take and develop x-ray photographs for medical purposes.

Registered dietitians (RDs) are licensed to use dietary principles to maintain health and treat disease.

Respiratory therapists treat breathing problems under a doctor's supervision and help in respiratory rehabilitation.

Social workers help patients to handle social problems such as finances, housing, and social and family problems that arise out of illness or disability.

Speech pathologists diagnose and treat disorders of speech and communication.

SOURCE: "Allied Health Care Providers," U.S. Department of Commerce, Washington, DC

---

the frequency of drug therapy mishaps, which can have serious and even life-threatening consequences.

Studies citing the value of pharmacists in patient care describe pharmacists improving rates of immunization against disease (pharmacists can provide immunization in twenty-seven states), assisting patients to better control chronic diseases such as asthma and diabetes, reducing the frequency and severity of drug interactions and adverse reactions, and helping patients effectively manage pain and symptoms of disease, especially at the end of life. Pharmacists also offer public health education programs about prescription medication safety, prevention of poisoning, appropriate use of nonprescription (over-the-counter) drugs, and medical self-care.

The U.S. Bureau of Labor Statistics reported that pharmacists held about 230,000 jobs in 2002. More than 60% worked in community pharmacies—either independently owned or part of a drugstore chain, grocery store, department store, or mass merchandiser. Most full-time salaried pharmacists worked about forty hours a week; however, about 19% worked part time in 2002, and many self-employed pharmacists worked more than fifty hours a week. The median annual wage and salary earnings of pharmacists in 2002 was $77,050.

INCREASE IN HEALTH CARE EMPLOYMENT

In 2002 almost thirteen million persons worked in the health care services, about three times the number employed in health services in 1970, when 4.2 million worked in the health field. (See Table 2.8.) Workers in health care professions accounted for 8.8% of all employed Americans (excluding military personnel). In 1970 only 5.5% of employed civilians worked in health care services.

Since 1970, the proportion of health care workers employed in hospitals has dropped dramatically. More than six in ten (63.4%) of health services personnel worked in hospitals in 1970. By 1990 that number had dropped to 49.6% employed in hospitals, and by 2002 that number fell again, to 42.2%. While hospitals still employ a larger proportion of health workers than any other service locations, more patients are now able to receive treatment in physicians' offices, clinics, and other outpatient settings. In addition, insurers are less willing to pay for lengthy hospitalizations than they were in the past.

Why Is Health Care Booming?

Three major factors appear to have influenced the escalation in health care employment: advances in technology, the increasing amounts of money spent on health care, and the aging of the U.S. population. In other sectors of the economy, technology often replaces humans in the labor force. But health care technology has increased the demand for highly trained specialists to operate the sophisticated equipment. Because of technological advances, patients are likely to undergo more tests and diagnostic procedures, take more drugs, see more specialists, and be subjected to more aggressive treatments than ever before.

The second factor in the increase in health care employment involves the amount of money the nation spends on keeping its citizens in good health. Americans spent more than $1.6 trillion on health care in 2004 and the Centers for Medicare & Medicaid Services project that national health expenditures will reach $3.4 trillion in 2013. For each year that the amount of money spent on health care continues to grow, employment in the field grows as well. Some health care industry observers believe

TABLE 2.8

Persons employed in health service sites, selected years 1970–2002

[Data are based on household interviews of a sample of the civilian noninstitutionalized population]

Site	1970	1980	1990	1995[1]	1997	1998	1999	2000[2]	2001	2002
					Number of persons in thousands					
All employed civilians	76,805	99,303	117,914	124,900	129,558	131,463	133,488	136,891	136,933	136,485
All health service sites	4,246	7,339	9,447	10,928	11,525	11,504	11,646	11,742	12,110	12,653
Offices and clinics of physicians	477	777	1,098	1,512	1,559	1,581	1,624	1,697	1,799	1,907
Offices and clinics of dentists	222	415	580	644	662	666	694	676	699	740
Offices and clinics of chiropractors[3]	19	40	90	99	118	127	142	124	117	138
Hospitals	2,690	4,036	4,690	4,961	5,130	5,116	5,117	5,092	5,270	5,340
Nursing and personal care facilities	509	1,199	1,543	1,718	1,755	1,801	1,786	1,737	1,771	1,942
Other health service sites	300	872	1,446	1,995	2,301	2,213	2,283	2,414	2,454	2,585
					Percent of employed civilians					
All health service sites	5.5	7.4	8.0	8.7	8.9	8.8	8.7	8.6	8.8	9.3
					Percent distribution					
All health service sites	100.0	100.0	100.0	100.0	100.0	100.0	100.0	100.0	100.0	100.0
Offices and clinics of physicians	11.2	10.6	11.6	13.8	13.5	13.7	13.9	14.5	14.9	15.1
Offices and clinics of dentists	5.2	5.7	6.1	5.9	5.7	5.8	6.0	5.8	5.8	5.8
Offices and clinics of chiropractors[3]	0.4	0.5	1.0	0.9	1.0	1.1	1.2	1.1	1.0	1.1
Hospitals	63.4	55.0	49.6	45.4	44.5	44.5	43.9	43.4	43.5	42.2
Nursing and personal care facilities	12.0	16.3	16.3	15.7	15.2	15.7	15.3	14.8	14.6	15.3
Other health service sites	7.8	11.9	15.3	18.3	20.0	19.2	19.6	20.6	20.3	20.4

[1] Data for years prior to 1995 are not strictly comparable with data from 1995 onwards due to a redesign of the Current Population Survey.
[2] Starting in 2000, 2000-based population estimates are used as survey controls.
[3] Data for 1980 are from the American Chiropractic Association; data for all other years are from the U.S. Bureau of Labor Statistics.
Notes: Employment is full- or part-time work. Totals exclude persons in health-related occupations who are working in nonhealth industries, as classified by the U.S. Bureau of the Census, such as pharmacists employed in drugstores, school nurses, and nurses working in private households. Totals include Federal, State, and county health workers. In 1970–82, employed persons were classified according to the industry groups used in the 1970 Census of Population. In 1983–91, persons were classified according to the system used in the 1980 Census of Population. Beginning in 1992 persons were classified according to the system used in the 1990 Census of Population.

SOURCE: "Table 98. Persons Employed in Health Service Sites: United States, Selected Years 1970–2002," in *Health, United States, 2003,* National Center for Health Statistics, 2003, http://www.cdc.gov/nchs/data/hus/tables/2003/03hus098.pdf (accessed June 2, 2004)

that government and private financing for the health care industry, unlike most other fields, is virtually unlimited.

The third factor contributing to the rise in the number of health care workers is the aging of the nation's population. There are greater numbers of older adults in the United States than ever before, and they are living longer. According to the U.S. Bureau of the Census estimates, in 2005, 4.9 million Americans will be age eighty-five or older; and by 2030, 18.2 million people will be over the age of eighty-five.

The increase in the number of older people is expected to boost the demand for home health care services, assisted living, and nursing home care. Many nursing homes now offer special care for stroke patients, persons with Alzheimer's disease (progressive cognitive impairment), and persons who need a respirator to breathe. To care for such patients, nursing homes need more physical therapists, nurses' aides, and respiratory therapists—three of the fastest-growing occupations. The U.S. Bureau of Labor Statistics estimated that from 1996 to 2006 the number of physical therapists would increase 70.8%, to 196,000, and the number of respiratory therapists would grow 45.8%, to 119,000.

COMPLEMENTARY AND ALTERNATIVE MEDICINE

The National Center for Complementary and Alternative Medicine (NCCAM), an institute of the National Institutes of Health (NIH), defines alternative medicine as "a group of diverse medical and health care systems, practices, and products that are not presently considered to be part of conventional medicine." Though there is some overlap between them, the NCCAM further distinguishes between "complementary," "alternative," and "integrative" medicine in the following manner:

• Alternative medicine is therapy or treatment that is used instead of conventional medical treatment.

• Complementary medicine is nonstandard therapy or treatment that is used along with conventional medicine, not in place of it. Complementary medicine appears to offer health benefits but there is generally no scientific evidence to support its utility.

- Integrative medicine is the combination of conventional medical treatment and complementary and alternative medicine (CAM) therapies that have been scientifically researched and have demonstrated evidence that they are both safe and effective.

In general terms, alternative therapies are untested and unproven, while complementary and integrative practices that are used in conjunction with mainstream medicine often have substantial scientific basis of demonstrated safety and efficacy.

Growing Popularity of Complementary and Alternative Medicine

In the United States, there is increasing enthusiasm for and use of complementary and alternative medicine (CAM) approaches and practices. Surveys conducted in 1991 and 1997 by Harvard Medical School researcher Dr. David Eisenberg and his colleagues about the use of alternative medicine in the United States found that more than four in ten Americans had used at least one alternative therapy (including the services of nutritionists, Pilates and tai' chi instructors, and chiropractors, among others). The earlier survey published in the *New England Journal of Medicine* in 1993 found that:

- In 1990 about one third of Americans regularly used alternative medicine therapies and treatment.
- Americans made more office visits to alternative medical practitioners than to traditional primary care physicians.
- About $14 billion per year was spent on alternative medicine.

The November 1998 *Journal of the American Medical Association* survey revealed that:

- Americans' use of alternative medicine had skyrocketed since the prior survey, from 34% to 42%.
- Total visits to alternative medicine practitioners rose by 47%.
- About $27 billion was spent out-of-pocket (not paid by insurance) for alternative medicine, nearly twice as much as was spent in seven years earlier and about as much as Americans paid out-of-pocket for conventional treatments from physicians in the same year.
- The highest rates of CAM use were among college graduates living in the western United States, ages thirty-five to forty-nine, with incomes greater than $50,000 per year.

A telephone survey of thirty-one thousand adults conducted in 2002 by several government agencies including the NIH, NCCAM, and the Centers for Disease Control and Prevention (CDC), confirmed the findings of previous surveys—that a significant proportion of Americans, as high as 62%, were using CAM therapies and products ("Complementary and Alternative Medicine Use among Adults: United States 2002," http://altmed.od.nih.gov/news/report.pdf, May 24, 2004).

ALTERNATIVE MEDICINE SYSTEMS AND PRACTITIONERS

This section considers two alternative medicine systems that originated in Western culture—homeopathy and naturopathic medicine—and two alternative medicine systems that developed in non-Western cultures—acupuncture and traditional Chinese medicine. It also describes some of the CAM practitioners who are providing care for Americans.

Homeopathic Medicine

Homeopathic medicine (also called homeopathy) is based on the belief that "like cures like" and uses very diluted amounts of natural substances to encourage the body's own self-healing mechanisms. Homeopathy was developed by a German physician, Dr. Samuel Hahnemann, in the 1790s. Dr. Hahnemann found that he could produce symptoms of particular diseases by injecting small doses of various herbal substances. This discovery inspired him to administer to sick people extremely diluted formulations of substances that would produce the same symptoms they suffered from in an effort to stimulate natural recovery and regeneration.

According to Dr. Kenneth Pelletier, a clinical professor of medicine at Stanford University School of Medicine and director of the NIH-funded Complementary and Alternative Medicine Program at Stanford, homeopathy has demonstrated effectiveness for a variety of ailments. In his book *The Best of Alternative Medicine: What Works? What Does Not?* (New York, NY: Simon & Schuster, 2000), Dr. Pelletier reports that clinical trials of homeopathy found it effective for the treatment of disorders such as seasonal allergies, asthma, childhood diarrhea, fibromyalgia, influenza, and rheumatoid arthritis.

Naturopathic Medicine

As its name suggests, naturopathic medicine (also called naturopathy) uses naturally occurring substances to prevent, diagnose, and treat disease. Although it is now considered an alternative medicine system, it is one of the oldest medicine systems and has its origins in Native American culture and also draws from Greek, Chinese, and East Indian ideas about health and illness.

The guiding principles of modern naturopathic medicine are "first, do no harm" and "nature has the power to heal." Naturopathy seeks to treat the whole person, since disease is seen as arising from many causes rather than a single cause. Naturopathic physicians are taught that "prevention is as important as cure" and to view creating and maintaining health as equally important as curing disease. They are instructed to identify and treat the causes of diseases rather than acting only to relieve symptoms.

Naturopathic treatment methods include nutritional counseling. Methods also include the use of dietary supplements, herbs, and vitamins; hydrotherapy (water-based therapies, usually involving whirlpool or other baths); exercise; manipulation; massage; heat therapy; and electrical stimulation. Since naturopathy draws on Chinese and Indian medical techniques, naturopathic physicians often use Chinese herbs, acupuncture, and East Indian medicines to treat disease.

Dr. Pelletier's research found studies demonstrating that naturopathy was effective for conditions such as asthma, atherosclerosis, back pain, some cancers, depression, diabetes, eczema (a skin condition), middle ear infections, migraine headaches, natural childbirth, and osteoarthritis. Further, Dr. Pelletier asserted that licensed naturopathic physicians are among the best trained CAM practitioners and he predicted that research would continue to confirm the benefits and efficacy of the safe, inexpensive, and low-risk therapies they can provide.

Traditional Chinese Medicine

Traditional Chinese medicine (TCM) uses nutrition, acupuncture, massage, herbal medicine, and Qi Gong (exercises to improve the flow of vital energy through the body) to help people achieve balance and unity of their minds, bodies, and spirits. Practiced for more than three thousand years by about one quarter of the world's population, TCM has been adopted by naturopathic physicians, chiropractors, and other CAM practitioners in the United States.

TCM views balancing *qi* (pronounced "chee"), the vital life force that flows over the surface of the body and through internal organs, as central to health, wellness, disease prevention, and treatment. This vital force or energy is thought to flow through the human body in meridians, or channels. The Chinese believe that pain and disease develop when there is any sort of disturbance in the natural flow. TCM also seeks to balance the feminine and masculine qualities of yin and yang using other techniques such as moxibustion, which is the stimulation of acupuncture points with heat, and cupping, in which the practitioner increases circulation by putting a heated jar on the skin of a body part.

Herbal medicine is the most commonly prescribed treatment, and herbal preparations may be consumed as teas made from boiled fresh herbs or dried powders, or in combined formulations known as patent medicines. More than two hundred herbal preparations are used in TCM, and several (such as ginseng, ma huang, and ginger) have become popular in the United States. Ginseng is supposed to improve immunity and prevent illness; ma huang is a stimulant used to promote weight loss and relieve lung congestion; and ginger is prescribed to aid digestion, relieve nausea, reduce arthritic knee pain, and improve circulation. Many modern pharmaceutical drugs are derived from TCM herbal medicines. For example, ma

huang components are used to make ephedrine and pseudoephedrine; GBE made from ginkgo biloba is used to treat cerebral insufficiency (lack of blood flow to the brain); and researchers have reported some encouraging findings about the use of ginkgo biloba to improve memory and slow the progression of dementia in some patients (Edward Ernst, "The Risk-Benefit Profile of Commonly Used Herbal Therapies: Ginkgo, St. John's Wort, Ginseng, Echinacea, Saw Palmetto, and Kava," *Annals of Internal Medicine,* vol. 136, no. 1, January 2002).

Acupuncture

Acupuncture is a Chinese practice that dates back more than 5,000 years. Chinese medicine describes acupuncture—the insertion of extremely thin, sterile needles to any of 360 specific points on the body—as a way to balance *qi*. After a diagnosis of an imbalance in the flow of energy, the acupuncturist inserts needles at specific points along the meridians (pathways of energy flow throughout the body). Each point controls a different part of the body. Once the needles are in place, they are rotated gently or are briefly charged with a small electric current.

Traditional Western medicine explains the acknowledged effectiveness of acupuncture as the result of triggering the release of pain-relieving substances called endorphins that occur naturally in the body, as well as neurotransmitters and neuropeptides that influence brain chemistry. In addition to providing lasting pain relief, acupuncture has demonstrated success in helping people with substance abuse problems, relieving nausea, heightening immunity by increasing total white blood cells and T-cell production, and assisting patients to recover from stroke and other neurological impairments. Imaging techniques have confirmed that acupuncture acts to alter brain chemistry and function.

Chiropractic Physicians

Doctors of chiropractic (also known as chiropractors or DCs) treat patients whose health problems are associated mainly with the body's structural and neurological systems, especially the spine. These practitioners believe that interference with these systems can impair normal functions and lower resistance to disease. Chiropractic medicine asserts that misalignment or compression of the spinal nerves, for example, can alter many important body functions. According to the American Chiropractic Association (ACA), they "consider man as an integrated being and give special attention to the physiological and biochemical aspects including structural, spinal, musculoskeletal, neurological, vascular, nutritional, emotional, and environmental relationships." Doctors of chiropractic medicine do not use or prescribe pharmaceutical drugs or perform surgery. Instead, they rely on adjustment and manipulation of the musculoskeletal system, particularly the spinal column.

Many chiropractors use nutritional therapy and prescribe dietary supplements; some employ a technique known as applied kinesiology to diagnose and treat disease. Applied kinesiology is based on the belief that every organ problem is associated with weakness of a specific muscle. Chiropractors who use this technique claim they can accurately identify organ system dysfunction without any laboratory or other diagnostic tests.

In addition to manipulation, chiropractors also use a variety of other therapies to support healing and relax muscles before they make manual adjustments. These treatments include:

- heat and cold therapy to relieve pain, speed healing, and reduce swelling
- hydrotherapy to relax muscles and stimulate blood circulation
- immobilization such as casts, wraps, traction, and splints to protect injured areas
- electrotherapy to deliver deep tissue massage and boost circulation
- ultrasound to relieve muscle spasms and reduce swelling.

According to the ACA, chiropractic is the third-largest group of health care professionals after medicine and dentistry. The ACA predicts that there will be nearly twice as many practicing doctors of chiropractic by 2010 as there were in 1999 when approximately 50 million patients sought care from slightly more than seventy thousand chiropractors. Visits to chiropractors are most often for treatment of lower back pain, neck pain, and headaches.

Critics of chiropractic are concerned about injuries resulting from powerful manual adjustments, and some physicians question chiropractors' abilities to establish medical diagnoses. Others worry that persons seeking chiropractic care instead of traditional allopathic medical care may be forgoing lifesaving diagnoses and treatment.

Alternative Medicine Is More Than a Fad

Researchers from the Harvard Medical School looked at long-term trends in the use of CAM therapies in the United States and published their findings in the August 21, 2001, issue of the *Annals of Internal Medicine*. The researchers conducted more than two thousand surveys and traced patterns of CAM utilization since the 1960s. They questioned survey respondents about twenty different CAM practices such as acupuncture, aromatherapy, biofeedback, energy healing, massage, and yoga.

The study found that over the past forty years nearly all of the twenty CAM therapies had increased in popularity, though interest surged during the 1960s and 1970s. The researchers observed that specific CAM therapies gained acceptance during each decade. In the 1960s Americans discovered diet programs, vitamins, and self-help support groups, and in the 1970s they turned to herbal medicine, biofeedback, and energy healing. The 1980s saw growing popularity of massage and naturopathy, and during the 1990s the appeal of massage increased along with interest in aromatherapy, energy healing, herbal medicine, and yoga.

Unlike the earlier studies that found CAM users to be mostly educated adults living in Western states, the Harvard researchers found the use of alternative therapies was unrelated to education, gender, or ethnicity. They observed that the increases in acceptance and use of CAM during the past fifty years suggest that demand for CAM therapies will continue in the future.

More recent research reveals that Americans' interest in and enthusiasm for CAM practices continues to grow. CDC researchers report that nearly two-thirds (62.1%) of American adults used some form of complementary or alternative medicine in the past year. (See Table 2.9.) The 2002 survey of thirty-one thousand U.S. adults asked about twenty-seven types of therapies such as acupuncture and chiropractic, the use of herbs or botanical products, yoga, meditation, special diets, and megavitamin therapy.

About 36% of survey respondents had used at least one form of complementary and alternative medicine. When prayer specifically for health reasons was included on the list of alternative approaches, the number of U.S. adults using some form of CAM in the past year rose to 62%. Researchers found that people most likely to use CAM therapies were women; those with higher education; and those who had been hospitalized within the past year. (See Table 2.10.) Former smokers were also more likely than current smokers or those who had never smoked to use CAM therapies. The survey also found that African-Americans were more likely than whites or Asians to use CAM when megavitamin therapy and prayer were included in the definition. (See Table 2.10.)

In "Complementary and Alternative Medicine Use among Adults: United States, 2002," the CDC reported that alternative approaches were most often used to treat back pain or problems (16.8%), colds (9.5%), neck pain or problems (6.6%), joint pain or stiffness (4.9%), and anxiety or depression (4.5%). When asked the reason they had sought or used CAM treatments, more than half (55%) of the survey respondents said they were most likely to use CAM because they believed that it would help them when combined with conventional medical treatments. Half of the respondents thought CAM would be interesting to try, 26% used CAM because a conventional medical professional suggested they try it, and 13% used CAM because they felt that conventional medicine was too expensive.

The CDC survey also found that within the past twelve months, 43% of adults reported that they had prayed for their own health, 24% prayed for someone

TABLE 2.9

Adults who used complementary and alternative medicine, by type of therapy, 2002

Therapy	Ever used		Used during past 12 months	
	Number in thousands	Percent	Number in thousands	Percent
Any CAM[1] use	149,271	74.6	123,606	62.1
Alternative medical systems				
Acupuncture	8,188	4.0	2,136	1.1
Ayurveda	751	0.4	154	0.1
Homeopathic treatment	7,379	3.6	3,433	1.7
Naturopathy	1,795	0.9	498	0.2
Biologically based therapies				
Chelation therapy	270	0.1	66	0.0
Folk medicine	1,393	0.7	233	0.1
Nonvitamin, nonmineral, natural products	50,613	25.0	38,183	18.9
Diet-based therapies[2]	13,799	6.8	7,099	3.5
Vegetarian diet	5,324	2.6	3,184	1.6
Macrobiotic diet	1,368	0.7	317	0.2
Atkins diet	7,312	3.6	3,417	1.7
Pritikin diet	580	0.3	137	0.1
Ornish diet	290	0.1	76	0.0
Zone diet	1,062	0.5	430	0.2
Megavitamin therapy	7,935	3.9	5,739	2.8
Manipulative and body-based therapies				
Chiropractic care	40,242	19.9	15,226	7.5
Massage	18,899	9.3	10,052	5.0
Mind-body therapies				
Biofeedback	1,986	1.0	278	0.1
Meditation	20,698	10.2	15,336	7.6
Guided imagery	6,067	3.0	4,194	2.1
Progressive relaxation	8,518	4.2	6,185	3.0
Deep breathing exercises	29,658	14.6	23,457	11.6
Hypnosis	3,733	1.8	505	0.2
Yoga	15,232	7.5	10,386	5.1
Tai chi	5,056	2.5	2,565	1.3
Qi gong	950	0.5	527	0.3
Prayer for health reasons[3]	110,012	55.3	89,624	45.2
Prayed for own health	103,662	52.1	85,432	43.0
Others ever prayed for your health	62,348	31.3	48,467	24.4
Participate in prayer group	25,167	23.0	18,984	9.6
Healing ritual for own health	9,230	4.6	4,045	2.0
Energy healing therapy/Reiki	2,264	1.1	1,080	0.5

[1]CAM includes acupuncture; ayurveda; homeopathic treatment; naturopathy; chelation therapy; folk medicine; nonvitamin, nonmineral, natural products; diet-based therapies; megavitamin therapy; chiropractic care; massage; biofeedback; meditation; guided imagery; progressive relaxation; deep breathing exercises; hypnosis; yoga; tai chi; qi gong; prayer for health reasons; and energy healing therapy/Reiki. Respondents may have reported using more than one type of therapy.
[2]The totals of the numbers and percents of the categories listed under "Diet-based therapies" are greater than the number and percent of "Diet-based therapies" because respondents could choose more than one diet-based therapy.
[3]The totals of the numbers and percents of the categories listed under "Prayer for health reasons" are greater than the number and percent of "Prayer for health reasons" because respondents could choose more than one method of prayer.
Notes: CAM is complementary and alternative medicine. The denominators for statistics shown exclude persons with unknown CAM information. Estimates were age adjusted to the year 2000 U.S. standard population using four age groups: 18–24 years, 25–44 years, 45–64 years, and 65 years and over.

source: Patricia M. Barnes, Eve Powell-Griner, Kim McFann, and Richard L. Nahin, "Table 1. Frequencies and Age-Adjusted Percents of Adults 18 Years and Over Who Used Complementary and Alternative Medicine, by Type of Therapy: United States, 2002," in "Complementary and Alternative Medicine Use among Adults: United States, 2002," in *Advance Data from Vital and Health Statistics,* no. 343, Centers for Disease Control and Prevention, National Center for Health Statistics, May 27, 2004, www.cdc.gov/nchs/data/ad/ad343.pdf (accessed June 7, 2004)

else, 19% used products such as herbs, 12% practiced deep breathing, and 8% had meditated. Just about 12% of adults sought care from a licensed CAM practitioner—8% seek care from a chiropractor, 5% use massage therapeutically, and 4% use diet-based therapies for health.

CRITICS SAY ALTERNATIVE MEDICINE IS A WASTE OF TIME AND MONEY. Although complementary and alternative medicine practices are gaining in popularity throughout the United States and Europe, many allopathic physicians and scientists regard them with skepticism because they have not been rigorously tested or proven to be effective. In the May 15, 2002, issue of *Time* magazine, columnist Leon Jaroff asserted that the NCCAM budget of about $105 million per year is being misspent and that NCCAM is staffed with CAM practitioners and professionals who are biased in favor of CAM practices and unable to assess objectively their value to the American people.

Jaroff also contended that NCCAM monies are repeatedly given to the same alternative practitioners and researchers and that few of the results of NCCAM studies have been published. The *Time* columnist stated that NCCAM is always positive about CAM practices, and that he would like to see NCCAM publish at least one report that is critical or refutes the claims of CAM practitioners. Jaroff asserted that scientific repudiation of many CAM treatments would convince Americans that they are spending increasing sums of money on essentially worthless remedies and therapies.

Although detractors criticize the absence of scientific verification of the efficacy of CAM treatments, they also question whether some CAM approaches, which are generally not covered by health insurance and are paid for by the patient, exploit persons who are desperate, gullible, or otherwise vulnerable. Finally, critics of alternative medicine are concerned that CAM practices and practitioners are not adequately regulated. They point to variability of practitioners' training and expertise as well as the largely unregulated nature of the herbal and other remedies CAM practitioners may prescribe.

TABLE 2.10

Adults who used selected complementary and alternative medicine categories during the past year, by selected characteristics, 2002

Selected characteristic	Any use of — CAM including megavitamin therapy and prayer[1]	Biologically based therapies including megavitamin therapy[2]	Mind-body therapies including prayer[3]	CAM excluding megavitamin therapy and prayer[4]	Biologically based therapies excluding megavitamin therapy[5]	Mind-body therapies excluding prayer[6]	Alternative medical systems[7]	Energy therapies	Manipulative and body-based therapies[8]
Total[9,10]	**62.1**	**21.9**	**52.6**	**35.1**	**20.6**	**16.9**	**2.7**	**0.5**	**10.9**
Sex[10]									
Male	54.1	19.6	43.4	30.2	18.2	12.5	2.2	0.3	9.5
Female	69.3	24.1	61.1	39.7	22.9	21.1	3.2	0.7	12.2
Age									
18–29 years	53.5	19.6	44.2	32.9	18.8	17.7	2.3	0.4	9.5
30–39 years	60.7	23.2	49.8	37.8	22.1	18.3	3.3	0.6	12.8
40–49 years	64.1	24.7	53.3	39.4	23.3	18.9	3.2	0.7	13.0
50–59 years	66.1	26.2	56.1	39.6	24.7	19.6	3.3	0.8	11.3
60–69 years	64.8	21.3	56.3	32.6	19.6	14.4	2.1	0.4	9.8
70–84 years	68.6	15.3	63.3	25.1	13.3	9.4	1.4	0.1	7.7
85 years and over	70.3	9.1	66.0	14.9	8.4	6.4	0.9	0.3	2.1
Race[10]									
White, single race	60.4	22.3	50.1	35.9	20.9	17.0	2.8	0.5	12.0
Black or African American, single race	71.3	16.5	68.3	26.2	15.2	14.7	1.4	0.3	4.4
Asian, single race	61.7	29.5	48.1	43.1	28.9	20.9	4.5	0.6	7.2
Hispanic or Latino origin[10,11]									
Hispanic or Latino	61.4	20.6	55.1	28.3	19.8	10.9	2.4	0.4	5.8
Not Hispanic or Latino	62.3	22.3	52.4	36.1	20.9	17.7	2.8	0.6	11.6
Education[10]									
Less than high school	57.4	12.5	52.0	20.8	11.7	8.0	1.3	0.2	5.1
High school graduate/GED[12] recipient	58.3	17.8	49.6	29.5	16.8	12.4	1.6	0.3	9.4
Some college—no degree	64.7	24.1	54.8	38.8	22.6	19.1	2.7	0.7	12.5
Associate of arts degree	64.1	24.6	53.8	39.8	23.1	20.2	3.0	0.5	12.6
Bachelor of arts or science degree	66.7	29.8	54.9	45.9	27.7	25.0	4.6	0.9	15.3
Masters, doctorate, professional degree	65.5	31.5	52.7	48.8	29.8	26.5	5.2	1.6	12.8
Family income[10,13]									
Less than $20,000	64.9	18.9	58.8	29.6	18.0	14.8	2.4	0.4	6.7
$20,000 or more	61.6	23.1	51.2	37.0	21.6	17.9	2.9	0.6	12.1
$20,000–34,999	63.5	21.1	55.3	34.1	19.9	16.9	2.0	0.5	10.0
$35,000–54,999	62.8	22.6	52.8	36.6	21.2	17.9	2.9	0.6	11.8
$55,000–74,999	60.9	22.7	50.1	37.4	21.2	18.2	2.4	0.4	11.0
$75,000 or more	61.9	27.1	48.7	43.3	25.6	20.7	4.0	0.7	15.2
Poverty status[10,14]					Percents				
Poor	65.5	17.9	60.8	28.2	17.0	14.1	2.0	0.3	5.9
Near poor	64.3	19.1	57.1	30.4	18.3	14.7	1.9	0.4	7.7
Not poor	62.6	24.7	51.2	39.8	23.2	19.5	3.2	0.6	13.1
Health insurance[15]									
Under 65 years:									
Private	61.4	24.6	50.0	39.4	23.2	19.3	3.0	0.6	13.1
Public	65.1	17.9	59.8	31.1	16.5	18.0	2.3	0.4	7.3
Uninsured	57.7	21.1	49.5	31.2	20.4	14.7	3.1	0.7	8.0
65 years and over:									
Private	68.2	16.0	61.9	27.2	14.0	10.6	1.4	0.2	9.4
Public	65.9	14.6	61.1	21.3	13.4	8.4	1.3	0.1	4.5
Uninsured	74.4	18.2	73.2	19.7	18.2	3.0	0.7		0.7
Marital status[10]									
Never married	60.2	21.0	52.0	33.0	19.7	18.0	2.6	0.7	9.4
Married	62.4	21.8	52.7	35.0	20.5	15.6	2.7	0.4	11.1
Cohabiting	59.4	25.9	47.7	37.9	24.6	20.4	2.9	1.3	11.1
Divorced or separated	65.4	23.5	57.5	38.8	22.2	22.1	2.6	0.6	11.1
Widowed	72.8	22.6	65.5	33.9	21.0	18.5	2.0	0.1	8.4

TABLE 2.10

Adults who used selected complementary and alternative medicine categories during the past year, by selected characteristics, 2002

[CONTINUED]

Selected characteristic	CAM including megavitamin therapy and prayer[1]	Biologically based therapies including megavitamin therapy[2]	Mind-body therapies including prayer[3]	CAM excluding megavitamin therapy and prayer[4]	Biologically based therapies excluding megavitamin therapy[5]	Mind-body therapies excluding prayer[6]	Alternative medical systems[7]	Energy therapies	Manipulative and body-based therapies[8]
					Any use of —				
Urban/rural[10]									
Urban	62.6	22.9	53.2	36.0	21.5	18.0	2.9	0.6	10.8
Rural	60.4	19.3	50.9	32.6	18.3	13.9	2.1	0.4	11.1
Place of residence[10]									
MSA,[16] Central City	63.5	22.5	55.3	34.9	21.1	18.3	3.1	0.6	9.9
MSA,[16] not Central City	61.2	23.2	50.9	36.5	21.8	17.4	2.7	0.6	11.1
Not MSA[16]	62.1	18.2	53.1	31.9	17.2	13.9	2.1	0.3	11.6
Region[10]									
Northeast	57.9	22.6	46.9	35.7	21.1	16.9	3.1	0.7	10.9
Midwest	61.4	20.9	52.0	37.0	19.7	18.2	2.2	0.5	13.2
South	64.6	19.3	57.2	29.9	18.0	14.0	1.9	0.3	7.9
West	62.1	27.7	50.3	42.2	26.4	21.1	4.6	0.8	13.8
Pacific states[17]	64.0	27.7	52.4	43.0	26.4	22.4	4.8	0.8	13.3
Body weight status[10,18]									
Underweight	62.0	18.4	55.1	33.6	17.6	20.4	3.0	0.5	8.9
Healthy weight	62.7	23.3	53.2	37.2	21.9	19.5	3.4	0.7	11.6
Overweight	60.1	21.9	49.6	34.8	20.6	15.8	2.6	0.5	11.2
Obese	64.6	21.1	56.3	33.4	19.8	15.3	1.9	0.4	10.3
Life time cigarette smoking status[10,19]					Percents				
Current smoker	57.2	19.7	47.6	32.9	18.7	16.8	2.0	0.5	9.2
Former smoker	66.6	27.0	55.6	41.9	25.3	21.1	4.0	0.8	13.6
Never smoker	62.8	21.2	54.3	34.1	20.0	16.1	2.6	0.5	10.7
Lifetime alcohol drinking status[10,20]									
Lifetime abstainer	61.6	14.9	56.9	24.3	14.0	10.8	1.5	0.2	6.1
Former drinker	69.2	20.5	62.3	33.4	19.0	16.6	2.3	0.5	9.4
Current infrequent/light drinker	62.2	24.3	51.6	39.7	23.0	19.6	3.1	0.7	13.3
Current moderate/heavier drinker	57.0	25.5	43.5	38.5	24.0	18.4	3.4	0.6	12.1
Hospitalized in the last year[10]									
Yes	75.9	22.1	70.4	37.4	20.5	19.5	3.1	0.5	11.2
No	60.6	22.0	50.8	34.9	20.7	16.7	2.7	0.5	10.9

— Quantity zero.

[1]CAM including megavitamins and prayer includes acupuncture; ayurveda; homeopathic treatment; naturopathy; chelation therapy; folk medicine; nonvitamin, nonmineral, natural products; diet-based therapies; megavitamin therapy; chiropractic care; massage; biofeedback; meditation; guided imagery; progressive relaxation; deep breathing exercises; hypnosis; yoga; tai chi; qi gong; prayer for health reasons; and energy healing therapy/Reiki.

[2]Biologically based therapies including megavitamin therapy includes chelation therapy; folk medicine; nonvitamin, nonmineral, natural products; diet-based therapies; and megavitamin therapy.

[3]Mind body therapies including prayer includes biofeedback; meditation; guided imagery; progressive relaxation; deep breathing exercises; hypnosis; yoga; tai chi; qi gong; and prayer for health reasons.

[4]CAM excluding megavitamins and prayer includes acupuncture; ayurveda; homeopathic treatment; naturopathy; chelation therapy; folk medicine; nonvitamin, nonmineral, natural products; diet-based therapies; chiropractic care; massage; biofeedback; meditation; guided imagery; progressive relaxation; deep breathing exercises; hypnosis; yoga; tai chi; qi gong; and energy healing therapy/Reiki.

[5]Biologically based therapies excluding megavitamin therapy includes chelation therapy; folk medicine; nonvitamin, nonmineral natural products; diet-based therapies.

[6]Mind-body therapies excluding prayer includes biofeedback; meditation; guided imagery; progressive relaxation; deep breathing exercises; hypnosis; yoga; tai chi; qi gong.

[7]Alternative medical systems includes acupuncture; ayurveda; homeopathic treatment; and naturopathy.

[8]Manipulative and body-based therapies includes chiropratic care and massage.

[9]Total includes other races not shown separately and persons with unknown education, family income, poverty status, health insurance status, marital status, body weight status, lifetime smoking status, alcohol consumption status, and hospitalization status.

[10]Estimates were age adjusted to the year 2000 U.S. standard population using four age groups; 18–24 years, 25–44 years, 45–64 years, and 65 years and over.

[11]Persons of Hispanic or Latino origin may be of any race or combination of races. Similarly, the category "Not Hispanic or Latino" refers to all persons who are not of Hispanic or Latino origin, regardless of race.

[12]GED is General Education Development high school equivalency diploma.

[13]The categories "Less than $20,000" and "$20,000 or more" include both persons reporting dollar amounts and persons reporting only that their incomes were within one of these two categories. The indented categories include only those persons who reported dollar amounts.

[14]Poverty status is based on family income and family size using the Census Bureau's poverty thresholds for 2001. "Poor" persons are defined as below the poverty threshold. "Near poor" persons have incomes of 100% to less than 200% of the poverty threshold. "Not poor" persons have incomes that are 200% of the poverty threshold or greater.

TABLE 2.10

Adults who used selected complementary and alternative medicine categories during the past year, by selected characteristics, 2002

[CONTINUED]

[15]Classification of health insurance coverage is based on a hierarchy of mutually exclusive categories. Persons with more than one type of health insurance were assigned to the first appropriate category in the hierarchy. Persons under age 65 years and those age 65 years and over were classified separately due to the prominence of Medicare coverage in the older population. The category "Uninsured" includes persons who had no coverage as well as those who had only Indian Health Service coverage or had only a private plan that paid for one type of service such as accidents or dental care. Estimates are age-adjusted to the 2000 U.S. standard population using three age groups: 18–24 years, 25–44 years, and 45–64 years for persons under age 65, and two age groups: 65–74 years and 75 years and over for persons aged 65 years and over.
[16]MSA is metropolitan statistical area.
[17]Pacific states includes California, Oregon, Washington, Alaska, and Hawaii.
[18]Body weight status was based on Body Mass Index (BMI) using self-reported height and weight. The formula for BMI is kilograms/meters^2. Underweight is defined as a BMI of less than 18.5; healthy weight is defined as a BMI of at least 18.5 and less than 25; overweight but not obese, is defined as a BMI of at least 25 and less than 30: and obese is defined as a BMI of 30 or more.
[19]Lifetime cigarette smoking status: Current smoker: smoked at least 100 cigarettes in lifetime and currently smoked cigarettes every day or some days; Former smoker: smoked at least 100 cigarettes in lifetime but did not currently smoke; Never smoker: never smoked at all or smoked at all or smoked less than 100 cigarettes in lifetime.
[20]Lifetime alcohol drinking status: Lifetime abstainer is less than 12 drinks in lifetime; former drinker is 12 or more drinks in lifetime, but no drinks in past year; current infrequent/light drinker is defined as at least 12 drinks in lifetime and 1–11 drinks in past year (infrequent) or 3 drinks or fewer per week, on average (light); current moderate/heavier is defined as at least 12 drinks in lifetime and more than 3 drinks per week up to 14 drinks per week, on average for men and more than 3 drinks per week up to 7 drinks per week on average for women (moderate) or more than 14 drinks per week on average for men and more than 7 drinks per week on average for women (heavier).
Note: CAM is complementary and alternative medicine. The denominators for statistics shown exclude persons with unknown CAM information.

SOURCE: Patricia M. Barnes, Eve Powell-Griner, Kim McFann, and Richard L. Nahin, "Table 4. Age-Adjusted Percents of Adults 18 Years and Over Who Used Selected Complementary and Alternative Medicine Categories during the Past 12 Months, by Selected Characteristics: United States, 2002," in "Complementary and Alternative Medicine Use among Adults: United States, 2002," in *Advance Data from Vital and Health Statistics,* no. 343, Centers for Disease Control and Prevention, National Center for Health Statistics, May 27, 2004, www.cdc.gov/nchs/data/ad/ad343.pdf (accessed June 7, 2004)

CHAPTER 3
HEALTH CARE INSTITUTIONS

A hospital is no place to be sick.
—Samuel Goldwyn (1879–1974)

HOSPITALS

The first hospitals in the United States were established more than two hundred years ago. No records of hospitals in the early colonies exist, but almshouses, which sheltered the poor, also cared for those who were ill. The first almshouse opened in 1662 in the Massachusetts Bay Colony. In 1756 the Pennsylvania Hospital in Philadelphia became the first American institution devoted entirely to care of the sick.

Until the late 1800s, American hospitals had a bad reputation. The upper classes viewed hospitals as places for the poor who could not afford home care, and the poor saw hospitalization as a humiliating consequence of personal economic failure. People from all walks of life thought hospitals were places to go to die.

TYPES OF HOSPITALS

There are more than sixty-five hundred hospitals in the United States that are described as short-stay or long-term, depending on the length of time a patient spends before discharge. Short-stay facilities include community, teaching, and public hospitals. Sometimes short-stay hospitals are referred to as acute care facilities because the services provided within them aim to help resolve pressing problems or medical conditions, such as a heart attack, rather than long-term chronic conditions such as the need for rehabilitation following a head injury. Long-term hospitals are usually rehabilitation and psychiatric hospitals or facilities for the treatment of tuberculosis or other pulmonary (respiratory) diseases.

Hospitals also are distinguished by their ownership, scope of services, and whether they are teaching hospitals with academic affiliations. Hospitals may be operated as proprietary (for-profit) businesses, owned either by corporations or individuals such as the physicians on staff, or they may be voluntary—owned by not-for-profit corporations, religious organizations, or operated by federal, state, or city governments. Voluntary, not-for-profit hospitals are usually governed by a board of trustees, selected from among community business and civic leaders, who serve without pay to oversee hospital operations.

Most community hospitals offer emergency services as well as a range of inpatient and outpatient medical and surgical services. There are more than one thousand "tertiary" hospitals in the United States, which provide highly specialized services such as neonatal intensive care units (for care of sick newborns), trauma services, or cardiovascular surgery programs. The majority of tertiary hospitals serve as teaching hospitals.

Teaching hospitals are those community and tertiary hospitals affiliated with medical schools, nursing schools, or allied-health professions training programs. Teaching hospitals are the primary sites for training new physicians where interns and residents work under the supervision of experienced physicians. Nonteaching hospitals also may maintain affiliations with medical schools and some also serve as sites for nursing and allied-health professions students as well as physicians-in-training.

Community Hospitals

The most common type of hospital in the United States is the community, or general, hospital. Community hospitals, where most people receive care, are typically small, with fifty to five hundred beds. These hospitals normally provide quality care for routine medical and surgical problems. Since the early 1980s, many smaller hospitals were closed down because they were no longer profitable. The larger ones, usually located in cities and adjacent suburbs, are often equipped with a full complement of medical and surgical personnel and state-of-the-art equipment.

Some community hospitals are nonprofit corporations, supported by local funding. These include hospitals supported by religious, cooperative, or osteopathic organizations. In the 1990s, increasing numbers of not-for-profit community hospitals have converted their ownership status, becoming proprietary hospitals that are owned and operated on a for-profit basis by corporations. These hospitals have joined investor-owned corporations because they need additional financial resources to maintain their existence in an increasingly competitive industry. Investor-owned corporations acquire not-for-profit hospitals to build market share, expand their provider networks, and penetrate new health care markets.

Teaching Hospitals

Most teaching hospitals, which provide clinical training for medical students and other health care professionals, are affiliated with a medical school and may have several hundred beds. Many of the physicians on staff at the hospital also hold teaching positions at the university affiliated with the hospital, in addition to teaching physicians-in-training at the bedsides of the patients. Patients in teaching hospitals understand that they may be examined by medical students and residents in addition to their primary "attending" physicians.

One advantage of obtaining care at a university-affiliated teaching hospital is the opportunity to receive treatment from highly qualified physicians with access to the most advanced technology and equipment. A disadvantage is the inconvenience and invasion of privacy that may result from multiple examinations performed by residents and students. When compared with smaller community hospitals, some teaching hospitals have reputations for being very impersonal; however, patients with complex, unusual, or difficult diagnoses usually benefit from the presence of acknowledged medical experts and more comprehensive resources available at these facilities.

Public Hospitals

Public hospitals are owned and operated by federal, state, or city governments. Many have a continuing tradition of caring for the poor. They are usually located in the inner cities and are often in precarious financial situations because many of their patients are unable to pay for services. These hospitals depend heavily on Medicaid payments supplied by local, state, and federal agencies or on grants from local governments. Medicaid is a program run by both the state and federal government for the provision of health care insurance to persons younger than sixty-five years of age who cannot afford to pay for private health insurance. The federal government matches the states' contribution to provide a certain minimal level of available coverage, and the states may offer additional services at their own expense.

Well-known public hospitals include Bellevue Hospital Center (New York City), Parkland Memorial Hospital (Dallas, Texas), Truman Medical Center (Kansas City, Missouri), University of Southern California Medical Center (Los Angeles, California), and Temple University Hospital (Philadelphia, Pennsylvania). Many public hospitals are also university-affiliated teaching hospitals.

TREATING SOCIETY'S MOST VULNERABLE MEMBERS. Increasingly, public hospitals must bear the burden of the weaknesses in the nation's health care system. The major problems in U.S. society are readily apparent in the emergency rooms and corridors of public hospitals—poverty, drug and alcohol abuse, crime-related and domestic violence, and infectious diseases such as acquired immunodeficiency syndrome (AIDS) and tuberculosis.

LOSING MONEY. The typical public hospital provides millions of dollars in health care, and fails to recoup those costs from reimbursement by private insurance, Medicare (a program run by the federal government through which persons age sixty-five and older receive health care insurance), or Medicaid. The National Association of Public Hospitals and Health Systems (NAPH) estimated that nearly half of all public hospital charges are not ultimately paid. This figure has grown sharply as the number of uninsured Americans has also increased. State and local governments provide subsidies to help offset these expenses. However, even with the subsidies, the unpaid costs incurred by the nation's public hospitals add up to billions of dollars' worth of care each year.

PROVIDING NEEDED SERVICES. The NAPH believes that the mission of public hospitals is to respond to the needs of their communities. As a result, most provide a broad spectrum of services. Although the need for trauma care exists across all socioeconomic levels, the American Hospital Association reported that NAPH members are twice as likely to have trauma centers as other community hospitals.

Almost half of NAPH-member hospitals provide prison services, and some hospitals have dedicated beds for prisoners. County and city revenues provide most, if not all, of the funds available for prison services. Many of the NAPH-member hospitals are also major academic centers, training medical and dental residents as well as nursing and allied health professionals.

MORE THAN THEY CAN HANDLE. For many Americans, the public hospital emergency room has replaced the physician's office as the place to seek health care services. With no insurance and little money, many people go to the only place that will take them without question. Insurance companies and health care planners estimate that more than half of all emergency room visits are for nonemergency treatment.

Poor or near poor children up to eighteen years of age of all races were more likely to visit emergency rooms (25.2% and 22.1%, respectively) in 2001 than

TABLE 3.1

Emergency department visits within the past year among children under 18, by selected characteristics, selected years 1997–2001

[Data are based on household interviews of a sample of the civilian noninstitutionalized population]

Characteristic	Under 18 years of age			Under 6 years of age			6–17 years of age		
	1997	1999	2001	1997	1999	2001	1997	1999	2001
	Percent of children with 1 or more emergency department visits								
All children[1]	19.9	17.9	20.7	24.3	23.3	24.9	17.7	15.3	18.6
Race[2]									
White only	19.4	17.1	20.2	22.6	21.9	24.2	17.8	14.8	18.2
Black or African American only	24.0	22.5	22.6	33.1	32.3	29.2	19.4	18.2	19.7
American Indian and Alaska Native only	*24.1	33.3	27.0	*24.3	*29.5	*	*24.0	*36.2	*26.5
Asian only	12.6	9.4	11.4	20.8	*13.4	*8.6	8.6	*7.4	*13.0
Native Hawaiian and other Pacific Islander only	—	*	*	—	*	*	—	*	*
2 or more races	—	23.3	31.1	—	28.7	33.7	—	*19.7	29.2
Hispanic origin and race[2]									
Hispanic or Latino	21.1	15.9	19.4	25.7	21.4	26.1	18.1	12.6	15.4
Not Hispanic or Latino	19.7	18.3	20.9	24.0	23.8	24.7	17.6	15.7	19.2
White only	19.2	17.4	20.6	22.2	22.1	24.3	17.7	15.3	18.9
Black or African American only	23.6	22.5	22.6	32.7	32.5	28.8	19.2	18.2	19.8
Poverty status[3]									
Poor	25.4	24.4	25.2	29.9	31.6	28.1	22.5	20.6	23.5
Near poor	22.6	22.2	22.1	28.8	30.4	28.5	19.4	17.8	18.6
Nonpoor	17.4	15.4	19.5	21.0	19.0	23.5	15.8	13.8	17.7
Hispanic origin and race and poverty status[2,3]									
Hispanic or Latino:									
Poor	22.0	16.4	21.7	24.8	21.0	26.3	20.1	13.0	18.7
Near Poor	20.8	15.2	17.4	28.9	21.7	24.8	15.6	11.6	13.1
Nonpoor	20.3	17.2	21.0	22.7	23.0	28.4	18.9	14.3	16.8
Not Hispanic or Latino:									
White only:									
Poor	26.3	26.3	28.2	28.0	34.9	30.0	25.1	22.4	27.2
Near Poor	23.0	24.5	23.0	26.5	33.0	28.7	21.2	20.1	19.8
Nonpoor	17.4	15.1	19.4	20.6	18.1	23.1	15.9	13.8	17.7
Black of African American only:									
Poor	29.8	29.8	26.2	40.9	42.5	31.9	22.8	23.4	23.3
Near Poor	23.6	23.5	26.0	33.6	33.7	35.8	19.1	18.7	21.2
Nonpoor	17.8	18.8	20.2	23.8	27.1	27.0	15.5	15.6	17.3
Health insurance status[4]									
Insured	19.8	18.1	21.0	24.4	23.1	25.1	17.5	15.7	18.9
Private	17.5	15.4	18.6	20.9	18.9	22.0	15.9	13.9	17.1
Medicaid	28.2	28.8	28.5	33.0	35.2	32.4	24.1	24.2	25.9
Uninsured	20.2	16.4	17.4	23.0	25.5	22.1	18.9	12.7	15.5
Poverty status and health insurance status[3]									
Poor:									
Insured	26.6	26.9	27.6	31.4	32.8	30.3	23.2	23.4	26.0
Uninsured	20.9	15.8	15.0	20.9	25.8	*16.7	20.9	11.9	14.2
Near poor:									
Insured	22.7	23.3	22.6	29.2	31.2	28.8	19.2	18.7	19.0
Uninsured	22.2	18.3	19.3	27.3	26.6	*25.8	20.1	14.8	16.7
Nonpoor:									
Insured	17.3	15.4	19.3	20.8	18.7	23.3	15.7	13.9	17.5
Uninsured	18.8	16.1	19.8	23.7	25.8	24.3	16.7	12.0	18.3
Geographic region									
Northeast	18.5	17.1	20.1	20.7	20.3	23.7	17.4	15.5	18.6
Midwest	19.5	18.4	21.2	26.0	24.1	25.6	16.4	15.8	19.2
South	21.8	19.2	22.2	25.6	25.7	27.0	19.9	16.1	19.8
West	18.5	15.9	18.1	23.5	21.4	22.1	15.9	13.1	15.9
Location of residence									
Within MSA[5]	19.7	16.7	19.8	23.9	22.0	24.1	17.4	14.0	17.6
Outside MSA[5]	20.8	22.4	24.3	26.2	29.1	28.5	18.6	19.7	22.4

those who were not poor (19.5%). (See Table 3.1.) About 28.5% of children on Medicaid visited emergency rooms at least once in 2001, as opposed to 18.6% of children who were privately insured and 17.4% of uninsured children. In the eighteen and older age group, 27.5% of poor persons made one or more emergency department visits and 26.2% of the near poor made one or more visits. Of adults age eighteen to sixty-four, 17.2% of people who were privately insured made one or more emergency room visits during 2001, as opposed to 39.7% of those who had Medicaid and 18.9% of those who were uninsured. (See Table 3.2.)

TABLE 3.1

Emergency department visits within the past year among children under 18, by selected characteristics, selected years 1997–2001 [CONTINUED]

[Data are based on household interviews of a sample of the civilian noninstitutionalized population]

Characteristic	Under 18 years of age			Under 6 years of age			6–17 years of age		
	1997	1999	2001	1997	1999	2001	1997	1999	2001
	Percent of children with 2 or more emergency department visits								
Geographic region									
Northeast	6.2	4.9	6.1	7.6	6.5	6.8	5.4	4.0	5.8
Midwest	6.6	5.8	7.1	10.4	9.8	11.3	4.8	4.0	5.1
South	8.0	6.1	7.8	10.1	9.8	11.3	6.9	4.3	6.0
West	7.1	4.7	5.6	10.0	7.6	7.0	5.6	3.3	4.8
Location of residence									
Within MSA[5]	7.2	5.0	6.8	9.6	8.0	9.2	5.9	3.4	5.5
Outside MSA[5]	6.8	7.4	7.1	9.7	11.3	10.8	5.6	5.8	5.5

*Estimates are considered unreliable.
— Data not available.
[1]Includes all other races not shown separately, unknown poverty status, and unknown health insurance status.
[2]The race groups, white, black, American Indian and Alaska Native (AI/AN), Asian, Native Hawaiian and Other Pacific Islander, and 2 or more races, include persons of Hispanic and non-Hispanic origin. Persons of Hispanic origin may be of any race. Starting with data year 1999 race-specific estimates are tabulated according to 1997 Standards for federal data on Race and Ethnicity and are not strictly comparable with estimates for eariler years. The five single race categories plus multiple race categories shown in the table conform to 1997 Standards. The 1999 race-specific estimates are for persons who reported only one racial group; the category "2 or more races" includes persons who reported more than one racial group. Prior to data year 1999, data were tabulated according to 1977 Standards with four racial groups and the category "Asian only" included Native Hawaiian and Other Pacfic Islander. Estimates for single race categories prior to 1999 included persons who reported one race or, if they reported more than one race, identified one race as best representing their race. The effect of the 1997 Standard on the 1999 estimates can be seen by comparing 1999 data tabulated according to the two Standards: Estimates based on the 1977 Standard of the percent of children under 18 years of age with 1 or more emergency department visits are: 0.1 percentage points higher for white children; 0.2 percentage points higher for black children; 2.1 percentage points lower for AI/AN children; and 2.0 percentage points higher for Asian and Pacific Islander children than estimates based on the 1997 Standards.
[3]Poor persons are defined as below the poverty threshold. Near poor persons have incomes of 100 percent to less than 200 percent of the poverty threshold. Nonpoor persons have incomes of 200 percent or greater than the poverty threshold. Poverty status was unknown for 17 percent of children in the sample in 1997, 21 percent in 1998, 24 percent in 1999, 23 percent in 2000, and 23 percent in 2001.
[4]Health insurance categories are mutually exclusive. Persons who reported both Medicaid and private coverage are classfied as having private coverage. Starting in 1997 Medicaid includes state-sponsored health plans and State Child Health Insurance Program (SCHIP). The category "insured" also includes military, other state, and Medicare coverage.
[5]MSA is metropolitan statistical area.

SOURCE: "Table 75. Emergency Department Visits within the Past 12 Months among Children under 18 years of Age, according to Selected Characteristics: United States, Selected Years 1997–2001," in *Health, United States, 2003,* National Center for Health Statistics, 2003, http://www.cdc.gov/nchs/data/hus/tables/2003/03hus075.pdf (accessed June 22, 2004)

Public hospitals are frequently underfunded and understaffed, and service can be exceedingly slow. All-day waits in the emergency room for initial treatment are not uncommon. A NAPH survey found that the average wait to get a hospital bed upon admission from the emergency room was 5.6 hours, although waits of three to four days were not unusual. Seriously ill patients could wait an average of 3.2 hours to be admitted into intensive care units.

PUBLIC HOSPITALS IN PERIL OF CLOSING. According to the California Department of Health Services, since the early 1990s, sixty hospitals in the state have closed while twenty-six have opened. Many urban public hospitals are located in inner cities and are often the only resources for twenty-four-hour standby emergency and trauma care. As a result, they care for a disproportionate number of victims of violence. Between 1983 and 1999, ten of the original twenty-three hospitals with designated trauma centers in Los Angeles closed their trauma units, causing severe overcrowding in those that remained. During the 1992 Los Angeles riots, King/Drew Medical Center treated ninety-four lacerations, fifty-four gunshot wounds, eighty-seven assaults, and nineteen stab wounds over the course of six days.

During 2002 Los Angeles faced another public hospital crisis with the threatened closure of two more county hos-

pitals, Harbor-UCLA Medical Center and Olive View-UCLA Medical Center, facilities that provide trauma and emergency care and are considered "lifelines" for the working poor. Though both remain open, the county's public hospitals operate under continuing threats of closure. Three quarters of the Los Angeles county health system's patients are uninsured, and some industry observers believe that the remaining three hospitals that form the core of the county health system would be unable to accommodate them.

In 2003 the NAPH urged Congress to take immediate steps to relieve the financial crisis that threatened to close more public hospitals, further compromising the nation's "safety net"—its essential role in the provision of care for uninsured Americans. Citing economic uncertainty and heightened awareness about matters of national security, NAPH called upon the administration of President George W. Bush to reverse Medicaid and Medicare cuts that went into effect in fiscal year 2003; remove regulatory obstacles to enable public hospitals to negotiate lower pharmaceutical drug prices; expand access to health insurance coverage; and ensure adequate financing for emergency preparedness.

REASONS FOR HOSPITALIZATION

The National Hospital Discharge Survey (NHDS) has been performed annually since 1965 by the National Cen-

TABLE 3.2

Emergency department visits within the past year among adults, by selected characteristics, selected years 1997–2001

[Data are based on household interviews of a sample of the civilian noninstitutionalized population]

Characteristic	1 or more emergency department visits				2 or more emergency department visits			
	1997	1999	2000	2001	1997	1999	2000	2001
	Percent of adults with emergency department visit							
All adults 18 years of age and over[1,2]	19.6	17.2	20.2	19.7	6.7	5.2	6.9	6.4
Age								
18–44 years	20.7	17.7	20.6	19.8	6.8	5.6	7.0	6.5
18–24 years	26.3	21.7	25.9	24.0	9.1	7.3	8.9	8.7
25–44 years	19.0	16.5	18.9	18.4	6.2	5.0	6.4	5.8
45–64 years	16.2	14.6	17.6	18.0	5.6	4.3	5.6	5.6
45–54 years	15.7	14.3	17.9	17.7	5.5	4.3	5.8	5.5
55–64 years	16.9	15.1	17.0	18.5	5.7	4.3	5.3	5.9
65 years and over	22.0	19.9	23.7	22.3	8.1	5.6	8.6	7.5
65–74 years	20.3	17.3	21.6	19.7	7.1	4.7	7.4	7.1
75 years and over	24.3	23.1	26.2	25.4	9.3	6.7	10.1	8.0
Sex[2]								
Male	19.1	16.1	18.8	18.9	5.9	4.3	5.8	5.7
Female	20.2	18.2	21.6	20.5	7.5	6.0	8.0	7.2
Race[2,3]								
White only	19.0	16.6	19.4	19.1	6.2	4.7	6.4	6.1
Black or African American only	25.9	22.2	26.5	25.2	11.1	8.8	10.7	9.4
American Indian and Alaska Native only	24.8	29.2	30.5	33.9	13.1	11.7	12.8	15.5
Asian only	11.6	9.7	13.6	12.7	2.9		3.8	2.6
Native Hawaiian and Other Pacific Islander only	—				—			
2 or more races	—	24.4	32.9	25.5	—	11.4	11.4	8.8
American Indian and Alaska Native; White	—	26.0	33.9	25.4	—	13.9	9.2	6.1
Hispanic origin and race[2,3]								
Hispanic or Latino	19.2	15.3	18.4	18.4	7.4	4.5	7.1	7.0
Mexican American	17.8	14.4	17.4	15.6	6.4	4.1	7.1	5.6
Not Hispanic or Latino	19.7	17.5	20.6	20.0	6.7	5.3	6.9	6.4
White only	19.1	16.9	19.8	19.4	6.2	4.8	6.4	6.1
Black or African American only	25.9	22.2	26.5	25.3	11.0	8.8	10.7	9.4
Poverty status[2,4]								
Poor	29.2	27.6	30.2	27.5	13.7	11.7	14.3	13.1
Near poor	24.9	21.7	25.1	26.2	10.0	8.0	10.6	10.4
Nonpoor	17.5	15.4	18.6	18.2	5.0	4.1	5.3	5.1
Hispanic origin and race and poverty status[2,3,4]								
Hispanic or Latino:								
Poor	22.9	17.1	24.4	19.9	10.2	6.6	11.3	10.1
Near poor	19.2	15.9	19.4	20.1	8.4	5.0	7.6	7.7
Nonpoor	17.9	14.5	17.1	17.6	5.5	3.8	6.1	5.3
Not Hispanic or Latino:								
White only:								
Poor	30.8	29.4	30.6	29.6	14.1	11.7	14.3	13.7
Near poor	25.5	22.2	26.8	27.9	9.8	7.6	11.5	11.0
Nonpoor	17.2	15.5	18.2	18.0	4.8	4.1	5.0	5.1
Black or African American only:								
Poor	35.5	33.5	38.0	32.1	17.9	16.8	19.0	15.7
Near poor	30.8	27.8	29.9	28.8	12.9	13.0	13.1	12.8
Non poor	20.7	18.4	24.1	22.3	7.8	5.7	8.4	7.0
Health insurance status[5,6]								
18–64 years of age:								
Insured	18.8	16.1	19.5	19.2	6.1	4.7	6.4	6.2
Private	16.9	14.5	17.6	17.2	4.7	3.7	5.1	4.7
Medicaid	37.6	35.4	42.3	39.7	19.7	17.4	21.0	21.7
Uninsured	20.0	18.3	19.6	18.9	7.5	7.0	7.0	6.6
65 years of age and over:								
Medicare HMO	20.2	20.1	24.4	23.6	6.7	5.7	8.5	8.8
Private	21.3	19.3	23.3	21.0	6.9	5.3	7.9	6.4
Medicaid	35.2	30.0	35.9	36.0	20.2	12.8	18.3	18.7
Medicare fee-for-service only	22.0	19.2	20.1	21.5	9.4	4.4	7.3	6.9

ter for Health Statistics. The NHDS is the longest continuously running nationally representative survey of hospital utilization and is considered the preeminent source for national data describing the characteristics of patients discharged from nonfederal short-stay hospitals. The 2002 NHDS found an estimated 33.7 million inpatients discharged, excluding newborns, from nonfederal short-stay hospitals in the United States.

TABLE 3.2

Emergency department visits within the past year among adults, by selected characteristics, selected years 1997–2001 [CONTINUED]

[Data are based on household interviews of a sample of the civilian noninstitutionalized population]

	1 or more emergency department visits				2 or more emergency department visits			
Characteristic	1997	1999	2000	2001	1997	1999	2000	2001
Poverty status and health insurance status[4,5]	Percent of adults with emergency department visit							
18–64 years of age:								
Poor:								
Insured	32.1	29.8	33.6	30.8	15.9	13.3	17.4	15.5
Uninsured	24.4	22.7	26.0	20.0	10.0	10.3	10.6	8.5
Near poor:								
Insured	26.6	23.1	27.3	28.0	10.3	8.7	11.6	11.7
Uninsured	21.3	18.6	20.1	23.6	9.1	7.5	7.7	9.0
Nonpoor:								
Insured	16.6	14.7	17.6	17.2	4.5	3.7	4.9	4.6
Uninsured	19.0	16.3	19.2	17.8	5.4	6.5	6.4	5.0
Geographic region[2]								
Northeast	19.5	16.9	20.0	19.8	6.9	5.1	6.2	6.1
Midwest	19.3	17.2	20.1	19.6	6.2	5.1	6.9	6.0
South	20.9	17.7	21.3	20.9	7.3	5.7	7.6	7.3
West	17.7	16.4	18.7	17.6	6.0	4.5	6.3	5.6
Location of residence[2]								
Within MSA[7]	19.1	16.6	19.6	19.4	6.4	1.9	6.6	6.3
Outside MSA[7]	21.5	19.5	22.5	21.3	7.8	6.4	7.8	7.0

— Data not available.

[1]Includes all other races not shown separately, unknown poverty status, and unknown health insurance status.

[2]Estimates are for persons 18 years of age and over and are age adjusted to the year 2000 standard using five age groups: 18–44 years, 45–54 years, 55–64 years, 65–74 years, and 75 years and over.

[3]The race groups, white, black, American Indian and Alaska Native (AI/AN), Asian, Native Hawaiian and Other Pacific Islander, and 2 or more races, include persons of Hispanic and non-Hispanic origin. Persons of Hispanic origin may be of any race. Starting with data year 1999 race-specific estimates are tabulated according to 1997 Standards for Federal data on Race and Ethnicity and are not striclty comparable with estimates for earlier years. The five single race categories pluse multiple race categories shown in the table conform to 1997 Standards. The 1999 race-specific estimates are for persons who reported only one racial group; the category "2 or more races" includes persons who reported more than one racial group. Prior to data years 1999, data were tabulated according to 1977 Standards with four racial groups and the category "Asian only" included Native Hawaiian and Other Pacific Islander. Estimates for single race categories prior to 1999 included persons who reported one race or, if they reported more than one race, identified one race as best representing their race. The effect of the 1997 Standard on the 1999 estimates can be seen by comparing 1999 data tabulated according to the two Standards: Age-adjusted estimates based on the 1977 Standard of the percent of adults with 1 or more emergency department visits are: 0.1 percentage points higher for white and black adults; 2.0 percentage points lower for AI/AN adults; and 0.3 percentage points higher for Asian and Pacific Islander adults than estimates based on the 1997 Standards.

[4]Poor persons are defined as below the poverty threshold. Near poor persons have incomes of 100 percent to less than 200 percent of the poverty threshold. Nonpoor persons have incomes of 200 percent or greater than the poverty threshold. Poverty status was unknown for 22 percent of adults in the sample in 1997, 27 percent in 1998, 29 percent in 1999 and 2000, and 30 percent in 2001.

[5]Estimates for persons 18–64 years of age are age adjusted to the year 2000 Standard using three age groups: 18–44 years, 45–54 years, and 55–64 years of age. Estimates for persons 65 years of age and over are age adjusted to the year 2000 Standard using two age groups: 65–74 years and 75 years and over.

[6]Health insurance categories are mutually exclusive. Persons who reported both Medicaid and private coverage are classified as having private coverage. Persons 65 years of age and over who reported Medicare HMO (health maintenance organization) and some other type of health insurance coverage are classified as having Medicare HMO. Starting in 1997 Medicaid includes states-sponsored health plans and State Child Health Insurance Program (SCHIP). The Category "insure" also includes military, other State, and Medicare coverage.

[7]MSA is metropolitan statistical area.

SOURCE: "Table 77. Emergency Department Visits within the Past 12 Months among Adults 18 Years of Age and Over, according to Selected Characteristics: United States, Selected Years 1997–2001," in *Health, United States, 2003,* National Center for Health Statistics, 2003, http://www.cdc.gov/nchs/data/hus/tables/2003/03hus077.pdf (accessed June 22, 2004)

In 2002 persons less than fifteen years old accounted for just 8% of hospital discharges and persons between fifteen and forty-four comprised 32% of discharges. Adults aged forty-five to sixty-four accounted for 23% of discharges and those age sixty-five and older made the largest contribution—38% of hospital discharges. (See Figure 3.1.) Figure 3.2 shows how the average age of persons discharged from the hospital has increased from 40.7 in 1970 to 52.1 in 2002.

The discharge rate was 1,174.6 per ten thousand population. The rate for females only was 1,388 per ten thousand; for males the rate was 952.3 per ten thousand. The numbers were higher for females primarily because women are hospitalized for childbirth and pregnancy-related conditions. (See Table 3.3.) The 2002 NHDS also reveals that male patients had longer average lengths of stay (ALOS) than

female patients—5.3 days compared with 4.6 days. Lengths of stay and discharge rates varied by geography—ALOS ranged from 4.4 days in the Midwest to 5.6 days in the Northeast. The discharge rate per ten thousand population ranged from 955.4 in the West to 1,290.3 in the Northeast.

By Diagnosis

Heart disease is the number-one killer of Americans. In 2002 diseases of the circulatory system, which include heart disease, ranked first among diagnoses for patients discharged from nonfederal short-stay hospitals, and it accounted for 4.4 million discharges. Nearly two-thirds (2.8 million) of these patients discharged with a diagnosis of heart disease were age sixty-five or older, and among older adults there were 798.7 discharges per ten thousand population with a first-listed diagnosis of heart disease. (See Table 3.4.)

FIGURE 3.1

FIGURE 3.2

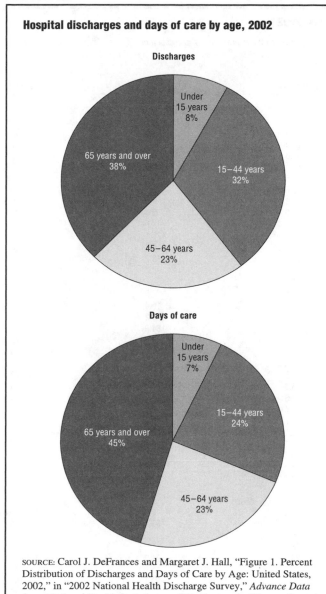

Hospital discharges and days of care by age, 2002

SOURCE: Carol J. DeFrances and Margaret J. Hall, "Figure 1. Percent Distribution of Discharges and Days of Care by Age: United States, 2002," in "2002 National Health Discharge Survey," *Advance Data from Vital and Health Statistics,* no. 342, Centers for Disease Control and Prevention, National Center for Health Statistics, May 21, 2004, http://www.cdc.gov/nchs/data/ad/ad342.pdf (accessed September 8, 2004)

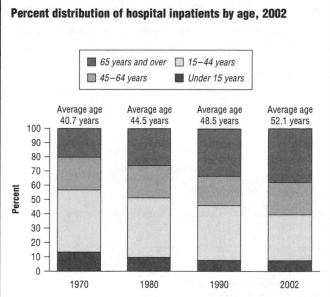

Percent distribution of hospital inpatients by age, 2002

SOURCE: Carol J. DeFrances and Margaret J. Hall, "Percent Distribution of Hospital Inpatients by Age: United States, 2002," in "2002 National Health Discharge Survey," *Advance Data from Vital and Health Statistics,* no. 342, Centers for Disease Control and Prevention, National Center for Health Statistics, May 21, 2004, http://www.cdc.gov/nchs/data/ad/ad342.pdf (accessed September 8, 2004)

discharged from short-stay hospitals. Nearly 75% of all procedures fell into just four broad categories: obstetrical procedures, operations of the digestive system, operations of the cardiovascular system, and miscellaneous diagnostic and therapeutic procedures that included computerized tomography (usually referred to as CT scan), arteriography and angiocardiography, diagnostic ultrasounds, and respiratory therapy.

Figure 3.4 reveals that about one-quarter of all procedures performed on females were obstetrical while the same proportion of procedures performed on men were cardiovascular. It also shows that males had more cardiovascular procedures than females (4 million versus 2.8 million) and females underwent more procedures of the digestive system than males (3.2 million versus 2.4 million).

The most commonly performed procedures for males were cardiovascular—removal of coronary artery obstruction and insertion of stents, cardiac catheterization, and coronary artery bypass graft—along with arteriography, angiocardiography, and endoscopy of the small intestine and diagnostic ultrasound. Female patients most frequently had obstetrical procedures—repair of obstetrical laceration, cesarean section, artificial rupture of membranes, episiotomy, and hysterectomy—as well as arteriography and angiography and endoscopy of the small intestine. (See Table 3.6.)

Organ Transplants

Organ transplants are a viable means of saving lives, and in 2003, 25,448 transplants were performed in 255

Table 3.5 shows that the second-leading discharge diagnosis was obstetric delivery, which accounted for nearly one-fifth (four million) of female patient discharges. Three other diagnostic categories also produced more than a million hospital discharges—1.7 million discharges attributable to psychoses (mental illness), 1.3 million discharges for pneumonia, and 1.2 million discharges for malignant neoplasms, or tumors. (See Table 3.4.) Figure 3.3 shows that ALOS varied by diagnosis from highs of eight days for psychoses and 7.1 days for malignant neoplasms to 2.6 days for delivery and 4.6 days for heart disease.

By Procedures

The NHDS revealed that in 2002 42.5 million surgical and nonsurgical procedures were performed on patients

TABLE 3.3

Rate of discharges from short-stay hospitals by sex and first-listed diagnosis, 2002

[Discharges of inpatients from non-federal hospitals. Excludes newborn infants. Diagnostic groupings are based on the *International Classification of Diseases, 9th Revision, Clinical Modification*]

Category of first-listed diagnosis	Both sexes	Male	Female
	Rate per 100,000 population		
All conditions	1,174.6	952.3	1,388.0
Infectious and parasitic diseases	30.5	29.7	31.4
Septicemia	11.9	11.1	12.7
Neoplasms	58.6	46.2	70.5
Malignant neoplasms	42.1	41.2	42.9
Malignant neoplasm of large intenstine and rectum	5.5	5.4	5.6
Malignant neoplasm of trachea, bronchus, and lung	5.6	6.1	5.1
Malignant neoplasm of breast	3.0		5.8
Benign neoplasms	14.9	3.5	25.8
Endocrine, nutritional and metabolic diseases, and immunity disorders	56.4	47.0	65.4
Diabetes mellitus	20.1	20.1	20.1
Volume depletion	17.7	14.5	20.7
Diseases of the blood and blood-forming organs	15.5	13.7	17.3
Mental disorders	85.8	87.9	83.8
Psychoses	59.4	58.1	60.5
Alcohol dependence syndrome	5.1	7.2	3.0
Diseases of the nervous system and sense organs	18.0	15.4	20.6
Diseases of the circulatory system	222.0	228.2	216.0
Heart disease	154.8	164.9	145.2
Acute myocardial infarction	28.5	34.1	23.1
Coronary atherosclerosis	38.2	47.4	29.3
Other ischemic heart disease	7.3	7.4	7.3
Cardiac dysrhythmias	27.5	26.8	28.0
Congestive heart failure	33.8	31.4	36.1
Cerebrovascular disease	32.8	30.7	34.8
Diseases of the respiratory system	123.4	119.3	127.2
Acute bronchitis and bronchiolitis	9.7	10.8	8.7
Pneumonia	45.7	44.0	47.3
Chronic bronchitis	18.1	16.3	19.8
Asthma	16.8	13.9	19.7
Diseases of the digestive system	115.6	104.3	126.5
Appendicitis	10.3	11.9	8.8
Noninfectious enteritis and colitis	10.8	9.1	12.4
Diverticula of intestine	9.1	7.5	10.7
Cholelithiasis	12.5	8.0	16.8
Diseases of the genitourinary system	63.3	39.8	85.8
Calculus of kidney and ureter	6.1	7.0	5.3
Complactions of pregnancy, childbirth, and the puerperium	18.4	. . .	36.0
Diseases of the skin and subcutaneous tissue	20.9	21.2	20.6
Cellulitis and abscess	14.7	15.0	14.4
Diseases of the musculoskeletal system and connective tissue	60.5	53.1	67.5
Osteoarthrosis and allied disorders	19.8	15.7	23.7
Intervertebral disc disorders	12.3	12.8	11.8
Congenital anomalies	6.2	6.9	5.5
Certain conditions originating in the perinatal period	5.8	6.6	5.0
Symptoms, signs, and ill-defined conditions	9.9	9.4	10.3
Injury and poisoning	93.9	94.7	93.2
Fractures, all sites[1]	34.7	30.8	38.4
Fracture of neck of femur	11.0	6.0	15.7
Poisonings	7.4	6.8	8.0
Supplementary classifications	170.0	28.7	305.5
Females with deliveries	137.6	—	269.7

— Category not applicable.

[1]Rates were calculated using U.S. Census Bureau estimates of the civilian population based on the 2000 census.

SOURCE: Carol J. DeFrances and Margaret J. Hall, "Table 6. Rate of Discharges from Short-Stay Hospitals by Sex and First-Listed Diagnosis: United States, 2002," in "2002 National Health Discharge Survey," *Advance Data from Vital and Health Statistics,* no. 342, Centers for Disease Control and Prevention, National Center for Health Statistics, May 21, 2004, http://www.cdc.gov/nchs/data/ad/ad342.pdf (accessed September 8, 2004)

hospital transplant centers across the country. The United Network for Organ Sharing (UNOS) compiles data on organ transplants, distributes organ donor cards, and maintains a registry of patients awaiting organ transplants. UNOS reported that as of July 2004, 85,867 Americans were waiting for transplants. According to UNOS about five thousand people die each year while waiting for an organ transplant because demand for organs continues to outpace supply.

Governors of many states began a variety of programs aimed at increasing public awareness of the lack of donor organs and honoring those who have chosen to become

TABLE 3.4

Number of discharges from short-stay hospitals by first-listed diagnosis and age, 2002

[Discharges of inpatients from non-federal hospitals. Excludes newborn infants. Diagnostic groupings are based on the *International Classification of Diseases, 9th Revision, Clinical Modification*]

Category of first-listed diagnosis	All ages	Under 15 years	15–44 years	45–64 years	65 years and over
			Number in thousands		
All conditions	33,727	2,540	10,736	7,723	12,727
Infectious and parasitic diseases	877	156	204	185	332
Septicemia	341	12	34	76	219
Neoplasms	1,682	33	313	611	725
Malignant neoplasms	1,208	25	121	419	643
Malignant neoplasm of large intestine and rectum	159		5	46	107
Malignant neoplasm of trachea, bronchus, and lung	160		5	55	100
Malignant neoplasm of breast	85		11	36	38
Benign neoplasms	427		183	178	61
Endocrine, nutritional and metabolic diseases, and immunity disorders	1,619	187	328	454	649
Diabetes mellitus	577	33	147	205	193
Volume depletion	508	129	53	77	249
Diseases of the blood and blood-forming organs	446	71	106	81	188
Mental disorders	2,464	149	1,422	620	273
Psychoses	1,704		957	431	224
Alcohol dependence syndrome	145		87	53	
Diseases of the nervous system and sense organs	518	81	134	114	189
Diseases of the circulatory system	6,373	31	434	1,871	4,037
Heart disease	4,446	17	273	1,313	2,843
Acute myocardial infarction	818		57	259	501
Coronary atherosclerosis	1,096		48	432	615
Other ischemic heart disease	211		18	86	107
Cardiac dysrhythmias	788		45	174	562
Congestive heart failure	970		32	219	717
Cerebrovascular disease	942		40	229	669
Diseases of the respiratory system	3,542	730	382	697	1,732
Acute bronchitis and bronchiolitis	279	209	8	22	40
Pneumonia	1,312	204	116	216	776
Chronic bronchitis	520		16	161	343
Asthma	484	187	109	109	80
Diseases of the digestive system	3,320	216	839	955	1,310
Appendicitis	295	70	155	50	21
Noninfectious enteritis and colitis	310	54	89	66	100
Diverticula of intestine	262		36	77	149
Cholelithiasis	359		116	109	133
Diseases of the genitourinary system	1,817	88	580	458	690
Calculus of kidney and ureter	176		81	62	29
Complications of pregnancy, childbirth, and the puerperium	528		524		—
Diseases of the skin and subcutaneous tissue	601		158	151	199
Cellulitis and abscess	422	41	109	126	147
Diseases of the musculoskeletal system and connective tissue	1,736	41	326	598	770
Osteoarthrosis and allied disorders	568		20	193	356
Intervertebral disc disorders	353		133	153	67
Congenital anomalies	178	124	31	15	7
Certain conditions originating in the perinatal period	166	165			
Symptoms, signs, and ill-defined conditions	283	63	99	68	54
Injury and poisoning	2,697	233	780	621	1,063
Fractures, all sites	995	68	239	165	524
Fracture of neck of femur	315		6	24	282
Poisonings	214	18	120	48	28
Supplementary classifications	4,880	75	4,073	224	508
Females with deliveries	3,951	12	3,934	5	—

— Category not applicable.

SOURCE: Carol J. DeFrances and Margaret J. Hall, "Table 2. Number of Discharges from Short-Stay Hospitals by First-Listed Diagnosis and Age: United States, 2002," in "2002 National Health Discharge Survey," *Advance Data from Vital and Health Statistics,* no. 342, Centers for Disease Control and Prevention, National Center for Health Statistics, May 21, 2004, http://www.cdc.gov/nchs/data/ad/ad342.pdf (accessed September 8, 2004)

donors. For example, Alabama Governor Don Siegelman created an Alabama Donor Registry, Georgia Governor Roy Barnes designated March as Eye Donor Month, and Utah Governor Michael O. Leavitt and the state legislature adopted a resolution to improve public awareness about organ and tissue donation. Governors of at least nine states forged partnerships with local advocacy, med-

ical, religious, and business groups to strengthen support for transplant programs.

State programs were also reinforced by a national organ donation initiative announced by Health and Human Services (HHS) Secretary Tommy G. Thompson in April 2001. Secretary Thompson vowed to create a national medal to honor families of organ donors, and

TABLE 3.5

Number of discharges from short-stay hospitals by sex and first-listed diagnosis, 2002

[Discharges of inpatients from non-federal hospitals. Excludes newborn infants. Diagnostic groupings are based on the *International Classification of Diseases, 9th Revision, Clinical Modification*]

Category of first-listed diagnosis	Both sexes	Male	Female
	Number in thousands		
All conditions	33,727	13,389	20,338
Infectious and parasitic diseases	877	417	460
Septicemia	341	156	186
Neoplasms	1,682	650	1,033
Maligant neoplasms	1,208	579	629
Malignant neoplasm of large intestine and rectum	159	76	83
Malignant neoplasm of trachea, bronchus, and lung	160	86	74
Malignant neoplasm of breast	85		85
Benign neoplasms	427	49	378
Endocrine, nutritional and metabolic diseases, and immunity disorders	1,619	661	958
Diabetes mellitus	577	283	294
Volume depletion	508	204	304
Diseases of the blood and blood-forming organs	446	192	254
Mental disorders	2,464	1,236	1,227
Psychoses	1,704	817	887
Alcohol dependence syndrome	145	101	44
Diseases of the nervous system and sense organs	518	217	301
Diseases of the circulatory system	6,373	3,209	3,164
Heart disease	4,446	2,319	2,127
Acute myocardial infarction	818	480	338
Coronary atherosclerosis	1,096	666	429
Other ischemic heart disease	211	103	108
Cardiac dysrhythmias	788	377	411
Congestive heart failure	970	441	529
Cerebrovascular disease	942	432	509
Diseases of the respiratory system	3,542	1,678	1,864
Acute bronchitis and bronchiolitis	279	152	127
Pneumonia	1,312	618	694
Chronic bronchitis	520	230	291
Asthma	484	196	288
Diseases of the digestive system	3,320	1,466	1,854
Appendicitis	295	167	129
Noninfectious enteritis and colitis	310	128	182
Diverticula of intestine	262	106	157
Cholelithiasis	359	113	246
Diseases of the genitourinary system	1,817	560	1,257
Calculus of kidney and ureter	176	99	77
Complications of pregnancy, childbirth, and the puerperium	528	—	528
Diseases of the skin and subcutaneous tissue	601	299	303
Cellulitis and abscess	422	211	212
Diseases of the musculoskeletal system and connective tissue	1,736	747	989
Osteoarthrosis and allied disorders	568	221	347
Interverterbral disc disorders	353	180	174
Congenital anomalies	178	97	80
Certain conditions originating in the perinatal period	166	93	73
Symptoms, signs, and ill-defined conditions	283	132	151
Injury and poisoning	2,697	1,331	1,366
Fractures, all sites	995	433	562
Fracture of neck of femur	315	85	230
Poisonings	214	96	118
Supplementary classifications	4,880	403	4,477
Females with deliveries	3,951	—	3,951

— Category not applicable.

SOURCE: Carol J. DeFrances and Margaret J. Hall, "Number of Discharges from Short-Stay Hospitals by Sex and First-Listed Diagnosis: United States, 2002," in "2002 National Health Discharge Survey," *Advance Data from Vital and Health Statistics*, no. 342, Centers for Disease Control and Prevention, National Center for Health Statistics, May 21, 2004, http://www.cdc.gov/nchs/data/ad/ad342.pdf (accessed September 8, 2004)

called upon the traditional alliances between employers and labor unions to promote donation-awareness efforts. Called the "Workplace Partnership for Life," this coalition included some of the largest U.S. employers and organizations, such as Aetna, American Airlines, Bank of America, Daimler-Chrysler Corporation, United Auto Workers, Ford Motor Company, General Motors, 3M, MetLife, Verizon, and the United States Postal Service.

In March 1998 UNOS was ordered to change its organ allocation policy to more equitably distribute organs to various regions of the country. Under the previous system, when an organ became available in a local area, that organ was offered to the sickest patient in that area. If no local patient needed the organ, then it was offered regionally, then nationally. The government wanted organs distributed to the sickest patients first, regard-

FIGURE 3.3

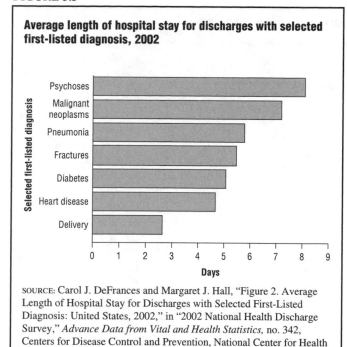

Average length of hospital stay for discharges with selected first-listed diagnosis, 2002

SOURCE: Carol J. DeFrances and Margaret J. Hall, "Figure 2. Average Length of Hospital Stay for Discharges with Selected First-Listed Diagnosis: United States, 2002," in "2002 National Health Discharge Survey," *Advance Data from Vital and Health Statistics,* no. 342, Centers for Disease Control and Prevention, National Center for Health Statistics, May 21, 2004, http://www.cdc.gov/nchs/data/ad/ad342.pdf (accessed September 8, 2004)

FIGURE 3.4

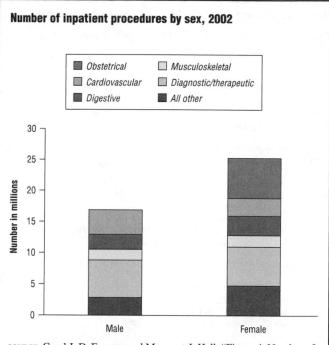

Number of inpatient procedures by sex, 2002

SOURCE: Carol J. DeFrances and Margaret J. Hall, "Figure 4. Number of All-Listed Inpatient Procedures by Sex: United States, 2002," in "2002 National Health Discharge Survey," *Advance Data from Vital and Health Statistics,* no. 342, Centers for Disease Control and Prevention, National Center for Health Statistics, May 21, 2004, http://www.cdc.gov/nchs/data/ad/ad342.pdf (accessed September 8, 2004)

less of where they lived. The HHS Secretary at that time, Donna Shalala, stated, "People are dying unnecessarily, not because they don't have health insurance, not because they don't have access to care, but simply because of where they happen to live in the country. We need a level playing field for all patients."

The new regulations changed the allocation of organs from a regional system to a national system in which medical necessity, rather than geography, was the primary factor determining who received organs. The new rules met with great resistance in Congress. Some members felt that the government should have no role in deciding life and death issues, and others insisted that a national program would result in the closure of smaller transplant centers, forcing some transplant recipients to travel great distances for life-saving care. UNOS opposed the regulations, arguing that the new system would obstruct their ability to supply donated organs.

The new system, based on need rather than location, took effect in March 2000, although the issue of precisely who would decide the allocation of organs remained unresolved until April 2000, when the U.S. House of Representatives passed a proposal to restore decision-making to UNOS, where it has remained. In September 2000 UNOS signed a new three-year contract with the government that compelled the network to put the new rules into effect. By 2002 UNOS policies reflected the shift to a more equitable national organ distribution system.

In February 2004 the Organ Procurement and Transplantation Network/United Network for Organ Sharing (OPTN/UNOS) revised and strengthened its policies to guard against potential medical errors in transplant candidate and donor matching. The policy revisions were developed in response to a systematic review begun after a medical error in February 2003, when a teenager named Jesica Santillan received a heart-lung transplant from a blood-type incompatible donor at Duke University Medical Center. News of this tragic error immediately prompted transplant centers throughout the United States to perform internal audits of their protocols and procedures to ensure appropriate donor/recipient matching.

The key policy revisions included stipulations that:

• The blood type of each transplant candidate and donor must be independently verified by two staff members at the institution involved at the time blood type is entered into the national database.

• Each transplant program and organ procurement organization (OPO) must establish a protocol to ensure blood type data for transplant candidates and donors are accurately entered into the national database and communicated to transplant teams. UNOS will verify the existence and effective use of these protocols during routine audits of OPOs and transplant programs.

• Organs must only be offered to candidates specifically identified on the computer-generated list of medically

TABLE 3.6

Number of procedures for discharges from short-stay hospitals, by procedure category and sex, 2002

[Discharges of inpatients from non-federal hospitals. Excludes newborn infants. Procedure groupings are based on the *International Classification of Diseases, 9th Revision, Clinical Modification*]

Procedure category	Both sexes	Male	Female
		Number in thousands	
All procedures	42,533	16,834	25,700
Operations on the nervous system	1,101	514	587
Spinal tap	316	161	156
Operations on the endocrine system	102	30	72
Operations on the eye	86	47	39
Operations on the ear	46	24	22
Operations on the nose, mouth, and pharynx	269	159	110
Operations on the respiratory system	1,022	283	439
Bronchoscopy with or without biopsy	251	147	104
Operations on the cardiovascular system	6,813	3,967	2,845
Removal of coronary artery obstruction and insertion of stents(s)	1,204	802	402
Coronary artery bypass graft[1]	515	373	142
Cardiac catheterization	1,328	799	529
Insertion, replacement, removal, and revision of pacemaker leads or device	420	213	207
Hemodialysis	552	288	264
Operations on the hemic and lymphatic system	354	178	175
Operations on the digestive system	5,597	2,350	3,247
Endoscopy of small intestine with or without biopsy	1,032	450	582
Endoscopy of large intestine with or without biopsy	278	235	343
Partial excision of large intestine	263	113	150
Appendectomy, excluding incidental	329	173	156
Cholecystectomy	436	143	293
Lysis of peritoneal adhesions	342	62	280
Operations on the urinary system	955	454	501
Cystoscopy with or without biopsy	173	86	87
Operations on the male genital organs	262	262	—
Prostatectomy	195	195	—
Operations on the female genital organs	2,161	—	2,161
Oophorectomy and salpingo-oophorectomy	533	—	533
Bilateral destruction or occlusion of fallopian tubes	329	—	329
Hysterectomy	669	—	669
Obstetrical procedures	6,646	—	6,646
Episiotomy with or without forceps or vacuum extraction	780	—	780
Artificial rupture of membranes	901	—	901
Cesarean section	1,059	—	1,059
Repair of current obstetric laceration	1,234	—	1,234
Operations on the musculoskeletal system	3,442	1,652	1,790
Partial excision of bone	218	112	106
Reduction of fracture	606	288	318
Open reduction of fracture with internal fixation	414	186	229
Excision or destruction of intervertebral disc	323	171	152
Total hip replacement	193	81	112
Total knee replacement	381	146	235
Operations on the integumentary system	1,348	616	732
Debridement of wound, infection, or burn	361	199	161
Miscellaneous diagnostic and therapeutic procedures	12,332	5,996	6,336
Computerized axial tomography	703	324	378
Arteriography and angiocardiography using contrast material	2,058	1,142	915
Diagnostic ultrasound	773	347	427
Respiratory therapy	1,070	546	524
Insertion of endotracheal tube	477	247	229
Injection or infusion of cancer chemotherapeutic substance	217	124	94

— Category not applicable.

[1]The number of discharges with a coronary artery bypass graft was 306,000.

SOURCE: Carol J. DeFrances and Margaret J. Hall, "Table 10. Number of All-Listed Procedures for Discharges from Short-Stay Hospitals by Procedure Category and Sex: United States, 2002," in "2002 National Health Discharge Survey," *Advance Data from Vital and Health Statistics,* no. 342, Centers for Disease Control and Prevention, National Center for Health Statistics, May 21, 2004, http://www.cdc.gov/nchs/data/ad/ad342.pdf (accessed September 8, 2004)

suitable transplant candidates for a given organ offer. If the organ offer is not accepted for any candidate on a given match run, an OPO may give transplant programs the opportunity to update transplant candidate data and re-run a match to see if any additional candidates are identified.

UNOS resolved to continuously review national policies and procedures for organ placement and to recommend policy and procedure enhancements to maximize the efficiency of organ placement and the safety of transplant candidates and recipients, as well as to ensure public confidence in the transplant system. As of July 2004, there had been no further reported occurrences of unintentional blood-type incompatible transplants.

SURGICAL CENTERS AND URGENT CARE CENTERS

Ambulatory surgery centers, often called surgicenters, are equipped to perform routine surgical procedures that do not require an overnight hospital stay. A surgical center requires less sophisticated and expensive equipment than a hospital operating room. Minor surgery, such as biopsies, abortions, hernia repair, and many cosmetic surgery procedures, are performed at outpatient surgical centers. Most procedures are done under local anesthesia, and the patient goes home the same day.

Most ambulatory surgery centers are freestanding, but some are located on hospital campuses or are adjacent to physicians' offices or clinics. Facilities are licensed by their states, and they must be equipped with at least one operating room, an area for preparing patients for procedures, a patient recovery area, and X-ray and clinical laboratory services. Surgical centers must have a registered nurse on the premises when patients are in the facility.

Urgent care centers (also called urgicenters) are usually operated by private for-profit organizations and provide up to twenty-four-hour care on a walk-in basis. These centers fill several special needs in a community. They provide convenient, timely, and easily accessible care in an emergency when the nearest hospital is miles away. The centers are normally open during the hours when most physicians' offices are closed, and they are economical to operate because they do not provide hospital beds. They usually treat problems such as cuts that require sutures, sprains and bruises from accidents, and various infections. Many provide inexpensive immunization, and some offer routine health care for persons who do not have a regular source of medical care. Urgent care tends to be more expensive than a visit to the family physician, but an urgent care center visit is usually less expensive than treatment from a traditional hospital emergency department.

LONG-TERM CARE FACILITIES

Families are still the major caretakers of older, dependent, and disabled members of American society. The number of people age sixty-five and older living in long-term care facilities such as nursing homes, however, is rising because the population in this age group is increasing rapidly. Even though many older people now live longer, healthier lives, the increase in overall length of life has increased the need for long-term care facilities.

Growth of the home health care industry in the early 1990s only slightly slowed the increase in the numbers of Americans entering nursing homes. Assisted living and continuing-care retirement communities offer other alternatives to nursing home care. When it is possible, many older adults prefer to remain in the community and receive health care in their homes.

Types of Nursing Homes

Nursing homes fall into three broad categories: residential care facilities, intermediate care facilities, and skilled nursing facilities. Each provides a different range and intensity of services:

- A residential care facility (RCF) normally provides meals and housekeeping for its residents, plus some basic medical monitoring, such as administering medications. This type of home is for persons who are fairly independent and do not need constant medical attention but need help with tasks such as laundry and cleaning. Many RCFs also provide social activities and recreational programs for their residents.

- An intermediate care facility (ICF) offers room and board and nursing care as necessary for persons who can no longer live independently. As in the RCF, exercise and social programs are provided, and some ICFs offer physical therapy and rehabilitation programs as well.

- A skilled nursing facility (SNF) provides around-the-clock nursing care, plus on-call physician coverage. The SNF is for patients who need intensive nursing care, as well as such services as occupational therapy, physical therapy, respiratory therapy, and rehabilitation.

Number of Nursing Home Residents Rising

The National Nursing Home Survey (NNHS) is a continuing series of national sample surveys of nursing homes, their residents, and their staff. The surveys were conducted in 1973–74, 1977, 1985, 1995, 1997, and 1999. Although each survey focused on different aspects of care, they all provided some common basic information about nursing homes, their residents, and their staff from two perspectives—that of the provider of services and that of the recipient. Data about the facilities include characteristics such as size, ownership, Medicare/Medicaid certification, occupancy rate, number of days of care provided, and expenses. The surveys gathered demographic data, health status, and services received by nursing home residents. The most recent NNHS was conducted in 1999. The nursing homes included in this survey had at least three beds and were either certified (by Medicare or Medicaid) or had a state license to operate as a nursing home.

According to the 1999 NNHS, the nation's eighteen thousand nursing homes had occupancy rates of almost 87% in 1999. Nursing homes averaged about 105 beds per facility. In 1999 about 1.5 million adults age sixty-five and older were nursing home residents. Of those, most were white (87.1%) and female (74.3%). If the 158,700 residents under sixty-five are added to the total, there were 1.6 million nursing home residents in 1999, with women (nearly 1.2 million) outnumbering men (457,900) by almost three to one. There were more than six times as many white nursing home residents as African-Americans and other racial minorities.

By 2001 the nation's 16,675 certified nursing homes housed 1,779,924 beds and had occupancy rates of 82.5%. The distribution of nursing home beds and occupancy rates varied by geography—the East North Central states boasted 364,309 beds while the less populated Mountain states had just 74,034 beds. Occupancy rates ranged from a high of 90.3% in the Middle Atlantic states to a low of 71.3% in the West South Central states of Arkansas, Louisiana, Oklahoma, and Texas. (See Table 3.7.)

Most residents of nursing homes are the "oldest old." Out of the total 1.6 million nursing home residents in 1999, 90% were sixty-five years old and older, according to the 1999 NNHS. People age eighty-five and older (the so-called oldest old) are a fast-growing segment of the population and accounted for almost half (46%) of all nursing home residents.

In 1999, 92% of all nursing homes were privately owned, according to NNHS data. Most (67%) nursing homes were company-owned and operated on a for-profit basis. Another 27% were operated by nonprofit, volunteer organizations, and only 12% were operated by governmental agencies. More than 80% were certified (approved for payment) by both Medicare and Medicaid. About half of all current nursing home residents were admitted directly from a hospital, and about 30% came from the community.

Diversification of Nursing Homes

To remain competitive with home health care and the increasing array of alternative living arrangements for the elderly, many nursing homes began to offer alternative services and programs. New services include adult day care and visiting nurse services for persons who still live at home. Other programs include respite plans that allow caregivers who need to travel for business or vacation to leave an elderly relative in the nursing home temporarily.

One of the most popular nontraditional services is subacute care, which is comprehensive inpatient treatment for people recovering from acute illnesses such as pneumonia, injuries such as a broken hip, and chronic diseases such as arthritis that do not require intensive, hospital-level treatment. This level of care also enables nursing homes to expand their markets by offering services for younger patients.

Innovation Improves Quality of Nursing Home Care

While industry observers and the media frequently raise concerns about the care provided in nursing homes and publicize instances of elder abuse and other quality of care issues, several organizations have actively sought to develop models of health service delivery that improve the clinical care and quality of life for nursing home residents. In August 2002 the Commonwealth Fund published a report examining one such model in eastern Wisconsin, *Evaluation of the Wellspring Model for Improving Nursing Home Quality*. Researchers from the Institute for the Future of Aging Services and American Association of Homes and Services for the Aging evaluated the Wellspring model of nursing home quality improvement.

Wellspring is a group of eleven not-for-profit nursing homes governed by a group called the Wellspring Alliance. Founded in 1994, the alliance aimed to improve simultaneously clinical care delivered to its nursing home residents and the work environment for its employees. Education and collaboration are hallmarks of the Wellspring philosophy, and this program began by equipping nursing home personnel with the skills needed to perform their jobs and organizing employees in teams working toward shared goals. The Wellspring model of service delivery uses a multidisciplinary clinical team approach—nurse practitioners, social service, food service personnel, nursing assistants, facility and housekeeping personnel—to solve problems and develop approaches to better meet residents' needs. The teams represent an important innovation because they allow health professionals and other workers to interact as peers and share resources, information, and decision-making in a cooperative, supportive environment.

Shared resources, training, ideas, and goals have had a powerful impact on care at the Wellspring facilities. The researchers observed more cooperation, responsibility, and accountability within the teams and the institutions than observed at other comparable facilities. In addition to finding a strong organizational culture that seemed committed to quality patient care, the researchers also documented measurable improvements in specific areas including:

• Wellspring facilities had lower rates of staff turnover than comparable Wisconsin facilities during the same time period, probably because Wellspring workers felt valued by management and experienced greater job satisfaction than other nursing home personnel.

• The Wellspring model did not require additional resources to institute, and Wellspring facilities operated at lower costs than comparable facilities.

• Wellspring facilities' performance, as measured by a federal survey, improved.

• Generally, Wellspring personnel appeared more attentive to residents' needs and problems and sought to anticipate and promptly resolve problems.

The researchers concluded that the organizational commitment to training and shared decision-making along with improved quality of interactions and relationships among staff and between staff and residents significantly contributed to enhanced quality of life for residents.

TABLE 3.7

Nursing homes, beds, occupancy, and residents by geographic division and state, 1995–2001

[Data are based on a census of certified nursing facilities]

Geographic division and state	Nursing homes			Beds			Residents			Occupancy rate[1]			Resident rate[2]	
	1995	2000	2001	1995	2000	2001	1995	2000	2001	1995	2000	2001	1995	2000
United States	16,389	16,886	16,675	1,751,302	1,795,388	1,779,924	1,479,550	1,480,076	1,469,001	84.5	82.4	82.5	404.5	349.1
New England	1,140	1,137	1,110	115,488	118,562	115,939	105,792	106,308	104,573	91.6	89.7	90.2	474.2	419.5
Maine	132	126	126	9,243	8,248	8,002	8,587	7,298	7,189	92.9	88.5	89.8	417.9	313.0
New Hampshire	74	83	83	7,412	7,837	7,883	6,877	7,158	7,126	92.8	91.3	90.4	434.1	392.6
Vermont	23	44	44	1,862	3,743	3,636	1,792	3,349	3,293	96.2	89.5	90.6	207.0	335.0
Massachusetts	550	526	506	54,532	56,030	54,514	49,765	49,805	48,876	91.3	88.9	89.7	477.3	426.8
Rhode Island	94	99	97	9,612	10,271	10,183	8,823	9,041	8,923	91.8	88.0	87.6	476.9	432.6
Connecticut	267	259	254	32,827	32,433	31,721	29,948	29,657	29,166	91.2	91.4	91.9	541.7	461.4
Middle Atlantic	1,650	1,796	1,799	244,342	267,772	268,888	228,649	242,674	242,784	93.6	90.6	90.3	384.0	354.2
New York	624	665	669	107,750	120,514	121,592	103,409	112,957	114,141	96.0	93.7	93.9	371.8	362.6
New Jersey	300	361	364	43,967	52,195	52,463	40,397	45,837	45,672	91.9	87.8	87.1	351.6	337.0
Pennsylvania	726	770	766	92,625	95,063	94,833	84,843	83,880	82,971	91.6	88.2	87.5	419.2	353.1
East North Central	3,171	3,301	3,265	367,879	369,657	364,309	294,319	289,404	284,563	80.0	78.3	78.1	476.1	414.3
Ohio	943	1,009	998	106,884	105,038	103,974	79,026	81,946	80,930	73.9	78.0	77.8	499.5	463.5
Indiana	556	564	560	59,538	56,762	56,861	44,328	42,328	41,946	74.5	74.6	73.8	548.9	462.3
Illinois	827	869	854	103,230	110,766	108,287	83,696	83,604	81,749	81.1	75.5	75.5	495.3	435.4
Michigan	432	439	434	49,473	50,696	49,535	43,271	42,615	41,508	87.5	84.1	83.8	345.0	299.1
Wisconsin	413	420	419	48,754	46,395	45,652	43,998	38,911	38,430	90.2	83.9	84.2	518.9	406.9
West North Central	2,258	2,281	2,247	200,109	193,754	191,091	164,660	157,224	154,804	82.3	81.1	81.0	489.6	429.8
Minnesota	432	433	427	43,865	42,149	40,836	41,163	38,813	38,052	93.8	92.1	93.2	537.4	453.4
Iowa	419	467	466	39,959	37,034	36,944	27,506	29,204	28,825	68.8	78.9	78.0	458.0	448.5
Missouri	546	551	545	52,679	54,829	54,882	39,891	38,586	38,706	75.7	70.4	70.5	432.8	391.5
North Dakota	87	88	87	7,125	6,954	6,757	6,868	6,343	6,279	96.4	91.2	92.9	522.0	430.7
South Dakota	114	114	112	8,296	7,844	7,568	7,926	7,059	6,952	95.5	90.0	91.9	543.3	438.8
Nebraska	231	236	230	18,169	17,877	17,369	16,166	14,989	14,492	89.0	83.8	83.4	501.4	441.5
Kansas	429	392	380	30,016	27,067	26,735	25,140	22,230	21,498	83.8	82.1	80.4	528.9	429.4
South Atlantic	2,215	2,418	2,410	243,069	264,147	265,149	217,303	227,818	228,961	89.4	86.2	86.4	335.4	291.9
Delaware	42	43	42	4,739	4,906	4,736	3,819	3,900	3,950	80.6	79.5	83.4	448.7	369.7
Maryland	218	255	251	28,394	31,495	30,507	24,716	25,629	25,361	87.0	81.4	83.1	432.7	383.1
District of Columbia	19	20	21	3,206	3,078	3,136	2,576	2,858	2,863	80.3	92.9	91.3	297.6	318.4
Virginia	271	278	277	30,070	30,595	31,102	28,091	27,091	26,875	93.5	88.5	86.4	385.2	310.4
West Virginia	129	139	139	10,903	11,413	11,373	10,216	10,304	10,304	93.7	90.5	90.6	355.2	325.2
North Carolina	391	410	413	38,322	41,376	42,194	35,511	36,658	37,106	92.7	88.6	87.9	401.1	347.6
South Carolina	166	178	179	16,682	18,102	18,185	14,568	15,739	16,117	87.3	86.9	88.6	366.0	313.1
Georgia	352	363	361	38,097	39,817	39,806	35,933	36,559	36,356	94.3	91.8	91.3	496.0	416.1
Florida	627	732	727	72,656	83,365	84,110	61,845	69,050	70,029	85.1	82.8	83.3	228.2	208.4
East South Central	1,014	1,071	1,080	99,707	106,250	107,656	91,563	96,348	96,598	91.8	90.7	89.7	416.6	385.5
Kentucky	288	307	304	23,221	25,341	25,482	20,823	22,730	22,776	89.1	89.7	89.4	391.9	390.1
Tennessee	322	349	349	37,074	38,593	38,923	33,929	34,714	34,588	91.5	89.9	88.9	479.6	426.1
Alabama	221	225	228	23,353	25,248	25,797	21,691	23,089	23,538	92.9	91.4	91.2	370.1	343.1
Mississippi	183	190	199	16,059	17,068	17,454	15,247	15,815	15,696	94.9	92.7	89.9	405.3	368.7
West South Central	2,264	2,199	2,143	224,695	224,100	220,048	169,047	159,160	156,961	75.2	71.0	71.3	486.1	397.6
Arkansas	256	255	250	29,952	25,715	25,061	20,823	19,317	18,677	69.5	75.1	74.5	508.3	415.5
Louisiana	337	337	332	37,769	39,430	38,861	32,493	30,735	30,127	86.0	77.9	77.5	639.3	523.8
Oklahoma	405	392	379	33,918	33,903	32,776	26,377	23,833	22,640	77.8	70.3	69.1	499.1	416.8
Texas	1,266	1,215	1,182	123,056	125,052	123,350	89,354	85,275	85,517	72.6	68.2	69.3	439.9	358.4

TABLE 3.7

Nursing homes, beds, occupancy, and residents by geographic division and state, 1995–2001 [CONTINUED]

[Data are based on a census of certified nursing facilities]

Geographic division and state	Nursing homes			Beds			Residents			Occupancy rate[1]			Resident rate[2]	
	1995	2000	2001	1995	2000	2001	1995	2000	2001	1995	2000	2001	1995	2000
Mountain	800	827	806	70,134	75,152	74,034	58,738	59,379	59,395	83.8	79.0	80.2	335.9	271.2
Montana	100	104	103	7,210	7,667	7,594	6,415	5,973	5,928	89.0	77.9	78.1	491.4	389.5
Idaho	76	84	84	5,747	6,181	6,368	4,697	5,640	4,619	81.7	75.1	72.5	321.7	257.0
Wyoming	37	40	39	3,035	3,119	3,098	2,661	2,605	2,546	87.7	83.5	82.2	468.2	386.8
Colorado	219	225	223	19,912	20,240	20,119	17,055	17,045	16,855	85.7	84.2	83.8	420.6	353.5
New Mexico	83	80	80	6,969	7,289	7,263	6,051	6,503	6,364	86.8	89.2	87.6	332.0	279.0
Arizona	152	150	139	16,162	17,458	16,836	12,382	13,253	13,455	76.6	75.9	79.9	233.3	193.4
Utah	91	93	92	7,101	7,651	7,683	5,832	5,703	5,592	82.1	74.5	72.8	323.5	262.2
Nevada	42	51	46	3,998	5,547	5,073	3,645	3,657	4,036	91.2	65.9	79.6	312.0	215.3
Pacific	1,871	1,856	1,815	185,879	175,994	172,810	149,479	141,761	140,362	80.4	80.5	81.2	302.4	241.3
Washington	285	277	268	28,464	25,905	24,983	24,954	21,158	20,663	87.7	81.7	82.7	362.5	251.6
Oregon	161	150	145	13,885	13,500	12,977	11,673	9,990	9,444	84.1	74.0	72.8	244.9	173.9
California	1,382	1,369	1,342	140,203	131,762	129,928	109,805	106,460	105,923	78.3	80.8	81.5	302.9	250.1
Alaska	15	15	15	814	821	882	634	595	638	77.9	72.5	72.3	348.0	225.9
Hawaii	34	45	45	2,513	4,006	4,040	2,413	3,558	3,694	96.0	88.8	91.4	178.5	202.6

Notes: Annual numbers of nursing homes, beds, and residents are based on the Centers for Medicare & Medical Services (CMS) 15-month Online Survey, Certification, and Reporting (OSCAR) database reporting cycle.

[1]Percent of beds occupied (number of nursing home residents per 100 nursing home beds).

[2]Number of nursing home residents (all ages) per 1,000 resident population 85 years of age and over.

SOURCE: "Table 110. Nursing Homes, Beds, Occupancy, and Residents, according to Geographic Division and State: United States, 1995–2001," in Health, United States, 2003, National Center for Health Statistics, 2003, http://www.cdc.gov/nchs/data/hus/tables/2003/2003/03hus110.pdf (accessed July 2, 2004)

MENTAL HEALTH FACILITIES

In earlier centuries, mental illness was often considered a sign of possession by the devil or, at best, moral weakness. A change in these attitudes began in the late eighteenth century, when mental illness began to be perceived as a treatable condition. It was then that the concept of "asylums" was developed, not simply to lock the mentally ill away, but also to provide them with "relief" from the conditions they found troubling.

Who Are the Mentally Ill?

Providers of mental health care distinguish between people who are severely mentally ill (defined by diagnosis), those who are mentally disabled (defined by level of disability), and those who are chronic mental patients (defined by duration of hospitalization). These three dimensions—diagnosis, disability, and duration—are the models used to describe the mentally ill population in the United States.

Mental Health: A Report of the Surgeon General, 1999 defines mental disorders as "health conditions that are characterized by alterations in thinking, mood, or behavior (or some combination thereof) associated with distress and/or impaired functioning." The report distinguishes mental disorders from mental problems, describing the signs and symptoms of mental health problems as less intense and of shorter duration than those of mental health disorders; it acknowledges, however, that both mental health disorders and problems may be distressing and disabling.

The U.S. Public Health Service uses this definition:

The chronically mentally ill population includes persons who suffer from emotional disorders that interfere with their functional capacities in relation to such primary aspects of daily life as self-care, interpersonal relationships, and work or schooling, and that may often necessitate prolonged mental health care.

The U.S. Surgeon General's Report asserts that at the close of the twentieth century, the nation's ability to prevent, identify, and treat mental disorders had outpaced the system for delivering mental health care to all those in need of it. The report estimated that one in five Americans suffers from a mental disorder in any given year and 15% of adults make use of mental health services during the year—8% seek care for a mental disorder and 7% have mental health problems.

Where Are the Mentally Ill?

The chronically mentally ill reside either in mental hospitals or in community settings, such as with families, in boarding homes and shelters, in single-room-occupancy hotels (usually cheap hotels or boardinghouses), in jail, or even on the streets as part of the homeless population. The institutionalized mentally ill are those persons with psychiatric diagnoses who have lived in mental hospitals for more than one year or those with diagnosed mental conditions who are living in nursing homes.

Between 1986 and 1998 the number of patients housed in county mental health institutions declined, although the number of mental health organizations rose by almost 975 during this time. The total number of beds dropped from 267,613 to 266,729, and from 111.7 beds to 99.1 beds per one hundred thousand persons. State and county mental hospital beds were reduced most dramatically, by more than one-half, from fifty to twenty-four beds per one hundred thousand persons. (See Table 3.8.) This is not necessarily a result of better treatment for the mentally ill, but rather a consequence of reduced funding for those institutions and individuals. Unfortunately, many of the patients who were once housed in mental institutions (including some who had been lifelong residents in these facilities) now fend for themselves on the streets or in prisons.

Declining mental health expenditures have resulted in fewer available services for specific populations of the mentally ill, particularly those who could benefit from inpatient or residential care. Even for persons without conditions requiring institutional care there are barriers to access. The Surgeon General's Report describes the U.S. mental health service system as largely uncoordinated and fragmented, in part because it involves so many different sectors—health and social welfare agencies, public and private hospitals, housing, criminal justice, education—and it is funded through many different sources. Finally, inequalities in insurance coverage for mental health, coupled with the stigma associated with mental illness and treatment, have also limited access to services.

HOME HEALTH CARE

The concept of home health care began as post-acute care after hospitalization, an alternative to longer, costlier lengths of stay in regular hospitals. Home health care services have grown tremendously since the 1980s when prospective payment (payments made before, rather than after, care is received) for Medicare patients sharply reduced hospital lengths of stay. During the mid-1980s Medicare began to reimburse hospitals using a rate scale based on diagnosis related groups (DRGs)—hospitals received a fixed amount for providing services to Medicare patients based on their diagnoses. This form of payment gave hospitals powerful financial incentives to utilize fewer resources since they could keep the difference between the prepayment and the amount they actually spent to provide care. Hospitals suffered losses when patients had longer lengths of stay and used more services than were covered by the standardized DRG prospective payment.

Home health care grew faster in the early 1990s than any other segment of health services. Its growth may be attributable to the observation that in many cases, caring for patients at home is preferable to and more cost-effective than care provided in a hospital, nursing home, or some other residential facility. Oftentimes older adults are more comfortable and much happier living in their own homes or with family

TABLE 3.8

Mental health organizations and beds for residential treatment by type of organization, selected years 1986–98

(Data are based on inventories of mental health organizations)

Type of organization	1986	1990	1992	1994[1]	1998[1]
			Number of mental health organizations		
All organizations	4,747	5,284	5,498	5,392	5,722
State and county mental hospitals	285	273	273	256	229
Private psychiatric hospitals	314	462	475	430	348
Non-federal general hospital psychiatric services	1,351	1,674	1,616	1,612	1,707
Department of Veterans Affairs medical centers[2]	139	141	162	161	145
Residential treatment centers for emotionally disturbed children	437	501	497	459	461
All other organizations[3]	2,221	2,233	2,475	2,474	2,832
			Number of beds		
All organizations	267,613	272,253	270,867	290,604	266,729
State and county mental hospitals	119,033	98,789	93,058	81,911	63,769
Private psychiatric hospitals	30,201	44,871	43,684	42,399	34,154
Non-federal general hospital psychiatric services	45,808	53,479	52,059	52,984	55,145
Department of Veterans Affairs medical centers[2]	26,874	21,712	22,466	21,146	13,742
Residential treatment centers for emotionally disturbed children	24,547	29,756	30,089	32,110	33,997
All other organizations[3]	21,150	23,646	29,511	60,054	65,922
			Beds per 100,000 civilian population		
All organizations	111.7	111.6	107.5	112.1	99.1
State and county mental hospitals	49.7	40.5	36.9	31.6	23.7
Private psychiatric hospitals	12.6	18.4	17.3	16.4	12.7
Non-federal general hospital psychiatric services	19.1	21.9	20.7	20.4	20.5
Department of Veterans Affairs medical centers[2]	11.2	8.9	8.9	8.2	5.1
Residential treatment centers for emotionally disturbed children	10.3	12.2	11.9	12.4	12.6
All other organizations[3]	8.8	9.7	11.7	23.2	24.6

Notes: Data for 1998 are revised and differ from the previous edition of *Health, United States*. These data exclude mental health care provided in non-psychiatric units of hospitals such as general medical units.
[1]Beginning in 1994 data for supportive residential clients (moderately staffed housing arrangements such as supervised apartments, group homes, and halfway houses) are included in the totals and all other organizations. This change affects the comparability of trend data prior to 1994 with data for 1994 and later years.
[2]Includes Department of Veterans Affairs (VA) neuropsychiatric hospitals, VA general hospital psychiatric services, and VA psychiatric outpatient clinics.
[3]Includes freestanding psychiatric outpatient clinics, partial care organizations, and multiservice mental health organizations.

SOURCE: "Table 107. Mental Health Organizations and Beds for 24-hour Hospital and Residential Treatment according to Type of Organization: United States, Selected Years 1986–98," in *Health, United States, 2003*, National Center for Health Statistics, 2003, http://www.cdc.gov/nchs/data/hus/tables/2003/03hus107.pdf (accessed July 2, 2004)

members. Disabled persons may also be able to function better at home with limited assistance than in a residential setting with full-time monitoring ("Home Health Care," *Family Economics and Nutrition Review*, vol. 9, no. 2, 1996).

Home health care agencies provide a wide variety of services. Services range from helping with activities of daily living, such as bathing, light housekeeping, and meals, to skilled nursing care, such as the nursing care needed by AIDS or cancer patients. About 20% of the personnel employed by home health agencies are registered nurses, another 7% are licensed practical nurses, and 13% are nursing or home health aides. Other personnel involved in home health care include physical therapists, social workers, and speech-language pathologists.

In 1972 Medicare extended home care coverage to persons under sixty-five years of age only if they were disabled or suffered from end-stage renal disease (ESRD). Prior to the year 2000, Medicare coverage for home

health care was limited to patients immediately following discharge from the hospital. By the year 2000 Medicare covered beneficiaries' home health care services with no requirement for prior hospitalization. There were also no limits to the number of professional visits or to the length of coverage. As long as the patient's condition warranted it, the following services were provided:

- Part-time or intermittent skilled nursing and home health aide services
- Speech-language pathology services
- Physical and occupational therapy
- Medical social services
- Medical supplies
- Durable medical equipment (with a 20% co-payment)

Over time, the population receiving home care services has changed. Today much of home health care is associated with rehabilitation from critical illnesses, and

TABLE 3.9

Home health care patients, by age, sex, and diagnosis, selected years 1992–2000

(Data are based on a survey of current home health care patients)

Age, sex, and diagnosis	1992	1994	1996	1998	2000
			Number of current patients		
Total home health care patients	1,232,200	1,889,327	2,427,483	1,881,768	1,355,290
			Current patients per 10,000 population		
Total	**47.8**	**71.8**	**90.6**	**69.6**	**48.7**
Age at time of survey:					
Under 65 years, crude	12.6	21.0	27.8	25.0	16.4
65 years and over, crude	295.4	424.9	526.3	375.7	277.0
65 years and over, age adjusted	315.8	449.6	546.6	381.0	276.5
65–74 years	151.7	209.1	240.1	202.0	130.2
75–84 years	398.3	542.2	753.6	470.3	347.6
85 years and over	775.9	1,206.1	1,253.4	885.4	694.1
Sex:					
Male, total	**32.6**	**47.8**	**60.9**	**47.9**	**35.1**
Under 65 years, crude	10.9	17.8	22.1	22.9	15.6
65 years and over, crude	219.2	303.1	386.4	255.2	199.6
65 years and over, age adjusted	255.8	350.0	438.3	277.6	216.4
65–74 years	121.8	169.9	187.0	159.7	100.7
75–84 years	322.0	427.5	598.7	321.4	270.0
85 years and over	635.2	893.1	1,044.3	653.0	553.9
Female, total	**62.4**	**94.7**	**118.9**	**90.4**	**61.8**
Under 65 years, crude	14.3	24.2	33.6	27.0	17.2
65 years and over, crude	347.4	508.9	623.9	460.4	332.6
65 years and over, age adjusted	351.5	506.6	615.0	445.8	315.5
65–74 years	175.3	240.6	283.2	236.3	154.6
75–84 years	445.3	614.5	854.0	568.8	400.4
85 years and over	830.7	1,327.6	1,337.0	981.7	754.9
			Percent distribution		
Age at time of survey:					
Under 65 years	23.1	25.7	27.0	31.3	29.5
65 years and over	76.9	74.3	73.0	68.7	70.5
65–74 years	22.6	20.6	18.4	19.7	17.3
75–84 years	33.9	31.2	35.3	29.9	31.3
85 years and over	20.4	22.4	19.4	19.1	21.9
Sex:					
Male	33.2	32.5	32.9	33.6	35.2
Female	66.8	67.5	67.1	66.4	64.8
Primary admission diagnosis:					
Malignant neoplasms	5.7	5.7	4.8	3.8	4.9
Diabetes	7.7	8.1	8.5	6.1	7.8
Diseases of the nervous system and sense organs	6.3	8.0	5.8	7.6	6.1
Diseases of the circulatory system	25.9	27.2	25.6	23.6	23.6
Diseases of heart	12.6	14.3	10.9	12.3	10.9
Cerebrovascular diseases	5.8	6.1	7.8	5.1	7.3
Diseases of the respiratory system	6.6	6.1	7.7	7.9	6.8
Decubitus ulcers	1.9	1.1	1.0	1.2	1.9
Diseases of the musculoskeletal system and connective tissue	9.4	8.3	8.8	8.3	9.8
Osteoarthritis	2.5	2.8	3.2	2.7	3.5
Fractures, all sites	3.8	3.7	3.3	4.0	4.1
Fracture of neck of femur (hip)	1.4	1.7	1.3	1.1	1.5
Other	32.7	31.8	34.6	37.5	34.9

Notes: Current home health care patients are those who were on the rolls of the agency as of midnight on the day immediately before the date of the survey. Rates are based on the civilian population as of July 1. Diagnostic categories are based on the *International Classification of Diseases, 9th Revision, Clinical Modification.*

SOURCE: "Table 87. Home Health Care Patients, according to Age, Sex, and Diagnosis: United States, Selected Years, 1992–2000," in *Health, United States, 2003,* National Center for Health Statistics, 2003, http://www.cdc.gov/nchs/data/hus/tables/2003/03hus087.pdf (accessed July 2, 2004)

fewer users are long-term patients with chronic conditions. This changing pattern of utilization reflects a shift from longer-term care for chronic conditions to short-term, post-acute care. Compared with post-acute care users, the long-term patients are older, more functionally disabled, more likely to be incontinent, and more expensive to serve.

In 2000 nearly 1.4 million persons received home health services. Women outnumbered men two to one and more than two-thirds of all home health care recipients were age sixty-five or older. The number of home health care patients per ten thousand population increased with advancing age, and CDC data revealed that nearly 10% of women age eighty-five and over used home health care services. (See Table 3.9.)

Medicare Limits Home Care Services

From 1990 to 2001 annual Medicare spending for home health care rose from $3.7 billion to $4.2 billion. Relaxed eligibility criteria for home health care, including elimination of the requirement of an acute hospitalization before receiving home care, enabled an increased number of beneficiaries to use services. Home health care utilization among those over the age of sixty-five peaked in 1996 and began to decline during 1997.

The Balanced Budget Act of 1997 (PL 105-33) aimed to cut approximately $16.2 billion from the federal government's home care expenditures over a period of five years. The act sought to return home health care to its original concept of short-term care plus skilled nursing and therapy services. According to Medicare's administrator, Nancy-Ann DeParle, some of the 4.8 million Medicare beneficiaries who received home health care would lose certain personal care services, such as assistance with bathing, dressing, and eating.

The Balanced Budget Act sharply curtailed the growth in home-care spending, greatly affecting health care providers. Annual Medicare home health care spending fell 32% between 1998 and 1999 in response to tightened eligibility requirements for skilled nursing services, limited per-visit payments, and increasingly stringent claims review. The changes forced many agencies to close and transfer their patients to other home-health companies. Nationwide, the Centers for Medicare and Medicaid Services (CMS, formerly known as the Health Care Financing Administration or HCFA) estimated that twelve hundred agencies went out of business during 1998.

Nonetheless, the aging population and financial imperative to prevent or minimize institutionalization—hospitalization or placement in a long-term care facility—combined to generate increasing expenditures for home health care services. Even though home health care decreased from 5.5% to just 2.9% of Medicare expenditure from 1999 to 2001, Medicare expenditures for home health care more than tripled from $1.2 billion to $4.3 billion during the same period. (See Table 3.10.)

HOSPICE CARE

In medieval times hospices were refuges for the sick, the needy, and travelers. The modern hospice movement developed in response to the need to provide humane care to terminally ill patients, while at the same time offering support to their families. An English physician, Dame Cicely Saunders, pioneered the hospice concept in Britain in the late 1960s and helped introduce it in the United States over the next decade. The care provided by hospice workers is called palliative care, and it aims to relieve patients' pain and the accompanying symptoms of terminal illness without seeking to cure the illness.

Hospice is a philosophy, an approach to care for the dying, and it is not necessarily a physical facility. Hospice may refer to a place—a freestanding facility or designated floor in a hospital or nursing home—or to a program such as hospice-home care, where a team of health professionals helps the dying patient and family at home. Hospice teams may involve physicians, nurses, social workers, pastoral counselors, and trained volunteers. The goal of hospice care is to provide support and care for people at the end of life, enabling them to remain as comfortable as possible.

Hospice workers consider the patient and family as the "unit of care" and focus their efforts on attending to emotional, psychological, and spiritual needs as well as physical comfort and well-being. The programs provide respite care, which offers relief at any time for families who may be overwhelmed and exhausted by the demands of caregiving and may be neglecting their own needs for rest and relaxation. Finally, hospice programs work to prepare relatives and friends for the loss of their loved ones. Hospice offers bereavement support groups and counseling to help deal with grief and may even help with funeral arrangements.

The hospice concept is different from most other health care services because it focuses on care rather than cure. Hospice workers try to minimize the two greatest fears associated with dying: fear of isolation and fear of pain. Potent, effective medications are offered to patients in pain, with the goal of controlling pain without impairing alertness so that patients may be as comfortable as possible.

Hospice care also emphasizes living life to its fullest. Patients are encouraged to stay active for as long as possible, to do things they enjoy, and to learn something new each day. Quality of life, rather than length of life, is the focus. In addition, whenever it is possible, family and friends are urged to be the primary caregivers in the home. Care at home helps both patients and family members enrich their lives and face death together.

Dr. Ira Byock, former president of the American Academy of Hospice and Palliative Medicine, explains the concept of hospice care in *Dying Well: The Prospect for Growth at the End of Life* (New York, NY: G. P. Putnam's Sons, 1997):

> Hospice care differs noticeably from the modern medical approach to dying. Typically, as a hospice patient nears death, the medical details become almost automatic and attention focuses on the personal nature of this final transition—what the patient and family are going through emotionally and spiritually. In the more established system, even as people die, medical procedures remain the first priority. With hospice, they move to the background as the personal comes to the fore.

Studies show that about 80% of terminally ill patients die in a hospital or a nursing home, many of them the

TABLE 3.10

Medicare enrollees and expenditures by type of service, selected years 1970–2001

Type of service	1970	1980	1990	1995	1997	1998	1999	2000	2001[1]
Enrollees					**Number in millions**				
Total[2]	**20.4**	**28.4**	**34.3**	**37.6**	**38.5**	**38.9**	**39.2**	**39.7**	**40.0**
Hospital insurance	20.1	28.0	33.7	37.2	38.1	38.5	38.8	39.3	39.6
Supplementary medical insurance	19.5	27.3	32.6	35.6	36.4	36.8	37.0	37.3	37.6
Expenditures					**Amount in billions**				
Total	**$7.5**	**$36.8**	**$111.0**	**$184.2**	**$213.6**	**$213.4**	**$212.9**	**$221.8**	**$244.8**
Total hospital insurance (HI)	5.3	25.6	67.0	117.6	139.5	135.8	130.6	131.1	143.4
HI payments to managed care organizations[3]	—	0.0	2.7	6.7	16.3	19.0	20.9	21.4	20.8
HI payments for fee-for-service utilization	5.3	25.6	64.3	110.9	123.1	116.8	109.8	109.7	122.6
Inpatient hospital	4.8	24.1	56.9	82.3	89.2	57.4	86.5	87.3	95.6
Skilled nursing facility	0.2	0.4	2.5	9.1	12.5	13.1	10.9	10.9	13.4
Home health agency	0.1	0.5	3.7	16.2	17.5	11.6	7.3	3.9	4.2
Home health agency transfer[4]	—	—	—	—	—	0.5	0.6	1.7	3.1
Hospice	—	—	0.3	1.9	2.1	2.2	2.6	3.0	3.7
Administrative expenses[5]	0.2	0.5	0.9	1.4	1.9	2.0	2.0	2.9	2.5
Total supplementary medical insurance (SMI)	2.2	11.2	44.0	66.6	74.1	77.6	82.3	90.7	101.4
SMI payments to managed care organizations[3]	0.0	0.2	2.8	6.6	11.0	15.3	17.7	18.4	17.6
SMI payments for fee-for-service utilization[6]	2.2	11.0	41.2	60.0	63.2	62.3	64.6	72.3	83.8
Physician/supplies[7]	1.8	8.2	29.6	—	—	—	—	—	—
Outpatient hospital[8]	0.1	1.9	8.5	—	—	—	—	—	—
Independent laboratory[9]	0.0	0.1	1.5	—	—	—	—	—	—
Physician fee schedule	—	—	—	31.7	31.9	32.4	33.4	37.0	42.0
Durable medical equipment	—	—	—	3.7	4.2	4.0	4.3	4.7	5.4
Laboratory[10]	—	—	—	4.3	3.9	3.6	3.8	4.0	4.5
Other[11]	—	—	—	9.9	12.2	12.3	12.2	13.7	16.9
Hospital[12]	—	—	—	8.7	9.4	8.7	8.8	8.5	11.9
Home health agency	0.0	0.2	0.1	0.2	0.2	0.2	1.2	4.4	4.3
Home health agency transfer[4]	—	—	—	—	—	−0.5	−0.6	−1.7	−3.1
Administrative expenses[5]	0.2	0.6	1.5	1.6	1.4	1.5	1.6	1.8	1.7
					Percent distribution of expenditures				
Total hospital insurance (HI)	100.0	100.0	100.0	100.0	100.0	100.0	100.0	100.0	100.0
HI payments to managed care organizations[3]	—	0.0	4.0	5.7	11.7	14.0	16.0	16.3	14.5
HI payments for fee-for-service utilization	100.0	100.0	96.0	94.3	88.2	86.0	84.1	83.7	85.5
Inpatient hospital	90.6	94.1	84.9	70.0	63.9	64.4	66.2	66.6	66.7
Skilled nursing facility	3.8	1.6	3.7	7.8	9.0	9.6	8.3	8.3	9.3
Home health agency	1.9	2.0	5.5	13.8	12.5	8.5	5.5	3.0	2.9
Home health agency transfer[4]	—	—	—	—	—	0.4	0.5	1.3	2.2
Hospice	—	—	0.4	1.6	1.5	1.6	2.0	2.3	2.6
Administrative expenses[5]	3.8	2.0	1.3	1.2	1.4	1.5	1.5	2.2	1.7
					Percent distribution of expenditures				
Total supplementary medical insurance (SMI)	100.0	100.0	100.0	100.0	100.0	100.0	100.0	100.0	100.0
SMI payments to managed care organizations[3]	0.0	1.8	6.4	9.9	14.8	19.7	21.5	20.3	17.4
SMI payments for fee-for-service utilization[6]	100.0	98.2	93.6	90.1	85.3	80.3	78.5	79.7	82.6
Physician/supplies[7]	81.8	73.2	67.3	—	—	—	—	—	—
Outpatient hospital[8]	4.5	17.0	19.3	—	—	—	—	—	—
Independent laboratory[9]	0.0	0.9	3.4	—	—	—	—	—	—
Physician fee schedule	—	—	—	47.6	43.0	41.8	40.6	40.8	41.4
Durable medical equipment	—	—	—	5.6	5.7	5.2	5.2	5.2	5.3
Laboratory[10]	—	—	—	6.5	5.3	4.6	4.6	4.4	4.4
Other[11]	—	—	—	14.9	16.5	15.9	14.8	15.1	16.7
Hospital[12]	—	—	—	13.0	12.7	11.2	10.7	9.4	11.7
Home health agency	0.0	1.8	0.2	0.3	0.3	0.3	1.5	4.9	4.2
Home health agency transfer[4]	—	—	—	—	—	−0.6	−0.7	−1.9	−3.1
Administrative expenses[5]	9.1	5.4	3.4	2.4	1.9	1.9	1.9	2.0	1.7

— Data not available.
0.0 Quantity greater than 0 but less than 0.05.
[1]Preliminary figures.
[2]Average number enrolled in the hospital insurance (HI) and/or supplementary medical insurance (SMI) programs for the period.
[3]Medicare-approved managed care organizations.
[4]Reflects annual home health HI to SMI transfer amounts for 1998 and later.
[5]Includes research, costs of experiments and demonstration projects, and peer review activity.
[6]Type of service reporting categories for fee-for-service reimbursement differ before and after 1991.
[7]Includes payment for physicians, practitioners, durable medical equipment, and all suppliers other than Independent laboratory, which is shown separately through 1990. Beginning in 1991, those physician services subject to the physician fee schedule are so broken out. Payments for laboratory services paid under the Laboratory fee schedule and performed in a physician office are included under "Laboratory" beginning in 1991. Payments for durable medical equipment are broken out and so labeled beginning in 1991. The remaining services from the "Physician" category are included in "Other."
[8]Includes payments for hospital outpatient department services, for skilled nursing facility outpatient services, for Part B services received as an inpatient in a hospital or skilled nursing facility setting, and for other types of outpatient facilities. Beginning 1991, payments for hospital outpatient department services, except for laboratory services, are listed under

TABLE 3.10

Medicare enrollees and expenditures by type of service, selected years 1970–2001 [CONTINUED]

"Hospital." Hospital outpatient laboratory services are included in the "Laboratory" line.
[9]Beginning in 1991 those independent laboratory services that were paid under the Laboratory fee schedule (most of independent lab) are included in the "Laboratory" line; the remaining services are included in "Physician fee schedule" and "Other" lines.
[10]Payments for laboratory services paid under the Laboratory fee schedule performed in a physician office, independent lab, or in a hospital outpatient department.
[11]Includes payments for physician-administered drugs, free-standing ambulatory surgical center facility services; ambulance services; supplies; free-standing end-stage renal disease (ESRD) dialysis facility services; rural health clinics; outpatient rehabilitation facilities; psychiatric hospitals; and federally qualified health centers.
[12]Includes the hospital facility costs for Medicare Part B services that are predominantly in the outpatient department, with the exception of hospital outpatient laboratory services, which are included on the "Laboratory" line. The physician reimbursement is included on the "Physician fee schedule" line.
Notes: Table includes service disbursements as of January 2003 for Medicare enrollees residing in Puerto Rico, Virgin Islands, Guam, other outlying areas, foreign countries, and unknown residence. Totals do not necessarily equal the sum of rounded components.

SOURCE: "Table 134. Medicare Enrollees and Expenditures and Percent Distribution, according to Type of Service: United States and Other Areas, Selected Years 1970–2001," in *Health, United States, 2003,* National Center for Health Statistics, 2003, http://www.cdc.gov/nchs/data/hus/tables/2003/03hus134.pdf (accessed July 2, 2004)

---

object of over-treatment. The Institute of Medicine's Committee on Care at the End of Life described this over-treatment as involving both care that is inappropriate and care that is not wanted by the patient, even if some clinical benefit could be expected.

Utilization of hospice care is increasing in the United States. From 1992 to 2000 the number of persons receiving hospice care doubled from 52,100 to 105,496. The majority of hospice patients were age sixty-five or older, slightly more than half (51.9%) of the hospice patients had cancer, and more women than men received hospice care (57.4% versus 42.6%). (See Table 3.11.)

Hospice Isn't the Answer for Everyone

Hospice, however, is not the ideal program for everyone. To some, choosing hospice care might mean giving up hope and succumbing to death. Others might wish to endure their pain and suffering out of religious or philosophical convictions. Still others might opt for quantity rather than quality of life, as reported by Joel Tsevat et al. in "Health Values of Hospitalized Patients 80 Years or Older" (*Journal of the American Medical Association,* vol. 279, no. 5, February 4, 1998). In this study 414 hospitalized patients age eighty to ninety-eight were interviewed. Nearly 41% of patients were unwilling to exchange any time in their current state of health for a shorter life in excellent health.

MANAGED CARE ORGANIZATIONS

Managed health care is the sector of the health insurance industry in which health care providers are not independent businesses run by, for example, private medical practitioners, but by administrative firms that manage the allocation of health care benefits. In contrast to conventional indemnity insurers that do not govern the provision of medical care services and simply pay for them, managed care firms have a significant voice in how services are administered to enable them to exert better control over health care costs. (Indemnity insurance is traditional fee-for-service coverage in which providers are paid according to the service performed.)

Managed care, which has a primary purpose of controlling service utilization and costs, represents a rapidly growing segment of the health care industry. The beneficiaries of employer-funded health plans (persons who receive health benefits from their employers), as well as Medicare and Medicaid recipients, often find themselves in this type of health care program. The term "managed care organization" covers several types of health care delivery systems, such as health maintenance organizations (HMOs), preferred provider organizations (PPOs), and "utilization review" (UR) groups that oversee diagnoses, recommend treatments, and manage costs for their beneficiaries.

Health Maintenance Organizations

Health maintenance organizations (HMOs) began to grow in the 1970s as alternatives to traditional health insurance, which was becoming increasingly expensive. The HMO Act of 1973 was a federal law requiring employers with more than twenty-four employees to offer an alternative to conventional indemnity insurance in the form of a federally qualified HMO. The intent of the act was to stimulate HMO development, and the federal government has been promoting HMOs since the administration of President Richard Nixon (1969–74), maintaining that groups of physicians following certain rules of practice could slow rising medical costs and improve health care quality.

HMOs are health insurance programs organized to provide complete coverage for subscribers' (also known as enrollees or members) health needs for negotiated, prepaid prices. The subscribers (and/or their employers) pay a fixed amount each month; in turn, the HMO group provides, at no extra charge or at a very minimal charge, preventive care, such as routine checkups and immunizations, and care for any illness or accident. Inpatient hospitalization and referral services are also covered by the monthly fee. HMO members benefit from reduced out-of-pocket costs (they do not pay deductibles), they do not have to file claims or fill out insurance forms, and they generally pay only a small co-payment for each office visit. Members are usually "locked into" the plan for a specified period—usu-

TABLE 3.11

Hospice patients, according to age, sex, and diagnosis, selected years 1992–2000

(Data are based on a survey of hospice patients)

Age, sex, and diagnosis	1992	1994	1996	1998	2000
			Number of current patients		
Total hospice patients	52,100	60,783	59,363	79,837	105,496
			Current patients per 10,000 population		
Total	**2.0**	**2.3**	**2.2**	**3.0**	**3.8**
Age at time of survey:					
Under 65 years, crude	0.5	0.8	0.5	0.7	0.8
65 years and over, crude	13.1	12.9	13.9	18.2	24.9
65 years and over, age adjusted[1]	13.7	13.6	14.4	18.4	24.9
65–74 years	7.8	7.3	7.8	9.9	10.1
75–84 years	19.2	16.9	16.9	22.0	31.9
85 years and over	23.4	30.6	34.7	44.7	67.3
Sex:					
Male, total	1.9	2.1	2.0	2.6	3.3
Under 65 years, crude	0.5	0.9	0.5	0.7	0.8
65 years and over, crude	13.9	12.5	14.8	18.5	24.8
65 years and over, age adjusted[1]	16.0	14.4	16.1	20.3	26.9
65–74 years	6.3	7.0	10.4	10.2	13.0
75–84 years	25.8	18.2	18.5	25.2	32.6
85 years and over	28.8	34.8	33.9	49.2	69.9
Female, total	2.1	2.5	2.4	3.3	4.3
Under 65 years, crude	0.4	0.7	0.6	0.8	0.9
65 years and over, crude	12.6	13.2	13.2	18.0	25.0
65 years and over, age adjusted[1]	12.6	13.2	12.9	17.3	23.3
65–74 years	8.9	7.5	5.8	9.6	7.6
75–84 years	15.1	16.1	15.9	19.9	31.5
85 years and over	21.4	29.0	35.0	42.9	66.2
			Percent distribution		
Age at time of survey:[2]					
Under 65 years	19.5	30.1	21.3	21.6	18.6
65 years and over	80.5	69.9	78.7	78.4	81.4
65–74 years	27.3	22.2	24.5	22.7	17.2
75–84 years	38.6	30.1	32.4	32.9	37.0
85 years and over	14.6	17.6	21.9	22.7	27.3
Sex:					
Male	46.1	44.7	44.9	42.7	42.6
Female	53.9	55.3	55.1	57.3	57.4
Primary admission diagnosis:[3]					
Malignant neoplasms	65.7	57.2	58.3	55.5	51.9
Large intestine and rectum	9.0	8.0	4.0	6.4	4.9
Trachea, bronchus, and lung	21.1	12.5	15.8	13.0	12.3
Breast	3.9	4.8	6.2	4.9	4.8
Prostate	6.0	5.9	6.6	6.1	7.7
Diseases of heart	10.2	9.3	8.3	9.7	12.8
Diseases of the respiratory system	4.3	6.6	7.3	10.6	6.5
Other	19.8	27.0	26.1	24.3	28.8

[1]Age adjusted by the direct method to the year 2000 standard population using the following three age groups: 65–74 years, 75–84 years, and 85 years and over.
[2]Denominator excludes persons with unknown age.
[3]Denominator excludes persons with unknown diagnosis.
Notes: Current hospice patients are those who were on the rolls of the agency as of midnight on the day immediately before the date of the survey. Rates are based on the civilian population as of July 1. Population figures are adjusted for net underenumeration using the 1990 National Population Adjustment Matrix from the U.S. Bureau of the Census. Diagnostic categories are based on the *International Classification of Diseases, 9th Revision, Clinical Modification.*

SOURCE: "Table 88. Hospice Patients, According to Age, Sex, and Diagnosis: United States, Selected Years 1992–2000," in *Health, United States, 2003,* National Center for Health Statistics, 2003, http://www.cdc.gov/nchs/data/hus/tables/2003/03hus088.pdf (accessed July 2, 2004)

ally one year. If the necessary service is available within the HMO, patients normally must use an HMO doctor. There are several types of HMOs:

- Staff model HMO—the "purest" form of managed care. All primary care physicians are employees of the HMO and practice in a centralized location such as an outpatient clinic that also may house a laboratory, pharmacy, and facilities for other diagnostic testing. The staff

model offers the HMO the greatest opportunities to manage both cost and quality of health care services.

- Group model—in which the HMO contracts with a group of primary care and multi-specialty health providers. The group is paid a fixed amount per patient to provide specific services. This model is the one used by Kaiser Permanente and Group Health Cooperative of Puget Sound (Group Health Cooperative of Puget

Sound affiliated with Kaiser Permanente in 2000), early pioneers in the HMO movement. The administration of the medical group determines how the HMO payments will be distributed among the physicians and other health care providers. Group model HMOs are usually located in hospitals or clinic settings and have on-site pharmacies. Participating physicians usually do not have any fee-for-service patients.

- Network model—in which the HMO contracts with two or more groups of health providers that agree to provide health care at negotiated prices to all members enrolled in the HMO.

- Independent practice association model (IPA)—in which the HMO contracts with individual physicians or medical groups that then provide medical care to HMO members at their own offices. The individual physicians agree to follow the practices and procedures of the HMO when caring for the HMO members; however, they generally also maintain their own private practices and see fee-for-service patients as well as HMO members. IPA physicians are paid by capitation (literally, "per head") for the HMO patients and by conventional methods for their fee-for-service patients. Physician members of the IPA guarantee that the care for each HMO member for which they are responsible will be delivered within a fixed budget. They guarantee this by allowing the HMO to withhold an amount of their payments (usually about 20% per year). If at year's end the physician's cost for providing care falls within the preset amount, then the physician receives all the monies withheld. If the physician's costs of care exceed the agreed-upon amount, the HMO may retain any portion of the monies it has withheld. This arrangement places physicians and other providers such as hospitals, laboratories, and imaging centers "at risk" for keeping down treatment costs, and this "at risk" formula is key to HMO cost-containment efforts.

Some HMOs offer an open-ended or point-of-service (POS) option that allows members to choose their own physicians and hospitals, either within or outside the HMO. A member who chooses an outside provider, however, will generally have to pay a larger portion of the expenses. Physicians not contracting with the HMO but who see HMO patients are paid according to the services performed. POS members are given incentive to seek care from contracted network physicians and other health care providers through comprehensive coverage offerings.

The number of people enrolled in HMOs more than tripled between 1980 and 1990. In 1980 HMOs covered only 9.1 million people. By 1990, thirty-three million Americans were enrolled in HMOs. Enrollment continued to explode through the 1990s, and by 1999, there were 643 HMOs covering 81.3 million persons—30% of the American population. Since 1999 both the number of HMOs and the number of people covered declined. By 2003, the number of HMOs had dropped to five hundred, and enrollment had declined from the 1999 peak by about five million, to 76.1 million—more than one quarter of the U.S population. (See Table 3.12.)

HMOs Have Fans and Critics

HMOs have been the subject of considerable debate among physicians, payers, policymakers, and health care consumers. Many physicians feel HMOs interfere in the physician-patient relationship and effectively prevent them from practicing medicine the way they have traditionally practiced. These physicians claim they know their patients' conditions and are, therefore, in the best position to recommend treatment. The physicians resent being advised and overruled by insurance administrators. (Physicians can recommend the treatment they believe is best, but if the insurance company will not cover the costs, patients may be unwilling to undergo the recommended treatment.)

The HMO industry counters that its evidence-based determinations (judgments about the appropriateness of care that reflect scientific research) are based on the experiences of many thousands of physicians and, therefore, it knows which treatment is most likely to be successful. The industry maintains that, in the past, physicians' chosen treatments have not been scrutinized or even assessed for effectiveness, and as a result most physicians do not really know whether the treatment they have prescribed is optimal for the specific medical condition.

Further, the HMO industry cites the slower increase in health care expenses as another indicator of its management success. Industry spokespersons have noted that any major change in how the industry is run would lead to increasing costs. They claim that HMOs and other managed care programs are bringing a more rational approach to the health care industry while maintaining health care quality and controlling costs.

Still, many physicians resent that, with a few exceptions, HMOs are not financially liable for their decisions. When a physician chooses to forgo a certain procedure and negative consequences result, the physician may well be held legally accountable. When an HMO informs a physician that it will not cover a recommended procedure and the HMO's decision is found to be wrong, it cannot be held directly liable. Many physicians assert that because HMOs make such choices, they are practicing medicine, and should, therefore, be held accountable. The HMOs counter that these are administrative decisions, and they deny that they are practicing medicine.

The legal climate, however, began to change for HMOs during the mid-1990s. Both the Third Circuit Fed-

TABLE 3.12

Health maintenance organizations (HMOs) and enrollment, according to type, region, and federal program, selected years 1976–2002

[Data are based on a census of health maintenance organizations]

Plans and enrollment	1976	1980	1990	1995	1997	1998	1999	2000	2001	2002
Plans					**Number**					
All plans	174	235	572	562	652	651	643	568	541	500
Model type:[1]										
Individual practice association[2]	41	97	360	332	284	317	309	278	257	229
Group[3]	122	138	212	108	98	116	123	101	104	100
Mixed	—	—	—	122	258	212	208	188	180	171
Geographic region:										
Northeast	29	55	115	100	110	107	110	98	96	87
Midwest	52	72	160	157	184	185	179	161	190	140
South	23	45	176	196	236	237	239	203	158	178
West	70	63	121	109	121	122	115	106	97	95
Enrollment[1]					**Number of persons in millions**					
Total	**6.0**	**9.1**	**33.0**	**50.9**	**66.8**	**76.6**	**81.3**	**80.9**	**79.5**	**76.1**
Model type:[1]										
Individual practice association[2]	0.4	1.7	13.7	20.1	26.7	32.6	32.8	33.4	33.1	31.6
Group[3]	5.6	7.4	19.3	13.3	11.0	13.8	15.9	15.2	15.6	15.0
Mixed	—	—	—	17.6	29.0	30.1	32.6	32.3	30.9	29.6
Federal program:[4]										
Medicaid[5]	—	0.3	1.2	3.5	5.6	7.8	10.4	10.8	11.4	12.8
Medicare	—	0.4	1.8	2.9	4.8	5.7	6.5	6.6	6.1	5.4
					Percent of HMO enrollees					
Model type:[1]										
Individual practice association[2]	6.6	18.7	41.6	39.4	39.9	42.6	40.3	41.3	41.6	41.5
Group[3]	93.4	81.3	58.4	26.0	16.5	18.0	19.6	18.9	19.5	19.4
Mixed	—	—	—	34.5	43.4	39.2	40.1	39.9	38.8	38.8
Federal program:[4]										
Medicaid[5]	—	2.9	3.5	6.9	8.2	10.2	12.7	13.3	14.3	16.9
Medicare	—	4.3	5.4	5.7	7.2	7.4	8.0	8.1	7.7	7.1
					Percent of population enrolled in HMOs					
Total	**2.8**	**4.0**	**13.4**	**19.4**	**25.2**	**28.6**	**30.1**	**30.0**	**28.3**	**26.4**
Geographic region:										
Northeast	2.0	3.1	14.6	24.4	32.4	37.8	36.7	36.5	35.1	33.4
Midwest	1.5	2.8	12.6	16.4	19.5	22.7	23.3	23.2	21.7	20.6
South	0.4	0.8	7.1	12.4	17.9	21.0	23.9	22.6	21.0	19.8
West	9.7	12.2	23.2	28.6	36.4	39.1	41.4	41.7	40.7	38.2

— Data not available.

[1]Enrollment or number of plans may not equal total because some plans did not report these characteristics.
[2]An HMO operating under an individual practice association model contracts with an association of physicians from various settings (a mixture of solo and group practices) to provide health services.
[3]Group includes staff, group, and network model types.
[4]Federal program enrollment in HMOs refers to enrollment by Medicaid or Medicare beneficiaries, where the Medicaid or Medicare program contracts directly with the HMO to pay the appropriate annual premium.
[5]Data for 1990 and later include enrollment in managed care health insuring organizations.

Notes: Data as of June 30 in 1976–80, and January 1 from 1990 onwards. Open-ended enrollemnt in HMO plans, amounting to 8 million on Jan 1, 2002, is included from 1994 onwards. HMOs in Guam are included starting in 1994; HMOs in Puerto Rico, starting in 1998. In 2002 HMO enrollment in Guam was 34,000 and in Puerto Rico, 1,825,000. Data for additional years are available.

SOURCE: "Table 132. Health Maintenance Organizations (HMOs) and Enrollment, according to Model Type, Geographic Region, and Federal Program: United States, Selected Years 1976–2002," in *Health, United States, 2003,* National Center for Health Statistics, 2003, http://www.cdc.gov/nchs/data/hus/tables/2003/03hus132.pdf (accessed July 2, 2004)

---

eral Court of Appeals in *Dukes v. U.S. Healthcare* (64 LW 2007, 1995) and the Tenth Circuit Federal Court of Appeals in *PacifiCare of Oklahoma, Inc., v. Burrage* (59 F.3rd 151, 1995) agreed that HMOs were liable for malpractice and negligence claims against the HMO and HMO physicians. In *Frappier Estate v. Wishnov* (Florida District Court of Appeals, Fourth District, No. 95-0669, May 8, 1996), the Florida court agreed with the earlier findings. It seemed these decisions would be backed by new laws when both houses of Congress passed legislation (the "Patients' Bill of Rights") giving patients more recourse to contest the decisions of HMOs, although the House of Representatives and the Senate disagreed about the specific rights and the actions patients could take to enforce their rights.

The Senate-passed bill ensured that patients could hold their HMOs accountable when their actions resulted in injury or death. The bill allows patients to sue their HMOs in state court over denied benefits or to contest quality of care issues. It also allows federal court lawsuits for issues unrelated to quality of care. The bill does not limit damages in state court, but damages are capped at $5 million in federal court.

The House version of the bill limits patients' access to courts and their ability to sue their HMOs by permitting lawsuits in state courts under restrictive rules and sets a cap for noneconomic damages at $1.5 million. Critics of the House-passed bill contended that it placed special interests above the interests of insured Americans.

By August 2002 the prospects for a patients' rights law passing during 2002 dimmed as senators and members of the House failed to resolve their differences about the legislation. The central issue that stalled the negotiations about the bill was the question of how much recourse patients should have in court when they believe their HMOs have not provided adequate care. Although the legislation was not officially "dead," and a conference committee was appointed to attempt to resolve the issues, many industry observers decided that the talks, and White House actions to encourage consensus, had failed.

In June 2004 Democrats renewed their efforts to press for passage of a law enabling patients to sue their HMOs over treatment denials in response to the Supreme Court rulings against such lawsuits in state courts. The Democrats want the right to sue in state courts because monetary damages are usually higher than in federal courts. Republicans generally want limits on lawsuits and damages and to confine them to federal courts.

Preferred Provider Organizations

During the 1990s, in response to HMOs and other efforts by insurance groups to cut costs, physicians began forming or joining preferred provider organizations (PPOs). PPOs are managed care organizations that offer integrated delivery systems—networks of providers—available through a wide array of health plans and are readily accountable to purchasers for access, cost, quality, and services of their networks. They use provider selection standards, utilization management, and quality assessment programs to complement negotiated fee reductions (discounted rates from participating physicians, hospitals, and other health care providers) as effective strategies for long-term cost control. Under a PPO benefit plan, covered persons retain the freedom of choice of providers but are offered financial incentives such as lower out-of-pocket costs to use the preferred provider network. PPO members may use other physicians and hospitals, but they usually have to pay a higher proportion of the costs. PPOs are marketed directly to employers and to third-party administrators (TPAs) who then market PPOs to their employer clients.

Exclusive provider organizations (EPOs) are a more restrictive variation of PPOs in which members must seek care from providers on the EPO panel. If a member visits an outside provider who is not on the EPO panel, then the EPO will offer either very limited or no coverage for the office or hospital visit.

While HMO enrollment has declined in recent years, according to the CDC National Center for Health Statistics (NCHS) the percentage of employers offering one or more PPO plans rose from 49% to 57% between 2001 and 2003, and PPO enrollment rose from 50% to 54% of covered employees. Growth in PPO enrollment occurred almost entirely in the West and Midwest regions. PPO enrollment is highest in the Midwest, at 64% and the South, at 55%.

CHAPTER 4
RESEARCHING, MEASURING, AND MONITORING THE QUALITY OF HEALTH CARE

More than twenty-five hundred agencies, institutions, and organizations are dedicated to researching, quantifying (measuring), monitoring, and improving health in the United States. Some are federally funded public entities such as the many institutes and agencies governed by the U.S. Department of Health and Human Services (HHS). Others are professional societies and organizations that develop standards of care, represent the views and interests of health care providers, and ensure the quality of health care facilities such as the American Medical Association (AMA) and the Joint Commission on Accreditation of Healthcare Organizations (JCAHO). Still other voluntary health organizations such as the American Heart Association, American Cancer Society, and the March of Dimes promote research and education about prevention and treatment of specific diseases.

THE U.S. DEPARTMENT OF HEALTH AND HUMAN SERVICES

HHS is the nation's lead agency for ensuring the health of Americans by planning, operating, and funding delivery of essential human services, especially for society's most vulnerable populations. HHS consists of more than three hundred programs, operated by eleven divisions, including eight agencies in the U.S. Public Health Service. It is the largest grant-making agency in the federal government, funding about sixty thousand grants each year as well as the HHS Medicare program, the nation's largest health insurer, which processes more than nine hundred million claims per year. For fiscal year 2004, HHS had a budget of $548 billion dollars and 66,639 employees.

HHS Milestones

HHS has a long, illustrious history beginning with the 1798 opening of the first Marine Hospital in Boston to care for sick and injured merchant seamen. Under President Abraham Lincoln, the agency that would become the Food and Drug Administration was established in 1862. The National Institutes of Health (NIH) dates back to 1887, and later became part of the Public Health Service. The 1935 enactment of the Social Security Act spurred the development of the Federal Security Agency in 1939 to direct programs in health, human services, insurance, and education. In 1946 the Communicable Disease Center, which would become the Centers for Disease Control and Prevention (CDC), was established, and almost twenty years later, in 1965, Medicare and Medicaid were enacted to improve access to health care for older, disabled, and low-income Americans. The same year, the "Head Start" program was developed to provide education, health, and social services to preschool-age children.

In 1970 the National Health Service Corps was established to help meet the health care needs of underserved areas and populations; the following year the National Cancer Act became law, which established cancer research as a national research priority. In 1984 the human immunodeficiency virus (HIV), the virus that causes acquired immunodeficiency syndrome (AIDS), was identified by the U.S. Public Health Service and French research scientists. The National Organ Transplant Act became law in 1984, and in 1990 the Human Genome Project was initiated.

During 1994 NIH-funded research isolated the genes responsible for inherited breast cancer, colon cancer, and the most frequently occurring type of kidney cancer. In 1998 efforts were launched to eliminate racial and ethnic disparities (differences) in health, and in 2000 the human genome sequencing was published. In 2001 the Health Care Financing Administration (HCFA) was replaced by the Centers for Medicaid & Medicare Services, and HHS responded to the first reported cases of bioterrorism—the 2001 anthrax attacks—and developed new strategies to prevent and detect threats of bioterrorism.

FIGURE 4.1

Cycle of health care research

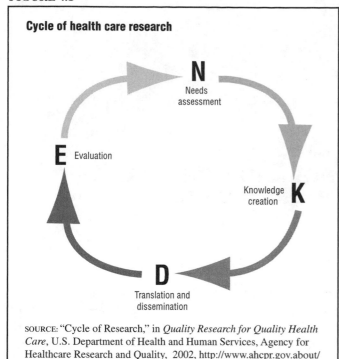

SOURCE: "Cycle of Research," in *Quality Research for Quality Health Care*, U.S. Department of Health and Human Services, Agency for Healthcare Research and Quality, 2002, http://www.ahcpr.gov.about/qualres.pdf (accessed July 2, 2004)

FIGURE 4.2

Health care research pipeline

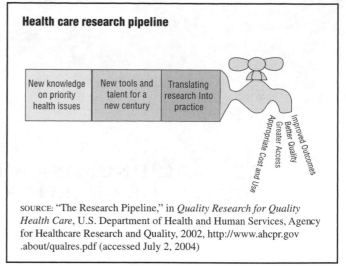

SOURCE: "The Research Pipeline," in *Quality Research for Quality Health Care*, U.S. Department of Health and Human Services, Agency for Healthcare Research and Quality, 2002, http://www.ahcpr.gov.about/qualres.pdf (accessed July 2, 2004)

HHS Agencies and Institutes Provide Comprehensive Health and Social Services

In addition to the CDC and NIH, the following HHS agencies research, plan, direct, oversee, administer, and provide health care services:

- Administration on Aging (AoA) provides services aimed at helping older Americans retain their independence. The AoA develops policies that support older adults and directs programs that provide transportation, in-home services, and other health and social services. In fiscal year 2004 the AoA had a budget of $1.4 billion and 120 employees.

- Administration for Children and Families (ACF) provides services for families and children in need, administers Head Start, and works with state foster care and adoption programs. ACF ran about sixty programs with a budget of $49 billion and 1,425 employees in 2004.

- Agency for Healthcare Research and Quality (AHRQ) researches access to health care, quality of care, and efforts to control health care costs. It also looks at the safety of health care services and ways to prevent medical errors. Figure 4.1 shows how AHRQ researches health system problems by performing a continuous process of needs assessment, gaining knowledge, interpreting and communicating information, and evaluating the effects of this process on the health problem. Figure 4.2 shows the process that transforms new information about health care issues into actions to improve access, costs, outcomes (what happens to patients as a result of the care they have received), and quality. AHRQ had a budget of $304 billion in fiscal year 2004 and 294 employees. AHRQ has invested $165 million in patient safety research and currently manages a patient safety research portfolio of more than one hundred projects.

- Agency for Toxic Substances and Disease Registry (ATSDR) seeks to prevent exposure to hazardous waste.

- Centers for Medicare & Medicaid Services (CMS) administer entitlement programs that provide health insurance for about seventy-five million Americans who are either age sixty-five or older or in financial need. It also operates the State Children's Health Insurance Program (SCHIP), which covers about ten million uninsured children, and it regulates all laboratory testing, except testing performed for research purposes, in the United States. CMS had a $453 billion budget in fiscal year 2004 and 4,586 employees.

- Food and Drug Administration (FDA) acts to ensure the safety and efficacy of pharmaceutical drugs and medical devices and monitors food safety and purity. The FDA had a budget of $1.7 billion in fiscal year 2004 and nearly 10,700 employees.

- Health Resource and Service Administration (HRSA) provides services for medically underserved populations such as migrant workers, the homeless, and residents in public housing. HRSA oversees the nation's organ transplant program, directs efforts to improve maternal and child health, and delivers services to persons with AIDS through the Ryan White CARE Act. More than eighteen hundred people work for HRSA; its fiscal year 2004 budget was $7.2 billion.

- Indian Health Service (IHS) serves more than 550 tribes through a network of forty-nine hospitals, 236 health centers, 309 health stations, and thirty-four urban Indian health centers. IHS employed 16,145 workers in 2004 and had a budget of $3.7 billion.

- Office of the Secretary of Health and Human Services (OSHHS) provides the department's leadership and oversees the eleven operating divisions of HHS. It also advises the president about health, welfare, human service, and income security issues.

- Program Support Center (PSC) administers operations, financial management, and human resources for HHS as well as other departments and federal agencies. The PSC staff of about twelve hundred processes approximately $200 billion in grant payments, provides personnel and payroll services for more than sixty-six thousand HHS employees, and performs accounting, management, information technology, and telecommunication services.

- Substance Abuse and Mental Health Service Administration (SAMHSA) seeks to improve access to, and availability of, substance abuse prevention and treatment programs as well as other mental health services. SAMHSA was budgeted $3.4 billion in fiscal year 2004 and had 546 employees.

HHS agencies work with state, local, and tribal governments as well as public and private organizations to coordinate and deliver a wide range of services including:

- Preventive health services such as surveillance to detect outbreaks of disease and immunization programs through efforts directed by the CDC and the NIH

- Ensuring food, drug, and cosmetic safety through efforts of the FDA

- Improving maternal and child health and preschool education in programs such as Head Start, which served more than nine hundred thousand children in 2004

- Preventing child abuse, domestic violence, and substance abuse, as well as funding substance abuse treatment through programs directed by the ACF

- Assuring delivery of health care services to nearly 1.6 million Native Americans and Alaska Natives through the IHS, a network of hospitals, health centers, and other programs and facilities

- Medicare (federal health insurance program for older adults and persons with disabilities) and Medicaid (state and federal health insurance for low-income people) are administered by the CMS

- Financial assistance and support services for low-income and older Americans, such as home-delivered meals ("Meals on Wheels") coordinated by the AoA.

SUBSTANTIAL BUDGET HELPS HHS TO ACHIEVE ITS OBJECTIVES. Figure 4.3 displays how the FY (fiscal year)

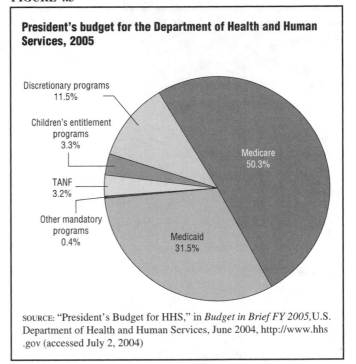

FIGURE 4.3

President's budget for the Department of Health and Human Services, 2005

SOURCE: "President's Budget for HHS," in *Budget in Brief FY 2005,* U.S. Department of Health and Human Services, June 2004, http://www.hhs.gov (accessed July 2, 2004)

2005 HHS budget will be allocated, and Table 4.1 shows budgets for the HHS agencies during 2003, 2004, and 2005. More than 80% of the FY 2005 HHS budget is designated for the Medicare and Medicaid programs. The FY 2005 budget aims to provide additional funds to assist state and local public health agencies to protect the nation against bioterrorism. The budget also is intended to: increase access to care for three million people through 614 new and expanded health center sites; complete the doubling of the NIH budget; modernize and strengthen Medicare by provision of subsidized prescription drug benefits; advance welfare reform efforts by supporting the Temporary Assistance to Needy Families (TANF) program; and improve public health by intensifying prevention programs to reduce the occurrence of diabetes, asthma, and obesity. HHS agencies also plan to improve budget and management performance of the agencies and to add approximately 185 employees to their ranks in 2005.

THE U.S. PUBLIC HEALTH SERVICE COMMISSIONED CORPS. The uniformed service component of the early Marine Hospital Service adopted a military model for a group of career health professionals who traveled from one marine hospital to another as their services were needed. A law enacted in 1889 established this group as the Commissioned Corps, and throughout the twentieth century the corps grew to include a wide range of health professionals. In addition to physicians, the corps employed nurses, dentists, research scientists, planners, pharmacists, sanitarians, engineers, and other public health professionals. The corps assisted the Marine Hospital Service to prevent infectious diseases from entering

TABLE 4.1

Health and Human Services budget by operating division, 2005

[Dollars in millions]

	2003	2004	2005	2005 +/−2004
Food & Drug Administration:				
Program level	$1,652	$1,695	$1,845	+$149
Budget authority	1,381	1,386	1,495	+109
Outlays	1,395	1,333	1,466	+133
Health Resources & Services Administration:				
Budget authority	6,741	6,695	6,099	−596
Outlays	6,118	6,370	6,411	+41
Indian Health Service:				
Budget authority	2,950	3,072	3,117	+45
Outlays	2,942	2,899	3,202	+303
Centers for Disease Control & Prevention:				
Budget authority	4,340	4,440	4,180	−260
Outlays	4,563	4,096	4,446	+350
National Institutes of Health:				
Budget authority	27,166	28,028	28,757	+729
Outlays	22,916	25,913	27,983	+2,070
Substance Abuse & Mental Health Services:				
Budget authority	3,138	3,234	3,429	+195
Outlays	3,038	3,133	3,295	+162
Agency for Healthcare Research & Quality:				
Program level	309	304	304	0
Budget authority	0	0	0	0
Outlays	203	0	0	0
Centers for Medicare & Medicaid Services:				
Budget authority	420,005	457,241	474,567	+17,326
Outlays	414,438	453,003	482,088	+29,085
Administration for Children & Families:				
Budget authority[1]	47,305	49,016	46,640	−2,376
Outlays	47,648	47,789	47,739	−50
Administration on Aging:				
Budget authority	1,367	1,374	1,377	+3
Outlays	1,367	1,313	1,377	+64
Departmental Management/Civil Rights/PHSSEF[2]:				
Budget authority	2,669	2,558	2,698	+140
Outlays	1,766	2,691	2,652	−39
Office of Inspector General:				
Budget authority	37	39	40	+1
Outlays	22	42	40	−2
Program Support Center:				
Budget authority	380	393	402	+9
Outlays	383	390	403	+13
Proprietary Receipts:				
Budget authority	−1,346	−1,230	−1,223	+7
Outlays	−1,346	−1,230	−1,223	+7
Total, Health & Human Services:				
Budget authority	$516,133	$556,246	$571,578	+$15,332
Outlays	$505,453	$547,742	$579,879	+$32,137
Full-time equivalents	64,919	66,620	66,805	+185
Commissioned corps detailed outside HHS	1,171	1,179	1,179	0

[1]In fiscal year 2004 Temporary Assistance to Needy Families includes; 1) $2 billion for the Contingency Fund to remain available for five years; and 2) $500 million for employment achievement bonuses providing $100 million per year to the States.
[2]Public Health and Social Services Emergency Fund

SOURCE: "HHS Budget by Operating Division," in *Budget in Brief FY 2005*, U.S. Department of Health and Human Services, June 2004, http://www.hhs.gov (accessed July 2, 2004).

the country by examining newly arrived immigrants and directing state quarantine (the period of time and place where persons suspected of having contagious diseases are detained and isolated) functions.

By 1912 the Marine Hospital Service was renamed the Public Health Service (PHS) to reflect its broader scope of activities. Today PHS is part of the Department of Health and Human Services. PHS-commissioned officers played important roles in disease prevention and detection, acted to ensure food and drug safety, conducted research, provided medical care to underserved groups such as Native Americans and Alaska Natives, and assisted in disaster relief programs. One of the uniformed services in the United States (others are the Navy, Army, Marines, Air Force, and Coast Guard), the PHS Commissioned Corps continues to perform all of these functions and also identifies environmental threats to health and safety, promotes healthy lifestyles for Americans, and is involved with international agencies to help address global health problems.

In 2004 the PHS Commissioned Corps numbered approximately six thousand health professionals. These people report to the U.S. Surgeon General, who holds the rank of vice admiral in the U.S. PHS Commissioned Corps. Corps officers work in PHS agencies and at other agencies including the Bureau of Prisons, U.S. Coast Guard, Environmental Protection Agency, and the Commission on Mental Health of the District of Columbia. The Surgeon General is the physician appointed by the U.S. president to serve in a medical leadership position in the nation for a four-year term of office. The Surgeon General reports to the assistant secretary for health, and the Office of the Surgeon General is part of the Office of Public Health and Science. Sixteen surgeons general have served since the 1870s. In August 2002 Dr. Richard Carmona was sworn in as the seventeenth Surgeon General.

CENTERS FOR DISEASE CONTROL AND PREVENTION

The CDC is the primary HHS agency responsible for ensuring the health and safety of the nation's citizens in the United States and abroad. CDC responsibilities include researching and monitoring health, detecting and investigating health problems, researching and instituting prevention programs, developing health policies, ensuring environmental health and safety, and offering education and training.

CDC headquarters are located in Atlanta, Georgia. However, two thousand of the more than eighty-five hundred CDC employees, representing 170 disciplines, serve throughout the country at forty-seven state health departments and forty-five locations outside the United States. In addition to research scientists, physicians, nurses, and

FIGURE 4.4

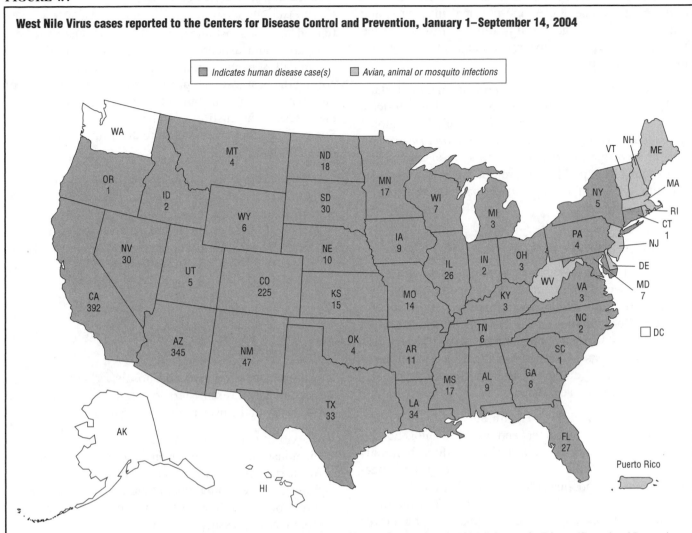

West Nile Virus cases reported to the Centers for Disease Control and Prevention, January 1–September 14, 2004

■ Indicates human disease case(s)   □ Avian, animal or mosquito infections

SOURCE: "2004 West Nile Virus Activity in the United States (reported to the CDC as of September 14, 2004)," Centers for Disease Control and Prevention, Division of Vector-Borne Infectious Diseases, September 14, 2004, http://www.cdc.gov/ncidod/dvbid/westnile/surv&control04Maps_PrinterFriendly.htm (accessed September 16, 2004)

other health practitioners, CDC employs epidemiologists, who study disease in human populations. Epidemiologists measure disease occurrences, such as incidence and prevalence of disease, and work with clinical researchers to answer questions about causation—how particular diseases arise and the factors that contribute to their development—whether new treatments are effective, and how to prevent specific diseases.

Twelve centers, institutes, and offices make up the CDC. Among the best known are the National Center for Health Statistics, which collects vital statistics, and the National Institute for Occupational Safety and Health (NIOSH), which seeks to prevent workplace injuries and accidents through research and prevention. Julie Louise Gerberding, MD, MPH, was named director of the CDC in 2002.

CDC Actions to Protect the Health of the Nation

The CDC is part of the first response to natural disasters, outbreaks of disease, and other public health emer-

gencies. One recent CDC action is the 1999 identification of the West Nile virus (encephalitis) and methods to control this disease. Figure 4.4 is a map created by the CDC Division of Vector-Borne Diseases that shows the distribution of reported cases of West Nile virus infection as of September 17, 2004. Other examples are identification and education about effective strategies for preventing school and domestic violence and the National Breast and Cervical Cancer Early Detection Program, which detected breast cancer and prevented cervical cancer in more than forty thousand women from 1991 to September 1999.

Examples of CDC efforts to educate and communicate vital health information are its publications *Morbidity and Mortality Weekly Report (MMWR)* and the *Emerging Infectious Disease Journal* that alert the medical community to the presence of health risks, outbreaks, and preventive measures. In addition to providing vital statistics (births, deaths, and related health data), the CDC monitors Americans' health using surveys to measure the frequency of behaviors that increase health risk, such as smoking, substance abuse, and physical inactivity, and compiles data about the use of health care resources such as inpatient hospitalization rates and visits to hospital emergency departments.

CDC partners with public and private, national, state, and local agencies and organizations to deliver services. Examples of these collaborative efforts include the global battle against HIV/AIDS via *Leadership and Investment in Fighting an Epidemic (LIFE)* and a ten-agency initiative to address the problem of preventing further increases in antimicrobial infections—infections that resist treatment with antibiotics.

NATIONAL INSTITUTES OF HEALTH

The NIH, which began as a one-room laboratory in 1887, is the world's premier medical research center. NIH conducts research in its own facilities and supports research in universities, medical schools, and hospitals throughout and outside the United States. NIH trains research scientists and other investigators and serves to communicate medical and health information to professional and consumer audiences.

Part of the U.S. Public Health Service, NIH is composed of twenty-seven centers and institutes and is housed in more than seventy-five buildings on a three-hundred-acre campus in Bethesda, Maryland. Among the better-known centers and institutes are the National Cancer Institute, National Human Genome Research Institute, National Institute of Mental Health, and the newer National Center for Complementary and Alternative Medicine. Figure 4.5 is an organizational chart of the NIH and shows all of its centers and institutes.

Patients arrive at the NIH Warren Grant Magnuson Clinical Center in Bethesda, Maryland, to participate in clinical research trials. About seven thousand patients per year are treated as inpatients here, and an additional seventy-two thousand receive outpatient treatment. The National Library of Medicine—which produces the *Index Medicus,* a monthly listing of articles from the world's top medical journals, and maintains *MEDLINE,* a comprehensive medical bibliographic database—is in the NIH Lister Hill Center.

The NIH budget has increased from about $300 per year in 1887 to $13.7 billion in 1998 and will reach nearly $29 billion in fiscal year 2005. NIH works to achieve its ambitious research objectives of "acquiring new knowledge to help prevent, detect, diagnose, and treat disease and disability, from the rarest genetic disorder to the common cold" by investing in promising biomedical research. NIH makes grants and contracts to support research and training in every state in the country, at more than two thousand institutions.

Establishing Research Priorities

By law, all twenty-seven institutes of the NIH must be funded, and each institute must allocate its funding to specific areas and aspects of research within its domain. About half of each institute's budget is dedicated to supporting the best research proposals presented, in terms of their potential to contribute to advances that will combat the diseases the institute is charged with researching. Some of the other criteria used to determine research priorities include:

- Public health need—The NIH responds to health problems and diseases based on their incidence (the rate of development of a disease in a group during a given period of time), severity, and the costs associated with them. Examples of other measures used to weigh and assess need are the mortality rate (the number of deaths caused by the disease), the morbidity rate (the degree of disability caused by the disease), the economic and social consequences of the disease, and whether rapid action is required to control the spread of the disease.

- Rigorous peer review—Proposals are scrutinized by accomplished researchers to determine their potential to return on the investment of resources.

- Flexibility and expansiveness—NIH experience has demonstrated that important findings for commonly occurring diseases may come from research about rarer ones. NIH attempts to fund the broadest possible array of research opportunities to stimulate creative solutions to pressing problems.

- Commitment to human resources and technology—NIH invests in people, equipment, and even some construction projects in the pursuit of scientific advancements.

Since not even the most gifted scientists can accurately predict the next critical discovery or stride in biomedical research, NIH must analyze each research opportunity in terms of competition for the same resources, public interests, scientific merit, and the potential to build upon current knowledge. Figure 4.6 shows all of the stakeholders whose interests and opinions are considered when NIH resource allocation and grant funding decisions are made.

NIH Achievements

As of 2004, NIH supports about one thousand principal investigators—researchers directing projects—and forty-five thousand trainees at academic institutions and research laboratories across the United States. The NIH recruits and attracts the most capable research scientists in the world. In fact, 104 scientists who conducted NIH research or were supported by NIH grants have received Nobel Prizes. Five Nobel winners made their prize-winning discoveries in NIH laboratories.

FIGURE 4.5

National Institutes of Health

Office of the Director Staff Offices:
Office of Extramural Research (HNA3)
Office of Intramural Research (HNA4)
Office of Management/Chief Financial Officer (HNAM)
Office of Science Policy (HNA6)
Office of Budget (HNA7)
Office of Communications and Public Liaison (HNA8)
Office of Equal Opportunity and Diversity Management (HNAD)
Office of Program Coordination (HNAN)
Office of Legislative Policy and Analysis (HNAP)
Office of Community Liaison (HNAR)
Executive Office (HNAR)
Office of the Ombudsman/Ctr. for Cooperative Resolution (HNAS)

Office of the Director Program Offices:
Office of Research on Women's Health (HNAG)
Office of AIDS Research (HNA5)
Office of Behavioral and Social Sciences Research (HNAH)
Office of Disease Prevention (HNA2)

Immediate Office of the Director (HNA)

National Cancer Institute (HNC)

National Eye Institute (HNW)

National Heart, Lung, and Blood Institute (HNH)

National Human Genome Research Institute (HN4)

National Institute on Aging (HNN)

National Institute on Alcohol Abuse and Alcoholism (HN5)

National Institute of Allergy and Infectious Diseases (HNM)

National Institute of Arthritis and Musculoskeletal and Skin Diseases (HNB)

National Institute of Biomedical Imaging and Bioengineering (HN8)

National Institute of Child Health and Human Development (HNT)

National Institute on Deafness and Other Communication Disorders (HN3)

National Institute of Dental and Craniofacial Research (HNP)

National Institute of Diabetes and Digestive and Kidney Diseases (HNK)

National Institute on Drug Abuse (HN6)

National Institute of Environmental Health Sciences (HNV)

National Institute of General Medical Sciences (HNS)

National Institute of Mental Health (HN7)

National Institute of Neurological Disorders and Stroke (HNQ)

National Institute of Nursing Research (HN2)

National Library of Medicine (HNL)

John E. Fogarty International Center for Advanced Study in the Health Sciences (HNF)

National Center for Complementary and Alternative Medicine (HND)

National Center on Minority Health and Health Disparities (HNE)

National Center for Research Resources (HNR)

Clinical Center (HNJ)

Center for Information Technology (HNU)

Center for Scientific Review (HNG)

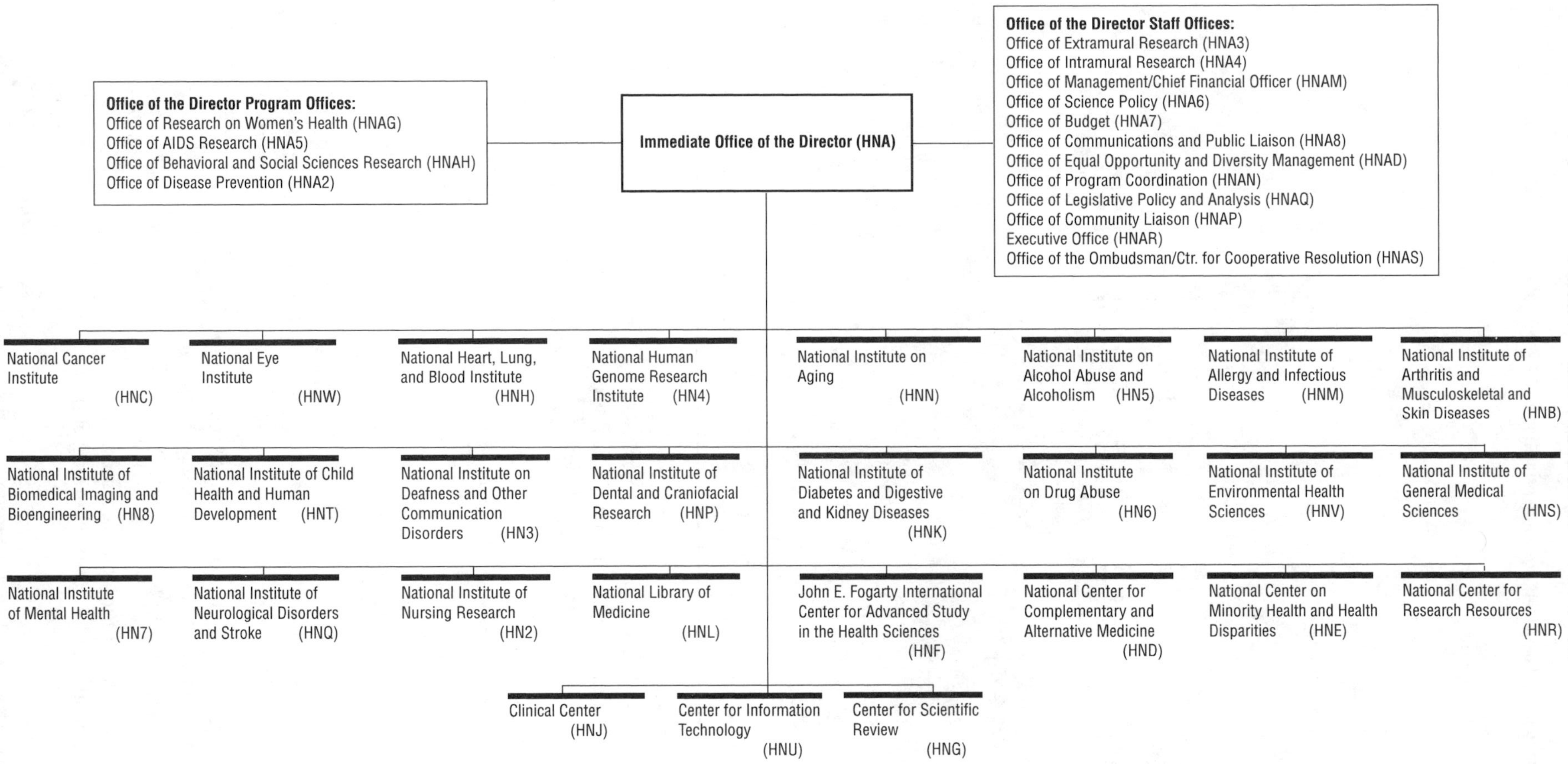

SOURCE: "National Institutes of Health," U.S. Department of Health and Human Services, National Institutes of Health, http://www1.od.nih.gov/oma/manualchapters/management/1123/nih.pdf (accessed September, 11, 2004)

FIGURE 4.6

Views taken into consideration in setting research priorities at the National Institutes of Health

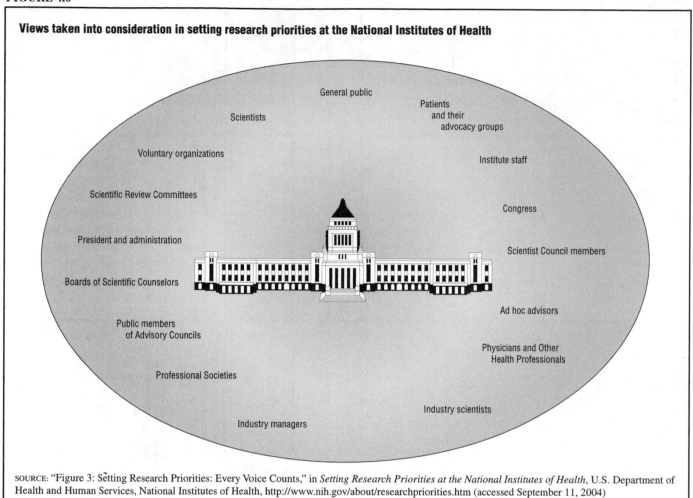

SOURCE: "Figure 3: Setting Research Priorities: Every Voice Counts," in *Setting Research Priorities at the National Institutes of Health*, U.S. Department of Health and Human Services, National Institutes of Health, http://www.nih.gov/about/researchpriorities.htm (accessed September 11, 2004)

Equally important, NIH research has contributed to great improvements in the health of the nation. Examples of past achievements credited to NIH effort include:

• U.S. deaths from cardiovascular disease—heart disease and stroke—were reduced significantly between 1975 and 2000, with heart disease deaths declining by 40% and stroke deaths by 51%.

• The number of AIDS-related deaths fell by about 70% between 1995 and 2001.

• Better detection and treatment increased the five-year survival rates for persons with cancer to 60%.

• Effective medication was explored to enable the estimated nineteen million Americans suffering from depression to regain quality of life.

• Immunization against a host of infectious diseases has markedly reduced deaths and disability among children and adults.

• Gene therapy, performed by NIH researchers for the first time in 1990, promises to produce more effective screening for genetic disorders and gene therapies for cancer and other diseases.

During 2004 NIH scientists initiated and expanded the scope of its medical research and reported significant findings resulting from new and ongoing research projects. Some of these important initiatives and findings were:

• The sequencing of the human genome set a new course for developing ways to diagnose and treat diseases such as cancer, Parkinson's disease and Alzheimer's disease, as well as rare diseases.

• In response to the anthrax attacks of 2001, the NIH launched and intensified research to prevent, detect, diagnose, and treat diseases caused by potential bioterrorism agents.

• Researchers aggressively pursued ways to make effective vaccines for deadly diseases like HIV/AIDS, tuberculosis, malaria, and potential agents of bioterrorism.

• New and improved imaging techniques enabled scientists to painlessly look inside the body and detect disease in its earliest stages when it is often most effectively treated.

- New, more precise ways to treat cancer are emerging, such as drugs that zero in on abnormal proteins in cancer cells.

- Novel research methods are being developed that can identify the causes of outbreaks, such as Severe Acute Respiratory Syndrome (SARS), in weeks rather than months or years.

- Persons at risk for developing type 2 diabetes can sharply reduce their risk by losing 5 to 7% of their body weight and exercising for thirty minutes every day.

- A vaccine that protects children ages two to five from typhoid fever was developed and tested. Typhoid fever strikes about sixteen million people per year worldwide and six hundred thousand die from it.

ACCREDITATION

Accreditation of health care providers—facilities and organizations—provides consumers, payers, and other stakeholders with the assurance that accredited facilities and organizations have been certified as meeting or exceeding predetermined standards. Accreditation refers to both the process during which the quality of care delivered is measured and the resulting official endorsement that quality standards have been met. In addition to promoting accreditation to health care consumers and other purchasers of care such as employer groups, accreditation assists health care facilities and organizations to recruit and retain qualified staff, increase organizational efficiencies in order to reduce costs, identify ways to improve service delivery, and reduce liability insurance premiums.

Joint Commission on Accreditation of Healthcare Organizations

As of 2004 the Joint Commission on Accreditation of Healthcare Organizations (JCAHO) surveys and accredits more than sixteen thousand health care organizations and programs throughout the United States. JCAHO is a not-for-profit organization, headquartered in Oakbrook Terrace, Illinois, with a satellite office in Washington, D.C. JCAHO has more than one thousand surveyors—physicians, nurses, pharmacists, hospital and health care organization administrators, and other health professionals— who are qualified and trained to evaluate specific aspects of health care quality.

Working closely with medical and other professional societies, purchasers of health care services, and management experts as well as other accrediting organizations, JCAHO develops the standards that health care organizations are expected to meet. In addition to developing benchmarks and standards of organizational quality, JCAHO is credited with promoting improvement in infection control, safety, and patients' rights.

JCAHO GROWS TO BECOME THE PREEMINENT ACCREDITING BODY. Early efforts to standardize and evaluate care delivered in hospitals began in 1910 by the American College of Surgeons, a group that forty years later would start the present-day Joint Commission on Accreditation of Healthcare Organizations, originally dubbed the Joint Commission on Accreditation of Hospitals (JCAH) in 1953. In 1965 JCAH began to offer long-term care facilities accreditation as well as hospitals, and in 1972 the Social Security Act was amended to require the secretary of HHS to validate JCAH findings and include them in the HHS annual report to the U.S. Congress.

In 1975 JCAH expanded its scope to include accreditation of ambulatory health care facilities, and in 1978 it began to evaluate and offer accreditation to hospital laboratories. In 1983 accreditation of hospice care organizations began and the accreditation schedule was changed from a two-year cycle to three years for hospitals, psychiatric facilities, substance abuse programs, community mental health centers, and long-term care organizations. In 1987 JCAH was renamed the Joint Commission on Accreditation of Healthcare Organizations to reflect its greatly expanded scope of accreditation services.

In 1990 hospice accreditation was integrated into home health care accreditation processes, and accreditation for managed care organizations was initiated within the ambulatory care accreditation program. During the 1990s JCAHO moved to emphasize performance-improvement standards, required accredited hospitals to prohibit smoking in the hospital, and began performing random, "surprise" surveys—unannounced site visits to accredited organizations. JCAHO also offered accreditation to health care networks, preferred provider organizations (PPOs), and managed behavioral health care organizations.

On April 1, 1998, in a move intended to stem the rising tide of medical errors, JCAHO revised its sentinel event policy, the requirement that accredited organizations immediately report and investigate the causes of medical errors and institute preventive and corrective measures. In 1999 JCAHO launched a toll-free telephone complaint hotline to encourage patients, families, caregivers, and other concerned citizens to report concerns about quality of care at accredited organizations.

During 2000 JCAHO established standards and survey requirements for agencies that provide foster care services and developed cooperative agreements with professional organizations that certify and accredit blood banks, cancer centers, and hospital rehabilitation programs. JCAHO also added standards for assisted-living facilities, pain assessment and management programs, and office-based surgery programs. In 2001, following the terrorist attacks of September 11, JCAHO set up a command center to provide round-the-clock advice and counsel to accredited hospitals and health care organizations.

On July 1, 2002, JCAHO required hospitals to begin collecting and reporting data about the care they provide for four specific diagnoses—acute myocardial infarction (heart attack), heart failure, community-acquired pneumonia, and pregnancy and related medical conditions. JCAHO has termed these "core measure data" and will use them to compare facilities and assess the quality of service delivered. In 2002 JCAHO also moved to make its recommendations more easily understood by consumers so they could make informed choices about health care providers.

In June 2004 JCAHO began to identify a set of performance measures for its new Health Care Staffing Services Certification Program. Staffing firms certified by the Joint Commission will be required to use the standardized set of measures, which will allow for national comparisons among agencies that provide temporary nurses and other professional personnel to health care organizations. The certification program was designed to meet quality oversight needs that have arisen in recent years as a result of significant, ongoing shortages of nurses and other professional personnel. These shortages have forced health care organizations to fill vacant positions with temporary personnel provided by staffing firms, which are not themselves subject to any quality oversight mechanism. The Joint Commission certification program will provide an independent, comprehensive evaluation of an agency's ability to provide competent staffing services.

National Committee for Quality Assurance

The National Committee for Quality Assurance (NCQA) is another well-respected accrediting organization that focuses its attention on the managed care industry. NCQA began surveying and accrediting managed care organizations in 1991. By 2004 the majority of all health maintenance organizations (HMOs) in the United States had been reviewed by NCQA, and about half of the states accepted NCQA accreditation in place of state review since accreditation indicated that the managed care plans met specific regulatory requirements.

When a managed care organization undergoes a NCQA survey, it is assessed using more than sixty different standards, each focusing on a specific aspect of health plan operations. The standards address access and service, the qualifications of providers, the organization's commitment to prevention programs and health maintenance, the quality of care delivered to members when they are ill or injured, and the organization's approaches for helping members manage chronic diseases such as diabetes, heart disease, and asthma.

To ensure fair comparisons between managed health care plans and to track their progress and improvement

over time, NCQA uses a tool called the Health Plan Employer Data and Information Set (HEDIS). The more than sixty HEDIS measures look at health care delivery issues such as:

- Management of asthma and effective use of medication

- Controlling hypertension (high blood pressure)

- Effective and appropriate use of antidepressant medications

- The frequency and consistency with which smokers are counseled to quit

- Rates of breast cancer screening

- The frequency and consistency with which beta blocker (drug treatment) is used following heart attack

- Rates of immunization among children and teens

NCQA combines HEDIS data with national and regional benchmarks of quality in a national database called Quality Compass. This national database enables employers and health care consumers to compare health plans to one another and make choices about coverage based on quality and value rather than simply price and participating providers (physicians, hospitals, and other providers that offer services to the managed care plan members).

NCQA issues health plan "report cards," rating HMOs and other managed care organizations (MCOs) that health care consumers and other stakeholders can access at the NCQA Web site. After NCQA review, MCOs may be granted NCQA's full accreditation for three years, indicating a level of excellence that exceeds NCQA standards. Those that need some improvement are granted one-year accreditation with recommendations about areas that need improvement, and those MCOs that meet some but not all NCQA standards may be denied accreditation or granted provisional accreditation.

In 2003 NCQA reported that managed care quality had improved dramatically for the fourth consecutive year. In 2003 participating health plans' performance on every measure was better than the previous year's results.

The 2003 NCQA *State of Health Care Quality* report was not nearly as positive as the report about the managed care. The NCQA found the nation's health care system plagued with "quality gaps" that prevent millions of Americans from receiving "best practice" care. These gaps result from factors such as poor use of technology and unreasonable payment systems, and they are responsible for more than fifty-seven thousand avoidable deaths each year. The report also documented the huge financial toll of commonplace failures to deliver appropriate care— nearly forty-one million sick days and more than $11 billion in lost productivity could be avoided annually if evidence-based "best practices" were more widely adopted. The "quality gaps" were not equally distributed throughout the system—health plans that measured and reported their performances were found to demonstrate higher levels of clinical quality.

Accreditation Association for Ambulatory Health Care, Inc.

Another accrediting organization, the Accreditation Association for Ambulatory Health Care, Inc. (AAAHC), was incorporated in 1979 and focuses exclusively on ambulatory (outpatient) facilities and programs. Outpatient clinics, group practices, college health services, occupational medicine clinics, and ambulatory surgery centers are among the organizations that are evaluated by AAAHC. The AAAHC accreditation process involves a self-assessment by the organization seeking accreditation and a survey conducted by AAAHC surveyors who are all practicing professionals. AAAHC grants accreditation for periods ranging from six months to three years.

In April 2002 the AAAHC and JCAHO signed a collaborative accreditation agreement that permits ambulatory health care organizations to use their AAAHC accreditation to satisfy JCAHO requirements. In June 2002 the Centers for Medicare & Medicaid Services (CMS) granted AAAHC authority to review health plans that provide coverage for Medicare beneficiaries. HMOs, PPOs, and ambulatory surgery centers are now considered Medicare-certified upon their receipt of accreditation from the AAAHC.

During 2003 and 2004 several states, including Florida, California, and Ohio, approved the AAAHC to conduct accreditation of office-based surgical centers, primary care practices, and freestanding radiology centers such as magnetic resonance imaging (MRI) services.

PROFESSIONAL SOCIETIES

There are professional and membership organizations and societies for all health professionals, such as physicians, nurses, psychologists, and hospital administrators, as well as for institutional health care providers, such as hospitals, managed care plans, and medical groups. These professional organizations represent the interests and concerns of their members, advocate on their behalf, and frequently compile data and publish information about working conditions, licensing, accreditation, compensation, and scientific advancements of interest to members.

The American Medical Association

The American Medical Association (AMA) is a powerful voice for U.S. physicians' interests. The AMA concerns itself with a wide range of health-related issues including medical ethics, medical education, physician and patient advocacy, and development of national health policy. The AMA publishes the highly regarded *Journal of the American Medical Association (JAMA)* and the *AMNews,* as well as journals in ten specialty areas called *Archives Journals.* The organization also maintains a Web site with full-text journal articles for its members.

Founded in 1847, the AMA has worked to upgrade medical education by expanding medical school curricula and establishing standards for licensing and accreditation of practitioners and postgraduate training programs. Recent activities of the AMA are advocating for passage of comprehensive Patients' Bill of Rights legislation, cohosting a world conference on preventing tobacco use, launching a "health literacy" campaign to improve patient-physician relationships, and managing a project aimed at reducing underage drinking.

The American Nurses Association

The American Nurses Association (ANA) is a professional organization that represents more than 2.6 million registered nurses (RNs) and promotes high standards of nursing practice and education as well as the roles and responsibilities of nurses in the workplace and the community. On behalf of its members, the ANA works to protect patients' rights, lobbies to advocate for nurses' interests, champions workplace safety, and provides career and continuing education opportunities. The ANA publishes the *American Journal of Nursing* and actively seeks to improve the public image of nurses among health professionals and the community at large.

The American Hospital Association

The American Hospital Association (AHA) represents nearly five thousand hospitals, health care systems, networks, and other health care providers as well as thirty-seven thousand individual members. Originally established as a membership organization for hospital superintendents in 1899, the AHA had expanded its mission by 1917 to address all facets of hospital care and quality. In addition to national advocacy activities and participation in the development of health policy, the AHA oversees research and pilot programs to improve health service delivery. It also gathers and disseminates hospital and other related health care data, publishes information of interest to its members, and sponsors educational opportunities for health care managers and administrators.

VOLUNTARY HEALTH ORGANIZATIONS

The American Heart Association

The mission of the American Heart Association is "to reduce disability and death from cardiovascular diseases and stroke." The association's national headquarters is in Dallas, Texas, and twelve regional affiliate offices serve the balance of the United States. More than twenty-three million volunteers and supporters were involved with association programs and activities during 2003–04.

The American Heart Association was started by a group of physicians and social workers in New York City in 1915. The early efforts of this group, called the Association for the Prevention and Relief of Heart Disease, were to educate physicians and the general public about heart disease. The first fundraising efforts were launched in 1948 during a radio broadcast, and since then the AHA has raised millions of dollars to fund research, education, and treatment programs.

In addition to research, fundraising, and generating public awareness about reducing the risk of developing heart disease, the American Heart Association has published many best-selling cookbooks featuring heart-healthy recipes and meal planning ideas. The American Heart Association is also considered one of the world's most trusted authorities about heart health among physicians and scientists. The organization publishes five print journals and one online professional journal, including *Circulation, Stroke, Hypertension,* and *Atherosclerosis, Thrombosis, and Vascular Biology.*

The American Cancer Society

The American Cancer Society (ACS) makes its headquarters in Atlanta, Georgia, and has more than thirty-four hundred offices across the country. The ACS mission is "to eliminate cancer as a major health problem by preventing cancer, saving lives, and diminishing suffering from cancer, through research, education, advocacy, and service."

The ACS is the biggest source of private, not-for-profit funding for cancer research—second only to the federal government. By 2004 the ACS had invested more than $2.5 billion in cancer research at leading centers throughout the United States. It also supports epidemiological research to provide cancer surveillance information about occurrence rates, risk factors, mortality, and availability of treatment services. The ACS publishes an array of patient information brochures and four clinical journals for health professionals—*Cancer, Cancer Cytopathology, CA—A Cancer Journal for Clinicians,* and *Cancer Practice.* The ACS also maintains a twenty-four-hour consumer telephone line staffed by trained cancer information specialists and a Web site with information for professionals, patients and families, and the media.

In addition to education, prevention, and patient services, the ACS advocates for the more than eight million cancer survivors, their families, and every potential cancer patient. The ACS seeks to obtain support and passage of laws, policies, and regulations that benefit persons affected by cancer. The ACS is especially concerned with developing strategies to better serve the poor and persons with little formal education, who historically have been disproportionately affected by cancer.

The March of Dimes

The March of Dimes was founded in 1938 by President Franklin Roosevelt to help protect America's young people from polio. In addition to supporting the research that produced the polio vaccine, the March of Dimes has advocated birth defects research and the fortification of food supplies with folic acid to prevent neural tube defects. The March of Dimes also has supported increasing access to quality prenatal care and the growth of neonatal intensive care units (NICUs) to help improve the chances of survival for babies born prematurely or those with serious medical conditions.

The March of Dimes continues to partner with volunteers, scientific researchers, educators, and community outreach workers to help prevent birth defects. March of Dimes funds genetic research, investigates the causes and treatment of premature birth, educates pregnant women, and provides health care services for women and children including immunization, checkups, and treatment for childhood illnesses.

In 2000 the March of Dimes set forth the following four goals for the immediate future:

- To reduce birth defects, the leading cause of infant mortality in the United States, by 10%

- To reduce infant mortality to seven deaths per one thousand live births. The United States ranks twenty-fifth in terms of infant mortality, trailing twenty-four countries where babies have greater chances of living until their first birthdays.

- To reduce low birth weight babies (less than 5.5 pounds) to no more than 5% of all live births since these babies are less likely to live until their first birthdays, and when they do may suffer serious health consequences

- Increase the proportion of women receiving prenatal care during the first trimester (the first three months of pregnancy) to 90% because early prenatal care is linked to healthier pregnancies and infants

In May 2004 the March of Dimes called on congressional leadership to increase federal support for prematurity research and education, and promoted passage of S.1726, known as the PREEMIE Act, to authorize expanded research, education, and services into the causes and prevention of premature birth.

CHAPTER 5

THE INCREASING COST OF HEALTH CARE

HOW MUCH DOES HEALTH CARE COST?

American society places a high value on human life, and generally wants—and expects—quality medical care. But quality care comes with an increasingly high cost. In 1970 the United States spent 7% of its gross domestic product (GDP; the value of all the goods and services produced by the nation) on health care. By 1999 health care had risen to 13% ($1.2 trillion) of the GDP, and in 2001 health care expenditures reached 14.1% ($1.4 trillion) of the GDP. Table 5.1 shows the growth in health care expenditures, the growth in the GDP, and the annual percent change from the previous year for the years from 1960 to 2001.

For many years the consumer price index (CPI; a measure of the average change in prices paid by consumers) increased at a greater rate for medical care than for any other commodity. From 1980 to 1990 the average annual increase in the overall CPI was 4.7%, while the average annual increase in the medical care index stood at 8.1%. By 1998 the average annual growth in the medical care index had fallen to 3.3%, but in 2002 it had risen again to 4.7%. The medical care index has consistently outpaced the CPI in each decade. Of all the components of health care delivery, the sharpest price increases in 2002 were in hospital outpatient services at 10.2%. (See Table 5.2.)

The Centers for Medicare & Medicaid Services (CMS was formerly known as the Health Care Financing Administration or simply HCFA), an agency of the U.S. Department of Health and Human Services (HHS), have projected that the national health expenditure will grow to $3.4 trillion by 2013, almost twice as much as the 2004 projection of $1.8 trillion. (See Table 5.3.) (Since the numbers in Table 5.3 are projections, they necessarily differ from the actual numbers presented in some other tables and figures.) Medicare was projected to reach $532.1 billion by 2013 and be responsible for almost 16% of all health care expenditures.

Generally, projections are most accurate for the near future and least accurate for the distant future. For example, predictions for 2030 should be viewed more cautiously than predictions for 2006. Since it is unlikely that the conditions on which the projections were based will remain the same, the HCFA cautioned that its projections should not be viewed as predictions for the future. Rather, they were intended to help policymakers evaluate the costs or savings of proposed legislative or regulatory changes.

Total Health Care Spending

The Center for Medicare & Medicaid Services, along with the Centers for Disease Control and Prevention (CDC) and the General Accounting Office (GAO), maintain most of the nation's statistics on health care costs. The CMS reported that the United States spent nearly $1.6 trillion for health care in 2002, up 9.3% from the previous year. (See Table 5.4.) This rate was higher than the lowest rates of increase since the late 1960s, which were documented in 1998 and 1999, but was not among the highest annual increases observed, such as the 11.7% rise in 1990.

About 54.1% of 2002 health care expenditures, or $839.6 billion, came from private funds, while the remaining 45.9% ($713.4 billion) was paid with public money. (See Table 5.4.) This means that 54 cents of every dollar spent on health care came from private funds, and the remainder came from federal (32.5 cents) or state and local governments (13.4 cents). The 2002 per capita cost for health care (the average per individual if spending was divided equally among all persons in the country) was $5,440. (See Table 5.4.)

A comparison of the sources of funds spent on health care in 1998 and 2002 reveals few significant changes. During 2002 private insurance paid slightly more than 2% more and Medicaid just over 1% more for health care services, and Americans' out-of-pocket expenses decreased by 1.5% from 1998. (See Table 5.3.)

TABLE 5.1

National health expenditures in comparison to gross domestic product and government expenditures, selected years 1960–2001

[Data are compiled from various sources by the Centers for Medicare & Medicaid Services]

Gross domestic product, government expenditures, and national health expenditures	1960	1970	1980	1990	1995	1998	1999	2000	2001
					Amount in billions				
Gross domestic product (GDP)	$527	$1,040	$2,796	$5,803	$7,400	$8,781	$9,274	$9,825	$10,082
Federal government expenditures	85.8	198.6	576.6	1,228.7	1,575.7	1,705.9	1,755.3	1,827.1	1,936.4
State and local government expenditures	38.1	107.5	307.8	660.8	902.5	1,033.7	1,105.8	1,196.2	1,292.6
National health expenditures	26.7	73.1	245.8	696.0	990.1	1,150.0	1,219.7	1,310.0	1,424.5
Private	20.1	45.4	140.9	413.5	532.5	628.4	669.7	718.7	777.9
Public	6.6	27.6	104.8	282.5	457.7	521.6	550.0	591.3	646.7
Federal government	2.8	17.6	71.3	192.7	323.5	368.7	386.2	415.1	454.8
State and local government	3.8	10.0	33.5	89.8	134.2	152.9	163.8	176.2	191.8
					Amount per capita				
National health expenditures	$143	$348	$1,067	$2,738	$3,697	$4,178	$4,392	$4,672	$5,035
Private	108	216	612	1,627	1,988	2,283	2,411	2,563	2,749
Public	35	131	455	1,111	1,709	1,895	1,980	2,109	2,286
					Percent				
National health expenditures as percent of GDP	5.1	7.0	8.8	12.0	13.4	13.1	13.2	13.3	14.1
				Health expenditures as a percent of total government expenditures					
Federal	3.3	8.9	12.4	15.7	20.5	21.6	22.0	22.7	23.5
State and local	9.9	9.3	10.9	13.6	14.9	14.8	14.8	14.7	14.8
					Percent distribution				
National health expenditures	100.0	100.0	100.0	100.0	100.0	100.0	100.0	100.0	100.0
Private	75.2	62.2	57.3	59.4	53.8	54.6	54.9	54.9	54.6
Public	24.8	37.8	42.7	40.6	46.2	45.4	45.1	45.1	45.4
				Average annual percent change from previous year shown					
Gross domestic product	—	7.0	10.4	7.6	5.0	5.9	5.6	5.9	2.6
Federal government expenditures	—	8.8	11.2	7.9	5.1	2.7	2.9	4.1	6.0
State and local government expenditures	—	10.9	11.1	7.9	6.4	4.6	7.0	8.2	8.1
National health expenditures	—	10.6	12.9	11.0	7.3	5.1	6.1	7.4	8.7
Private	—	8.5	12.0	11.4	5.2	5.7	6.6	7.3	8.2
Public	—	15.4	14.3	10.4	10.1	4.5	5.4	7.5	9.4
Federal government	—	20.1	15.0	10.5	10.9	4.5	4.7	7.5	9.6
State and local government	—	10.2	12.8	10.4	8.4	4.4	7.2	7.5	8.9
National health expenditures, per capita	—	9.3	11.9	9.9	6.2	4.2	5.1	6.4	7.8
Private	—	7.2	11.0	10.3	4.1	4.7	5.6	6.3	7.3
Public	—	14.0	13.2	9.3	9.0	3.5	4.5	6.5	8.4

— Category not applicable.

Notes: These data include revisions in health expenditures and differ from previous editions of *Health, United States*. They reflect U.S. Bureau of the Census resident population estimates as of July 2002. Federal and State and local government total expenditures reflect October 2002 revisions from the Bureau of Economic Analysis.

SOURCE: "Table 112. Gross Domestic Product, Federal and State and Local Government Expenditures, National Expenditures, and Average Annual Percent Change: United States, Selected Years 1960–2001," in *Health, United States, 2003,* National Center for Health Statistics, 2003, http://www.cdc.gov/nchs/data/hus/tables/2003/03hus112.pdf (accessed July 2, 2004)

Of the more than $1.5 trillion spent on health care in 2002, $1.3 trillion (89%) was spent on personal health services (expenses incurred by individuals as opposed to institutions). Some of the services included hospital care, physician and dental services, nursing and home health care, prescription drugs, and durable medical equipment. (See Table 5.5.)

Table 5.5 shows the trends and annual percent changes in personal health care expenditures by category. In 2002 the nation spent $501.5 billion on professional services, by far the largest chunk of health care spending, followed by $486.5 billion (about 32% of all health expenditures) on hospital costs. This expense was fol-

lowed by $339.5 billion for physician and clinical services, $162.4 billion for prescription drugs, and $103.2 billion for nursing home care. (See Table 5.5.) Figure 5.1 shows general percentages for how much was paid for medical spending in 2002.

WHO PAYS THE BILL?

In general, the government is the fastest-growing payer of health care expenses. From 1990 to 2002, total public share of the nation's total health care bill rose from 40.6% to 45.9%. (See Table 5.3.) This represented the largest increase in the government's contribution to health care since Medicare began covering the disabled population in the early 1970s.

TABLE 5.2

Consumer Price Index and average annual percent change for all items, selected items, and medical care costs, selected years 1960–2002

[Data are based on reporting by samples of providers and other retail outlets]

Items and medical care components	1960	1970	1980	1990	1995	1999	2000	2001	2002
					Consumer Price Index (CPI)				
All items	29.6	38.8	82.4	130.7	152.4	166.6	172.2	177.1	179.9
All items excluding medical care	30.2	39.2	82.8	128.8	148.6	162.0	167.3	171.9	174.3
All services	24.1	35.0	77.9	139.2	168.7	188.8	195.3	203.4	209.8
Food	30.0	39.2	86.8	132.4	148.4	164.1	167.8	173.1	176.2
Apparel	45.7	59.2	90.9	124.1	132.0	131.3	129.6	127.3	124.0
Housing	—	36.4	81.1	128.5	148.5	163.9	169.6	176.4	180.3
Energy	22.4	25.5	86.0	102.1	105.2	106.6	124.6	129.3	121.7
Medical care	22.3	34.0	74.9	162.8	220.5	250.6	260.8	272.8	285.6
Components of medical care									
Medical care services	19.5	32.3	74.8	162.7	224.2	255.1	266.0	278.8	292.9
Professional services	—	37.0	77.9	156.1	201.0	229.2	237.7	246.5	253.9
Physicians' services	21.9	34.5	76.5	160.8	208.8	236.0	244.7	253.6	260.6
Dental services	27.0	39.2	78.9	155.8	206.8	247.2	258.5	269.0	281.0
Eye glasses and eye care[1]	—	—	—	117.3	137.0	145.5	149.7	154.5	155.5
Services by other medical professionals[1]	—	—	—	120.2	143.9	158.7	161.9	167.3	171.8
Hospital and related services	—	—	69.2	178.0	257.8	299.5	317.3	338.3	367.8
Hospital services[2]	—	—	—	—	—	109.3	115.9	123.6	134.7
Inpatient hospital services[2]	—	—	—	—	—	107.9	113.8	121.0	131.2
Outpatient hospital services[1]	—	—	—	138.7	204.6	246.0	263.8	281.1	309.8
Hospital rooms	9.3	23.6	68.0	175.4	251.2	—	—	—	—
Other inpatient services[1]	—	—	—	142.7	206.8				
Nursing homes and adult day care	—	—	—	—	—	111.6	117.0	121.8	127.9
Medical care commodities	46.9	46.5	75.4	163.4	204.5	230.7	238.1	247.6	256.4
Prescription drugs and medical supplies	54.0	47.4	72.5	181.7	235.0	273.4	285.4	300.9	316.5
Nonprescription drugs and medical supplies[1]	—	—	—	120.6	140.5	148.5	149.5	150.6	150.4
Internal and respiratory over-the-counter drugs	—	42.3	74.9	145.9	167.0	175.9	176.9	178.9	178.8
Nonprescription medical equipment and supplies	—	—	79.2	138.0	166.3	176.7	178.1	178.2	177.5
					Average annual percent change from previous year shown				
All items	...	2.7	7.8	4.7	3.1	2.3	3.4	2.8	1.6
All items excluding medical care	...	2.6	7.8	4.5	2.9	2.2	3.3	2.7	1.4
All services	...	3.8	8.3	6.0	3.9	2.9	3.4	4.1	3.1
Food	...	2.7	8.3	4.3	2.3	2.5	2.3	3.2	1.8
Apparel	...	2.6	4.4	3.2	1.2	−0.1	−1.3	−1.8	−2.6
Housing	...	—	8.3	4.7	2.9	2.5	3.5	4.0	2.2
Energy	...	1.3	12.9	1.7	0.6	0.3	16.9	3.8	−5.9
Medical care	...	4.3	8.2	8.1	6.3	3.3	4.1	4.6	4.7

In 2002 private health insurance, the major non-government payer of health care costs, paid approximately 35.4% of all health expenditures, a proportion that has not changed significantly since 1990. The share of health care spending from private, out-of-pocket (paid by the patient) funds declined from 1990 to 2002, from nearly 20% to 13.7%. (See Table 5.3.)

Different sectors paid more for different types of health services. In 2002 the public sector paid for more than half (59%) of all hospital costs, with the federal government providing 47.2% of the nation's hospital bill. The public sector also paid 64% of all nursing home care and 60.6% of all home health care. Private health insurance paid for 49.1% of all physicians' services and 49.5% of dental bills. Patients paid 43.9% of their dental bills and 29.9% of their drug and prescription bills out-of-pocket. (See Table 5.6.)

The Personal Health Care Bill

Much of the increase in government spending has occurred in the area of personal health care. In 1980 gov-ernment sources paid 40.3% of personal health care expenditures; by 2002 they covered 44.2% ($592.2 billion) of the $1.34 trillion spent on personal health care services. (See Table 5.7.) Of the total expenditures, 33.6% came from the federal government and 10.6% came from state and local governments. A large proportion of the federal increase was attributed to Medicaid spending, which grew from 11.5% of all personal health care expenditures in 1980 to 17.3% in 2002.

WHY DID HEALTH CARE COSTS AND SPENDING INCREASE?

The increase in the cost of medical care is challenging to analyze because the methods and quality of health care change constantly and as a result are often not comparable. A hospital stay in 1960 did not include the same services offered in 2004. Further, the care received in a physician's office today is in no way comparable to that received a generation ago. One contributing factor to the

TABLE 5.2

Consumer Price Index and average annual percent change for all items, selected items, and medical care costs, selected years 1960–2002 [CONTINUED]

[Data are based on reporting by samples of providers and other retail outlets]

Items and medical care components	1960	1970	1980	1990	1995	1999	2000	2001	2002
Components of medical care									
Medical care services	...	5.2	8.8	8.1	6.6	3.3	4.3	4.8	5.1
Professional services	...	—	7.7	7.2	5.2	3.3	3.7	3.7	3.0
Physicians' services	...	4.6	8.3	7.7	5.4	3.1	3.7	3.6	2.8
Dental services	...	3.8	7.2	7.0	5.8	4.6	4.6	4.1	4.5
Eye glasses and eye care[1]	...	—	—	—	3.2	1.5	2.9	3.2	0.6
Services by other medical professionals[1]	...	—	—	—	3.7	2.5	2.0	3.3	2.7
Hospital and related services	...	—	—	9.9	7.7	3.8	5.9	6.6	8.7
Hospital services[2]	...	—	—	—	—	—	6.0	6.6	9.0
Inpatient hospital services[2]	...	—	—	—	—	—	5.5	6.3	8.4
Outpatient hospital services[1]	...	—	—	—	8.1	4.7	7.2	6.6	10.2
Hospital rooms	...	9.8	11.2	9.9	7.4	—	—	—	—
Other inpatient services[1]	...	—	—	—	7.7	—	—	—	—
Nursing homes and adult day care	...	—	—	—	—	—	4.8	4.1	5.0
Medical care commodities	...	−0.1	5.0	8.0	4.6	3.1	3.2	4.0	3.6
Prescription drugs and medical supplies	...	−1.3	4.3	9.6	5.3	3.9	4.4	5.4	5.2
Nonprescription drugs and medical supplies[1]	...	—	—	—	3.1	1.4	0.7	0.7	−0.1
Internal and respiratory over-the-counter drugs	...	—	5.9	6.9	2.7	1.3	0.6	1.1	−0.1
Nonprescription medical equipment and supplies	...	—	—	5.7	3.8	1.5	0.8	0.1	−0.4

— Data not available.
... Category not applicable.
[1]Dec. 1986 = 100.
[2]Dec. 1996 = 100.
Note: 1982–84 = 100, except where noted.

SOURCE: "Table 113. Consumer Price Index and Average Annual Percent Change for All Items, Selected Items, and Medical Care Components: United States, Selected Years 1960–2002," in *Health, United States, 2003,* National Center for Health Statistics, 2003, http://www.cdc.gov/nchs/data/hus/tables/2003/03hus113.pdf (accessed July 2, 2004)

rising cost of health care is the increase in biomedical technology, much of which is now available for use outside of a hospital.

Many other factors also contribute to the increase in health care costs. These include population growth, high salaries for physicians and some other health care workers, and the expense of malpractice insurance. Escalating malpractice insurance costs and professional liability premiums have prompted some physicians and other health care practitioners to refrain from performing high-risk procedures that increase their vulnerability or have caused them to relocate to states where malpractice premiums are lower. Furthermore, to protect themselves from malpractice suits, many health care practitioners routinely order diagnostic tests and prescribe treatments that are not medically necessary and do not serve to improve their patients' health. This practice is known as "defensive medicine," and while its precise contribution to rising health care costs is difficult to gauge, industry observers agree that it is a significant factor.

Although physicians have historically been the most vocal protesters of rising malpractice insurance premiums, hospitals and other health care providers also must purchase malpractice insurance to protect them from financial ruin in the event of lawsuits. An August 24, 2002, article in the *New York Times* reported that some

FIGURE 5.1

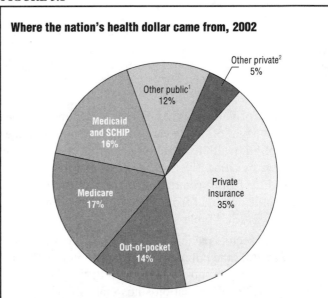

Where the nation's health dollar came from, 2002

Other private[2] 5%
Other public[1] 12%
Medicaid and SCHIP 16%
Medicare 17%
Out-of-pocket 14%
Private insurance 35%

[1]"Other public" includes programs such as workers' compensation, public health activity, Department of Defense, Department of Veterans Affairs, Indian Health Service, and State and local hospital subsidies and school health.
[2]"Other private" includes industrial in-plant, privately funded construction, and non-patient revenues, including philanthropy.
Note: Numbers shown may not add to 100 because of rounding.

SOURCE: "The Nation's Health Dollar: 2002; Where It Came From," Centers for Medicare and Medicaid Services, 2002, http://www.cms.hhs.gov/statistics/nhe/historical/chart.asp (accessed July 5, 2004)

TABLE 5.3

National health expenditures, by source of funds, selected years 1990–2013

Year	Total	Out-of-pocket payments	Total	Private health insurance	Other private funds	Total	Federal[2]	State and local[2]	Medicare[3]	Medicaid[4]
						Third-party payments				
							Public			
Historical estimates					**Amount in billions**					
1990	$696.00	$137.30	$558.70	$233.50	$42.80	$282.50	$192.70	$89.80	$110.20	$73.60
1998	1,150.30	175.3	975	382.9	70.8	521.3	368.4	152.9	210.2	171.5
1999	1,222.60	184.5	1,038.10	412.7	72.6	552.9	386.4	166.4	213.5	186.8
2000	1,309.40	192.6	1,116.90	449.3	72.9	594.6	416	178.6	225.1	203.4
2001	1,420.70	200.5	1,220.20	495.6	72.3	652.3	460.3	192	246.5	224.3
2002	1,553.00	212.5	1,340.50	549.6	77.5	713.4	504.7	208.7	267.1	250.4
Projected										
2003	1,673.60	227	1,446.60	606.7	80.9	759	535.2	223.8	280.9	269.2
2004	1,793.60	243	1,550.60	656.5	84.5	809.6	569.1	240.5	295.2	292.7
2005	1,920.80	260.9	1,660.00	707	88.7	864.2	605	259.3	309.3	319.2
2006	2,064.00	279.7	1,784.30	762.2	93.8	928.2	648.1	280.1	328.3	348.4
2007	2,219.20	299.3	1,919.90	821.9	99.5	998.5	695.5	303	349.3	380.4
2008	2,387.70	319.9	2,067.80	887.7	105.3	1,074.80	747.1	327.7	372.9	414.9
2009	2,565.00	341.7	2,223.30	954.6	111.3	1,157.40	803.5	354	399.3	452.2
2010	2,751.00	364.3	2,386.70	1,022.20	117.6	1,246.90	864.9	382	428.9	492.1
2011	2,945.60	387.4	2,558.20	1,092.00	123.7	1,342.50	930.6	411.9	460.8	534.8
2012	3,145.80	411.3	2,734.50	1,160.60	129.9	1,444.00	1,000.30	443.6	495.1	580.2
2013	3,358.10	436.2	2,921.80	1,233.40	136.3	1,552.10	1,074.80	477.3	532.1	628.5
Historical estimates					**Per capita amount**					
1990	$2,738	$540	$2,198	$919	$168	$1,111	$758	$353	—[5]	—[5]
1998	4,179	637	3,542	1,391	257	1,894	1,339	556	—[5]	—[5]
1999	4,402	664	3,738	1,486	261	1,991	1,391	599	—[5]	—[5]
2000	4,670	687	3,983	1,603	260	2,121	1,483	637	—[5]	—[5]
2001	5,021	709	4,313	1,752	256	2,306	1,627	679	—[5]	—[5]
2002	5,440	744	4,696	1,925	271	2,499	1,768	731	—[5]	—[5]
Projected										
2003	5,808	788	5,020	2,105	281	2,634	1,857	777	—[5]	—[5]
2004	6,167	836	5,332	2,257	291	2,784	1,957	827	—[5]	—[5]
2005	6,546	889	5,657	2,409	302	2,945	2,062	883	—[5]	—[5]
2006	6,972	945	6,027	2,575	317	3,135	2,189	946	—[5]	—[5]
2007	7,431	1,002	6,429	2,752	333	3,344	2,329	1,015	—[5]	—[5]
2008	7,928	1,062	6,866	2,947	350	3,569	2,481	1,088	—[5]	—[5]
2009	8,446	1,125	7,321	3,143	367	3,811	2,646	1,166	—[5]	—[5]
2010	8,984	1,190	7,795	3,338	384	4,072	2,825	1,248	—[5]	—[5]
2011	9,543	1,255	8,288	3,538	401	4,349	3,015	1,334	—[5]	—[5]
2012	10,110	1,322	8,789	3,730	417	4,641	3,215	1,426	—[5]	—[5]
2013	10,709	1,391	9,318	3,933	435	4,950	3,428	1,522	—[5]	—[5]
Historical estimates					**Percent distribution**					
1990	100	19.7	80.3	33.5	6.1	40.6	27.7	12.9	15.8	10.6
1998	100	15.2	84.8	33.3	6.2	45.3	32	13.3	18.3	14.9
1999	100	15.1	84.9	33.8	5.9	45.2	31.6	13.6	17.5	15.3
2000	100	14.7	85.3	34.3	5.6	45.4	31.8	13.6	17.2	15.5
2001	100	14.1	85.9	34.9	5.1	45.9	32.4	13.5	17.4	15.8
2002	100	13.7	86.3	35.4	5	45.9	32.5	13.4	17.2	16.1
Projected										
2003	100	13.6	86.4	36.3	4.8	45.4	32	13.4	16.8	16.1
2004	100	13.5	86.5	36.6	4.7	45.1	31.7	13.4	16.5	16.3
2005	100	13.6	86.4	36.8	4.6	45	31.5	13.5	16.1	16.6
2006	100	13.6	86.4	36.9	4.5	45	31.4	13.6	15.9	16.9
2007	100	13.5	86.5	37	4.5	45	31.3	13.7	15.7	17.1
2008	100	13.4	86.6	37.2	4.4	45	31.3	13.7	15.6	17.4
2009	100	13.3	86.7	37.2	4.3	45.1	31.3	13.8	15.6	17.6
2010	100	13.2	86.8	37.2	4.3	45.3	31.4	13.9	15.6	17.9
2011	100	13.2	86.8	37.1	4.2	45.6	31.6	14	15.6	18.2
2012	100	13.1	86.9	36.9	4.1	45.9	31.8	14.1	15.7	18.4
2013	100	13	87	36.7	4.1	46.2	32	14.2	15.8	18.7

hospitals had closed obstetric wards (units devoted to care of expectant mothers), clinics, and trauma services in response to soaring malpractice costs. The article cited an American Hospital Association (AHA) survey finding that more than thirteen hundred health care institutions had been affected by the costs of malpractice insurance, and the AHA claimed that in some states, such as New Jersey, insurance costs nearly doubled during 2001.

TABLE 5.3

National health expenditures, by source of funds, selected years 1990–2013 [CONTINUED]

			Third-party payments							
						Public				
Year	Total	Out-of-pocket payments	Total	Private health insurance	Other private funds	Total	Federal[2]	State and local[2]	Medicare[3]	Medicaid[4]
Historical estimates			Average annual percent change from previous year shown							
1990	—	—	—	—	—	—	—	—	—	—
1998	6.5	3.1	7.2	6.4	6.5	8	8.4	6.9	8.4	11.1
1999	6.3	5.2	6.5	7.8	2.5	6	4.9	8.8	1.6	8.9
2000	7.1	4.4	7.6	8.9	0.5	7.5	7.6	7.3	5.4	8.9
2001	8.5	4.1	9.2	10.3	−0.9	9.7	10.7	7.5	9.5	10.2
2002	9.3	6	9.9	10.9	7.2	9.4	9.7	8.7	8.4	11.7
Projected										
2003	7.8	6.8	7.9	10.4	4.4	6.4	6	7.2	5.2	7.5
2004	7.2	7.1	7.2	8.2	4.5	6.7	6.3	7.5	5.1	8.7
2005	7.1	7.3	7.1	7.7	4.9	6.8	6.3	7.8	4.8	9
2006	7.5	7.2	7.5	7.8	5.8	7.4	7.1	8	6.1	9.2
2007	7.5	7	7.6	7.8	6	7.6	7.3	8.2	6.4	9.2
2008	7.6	6.9	7.7	8	5.9	7.6	7.4	8.1	6.8	9.1
2009	7.4	6.8	7.5	7.5	5.7	7.7	7.5	8	7.1	9
2010	7.3	6.6	7.3	7.1	5.6	7.7	7.6	7.9	7.4	8.8
2011	7.1	6.3	7.2	6.8	5.3	7.7	7.6	7.8	7.5	8.7
2012	6.8	6.2	6.9	6.3	5	7.6	7.5	7.7	7.4	8.5
2013	6.7	6.1	6.9	6.3	5	7.5	7.4	7.6	7.5	8.3

[1]The health spending projections were based on the 2002 version of the National Health Expenditures (NHE) released in January 2004.
[2]Includes Medicaid SCHIP Expansion and SCHIP.
[3]Subset of Federal funds.
[4]Subset of Federal and State and local funds. Includes Medicaid SCHIP Expansion.
[5]Calculation of per capita estimates is inappropriate.
Notes: Per capita amounts based on July 1 Census resident based population estimates. Numbers and percents may not add to totals because of rounding.

SOURCE: "Table 3. National Health Expenditures; Aggregate and Per Capita Amounts, Percent Distribution and Average Annual Percent Change by Source of Funds: Selected Calendar Years 1990–2013," Centers for Medicare and Medicaid Services, 2002, http://www.cms.hhs.gov/statistics/nhe/projections-2003/t3.asp (accessed July 2, 2004)

Other factors include advanced biomedical procedures requiring high-technology expertise and equipment; redundant (excessive and unnecessary) technology in hospitals; cumbersome medical insurance programs and consumer demand for less restrictive insurance plans (ones that offer more choices, benefits, and coverage, but usually mean higher premiums); and consumer demand for the latest and most comprehensive testing and treatment. Legislation that increased Medicare spending and the growing number of older adults who utilize a disproportionate amount of health care services also acted to accelerate health care spending.

In an article in the August 10, 2002, issue of the *New York Times*, Drew Altman, president of the Kaiser Family Foundation, a health care research organization, expressed a concern shared by many health care industry observers "No one has a big new answer about what to do about health care costs. And it's all made worse because health costs are rising in bad economic times," Altman said. Some industry observers believe that combating health care inflation requires a major shift in how American health care providers and consumers approach health care delivery. They feel Americans must learn to use health care services wisely, choosing only treatments that have proven effective and accepting that bigger facilities and more treatment do not necessarily produce better health.

CONTROLLING HEALTH CARE SPENDING

In 1996 national health expenditures topped $1 trillion for the first time, and by 2002 national health expenditures exceeded $1.5 trillion. Despite the continuing growth in health care spending from year to year between 1998 and 2002—from 6.5% in 1998 to 9.3% in 2002—these figures represent a decline from the skyrocketing costs that marked the beginning of the 1990s. (See Table 5.5.) In 1990, for instance, health costs grew at a staggering 11.7% from the previous year.

In order to achieve these results, the nation's health care system underwent some dramatic changes. Beginning in the late 1980s, employers began looking for new ways to contain health benefit costs for their workers. Many enrolled their employees in managed care programs as alternatives to traditional, fee-for-service insurance. Managed care programs offered lower premiums by keeping a tighter control on costs and utilization, and by emphasizing the importance of preventive care. This allowed insurers to negotiate discounts with providers (physicians, hospitals, clinical laboratories, and others) in exchange for guaranteed access to employer-insured groups. Private insurance and other private sources such as privately funded construction and philanthropy pay for about 40% of the nation's health costs, according to 2002 data. Public sources pick up

TABLE 5.4

National health expenditures, by source of funds, selected years 1980–2002

Item	1980	1988	1990	1993	1994	1995	1996	1997	1998	1999	2000	2001	2002
							Amount in billions						
National health expenditures	$245.8	$558.1	$696.0	$888.1	$937.1	$990.2	$1,039.3	$1,092.8	$1,150.3	$1,222.6	$1,309.4	$1,420.7	$1,553.0
Private	140.9	331.7	413.5	497.7	509.7	533.6	556.8	589.2	629.0	669.7	714.9	768.4	839.6
Public	104.8	226.4	282.5	390.4	427.4	456.6	482.5	503.6	521.3	552.9	594.6	652.3	713.4
Federal	71.3	154.1	192.7	274.4	298.9	322.4	344.8	360.2	368.4	386.4	416.0	460.3	504.7
State and local	33.5	72.3	89.8	116.0	128.5	134.2	137.7	143.4	152.9	166.4	178.6	192.0	208.7
							Number in millions						
U.S. population[1]	230	249	254	263	265	268	270	273	275	278	280	283	285
							Amount in billions						
Gross domestic product[2]	$2,796	$5,108	$5,803	$6,642	$7,054	$7,401	$7,813	$8,318	$8,782	$9,274	$9,825	$10,082	$10,446
							Per capita amount						
National health expenditures	$1,067	$2,243	$2,738	$3,381	$3,534	$3,698	$3,847	$4,007	$4,179	$4,402	$4,670	$5,021	$5,440
Private	612	1,333	1,627	1,895	1,922	1,993	2,061	2,161	2,285	2,411	2,550	2,716	2,941
Public	455	910	1,111	1,486	1,612	1,705	1,786	1,846	1,894	1,991	2,121	2,306	2,499
Federal	310	619	758	1,045	1,127	1,204	1,276	1,321	1,339	1,391	1,483	1,627	1,768
State and local	146	290	353	442	485	501	510	526	556	599	637	679	731
							Percent distribution						
National health expenditures	100.0	100.0	100.0	100.0	100.0	100.0	100.0	100.0	100.0	100.0	100.0	100.0	100.0
Private	57.3	59.4	59.4	56.0	54.4	53.9	53.6	53.9	54.7	54.8	54.6	54.1	54.1
Public	42.7	40.6	40.6	44.0	45.6	46.1	46.4	46.1	45.3	45.2	45.4	45.9	45.9
Federal	29.0	27.6	27.7	30.9	31.9	32.6	33.2	33.0	32.0	31.6	31.8	32.4	32.5
State and local	13.6	13.0	12.9	13.1	13.7	13.6	13.2	13.1	13.3	13.6	13.6	13.5	13.4
							Percent of gross domestic product						
National health expenditures	8.8	10.9	12.0	13.4	13.3	13.4	13.3	13.1	13.1	13.2	13.3	14.1	14.9
							Average annual percent growth from previous year shown						
National health expenditures	11.7[3]	10.8	11.7	8.5	5.5	5.7	5.0	5.1	5.3	6.3	7.1	8.5	9.3
Private	10.2[3]	11.3	11.7	6.4	2.4	4.7	4.4	5.8	6.7	6.5	6.7	7.5	9.3
Public	14.8[3]	10.1	11.7	11.4	9.5	6.8	5.7	4.4	3.5	6.0	7.5	9.7	9.4
Federal	17.5[3]	10.1	11.8	12.5	9.0	7.8	7.0	4.4	2.3	4.9	7.6	10.7	9.7
State and local	11.5[3]	10.1	11.4	8.9	10.8	4.4	2.6	4.2	6.6	8.8	7.3	7.5	8.7
U.S. population	1.1[3]	1.0	1.1	1.1	1.0	1.0	0.9	0.9	0.9	0.9	1.0	0.9	0.9
Gross domestic product	8.7[3]	7.8	6.6	4.6	6.2	4.9	5.6	6.5	5.6	5.6	5.9	2.6	3.6

[1] July 1 census resident based population estimates for each year 1980–2002.
[2] U.S. Department of Commerce, Bureau of Economic Analysis.
[3] Average annual growth between 1960 and 1980.
Note: Numbers and percents may not add to totals because of rounding.

SOURCE: "Table 1. National Health Expenditures Aggregate and Per Capita Amounts, Percent Distribution and Average Annual Percent Change by Source of Funds: Selected Calendar Years 1980–2002," Centers for Medicare and Medicaid Services, 2002, http://www.cms.hhs.gov/statistics/nhe/projections-2003/t2.asp (accessed July 6, 2004)

about 45% of the nation's costs, and 14% of the costs come directly from consumers' pockets. (See Figure 5.1.)

There is heightened interest in developing treatments and technologies designed to reduce the health system's dependence on expensive, inpatient hospital care. After professional services ($501.5 billion), hospital care expenditures were the single-largest spending component of total health care expenses ($486.5), accounting for 31% of all national health care expenditures. (See Table 5.8 and Figure 5.2.) The annual hospital cost growth rate dropped from 12.8% per year in 1980 to around 3.4% between 1995 and 1998. In 2000, however, it spiked to 5%, and by 2002 it had nearly doubled to 9.5%. (See Table 5.8.)

Furthermore, higher hospital prices in 2002 resulted in the greatest increase in health care spending in a decade. Total health care costs increased 9.3% in 2002, compared with a 7.1% increase in 2000, and hospital care was responsible for nearly half of the increase. Economic analysis of the increase attributable to hospitals revealed that less than 40% was caused by rising hospital prices and slightly more than 60% by increased utilization of hospital services.

Physician and clinical services accounted for 22% ($339.5 billion) of 2002 national health spending. (See Table 5.8 and Figure 5.2.) The average annual physician spending, however, dropped steadily from 13.2% in 1988 to 4% in 1996. From 1997 to 2000 it fluctuated between 5 and 7.2% and while it spiked to 8.6% in 2001, it dropped to 7.7% in 2002. (See Table 5.8.) Managed care has played a large role in the slowed growth observed in this sector of health care delivery.

In 2002 spending for nursing home care totaled $103.2 billion, and spending for home health care reached $36.1 billion. (See Table 5.8.) Although in 2002 nursing home expenses increased just over 4%, this increase followed four consecutive years of decelerating growth from a high

TABLE 5.5

National health expenditures by type of expenditure, selected years 1990–2013

Type of expenditure	1990	1998	1999	2000	2001	2002	2003	2004	2005	2006	2007	Projected 2008	2009	2010	2011	2012	2013
							Amount in billions										
National health expenditures	$696.00	$1,150.50	$1,222.60	$1,309.40	$1,420.70	$1,553.00	$1,673.60	$1,793.60	$1,920.80	$2,064.00	$2,219.20	$2,387.70	$2,565.00	$2,751.00	$2,945.60	$3,145.80	$3,358.10
Health services and supplies	669.6	1,112.10	1,181.70	1,261.40	1,370.00	1,496.30	1,613.60	1,730.10	1,853.00	1,991.00	2,140.50	2,303.30	2,474.80	2,654.70	2,843.00	3,036.50	3,241.90
Personal health care	609.4	1,009.60	1,065.00	1,135.30	1,231.40	1,340.20	1,436.50	1,540.70	1,651.50	1,775.30	1,907.40	2,050.10	2,201.30	2,360.70	2,527.00	2,699.10	2,881.20
Hospital care	253.9	378.5	393.5	413.2	444.3	486.5	518.1	551.7	585.8	623.2	661.8	702.6	746.1	791.5	838.1	885.2	934.3
Professional services	216.9	371.7	397.6	426.5	464.3	501.5	535.8	572	611.2	656.2	705	759.2	816.2	876.7	940.3	1,006.00	1,075.80
Physician and clinical services	157.5	256.8	270.9	290.3	315.1	339.5	362.8	386.8	412	441.2	472.4	507.1	542.8	580.3	619.4	659.2	700.9
Other professional services	18.2	36.5	36.7	38.8	42.6	45.9	48.3	51	54.2	57.8	61.8	66.2	71	76.3	81.6	87	92.8
Dental services	31.5	53.2	56.4	60.7	65.6	70.3	74	78	82.3	87.1	92.2	97.6	103.1	108.8	114.6	120.2	126.3
Other personal health care	9.6	30.2	33.7	36.7	40.9	45.8	50.8	56.2	62.6	70.1	78.7	88.4	99.2	111.3	124.8	139.6	155.9
Nursing home and home health	65.3	127.7	121.9	125.5	132.8	139.3	145.2	152.2	160.2	169.5	179.6	190.5	202.5	215.3	228.8	243	258.2
Home health care	12.6	33.6	32.3	31.7	33.7	36.1	38.3	40.6	43.2	46.2	49.4	52.7	56.3	60.3	64.4	68.7	73.4
Nursing home care	52.7	83.1	89.6	93.8	99.1	103.2	107	111.7	116.9	123.3	130.2	137.8	146.1	155	164.4	174.3	184.8
Retail outlet sales of medical products	73.3	132.7	152	170.1	190	212.9	237.4	264.8	294.4	326.4	360.9	397.7	436.5	477.2	519.8	564.9	612.9
Prescription drugs	40.3	87.3	104.4	121.5	140.8	162.4	184.1	207.9	233.6	261.8	292.4	325.3	360.1	396.7	435.2	476.2	519.8
Other medical products	33.1	45.4	47.6	48.5	49.2	50.5	53.2	56.9	60.8	64.7	68.5	72.4	76.4	80.5	84.6	88.7	93.1
Durable medical equipment	10.6	16.9	17.2	17.7	18.2	18.8	19.6	20.6	21.5	22.6	23.8	25	26.4	27.8	29.3	30.9	32.6
Other non-durable medical products	22.5	28.6	30.3	30.8	31	31.7	33.6	36.4	39.3	42.1	44.7	47.4	50	52.7	55.3	57.8	60.5
Government administration and net cost of private health insurance	40	64.5	73	80.3	90.3	105	120.8	127.9	134.7	143.1	154.3	167.7	180.8	193.5	207.2	219.8	233.7
Government administration public health activities	20.2	38	43.7	45.8	48.3	51.2	56.3	61.4	66.8	72.6	78.8	85.5	92.7	100.5	108.8	117.6	127.1

TABLE 5.5

National health expenditures by type of expenditure, selected years 1990–2013 [CONTINUED]

Type of expenditure	1990	1998	1999	2000	2001	2002	2003	2004	2005	2006	2007	Projected 2008	2009	2010	2011	2012	2013
							Amount in billions										
Investment	26.4	38.3	40.9	48	50.6	56.7	60	63.5	67.8	72.9	78.7	84.5	90.3	96.3	102.6	109.2	116.1
Research[2]	12.7	20.5	23.4	28.8	31.5	34.3	36.3	38.6	41.5	45	48.8	52.7	56.8	61.2	65.7	70.4	75.4
Construction	13.7	17.7	17.6	19.2	19.2	22.4	23.7	25	26.3	27.9	29.9	31.7	33.4	35.1	36.9	38.8	40.8
							Average annual percent change from previous year shown										
National health expenditures	—	6.5	6.3	7.1	8.5	9.3	7.8	7.2	7.1	7.5	7.5	7.6	7.4	7.3	7.1	6.8	6.7
Health services and supplies	—	6.5	6.3	6.8	8.6	9.2	7.8	7.2	7.1	7.4	7.5	7.6	7.4	7.3	7.1	6.8	6.8
Personal health care	—	6.5	5.5	6.6	8.5	8.8	7.2	7.3	7.2	7.5	7.4	7.5	7.4	7.2	7	6.8	6.7
Hospital care	—	5.1	3.9	5	7.5	9.5	6.5	6.5	6.2	6.4	6.2	6.2	6.2	6.1	5.9	5.6	5.6
Professional services	—	7.1	5.8	7.3	8.8	8	6.8	6.8	6.8	7.4	7.4	7.7	7.5	7.4	7.3	7	6.9
Physician and clinical services	—	6.3	5.5	7.2	8.6	7.7	6.8	6.6	6.5	7.1	7.1	7.4	7	6.9	6.7	6.4	6.3
Other professional services	—	8.7	3.3	5.8	9.9	7.6	5.2	5.7	6.2	6.7	6.9	7.2	7.3	7.3	7	6.6	6.6
Dental services	—	6.8	6.1	7.7	8	7.2	5.2	5.4	5.6	5.8	5.9	5.8	5.7	5.5	5.3	55	5
Other personal health care	—	15.3	11.7	9	11.3	12.1	10.8	10.7	11.4	11.9	12.2	12.3	12.3	12.2	12.1	11.9	11.6
Nursing home and home health	—	8.2	−0.6	3	5.8	4.9	4.3	4.8	5.2	5.8	6	6.1	6.3	6.3	6.3	6.2	6.2
Home health care	—	13.1	−3.7	−1.8	6.2	7.2	5.9	6.1	6.6	6.8	6.9	6.8	6.8	7	6.8	6.8	6.8
Nursing home care	—	6.8	0.5	4.7	5.7	4.1	3.7	4.4	4.7	5.4	5.6	5.8	6.1	6.1	6.1	66	6
Retail outlet sales of medical products	—	7.7	14.5	11.9	11.7	12	11.5	11.6	11.2	10.9	10.5	10.2	9.7	9.3	8.9	8.7	8.5
Prescription drugs	—	10.1	19.7	16.4	15.9	15.3	13.4	12.9	12.4	12.1	11.7	11.3	10.7	10.2	9.7	9.4	9.2
Other medical products	—	4.1	4.7	2.1	1.3	2.6	5.5	6.9	6.8	6.4	5.9	5.7	5.5	5.3	5.1	4.8	4.9
Durable medical equipment	—	6	2.3	3	2.3	3.3	4.6	4.9	4.7	5	5.2	5.3	5.4	5.4	5.4	5.4	5.5
Other non-durable medical products	—	3.1	6.1	1.5	0.8	2.3	6	8.1	8	7.1	6.4	5.9	5.6	5.3	5	4.6	4.6

TABLE 5.5

National health expenditures by type of expenditure, selected years 1990–2013 [CONTINUED]

Type of expenditure	1990	1998	1999	2000	2001	2002	2003	2004	2005	2006	2007	2008	2009	2010	2011	2012	2013
													Projected				
							Average annual percentage change from previous year										
Government administration and net cost of private health insurance	—	6.1	13.2	10	12.5	16.2	15.1	5.9	5.3	6.2	7.9	8.7	7.8	7	7.1	6.1	6.3
Government public health activities	—	6.2	15.1	4.8	5.5	5.9	10	9.2	8.8	8.7	8.5	8.5	8.5	8.4	8.2	8.1	8
Investment	—	4.8	7	17.3	5.5	11.9	5.9	5.9	6.7	7.5	7.9	7.4	6.9	6.7	6.5	6.4	6.3
Research[2]	—	6.2	13.8	23.1	9.4	8.9	5.9	6.1	7.7	8.3	8.4	8.1	7.8	7.6	7.4	7.2	7
Construction	—	5.2	-0.9	9.5	-0.3	16.8	5.8	5.6	5.2	6.3	6.9	6.2	5.4	5.1	5.1	5.1	5.1

[1]The health spending projections were based on the 2002 version of the National Health Expenditures (NHE) released in January 2004.
[2]Research and development expenditures of drug companies and other manufacturers and providers of medical equipment and supplies are excluded from research expenditures. These research expenditures are implicitly included in the expenditure class in which the product falls, in that they are covered by the payment received for that product.
Note: Numbers may not add to totals because of rounding.

SOURCE: "Table 2. National Health Expenditure Amounts and Average Annual Percent Change by Type of Expenditure: Selected Calendar Years 1990–2013," Centers for Medicare and Medicaid Services, 2002, http://www.cms.hhs.gov/statistics/nhe/projections-2003/t2.asp (accessed July 2, 2004)

TABLE 5.6

National health expenditures, by source of funds and type of expenditure, 2001 and 2002

(In billions)

Year and type of expenditure	Total	All private funds	Private — Consumer — Total	Out-of-pocket payments	Private health insurance	Other	Public — Total	Federal	State and local
2001									
National health expenditures	1,420.7	768.4	696.1	200.5	495.6	72.3	652.3	460.3	192.0
Health services and supplies	1,370.0	751.0	696.1	200.5	495.6	54.9	619.0	434.6	184.4
Personal health care	1,231.4	691.4	637.8	200.5	437.2	53.7	540.0	412.1	127.8
Hospital care	444.3	181.7	162.6	13.1	149.5	19.1	262.6	211.6	51.1
Professional services	464.3	306.6	276.8	73.9	202.9	29.7	157.7	118.6	39.1
Physician and clinical services	315.1	208.7	186.5	33.1	153.4	22.2	106.4	88.1	18.3
Other professional services	42.6	31.7	28.8	12.4	16.4	2.9	10.9	7.0	3.9
Dental services	65.6	61.7	61.6	28.4	33.2	0.1	3.9	2.3	1.6
Other personal health care	40.9	4.4	—	—	—	4.4	36.4	21.1	15.3
Nursing home and home health	132.8	52.2	47.3	32.8	14.5	4.8	80.7	56.6	24.1
Home health care	33.7	14.1	13.0	6.1	6.9	1.1	19.6	14.4	5.2
Nursing home care	99.1	38.0	34.3	26.7	7.6	3.7	61.1	42.2	18.9
Retail outlet sales of medical products	190.0	151.0	151.0	80.7	70.3	—	39.0	25.4	13.6
Prescription drugs	140.8	109.3	109.3	42.5	66.8	—	31.5	18.0	13.5
Other medical products	49.2	41.7	41.7	38.2	3.5	—	7.5	7.3	0.2
Durable medical equipment	18.2	12.1	12.1	8.7	3.5	—	6.0	5.8	0.2
Other non-durable medical products	31.0	29.6	29.6	29.6	—	—	1.5	1.5	—
Government administration and net cost of private health insurance	90.3	59.6	58.3	—	58.3	1.3	30.7	17.2	13.6
Government public health activities	48.3	—	—	—	—	—	48.3	5.3	43.0
Investment	50.6	17.4	—	—	—	17.4	33.3	25.7	7.6
Research	31.5	2.7	—	—	—	2.7	28.8	25.0	3.8
Construction	19.2	14.7	—	—	—	14.7	4.5	0.7	3.8
2002									
National health expenditures	1,553.0	839.6	762.1	212.5	549.6	77.5	713.4	504.7	208.7
Health services and supplies	1,496.3	819.7	762.1	212.5	549.6	57.7	676.6	476.5	200.1
Personal health care	1,340.2	748.1	691.8	212.5	479.3	56.2	592.2	450.5	141.7
Hospital care	486.5	200.1	179.8	14.7	165.0	20.3	286.4	229.9	56.5
Professional services	501.5	328.4	297.0	78.2	218.9	31.3	173.2	129.7	43.4
Physician and clinical services	339.5	224.7	201.1	34.3	166.9	23.6	114.8	94.7	20.1
Other professional services	45.9	33.2	30.2	13.0	17.2	3.0	12.6	8.2	4.4
Dental services	70.3	65.8	65.7	30.9	34.8	0.1	4.5	2.7	1.8
Other personal health care	45.8	4.7	—	—	—	4.7	41.2	24.1	17.1
Nursing home and home health	139.3	51.4	46.8	32.4	14.4	4.6	87.9	61.7	26.2
Home health care	36.1	14.3	13.2	6.5	6.7	1.1	21.9	16.2	5.7
Nursing home care	103.2	37.1	33.6	25.9	7.7	3.5	66.1	45.5	20.5
Retail outlet sales of medical products	212.9	168.2	168.2	87.2	81.0	—	44.7	29.1	15.6
Prescription drugs	162.4	126.2	126.2	48.6	77.6	—	36.2	20.9	15.4
Other medical products	50.5	42.1	42.1	38.6	3.5	—	8.4	8.2	0.2
Durable medical equipment	18.8	11.9	11.9	8.5	3.5	—	6.8	6.6	0.2
Other non-durable medical products	31.7	30.1	30.1	30.1	—	—	1.6	1.6	—
Government administration and net cost of private health insurance	105.0	71.7	70.2	—	70.2	1.4	33.3	19.0	14.3
Government public health activities	51.2	—	—	—	—	—	51.2	7.0	44.1
Investment	56.7	19.8	—	—	—	19.8	36.8	28.3	8.6
Research	34.3	2.7	—	—	—	2.7	31.6	27.4	4.2
Construction	22.4	17.1	—	—	—	17.1	5.2	0.8	4.4

Note: Research and development expenditures of drug companies and other manufacturers and providers of medical equipment and supplies are excluded from research expenditures. These research expenditures are implicitly included in the expenditure class in which the product falls, in that they are covered by the payment received for that product. Numbers may not add to totals because of rounding.

SOURCE: Adapted from "Table 3. National Health Expenditures, by Source of Funds and Type of Expenditure: Selected Calendar Years 1997–2002," Centers for Medicare and Medicaid Services, 2002, http://www.cms.hhs.gov/statistics/nhe/projections-2003/t2.asp (accessed July 6, 2004)

of 9.1% annual growth in 1995. The increase was caused by legislation that increased Medicare payments to nursing homes for selected complex medical conditions and for facilities specializing in the care of patients with AIDS.

Home health care expenses also slowed, from 20.3% annual growth in 1993 to 2.8% in 1997. In 1998, 1999, and 2000 the annual growth was actually negative but rose 6.2% in 2001 and 7.2% in 2002. (See Table 5.8.) Like nursing home expenditures, home health spending increased in 2000 after several years of decelerating growth.

However, the fastest-growing component of health care was the market for prescription drugs. In 2002 Ameri-

TABLE 5.7

Personal health care expenditures, by source of funds, selected years 1980–2002

| | | | Third-party payments | | | | | | | |
| | | | | | | Public | | | | |
Year	Total	Out-of-pocket payments	Total	Private health insurance	Other private funds	Total	Federal[1]	State and local[1]	Medicare[2]	Medicaid[3]
					Amount in billions					
1980	$214.6	$58.2	$156.4	$60.6	$9.2	$86.6	$62.8	$23.8	$36.3	$24.7
1988	493.3	118.9	374.4	157.0	27.6	189.8	138.4	51.4	86.4	52.2
1993	775.8	146.9	628.8	259.9	38.4	330.5	250.6	79.9	144.4	115.7
1995	865.7	146.5	719.2	288.8	44.2	386.2	295.4	90.8	178.6	135.3
1996	911.1	151.9	759.3	302.2	47.3	409.8	316.5	93.3	193.1	144.5
1997	959.2	162.1	797.2	319.2	51.4	426.6	329.8	96.8	203.6	151.7
1998	1,009.6	175.3	834.3	342.0	54.4	437.9	334.7	103.2	204.0	160.0
1999	1,065.0	184.5	880.5	366.4	56.2	457.9	347.7	110.2	206.2	173.7
2000	1,135.3	192.6	942.8	398.7	54.2	489.8	372.0	117.8	217.5	188.3
2001	1,231.4	200.5	1,030.9	437.2	53.7	540.0	412.1	127.8	239.2	207.5
2002	1,340.2	212.5	1,127.7	479.3	56.2	592.2	450.5	141.7	259.1	232.4
					Per capita amount					
1980	$931.4	$252.8	$678.6	$263.1	$39.7	$375.7	$272.4	$103.3	[4]	[4]
1988	1,982.3	477.9	1,504.3	630.9	110.8	762.6	555.9	206.6	[4]	[4]
1993	2,953.6	559.5	2,394.1	989.4	146.4	1,258.3	954.0	304.3	[4]	[4]
1995	3,232.8	547.0	2,685.8	1,078.4	165.2	1,442.2	1,103.0	339.1	[4]	[4]
1996	3,372.6	562.2	2,810.4	1,118.6	174.9	1,516.9	1,171.4	345.5	[4]	[4]
1997	3,517.3	594.3	2,923.0	1,170.5	188.4	1,564.1	1,209.1	355.0	[4]	[4]
1998	3,668.1	636.9	3,031.1	1,242.7	197.5	1,590.9	1,216.0	375.0	[4]	[4]
1999	3,834.6	664.2	3,170.3	1,319.4	202.3	1,648.6	1,251.8	396.8	[4]	[4]
2000	4,049.1	686.8	3,362.3	1,422.1	193.4	1,746.8	1,326.7	420.1	[4]	[4]
2001	4,352.2	708.7	3,643.5	1,545.4	189.7	1,908.4	1,456.6	451.8	[4]	[4]
2002	4,694.6	744.4	3,950.2	1,679.0	196.9	2,074.3	1,577.9	496.4	[4]	[4]
					Percent distribution					
1980	100.0	27.1	72.9	28.3	4.3	40.3	29.3	11.1	16.9	11.5
1988	100.0	24.1	75.9	31.8	5.6	38.5	28.0	10.4	17.5	10.6
1993	100.0	18.9	81.1	33.5	5.0	42.6	32.3	10.3	18.6	14.9
1995	100.0	16.9	83.1	33.4	5.1	44.6	34.1	10.5	20.6	15.6
1996	100.0	16.7	83.3	33.2	5.2	45.0	34.7	10.2	21.2	15.9
1997	100.0	16.9	83.1	33.3	5.4	44.5	34.4	10.1	21.2	15.8
1998	100.0	17.4	82.6	33.9	5.4	43.4	33.2	10.2	20.2	15.8
1999	100.0	17.3	82.7	34.4	5.3	43.0	32.6	10.3	19.4	16.3
2000	100.0	17.0	83.0	35.1	4.8	43.1	32.8	10.4	19.2	16.6
2001	100.0	16.3	83.7	35.5	4.4	43.8	33.5	10.4	19.4	16.9
2002	100.0	15.9	84.1	35.8	4.2	44.2	33.6	10.6	19.3	17.3

[1]Includes Medicaid SCHIP (State Children's Health Insurance Program) Expansion & SCHIP.
[2]Subset of federal funds.
[3]Subset of federal and state and local funds.
[4]Calculation of per capita estimates is inappropriate.
Note: Per capita amounts based on July 1 census resident based population estimates for each year 1980–2002. Numbers and percents may not add to totals because of rounding.

SOURCE: "Table 4. Personal Health Care Expenditures Aggregate and Per Capita Amounts and Percent Distribution by Source of Funds: Selected Calendar Years 1980–2002," Centers for Medicare and Medicaid Services, 2002, http://www.cms.hhs.gov/statistics/nhe/projections-2003/t2.asp (accessed July 6, 2004)

cans spent $162.4 billion on prescription medication—a 15.3% increase from the previous year. (See Table 5.8.) A large part of the increase was financed by private insurers, which paid 48% of drug costs in 2002, up from 37.2% in 1995. (See Table 5.6.) Growth in this sector of health services has been fueled by the fact that prescription drugs are increasingly more often substituted for other types of health care. For example, antidepressant drugs have demonstrated effectiveness in place of more expensive psychotherapy.

Prescription Drug Prices Rose in 2004

A survey conducted by David Gross, Susan Raetzman, and Professor Stephen Schondelmeyer for the AARP (formerly known as the American Association of Retired Persons; AARP is a nonprofit, nonpartisan membership organization dedicated to making life better for persons aged fifty and older) found that pharmaceutical companies increased the prices they charge drug wholesalers for the top two hundred brand-name drugs an average of 3.4% in the first three months of 2004, while inflation in general was 1.2%. The study *Trends in Manufacturer Prices of Prescription Drugs Used by Older Americans* released in June 2004 by the AARP Public Policy Institute found that 29% of the drugs studied had increases in the first quarter (from December 31, 2003, to March 31, 2004) of more than 5%, or more than four times the rate of inflation for the same period. First-quarter increases of more than 7.5% were found in almost 11% of the drugs. Of the twenty-five brand-name drugs with the greatest sales in 2003, nearly two-thirds had price increases in the first quarter of 2004.

TABLE 5.8

National health expenditures by type of expenditure, selected years 1980–2002

Type of expenditure	1980	1988	1990	1993	1994	1995	1996	1997	1998	1999	2000	2001	2002
							Amount in billions						
National health expenditures	$245.8	$558.1	$696.0	$888.1	$937.1	$990.2	$1,039.3	$1,092.8	$1,150.3	$1,222.6	$1,309.4	$1,420.7	$1,553.0
Health services and supplies	233.5	535.4	669.6	856.3	904.7	957.6	1,005.1	1,055.5	1,112.1	1,181.7	1,261.4	1,370.0	1,496.3
Personal health care	214.6	493.3	609.4	775.8	816.5	865.7	911.1	959.2	1,009.6	1,065.0	1,135.3	1,231.4	1,340.2
Hospital care	101.5	209.4	253.9	320.0	332.4	343.6	355.2	367.6	378.5	393.5	413.2	444.3	486.5
Professional services	67.3	176.3	216.9	280.7	297.5	316.5	332.9	352.2	375.7	397.6	426.5	464.3	501.5
Physician and clinical services	47.1	127.4	157.5	201.2	210.5	220.5	229.4	241.0	256.8	270.9	290.3	315.1	339.5
Other professional services	3.6	14.3	18.2	24.5	25.7	28.6	30.9	33.4	35.5	36.7	38.8	42.6	45.9
Dental services	13.3	27.3	31.5	38.9	41.4	44.5	46.8	50.2	53.2	56.4	60.7	65.6	70.3
Other personal health care	3.3	7.3	9.6	16.1	19.9	22.9	25.8	27.7	30.2	33.7	36.7	40.9	45.8
Nursing home and home health	20.1	48.9	65.3	87.6	94.4	105.1	113.5	119.6	122.7	121.9	125.5	132.8	139.3
Home health care	2.4	8.4	12.6	21.9	26.1	30.5	33.6	34.5	33.6	32.3	31.7	33.7	36.1
Nursing home care	17.7	40.5	52.7	65.7	68.3	74.6	79.9	85.1	89.1	89.6	93.8	99.1	103.2
Retail outlet sales of medical products	25.7	58.7	73.3	87.5	92.2	100.5	109.5	119.8	132.7	152.0	170.1	190.0	212.9
Prescription drugs	12.0	30.6	40.3	51.3	54.6	60.8	67.2	75.7	87.3	104.4	121.5	140.8	162.4
Other medical products	13.7	28.1	33.1	36.2	37.6	39.7	42.4	44.0	45.4	47.6	48.5	49.2	50.5
Durable medical equipment	3.9	8.7	10.6	12.8	13.3	14.2	15.3	16.2	16.9	17.2	17.7	18.2	18.8
Other non-durable medical products	9.8	19.4	22.5	23.4	24.3	25.6	27.1	27.9	28.6	30.3	30.8	31.0	31.7
Government administration and net cost of private health insurance	12.1	26.6	40.0	53.3	58.2	60.5	61.0	60.9	64.5	73.0	80.3	90.3	105.0
Government public health activities	6.7	15.5	20.2	27.2	30.0	31.4	32.9	35.4	38.0	43.7	45.8	48.3	51.2
Investment	12.3	22.7	26.4	31.8	32.5	32.6	34.2	37.2	38.3	40.9	48.0	50.6	56.7
Research[1]	5.5	10.8	12.7	15.6	16.3	17.1	17.8	18.7	20.5	23.4	28.8	31.5	34.3
Construction	6.8	11.9	13.7	16.2	16.2	15.5	16.4	18.5	17.7	17.6	19.2	19.2	22.4
							Average annual percent change from previous year shown						
National health expenditures	11.7[2]	10.8	11.7	8.5	5.5	5.7	5.0	5.1	5.3	6.3	7.1	8.5	9.3
Health services and supplies	11.8[2]	10.9	11.8	8.5	5.7	5.9	5.0	5.0	5.4	6.3	6.8	8.6	9.2
Personal health care	11.7[2]	11.0	11.1	8.4	5.2	6.0	5.2	5.3	5.3	5.5	6.6	8.5	8.8
Hospital care	12.8[2]	9.5	10.1	8.0	3.9	3.4	3.4	3.5	3.0	3.9	5.0	7.5	9.5
Professional services	11.0[2]	12.8	10.9	9.0	6.0	6.4	5.2	5.8	6.7	5.8	7.3	8.8	8.0
Physician and clinical services	11.5[2]	13.2	11.2	8.5	4.6	4.8	4.0	5.0	6.6	5.5	7.2	8.6	7.7
Other professional services	11.7[2]	18.8	12.7	10.4	4.9	11.2	8.1	8.1	6.3	3.3	5.8	9.9	7.6
Dental services	10.0[2]	9.4	7.4	7.3	6.6	7.4	5.2	7.2	6.0	6.1	7.7	8.0	7.2
Other personal health care	8.6[2]	10.5	15.0	18.7	23.3	15.3	12.6	7.4	8.9	11.7	9.0	11.3	12.1
Nursing home and home health	16.8[2]	11.8	15.5	10.3	7.8	11.3	8.0	5.4	2.6	−0.6	3.0	5.8	4.9
Home health care	20.6[2]	17.1	22.1	20.3	19.1	17.1	10.1	2.8	−2.8	−3.7	−1.8	6.2	7.2
Nursing home care	16.4[2]	10.9	14.1	7.6	4.0	9.1	7.2	6.4	4.7	0.5	4.7	5.7	4.1
Retail outlet sales of medical products	8.6[2]	10.9	11.8	6.0	5.4	9.0	9.0	9.4	10.8	14.5	11.9	11.7	12.0
Prescription drugs	7.8[2]	12.4	14.7	8.4	6.6	11.2	10.5	12.8	15.2	19.7	16.4	15.9	15.3
Other medical products	9.4[2]	9.4	8.5	3.1	3.7	5.8	6.6	3.9	3.2	4.7	2.1	1.3	2.6
Durable medical equipment	9.3[2]	10.7	10.4	6.5	4.1	6.5	7.8	5.7	4.3	2.3	3.0	2.3	3.3
Other non-durable medical products	9.4[2]	8.9	7.7	1.4	3.6	5.4	6.0	2.9	2.6	6.1	1.5	0.8	2.3
Government administration and net cost of private health insurance	12.2[2]	10.3	22.7	10.0	9.2	4.0	0.9	−0.3	5.9	13.2	10.0	12.5	16.2
Government public health activities	15.3[2]	11.0	14.2	10.4	10.3	4.7	4.7	7.7	7.2	15.1	4.8	5.5	5.9
Investment	10.4[2]	8.0	7.8	6.4	2.1	0.3	5.1	8.8	2.7	7.0	17.3	5.5	11.9
Research[1]	10.9[2]	8.9	8.2	7.2	4.3	5.2	4.3	5.0	9.7	13.8	23.1	9.4	8.9
Construction	10.0[2]	7.2	7.4	5.7	0.1	−4.5	5.9	13.0	−4.4	−0.9	9.5	−0.3	16.8

[1]Research and development expenditures of drug companies and other manufacturers and providers of medical equipment and supplies are excluded from research expenditures. These research expenditures are implicitly included in the expenditure class in which the product falls, in that they are covered by the payment received for that product.
[2]Average annual growth between 1960 and 1980.
Note: Numbers may not add to totals because of rounding.

SOURCE: "Table 2. National Health Expenditures Aggregate Amounts and Average Annual Percent Change by Type of Expenditure: Selected Calendar Years 1980–2002," Centers for Medicare and Medicaid Services, 2002, http://www.cms.hhs.gov/statistics/nhe/projections-2003/t2.asp (accessed July 6, 2004)

Ironically, this increase occurred just after enactment of a new Medicare law intended to increase government spending for prescription drugs that promised prescription drug savings for older Americans and persons with disabilities. The price increase also preceded the June 2004 implementation of a pharmacy discount card program aimed at providing Medicare recipients savings on brand-name drugs ranging from 11 to 18%.

Medicare beneficiaries can buy the cards for up to $30 and obtain discounts on drugs they purchase at neighborhood pharmacies or by mail order. The most financially disadvantaged people receive the cards for free and are given $600 a year to fill their prescriptions. The card program is a temporary measure that will be replaced by prescription drug coverage under Medicare in 2006.

FIGURE 5.2

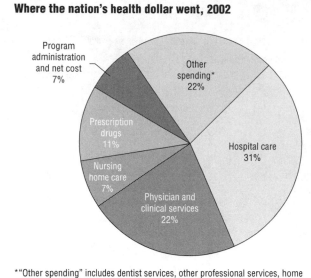

Where the nation's health dollar went, 2002

Program administration and net cost 7%

Other spending* 22%

Prescription drugs 11%

Nursing home care 7%

Hospital care 31%

Physician and clinical services 22%

*"Other spending" includes dentist services, other professional services, home health care, durable medical products, over-the-counter medicines and sundries, public health, research and construction.
Note: Numbers shown may not add to 100 because of rounding.

SOURCE: "The Nation's Health Dollar: 2002; Where It Went," Centers for Medicare and Medicaid Services, 2002, http://www.cms.hhs.gov/statistics/nhe/historical/chart.asp (accessed July 5, 2004)

HEALTH CARE FOR OLDER ADULTS, PERSONS WITH DISABILITIES, AND THE POOR

The United States is one of the few industrialized nations that does not have a national health care program. In most other developed countries, government national medical care programs cover almost all health-related costs, from maternity care to long-term care.

In the United States the major government health care entitlement programs are Medicare and Medicaid. They provide financial assistance for persons age sixty-five and older, the poor, and people with disabilities. Before the existence of these programs, a large number of older Americans could not afford adequate medical care. For older adults who are beneficiaries, the Medicare program provides reimbursement for hospital and physician care, while Medicaid pays for the cost of nursing home care.

Medicare

The Medicare program, enacted under Title XVIII (Health Insurance for the Aged) of the Social Security Act (PL 89-97), went into effect on July 1, 1966. The program is composed of two parts:

- Part A provides hospital insurance. Coverage includes physicians' fees, nursing services, meals, semiprivate rooms, special-care units, operating room costs, laboratory tests, and some drugs and supplies. Part A also covers rehabilitation services, limited post-hospital care in a skilled nursing facility, home health care, and hospice care for the terminally ill.

- Part B (Supplemental Medical Insurance, or SMI) is elective medical insurance; that is, enrollees must pay premiums to obtain coverage. SMI covers outpatient physicians' services, diagnostic tests, outpatient hospital services, outpatient physical therapy, speech pathology services, home health services, and medical equipment and supplies.

In 2002 more than $267 million was spent to provide coverage for the forty million persons enrolled in Medicare. (See Table 5.9.) Most Medicare recipients were sixty-five and older; more than half of these older adults were between the ages of sixty-five and seventy-four; a third were between the ages of seventy-five and eighty-four; and 12.1% were eighty-five and older. The CMS estimated that by 2050, sixty-nine million people age sixty-five and older would be eligible for Medicare; of those, fifteen million would be eighty-five or older.

In general, Medicare reimburses physicians on a fee-for-service basis, as opposed to per capita (per head) or per member per month (PMPM). In response to the increasing administrative burden of paperwork, reduced compensation, and delays in reimbursements, some physicians opt out of Medicare participation—they do not provide services under the Medicare program and choose not to accept Medicare patients into their practices. Others still provide services to Medicare beneficiaries but do not "accept assignment," meaning that patients must pay out-of-pocket for services and then seek reimbursement from Medicare.

Because of these problems, the Tax Equity and Fiscal Responsibility Act of 1982 (PL 97-248) authorized a "risk managed care" option for Medicare, based on agreed-upon prepayments. Beginning in 1985, the HCFA (now known as CMS) could contract to pay health care providers, such as HMOs or health care prepayment plans, to serve Medicare and Medicaid patients. These groups are paid a predetermined cost per patient for their services.

Medicare-Risk HMOs Control Costs, but Some Senior Health Plans Do Not Survive

During the 1980s and 1990s the federal government, employers that provided health coverage for retiring employees, and many states sought to control costs by encouraging Medicare and Medicaid beneficiaries to enroll in HMOs. From the early 1980s through the late 1990s "Medicare-risk HMOs" did contain costs because, essentially, the federal government paid the health plans that operated them with fixed fees—a predetermined dollar amount per member per month (PMPM). For this fixed fee, Medicare recipients were to receive a fairly comprehensive, preset array of benefits. PMPM payment provided financial incentives for Medicare-risk HMO physicians to control costs, unlike physicians who were reimbursed on a fee-for-service basis (paid for each visit, procedure, or treatment delivered).

TABLE 5.9

Expenditures for health services and supplies[1] under public programs, by type of expenditure and program, 2002

Program area	All expenditures	Personal health care											Administration	Public health activities
		Total	Hospital care	Physician and clinical services	Dental services	Other professional services	Home health care	Prescription drugs	Other nondurable medical products	Durable medical equipment	Nursing home care	Other personal health care		
		Amount in billions												
Public and private spending	$1,496.3	$1,340.2	$486.5	$339.5	$70.3	$45.9	$36.1	$162.4	$31.7	$18.8	$103.2	$45.8	$105.0	$51.2
All public programs	676.6	592.2	286.4	114.8	4.5	12.6	21.9	36.2	1.6	6.8	66.1	41.2	33.3	51.2
Federal funds	476.5	450.5	229.9	94.7	2.7	8.2	16.2	20.9	1.6	6.6	45.5	24.1	19.0	7.0
State and local funds	200.1	141.7	56.5	20.1	1.8	4.4	5.7	15.4	—	0.2	20.5	17.1	14.3	44.1
Medicare	267.1	259.1	149.2	68.8	0.1	6.4	11.4	2.6	1.6	5.9	12.9	—	8.0	—
Medicaid[2]	249.0	232.4	83.1	24.5	3.7	2.4	8.4	28.4	—	—	50.9	31.0	16.6	—
Federal	146.6	137.0	49.8	14.5	2.1	1.3	4.6	16.5	—	—	30.5	17.8	9.5	—
State and local	102.5	95.4	33.3	10.0	1.6	1.0	3.8	11.9	—	—	20.4	13.3	7.1	—
Other state and local public assistance programs	6.6	6.4	2.4	0.9	0.2	0.1	0.0	2.3	—	0.0	0.2	0.2	0.3	—
Department of Veterans Affairs	22.3	22.2	16.6	1.4	0.0	—	0.2	0.1	—	0.6	2.0	1.3	0.1	—
Department of Defense[3]	17.2	16.7	10.3	3.6	0.0	3.1	—	1.2	—	—	—	1.5	0.6	—
Workers' compensation	30.0	23.2	10.0	9.0	—	0.2	—	1.0	—	0.1	—	—	6.8	—
Federal	0.7	0.7	0.4	0.1	—	—	—	0.0	—	0.0	—	—	0.0	—
State and local	29.3	22.5	9.6	8.9	—	3.0	—	0.9	—	0.1	—	—	6.8	—
State and local hospitals[4]	15.2	15.2	11.0	—	—	—	1.8	—	—	—	—	2.4	—	—
Other public programs for personal health care[5]	18.0	17.0	3.9	6.5	0.5	0.6	0.0	0.6	—	0.2	0.0	4.7	0.9	—
Federal	15.5	14.8	3.7	6.3	0.5	0.3	0.0	0.5	—	0.1	0.0	3.5	0.7	—
State and local	2.4	2.2	0.2	0.2	0.0	0.4	—	0.1	—	0.1	0.0	1.2	0.2	—
Government public health activities	51.2	—	—	—	—	—	—	—	—	—	—	—	—	51.2
Federal	7.0	—	—	—	—	—	—	—	—	—	—	—	—	7.0
State and local	44.1	—	—	—	—	—	—	—	—	—	—	—	—	44.1
CMS programs														
Medicare, Medicaid SCHIP	521.8	496.3	234.1	94.6	4.4	8.9	19.9	31.6	1.6	6.0	63.8	31.4	25.5	—

[1]Includes durable medical products and over-the-counter medicines and sundries.
[2]Excludes funds paid into the Medicare trust funds by states under buy-in-agreements to cover premiums for Medicaid recipients.
[3]Includes care for retirees and military dependents.
[4]Expenditures not offset by revenues.
[5]Includes program spending for Medicaid SCHIP Expansion & SCHIP; maternal and child health; vocational rehabilitation medical payments; temporary disability insurance medical payments; Public Health Service and other Federal hospitals; Indian health services; alcoholism, drug abuse, and mental health; and school health. SCHIP is State Children's Health Insurance Program.
Notes: The figure 0.0 denotes amounts less than $50 million. Numbers may not add to total because of rounding.

SOURCE: "Table 10. Expenditures for Health Services and Supplies under Public Programs, by Type of Expenditure and Program: Calendar Year 2002," Centers for Medicare and Medicaid Services, 2002, http://www.cms.hhs.gov/statistics/nhe/projections-2003/t2.asp (accessed July 6, 2004)

Although Medicare recipients were generally pleased with these HMOs (even when enrolling meant they had to change physicians and thereby end longstanding relationships with their family doctors), many of the health plans did not fare well financially. The health plans suffered for a variety of reasons: some plans had underestimated the service utilization rates of older adults, and some were unable to provide the stipulated range of services as cost effectively as they had believed possible. Other plans found that the PMPM payment was simply not sufficient to enable them to cover all the clinical services and their administrative overhead.

Still, the health plans providing these "senior HMOs" competed fiercely to market to and enroll older adults. Some health plans feared that closing their Medicare-risk programs would be viewed negatively by employer groups, which, when faced with the choice of plans that offered coverage for both younger workers and retirees or one that only covered the younger workers, would choose the plans that covered both. Despite losing money, most health plans maintained their Medicare-risk programs to avoid alienating the employers they depended on to enroll workers who were younger, healthier, and less expensive to serve than the older adults.

About ten years into operations some of the Medicare-risk plans faced a challenge that proved daunting. Their enrollees had aged and required even more health care services than they had previously. For example, a senior HMO member who had joined as a healthy sixty-five-year old could now be a frail seventy-five-year-old with multiple chronic health conditions requiring many costly health services. While the PMPM had increased over the years, for some plans it was simply insufficient to cover their costs. Many Medicare-risk plans, especially those operated by smaller health plans, were forced to end their programs abruptly, leaving thousands of older adults scrambling to join other health plans. Others have endured to year 2004, offering older adults comprehensive care and generating substantial cost savings for employers and the federal government.

The Balanced Budget Act of 1997 produced another plan for Medicare recipients called "Medicare+Choice." These plans offer Medicare beneficiaries a wider range of managed care plan options than just HMOs—older adults may join preferred provider organizations (PPOs) and provider-sponsored organizations (PSOs) that generally offer greater freedom of choice of providers (physicians and hospitals) than available through HMO membership.

Medicaid

Medicaid was enacted by Congress in 1965 under "Grants to States for Medical Assistance Programs," Title XIX of the Social Security Act. It is a joint federal/state program that provides medical assistance to selected cate-gories of low-income Americans: the aged, persons who are blind, persons who are disabled, or financially struggling families with dependent children. Medicaid covers hospitalization, physicians' fees, laboratory and radiology fees, and long-term care in nursing homes.

In 2002 more than forty million people received Medicaid services—an estimated 13% of non-elderly females in the United States and about 11% of the non-elderly male population. Of 249 billion Medicaid dollars spent in 2002, 20.4% went to nursing home care, while 33.4% was spent on hospital care. (See Table 5.9.)

The Personal Responsibility and Work Opportunity Reconciliation Act (PL 104-193)—federal welfare reform—was signed into law in August 1996, replacing the Aid to Families with Dependent Children program (AFDC) with Temporary Assistance for Needy Families (TANF). Under TANF, Medicaid coverage was no longer guaranteed, as it had been for recipients of AFDC. The new law, however, required states to continue benefits to those who would have been eligible under the AFDC requirements that each state had in place on July 16, 1996.

Medicaid is the largest third-party payer of long-term care in the United States, financing about one half of all nursing home care. Under current law, an elderly person must have less than $2,500 in savings or assets (with some exceptions) to qualify for nursing home care paid for by Medicaid. Although home health services currently account for a small share of Medicaid expenditures for older adults, they are the fastest-growing expense.

LONG-TERM HEALTH CARE

One of the most urgent health care problems facing Americans today is the growing need for long-term care. Long-term care refers to health and social services for persons with chronic illnesses or mental or physical conditions so disabling that they cannot live independently without assistance—they require care on a daily basis. Longer life spans and improved life-sustaining technologies are increasing the likelihood that more people than ever before may eventually require costly, long-term care.

Limited and Expensive Options

Caring for chronically ill or elderly patients presents difficult and expensive choices for Americans: they must either provide long-term care at home or rely on nursing homes. Home health care was the fastest-growing segment of the health care industry during the first half of the 1990s. Although the rate of growth slowed during the late 1990s, the Centers for Medicare & Medicaid Services (CMS) project that the home health care sector will double, from $29.6 billion in 2002 to $60 billion in 2013.

The situation for disabled older adults who remain at home can be grim. Nine out of ten must rely on their families for some portion of their care, and 80% rely totally on their families, often creating tremendous financial and emotional strains on the household. Women are usually the caregivers, whether the older adults are their own parents or their in-laws, and sometimes they must sacrifice their jobs and incomes to care for elderly dependents. Hiring an unskilled worker to care for the sick or elderly in the home can cost more than $25,000 a year; skilled in-home care is even more expensive.

High Costs of Nursing Home Care

With the elderly population growing rapidly, the problems of long-term care and its costs have become urgent public policy and social issues. Nursing home care costs about $40,000 per year, and in some homes the costs can exceed $80,000 a year. Medicare does not cover routine nursing home care, and Medicaid is intended to cover expenses only for the poor. A *MetLife Market Survey on Nursing Home and Home Care Costs* (Westport, CT: MetLife Mature Market Institute, April 2002) found that the average daily charge was $168 for a private room and $143 for a semi-private room.

To be eligible for Medicaid, a person must have no more than $2,500 in assets. (In the case of a married couple where only one spouse is in a nursing home, the remaining spouse can retain a house, a car, up to $75,000 in assets, and $2,000 in monthly income.) Many elderly persons must "spend down" to deplete their entire life savings in order to qualify for Medicaid assistance. The term refers to a provision in Medicaid coverage that provides care for seniors whose income exceeds eligibility requirements. If their monthly income is $100 over the state Medicaid eligibility line, they can spend $100 a month on their medical care, and Medicaid will cover the remainder.

Although supplemental "Medigap" policies available through private insurers pay for some costs not covered by Medicare, most of these policies do not cover the average nursing home stay. Many older adults are eager to buy private insurance policies for long-term care. The average policy, covering two years of care after a one-hundred-day waiting period, costs about $300 a month for a couple in which the husband is in his early seventies and the wife in her late sixties. For many older adults with fixed incomes, the cost of long-term care insurance prevents them from obtaining it.

Coverage provided by these private policies varies widely. Some insurers refuse to pay for the first twenty days in a nursing home, and others require a waiting period of one-hundred days before they will pay. Some offer coverage for only one year; others allow longer stays. Because of the variations and limitations on coverage, some policyholders have had their claims denied or their policies cancelled. The purchasers of such policies must be very careful to understand the specific provisions and terms of their benefits.

A combination of federal, state, and private monies finance nursing home care. According to the Administration on Aging (AoA), in 2003 about half of the funds came from Medicaid, 25% were from Medicare, and the balance came from private payment and private insurance.

HIV/AIDS—Treatment Is Costly

HIV/AIDS treatment, like treatment of cancer and other chronic diseases, is expensive. Even though newer drug treatments—highly active antiretroviral therapy (HAART)—had higher per unit costs, their introduction in 1996 reduced total health care spending by reducing the rate of hospitalization and use of outpatient care. According to a study conducted by the Rand Corporation and published in the March 15, 2001, issue of the *New England Journal of Medicine,* the average HIV patient incurred medical costs of about $1,410 per month in 1998. In 1998 a year's worth of treatment for HIV could cost as much as $18,000 per patient. An individual with AIDS could spend up to $77,000 per year on medication alone.

Some HIV/AIDS patients rely on health insurance to help pay these costs, but many patients are not insured. Many policies exclude or deny coverage to persons with pre-existing conditions, and as a result many HIV-positive people are denied private health insurance.

Medicaid pays the costs of approximately half of all adults and nearly 90% of children living with HIV/AIDS, according to the Office of National AIDS Policy, a White House agency. Medicaid eligibility requirements vary from state to state; it generally covers people with incomes of less than $625 per month who cannot engage in substantial gainful employment due to physical or mental impairment that is expected to last at least one year or result in death. Medicaid programs vary widely by jurisdiction; many states supplement federal funding with state funds and each state determines not only the eligibility criteria for its program but also the benefits—the number and type of treatments—provided through the program.

Some expenses, however, have actually been reduced by relocating services from the hospital to a variety of outpatient settings. Examples of cost-saving services include outpatient transfusions and outpatient treatment for opportunistic infections such as *Pneumocystis carinii* pneumonia (PCP) and cryptococcal meningitis. Increased volunteer-based social service programs that enable patients to be cared for at home also serve to prevent prolonged, expensive hospital stays.

Federal government spending on HIV-related care and activities has increased steadily since 1985. In 2002 the Budget Office of the Public Health Service estimated that federal spending for HIV-related expenses was nearly $15 billion, $9.1 billion of which was spent on medical care. Other government costs included research ($2.6 billion), education and prevention ($1.6 billion), and cash assistance ($1.6 billion), which is provided through the Social Security Administration and the Department of Housing and Urban Development.

In fiscal year 2005 an estimated $19.8 billion will be spent on HIV-related care. Nearly 60% of the allocation is for care activities, 9% is for cash and housing assistance, and 12% is for global research, which does not include international research (when international research is included in the global category, it rises to 14%). About half of the budget ($10.1 billion) will fund entitlement programs—Medicaid, Medicare, Social Security disability Insurance (SSDI), and Supplemental Security Income (SSI).

The High Costs of Research

Medical and pharmaceutical research to develop and conduct clinical trials of antiretroviral drugs is expensive. In 2005 the National Institutes of Health (NIH) spent an estimated $2.9 billion for HIV/AIDS research, compared to about $440 million to investigate obesity prevention and treatment.

Decisions about how much is spent to research a particular disease are not based solely on how many people develop the disease or die from it. Rightly or wrongly, economists base the societal value of an individual on his or her earning potential and productivity—the ability to contribute to society as a worker. The bulk of the people who die from heart disease, stroke, and cancer are older adults. Many have retired from the workforce, and their potential economic productivity is usually low or even nil. (This is not an observation about how society values older adults; instead it is simply an economic measure of present and future financial productivity.)

In contrast, AIDS patients are usually much younger, dying in their twenties, thirties, and forties. Until they developed AIDS, their potential productivity, measured in economic terms, was high. The number of work years lost when they die is considerable. Using this economic equation to determine how disease research should be funded, it may be considered economically wise to invest more money to research AIDS since the losses, measured in potential work years rather than lives, is so much greater.

The primary goals of HIV/AIDS therapy are to prolong life and improve its quality. Few researchers expect any drug to cure HIV infection; their objective is to make the virus less deadly by foiling its efforts to reproduce within the body. A major obstacle to the discovery of such treatments is the cost of drug research and development. Pharmaceutical manufacturers spend millions of dollars researching and developing new medicines. According to the Pharmaceutical Research and Manufacturers of America, U.S. pharmaceutical companies spend more money

each year on research and development activities than the annual budget of the NIH.

Once a new drug receives federal Food and Drug Administration (FDA) approval, its manufacturer is ordinarily allowed to hold the patent on the drug in order to recoup its investment. During that time, the drug is priced much higher than if other manufacturers were allowed to compete by producing generic versions of the same drug. After the patent expires, competition between pharmaceutical manufacturers generally lowers the price. In contrast, HIV/AIDS drugs are granted only seven years of exclusivity under legislation aimed at encouraging research and promoting development of new treatments.

The pharmaceutical manufacturer must cover the cost not only of research and development for the approximately three out of ten drugs that succeed, but also for many—seven out of ten—that have failed. In contrast, the producer of generic drugs has the formula and must simply manufacture the drugs properly. The generic manufacturer does not have to pay for successful and unsuccessful research and development of new drugs, nor does it have to pursue the complicated, time-consuming process of seeking and obtaining FDA approval.

Cancer

Cancer, in all its forms, is extremely expensive to treat. Americans often resort to many different methods of treatment in search of a cure. In addition, it can be costly to treat the adverse side effects of radiation, chemotherapy, and other therapies. Pain management is also expensive for cancer patients. The National Institutes of Health (NIH) estimated the overall annual cost of cancer in 2002 as nearly $190 billion, of which $64.2 billion was for direct medical costs. The balance was attributed to indirect costs associated with lost productivity due to illness or death.

Generally, the younger a patient, the higher the cost, since younger patients can often fight the disease longer than older patients can. Most expenses for cancer treatment occur at the end of life: hospitalization for the initial phase of treatment costs only 38% as much as terminal care.

THE HARDSHIP OF HIGH HEALTH CARE COSTS ON FAMILIES

Families USA is a national, nonprofit, nonpartisan consumer organization based in Washington, D.C., dedicated to achieving affordable, quality health care and long-term care for all American families. The organization describes itself as "the voice for American consumers," and contends that American families pay about two-thirds of the nation's health care bill, while American businesses pay the other third. This ratio is based on the premise that families and businesses pay for health care in several ways:

- Directly, through out-of-pocket payments and insurance expenses, such as premiums, deductibles (annual amounts that must be paid by the employee before the insurance plan begins paying), and co-payments

- Indirectly, through Medicare payroll, income, and other federal, state, and local taxes that support public health programs. These include veterans' health benefits, military health benefits, the Medicaid program, and a variety of smaller public health programs.

As a result, Families USA estimates of per capita health spending differ from other reports, such as those from the CMS and the U.S. Census Bureau, which take into account only direct payments.

Families also purchase insurance themselves when they work for employers that do not offer group health insurance, or when insurers refuse to insure certain groups they consider to be at high risk (such as persons with chronic diseases). Workers who retire before reaching age sixty-five and are not yet eligible for Medicare coverage also must purchase insurance on their own. Further, many Medicare beneficiaries pay insurance premiums for supplemental (Medigap) insurance to cover the difference in charges that Medicare does not pay, as well as uncovered costs, such as prescription drugs.

The High Cost of Prescription Drugs

Spending for prescription drugs is the fastest-growing component of health care spending. Families USA decried the escalating costs of prescription drugs in a study that found that between January 2001 and January 2002 the prices of the fifty most commonly prescribed drugs for older adults rose nearly three times the rate of inflation. Since many older adults live on fixed incomes, these dramatic price increases may prevent them from obtaining life-saving medications. The Families USA report *Bitter Pill: The Rising Prices of Prescription Drugs for Older Americans* (Washington, DC, June 2002) observed that drug prices have outpaced inflation for at least a decade and that that generic drug prices rose more slowly than brand-name pharmaceuticals.

Families USA also refuted the pharmaceutical companies' claims that high drug prices simply reflect the companies' efforts to recoup their investments in drug research and development. Families USA asserted that prices for drugs that have been on the market for more than ten years continued to rise more sharply than the rate of inflation, long after the pharmaceutical companies should have regained their initial investments and realized substantial profits. Their 2001 analysis of the nine U.S. pharmaceutical companies that manufacture or market the fifty top-selling drugs for older adults revealed that profits consistently exceeded spending on research and development.

To control prescription drug expenditures, many hospitals, health plans, employers, and other group purchasers have attempted to obtain discounts and rebates for bulk purchases from pharmaceutical companies. Some have developed programs to encourage health care practitioners and consumers to use less costly generic drugs, and others have limited, reduced, or even eliminated prescription drug coverage.

More than half of Americans surveyed think prescription drug prices are high and should be controlled by the government. (See Table 5.10.) Research conducted by Harris Interactive in April 2003 found that 45% of survey respondents felt that prescription drug prices were "much higher here" in the United States than in Canada and Western Europe. Another 18% of respondents believed them to be "somewhat higher here." Just 5% of respondents considered drug prices "somewhat lower here," and 1% called them "much lower here" than in Canada and Europe. (See Table 5.11.)

A January 2004 Harris Interactive survey found that many Americans are aware that prescription drugs cost more in the United States than they do in Europe. Of the survey respondents, 39% felt that prescription drugs were "much more expensive" and 58% said they were merely "more expensive." (See Table 5.12.) Older adults were even more acutely aware of the price differential—very likely because they use and pay for prescription drugs more often than young adults. More than two-thirds (70%) of persons aged sixty-five and older know that prescription drugs cost more in the United States than in Europe and nearly half (49%) know that prescription drugs are "much more expensive" in the United States. (See Table 5.13.)

MANY OLDER ADULTS CANNOT AFFORD PRESCRIPTION DRUGS. A survey of nearly eleven thousand older adults in eight states conducted in 2001 by the Kaiser Family Foundation, the Commonwealth Fund, and Tufts-New England Medical Center found that cost prevented almost one quarter of all survey respondents from filling their prescriptions or caused them to skip doses of prescribed medications. The study also found that the percentage of all older adults surveyed who did not have prescription drug coverage varied among the eight states from highs of 31% in Illinois and Texas to lows of California (18%) and New York (19%).

A 2004 Families USA report, *Sticker Shock: Rising Prescription Drug Prices for Seniors* (Washington, DC, June 2004), predicted that older adults anticipating that the Medicare prescription drug law, enacted in 2003 to take effect in 2006, will afford them significant savings may be disappointed. The report found that the prices of

TABLE 5.10

Public opinion on federal government price controls for prescription drugs, 2003

WOULD YOU FAVOR OR OPPOSE FEDERAL GOVERNMENT PRICE CONTROLS OF... PRESCRIPTION DRUGS?

Base: All adults

	February 2000 %	June 2000 %	June 2001 %	March 2002 %	April 2003 %
Favor federal government price controls of prescription drugs	60	57	61	67	56
Oppose	37	39	34	29	39
Not sure	3	4	5	4	5

TABLE 5.11

Public opinion on prescription drug prices in the United States, Canada, and Western Europe, 2003

HOW DO YOU THINK THE PRICES OF PRESCRIPTION DRUGS IN THIS COUNTRY COMPARE WITH DRUG PRICES IN CANADA AND WESTERN EUROPE? ARE THE PRICES HERE MUCH HIGHER, SOMEWHAT HIGHER, ABOUT THE SAME, SOMEWHAT LOWER OR MUCH LOWER?

Base: All adults

	February 2000 %	June 2000 %	June 2001 %	March 2002 %	April 2003 %
Much higher here	25	29	35	37	45
About the same	8	7	7	4	5
Much lower here	2	2	1	1	1

Note: Columns may not add up to 100% due to rounding.

the top thirty brand-name prescription drugs dispensed to older adults had increased by almost 22% during the three years preceding the January 2004 study. Of the thirty frequently prescribed drugs, twenty-eight increased in price by two or more times the rate of inflation, twenty-one increased in price by three or more times the rate of inflation, and just one drug did not increase in price.

According to the report, the top five brand-name drugs prescribed for seniors rose especially quickly:

• Lipitor, prescribed to lower cholesterol, rose 5.5 times the rate of inflation.

• Plavix, intended to prevent blood clots, rose 5.3 times the rate of inflation.

• Fosamax, prescribed for persons with osteoporosis, rose 4.6 times the rate of inflation.

• Norvasc, used to treat high blood pressure, rose 6.6 times the rate of inflation.

• Celebrex, prescribed to relieve arthritis and joint pain, rose 5.4 times the rate of inflation.

Issued just days before the Medicare drug discount program took effect in June 2004, the report ventured that the one out of six (7.4 million) older adults who participate in this interim measure will continue to pay much higher prices for prescription drugs than they had in years past. The five out of six older adults who do not participate in the drug discount prices will suffer the full force of rapidly rising prescription drug prices. Even when the entire Medicare population is covered by the full implementation of the discount plan in 2006, many older adults will find their prescriptions unaffordable.

RATIONING HEALTH CARE

When health care rationing—allocating medical resources—is defined as "all care that is expected to be beneficial is not always available to all patients," most health care practitioners, policymakers, and consumers accept that rationing has been, and will continue to be, a feature of the American health care system. Most American opinion leaders and industry observers accept that even a country as wealthy as the United States cannot afford all the care that is likely to benefit its citizens. The practical considerations of allocating health care resources involve establishing priorities and determining how these resources should be rationed.

Opponents of Rationing

There is widespread agreement among Americans that rationing according to patients' ability to pay for health care services or insurance is unfair. Ideally, health care should be equitably allocated on the basis of need and the potential benefit derived from the care. Those who argue against rationing fear that society's most vulnerable populations—older adults, the poor, and persons with chronic illnesses—suffer most from the present rationing of health care.

Many observers believe that improving the efficiency of the U.S. health care system would save enough money to supply basic health care services to all Americans. They suggest that since expenditures for the same medical procedures vary greatly in different areas of the country, standardizing fees and costs could realize great savings. They also believe that money could be saved if greater emphasis was placed on preventive care and on effective strategies to prevent or reduce behaviors that increase

TABLE 5.12

Public opinion on the comparative cost of goods in the United States vs. Europe, 2004

HOW DO YOU THINK THE PRICES OF EACH OF THESE ITEMS IN THE UNITED STATES COMPARE WITH THE PRICES IN EUROPE?

Base: All adults

		Much cheaper here	Somewhat cheaper here	About the same	Somewhat more expensive here	Much more expensive here	Not sure	Cheaper here	More expensive here
Gasoline	%	33	20	7	6	8	26	54	14
Food	%	12	26	19	8	4	31	38	11
Clothes	%	9	21	24	9	4	33	30	14
Computers	%	9	19	21	7	3	40	28	11
Automobiles	%	9	17	17	14	7	36	26	21
Cameras	%	5	14	25	11	6	40	18	16
Medical care	%	4	6	5	18	37	30	10	55
Prescription drugs	%	3	4	5	19	39	29	7	58

SOURCE: "Table 1. Perceptions of What Is Cheaper and What Is More Expensive in U.S.A. vs. Europe," in *Health Care News: One Reason Why the Costs of Medical Care and Prescription Drugs are Under Scrutiny,* vol. 4, no. 3, Harris Interactive, March 2, 2004, http://www.harrisinteractive.com/news/newsletters/ healthnews/HI_HealthCareNews2004Vol4_Iss03.pdf (accessed July 7, 2004). © 2004, Harris Interactive Inc. All rights reserved. Reproduced with permission in 2004.

TABLE 5.13

Public opinion among people 65 and older on the comparative cost of goods in the United States vs. Europe, 2004

HOW DO YOU THINK THE PRICES OF EACH OF THESE ITEMS IN THE UNITED STATES COMPARE WITH THE PRICES IN EUROPE?

Base: People 65 and older

		Much cheaper here	Somewhat cheaper here	About the same	Somewhat more expensive here	Much more expensive here	Not sure	Cheaper here	More expensive here
Gasoline	%	45	32	5	1	7	10	76	9
Food	%	18	30	22	10	*	20	48	10
Clothes	%	15	29	28	9	—	18	44	9
Computers	%	12	19	30	8	—	31	31	8
Automobiles	%	16	21	21	15	4	22	37	19
Cameras	%	6	9	39	13	3	30	15	16
Medical care	%	3	14	—	26	40	17	17	66
Prescription drugs	%	7	5	1	21	49	17	12	70

*Less than 0.5%

SOURCE: "Table 2. Perceptions of People 65 and Older of What Is Cheaper and What Is More Expensive in U.S.A. vs. Europe," in *Health Care News: One Reason Why the Costs of Medical Care and Prescription Drugs Are Under Scrutiny,* vol. 4, no. 3, Harris Interactive, March 2, 2004, http://www .harrisinteractive.com/news/newsletters/healthnews/HI_HealthCareNews2004Vol4_Iss03.pdf (accessed July 7, 2004). © 2004, Harris Interactive Inc. All rights reserved. Reproduced with permission in 2004.

health risk such as smoking, alcohol and drug abuse, and unsafe sexual practices. Further, they insist that the high cost of administering the American health system could be streamlined by using a single payer for health care—as in the Canadian system.

Supporters of Rationing

Those who endorse rationing argue that the spiraling cost of health care stems from more than simple inefficiency. They attribute escalating costs to the aging population, rapid technological innovation, and the increasing price tags for labor and supplies.

Not everyone who supports rationing thinks that the U.S. health care system is working well. Some rationing supporters believe that the nation's health care system charges too much for the services it delivers, and that it fails altogether to deliver to millions of uninsured. In fact, they point out that the United States already rations health care by not covering the uninsured. Other health care rationing advocates argue that the problem is one of basic cultural assumptions, not the economics of the health care industry. Americans value human life, believe in the promise of health and quality health care for all, and insist that diseases can be cured. They contend that the issue is not whether health care should be rationed but rather how care is rationed. They believe that the United States spends too much on health compared to other societal needs; too much on the old rather than the young; more on curing and not enough on caring; too much on extending the length of life and not enough on enhancing the quality of life. Supporters of rationing argue instead for a system that guarantees a minimally acceptable level of health care for all, while reining in the expensive excesses of the current system, which often acts to prolong life at any cost.

THE OREGON PLAN. In 1987 the state of Oregon designed a new, universal health care plan that would simultaneously expand coverage and contain costs by limiting services. Unlike other states, which trimmed budgets by eliminating people from Medicaid eligibility, Oregon chose to eliminate low-priority services. The Oregon Health Plan, approved in August 1993, aimed to provide Medicaid to 120,000 additional residents living below the federal poverty level. The plan also established a high-risk insurance pool for persons refused health insurance coverage because of pre-existing medical conditions, offered more insurance options for small businesses, and improved employees' abilities to retain their health insurance benefits when they changed jobs. A 10-cent increase in the state cigarette tax (providing approximately $45 million annually) helped fund the additional estimated $400 million needed over the next several years.

Oregon developed a table of health care services and performed a cost-benefit analysis to rank them. (See Table 5.14.) It was decided that Oregon Medicaid would cover the top 565 services on a list of 696 medical procedures. Services that fell below the cutoff point and thus would not be covered included liver transplants for patients with liver cancer; nutritional counseling for obese people; fertility services; and treatment for the common cold, chronic back pain, and viral hepatitis.

When setting the priorities, disease prevention and quality of life were the factors that most influenced the ranking of the treatments. Quality of life (quality of well being, or QWB, in the Oregon plan) drew fire from those who felt such judgments could not be decided subjectively. Active medical or surgical treatment of terminally ill patients also ranked low on the QWB scale, while comfort and hospice care ranked high. The Oregon Health Services Commission emphasized that their QWB judgments were not based on an individual's quality of life at a given time; such judgments were considered ethically questionable. Instead they focused on the potential for change in an individual's life, posing questions such as, "After treatment, how much better or worse off would the patient be?"

Critics countered that the plan obtained its funding by reducing services that were currently offered to Medicaid recipients (often poor women and children) rather than by emphasizing cost control. Others objected to the ranking and the ethical questions raised by choosing to support some treatments over others.

By 1998 the Oregon Health Plan had encountered major problems. The state was no longer promising universal care; physicians were seeking and finding ways to get around the rationing restrictions; and friction with federal Medicaid regulators was blocking Oregon's efforts to deny more treatments. A plan to require that employers insure all their workers or contribute to a fund to cover them failed. Spend-

TABLE 5.14

Health care service categories and rankings

Rank	Category ID No.
"Essential" Services	
1. Acute fatal, prevents death, full recovery	15
Examples: Repair of deep, open wound of neck. Appendectomy for appendicitis. Medical therapy for myocarditis.	
2. Maternity care (including care for newborn in first 28 days of life)	12
Examples: Obstetrical care for pregnancy. Medical therapy for drug reactions and intoxications specific to newborn. Medical therapy for low birthweight babies.	
3. Acute fatal, prevents death, w/o full recovery	16
Examples: Surgical treatment for head injury with prolonged loss of consciousness. Medical therapy for acute bacterial meningitis. Reduction of an open fracture of a joint.	
4. Preventive care for children	01
Examples: Immunizations. Medical therapy for streptococcal sore throat and scarlet fever (reduces disability, prevents spread). Screening for specific problems such as vision or hearing problems, or anemia.	
5. Chronic fatal, improves life span and QWB (Quality of Well-Being)	20
Examples: Medical therapy for Type I Diabetes Mellitus. Medical and surgical treatment for treatable cancer of the uterus. Medical therapy for asthma.	
6. Reproductive services (excluding maternity and infertility)	13
Examples: Contraceptive management, vasectomy, tubal ligation.	
7. Comfort care	26
Example: Palliative therapy for conditions in which death is imminent.	
8. Preventive dental (children and adults)	03/07
Example: Cleaning and flouride.	
9. Preventive care for adults (A-B-C)	04
Examples: Mammograms, blood pressure screening, medical therapy and chemoprophylaxis for primary tuberculosis.	
"Very Important" Services	
10. Acute nonfatal, return to previous health	17
Examples: Medical therapy for acute thyroiditis. Medical therapy for vaginitis. Restorative dental service for dental caries.	
11. Chronic nonfatal, one time treatment improves QWB	23
Examples: Hip replacement. Laser surgery for diabetic retinopathy. Medical therapy for rheumatic fever.	
12. Acute nonfatal, w/o return to previous health	18
Examples: Relocation of dislocation of elbow. Arthroscopic repair of internal derangement of knee. Repair of corneal laceration.	
13. Chronic nonfatal, repetitive treatment improves QWB	24
Examples: Medical therapy for chronic sinusitis. Medical therapy for migraine. Medical therapy for psoriasis.	
Services "Valuable to Certain Individuals"	
14. Acute nonfatal, expedites recovery	19
Examples: Medical therapy for diaper rash. Medical therapy for acute conjunctivitis. Medical therapy for acute pharyngitis.	
15. Infertility services	14
Examples: Medical therapy for anovulation. Microsurgery for tubal disease. In-vitro fertilization.	
16. Preventive care for adults (D-E)	05
Examples: Dipstick urinalysis for hematuria in adults less than 60 years of age. Sigmoidoscopy for persons less than 40 years of age. Screening of nonpregnant adults for Type I Diabetes Mellitus.	
17. Fatal or nonfatal, minimal or no improvement in QWB (non-self-limited)	25
Examples: Repair fingertip avulsion that does not include fingernail. Medical therapy for gallstones without cholecystitis. Medical therapy for viral warts.	

SOURCE: "Health Care Service Categories and Rankings," in Oregon Basic Health Services Program, February 22, 1991

ing for the health plan climbed to $2.1 billion in the 1997–99 state budget period, up from $1.7 billion in the 1995–97 period. Higher cigarette taxes did not offset the increase, requiring more money from the state's general fund.

The Oregon Health Plan did serve to reduce the percentage of uninsured Oregonians, from 17% in 1992 to

11% in 1996, placing Oregon among the states with the lowest rates of uninsured residents. Still, by 1998, five years after the Oregon plan was initiated with the goal of having no uninsured people in the state, coverage was far from universal. Despite the Oregon plan's best efforts, there were still approximately 350,000 people in Oregon who had no insurance. The plan's supporters observed that the downward trend in the rates of uninsured was a measure of the plan's success and hailed the state's pioneering efforts.

The Oregon Health Services Commission (HSC) continued to modify the plan's covered benefits. The Commission's most recent effort to refine the list of covered services began in January 2002. The HSC sought to reduce the overall costs of the plan by eliminating less effective treatments and determining if any covered medical conditions could be more effectively treated using standardized clinical practice guidelines (step-by-step instructions for diagnosis and treatment of specific illnesses or disorders) while preserving basic coverage. The benefit review process will be ongoing with the HSC submitting a new prioritized list of benefits on July 1 of each even-numbered year for review by legislative assembly.

In 2001 the Oregon Health Plan was given a three-year grant of nearly $1.5 million from the Robert Wood Johnson Foundation, the nation's largest philanthropy devoted solely to health and health care, to help expand coverage to new populations within the state. The grant money acknowledged the success of the Oregon plan and supports statewide research and evaluation as the state moves to cover more people. In June 2004 the Robert Wood Johnson Foundation awarded the Office for Oregon Health Policy & Research (OHPR) a $260,000 grant to study the impacts of the benefit reductions and changes to the Oregon Health Plan. OHPR will collaborate with investigators from Portland State University and the Oregon Health & Science University over the next two years to develop a better understanding of these impacts on access to health care in the state. Researchers will look at shifts such as increased hospital and pharmacy costs resulting from the elimination of outpatient mental health coverage for OHP beneficiaries.

Rationing by HMOs

Until 2000, steadily increasing numbers of Americans received their health care from health maintenance organizations (HMOs) or other managed care systems. According to the Kaiser Family Foundation's *Trends and Indicators in the Changing Health Care Marketplace, 2004 Update,* by 1999 national enrollment in HMOs topped eighty-one million, nearly four times as many as were enrolled just a decade earlier (twenty-one million). The number of enrollees, however, declined during 2000 (78.9 million enrollees) and in July 2003 HMO enroll-ment was down to about seventy-six million. The number of HMOs operating in the United States also dropped from 560 in July 2000 to 500 in 2003.

Managed care programs have sought to control costs by limiting coverage for expensive experimental, duplicative, and unnecessary treatments. Before physicians can perform experimental procedures or prescribe new treatment plans, they must obtain prior authorization—approval from the patient's managed care plan to ensure that the expenses will be covered.

Increasingly, patients and physicians are battling HMOs for approval to use and receive reimbursement for new technology and experimental treatments. Judges and juries, moved by the desperate situations of patients, have generally decided cases against HMOs, regardless of whether the new treatment had been shown to be effective.

"SILENT RATIONING." Physicians and health care consumers are concerned that limiting coverage for new, high-cost technology will discourage research and development for new treatments before they have even been developed. This has been called "silent rationing," because patients will never know what they have missed.

While new technology is thought to contribute heavily to the growth of the nation's health care bill, its precise toll is unknown. Some estimates have put the share at 30–50%. Yet new technologies often save money by increasing the efficiency and effectiveness of medical care. These savings may, however, be offset when the new technology increases the volume of services delivered, resulting in an increase in total spending.

In an effort to control costs, some HMOs have discouraged physicians from informing patients about certain treatment options—those that are very expensive or not covered by the HMO. This has proved to be a highly controversial issue, both politically and ethically. In December 1996 HHS ruled that HMOs and other health plans cannot prevent physicians from telling Medicare patients about all available treatment options.

IS LESS HEALTH CARE BETTER THAN MORE? Although health care providers and consumers fear that rationing that sharply limits access to medical care will ultimately result in poorer health among affected Americans, researchers are also concerned about the effects of too much care on the health of the nation. Several recent studies suggest that an oversupply of medical care may be as harmful as an under-supply. They assert that supply appears to drive demand—in areas with more physicians and hospitals, people visit physicians more often and spend more days in hospitals with no apparent improvement in their health status.

Dr. John E. Wennberg, a physician and epidemiologist, and his colleagues at Dartmouth Medical School found tremendous regional variation in both utilization and the cost of health care that the researchers believe is explained, at least in part, by the distribution of health care providers. In an article published in the March 2002 issue of *Health Affairs,* Dr. Wennberg also suggests that variations in physicians' practice styles—whether they favor outpatient treatment over hospitalization for specific procedures such as biopsies (surgical procedures to examine tissue to detect cancer cells)—greatly affects demand for hospital care.

Variation in demand for health care services in turn produces variation in health care expenditures. Dr. Wennberg and his colleagues reported wide geographic variation in Medicare spending. Medicare paid more than twice as much to care for a sixty-five-year-old in Miami where the supply of health care providers is overabundant as it spent on care for a sixty-five-year-old in Minneapolis, a city with an average supply of health care providers. To be certain that the difference was not simply higher fees and charges in Miami, the investigators also compared rates of utilization and found that older adults in Miami visited physicians and hospitals much more often than their counterparts in Minneapolis.

The researchers also wanted to be sure that the differences were not caused by the severity of illness, so they compared care during the last six months of life to control for any underlying regional differences in the health of the population. Remarkably, the widest variations were observed in care during the last six months of life when older adults in Miami saw physician specialists six times as often as those in Minneapolis. Dr. Wennberg, who has studied variations in health service utilization for more than two decades, asserted that higher expenditures, particularly at the end of life, do not purchase better care. Instead, they finance generally unpleasant and futile interventions intended to prolong life rather than improve the quality of patients' lives.

The researchers concluded that areas with more medical care, higher utilization, and higher costs fared no better in terms of life expectancy, morbidity, or mortality, and the care they received was no different in quality from care received by persons in areas with average supplies of health care providers. The Dartmouth research and similar studies pose two important and as yet unanswered questions: "How much health care is needed to deliver the best health to a population?" and "Are Americans getting the best value for the dollars spent on health care?"

CHAPTER 6

INSURANCE—THOSE WITH AND THOSE WITHOUT

In 1798 Congress established the U.S. Marine Hospital Services for seamen. It was the first time an employer offered health insurance in the United States. Payments for hospital services were deducted from the sailors' salaries.

In the twenty-first century, many factors affect the availability of health insurance, including employment, income, personal health status, and age. As a result, an individual's or family's health insurance status often changes as circumstances change. In 2002 nearly seven of every ten Americans (69.6%) were covered during all or some part of the year by private insurance, mostly through their employers (61.3%). Medicare, the government's health insurance program for older adults and persons with disabilities, covered 13.4% of Americans, and Medicaid, the government health insurance program for the poor, covered 11.6%. (See Figure 6.1.) (Note that percentages come close to 100% because some persons are covered by more than one type of insurance program, yet in 2002 15.2% of people were not covered by any type of insurance.)

In 2002 the 15.2% of the American population without health coverage constituted a slight increase from the 14.6% uninsured in 2001, but a decrease from the 16.3% uninsured in 1998. (See Table 6.1.) The year 1998 was the first year since 1987 that the share of the population without health insurance declined. In the eleven-year period from 1987 (the first year comparable health statistics were available) to 1998, the uninsured rate either increased or remained unchanged from one year to the next. The number of uninsured children dropped in 2000, from 12.6% in 1999 to 11.6% (Robert J. Mills, "Health Insurance Coverage in the United States: 2000," in *Current Population Reports,* U.S. Census Bureau, September 2001).

According to the Centers for Disease Control and Prevention (CDC), 2003 marked the second consecutive yearly rise in the number of American adults without health insurance coverage. The percentage of uninsured adults rose to 20.1%, up from 19.1% in 2002. The proportion of uninsured adults in 2003 was 6.3% higher than in 1997, the peak of the U.S. economic boom and the first year for which these data were made available. Fewer children were uninsured—the percentage of uninsured children fell to 10.1% in 2003 compared to 13.9% in 1997. (See Figure 6.2.)

WHO WAS UNINSURED IN 2002 AND 2003?

Not surprisingly, the poor were the income group most likely to be without insurance coverage. In 2002, 30.4% of the nation's poor went without insurance. (See Table 6.2.) Across every demographic category—age, race, citizenship status, education, and work experience—higher proportions of the nation's poor were uninsured in 2002.

According to the U.S. Census Bureau 2002 and 2003 annual social and economic supplements to the Current Population Survey, almost eighty-two million people in the United States, or one in three people under age sixty-five, had no health insurance for at least one month during the past two years. Nearly two-thirds of the uninsured were without coverage for at least six months during 2002 and 2003, and just over half went without benefits for at least nine months.

The same U.S. Census data revealed that the proportion of people who did not have health insurance ranged from about 8.0% in Minnesota, Rhode Island, Wisconsin, and Iowa to 24.1% in Texas, based on three-year averages. New Mexico was the only state where the proportion of people without health coverage fell. In 2003 California had the greatest number of people without health insurance—11.9 million. Texas came in second with 8.5 million, followed by New York with 5.6 million.

Gender, Age, and Race/Ethnicity

More males than females lacked insurance in 2002—16.7% of males lacked insurance, compared to 13.9% of

FIGURE 6.1

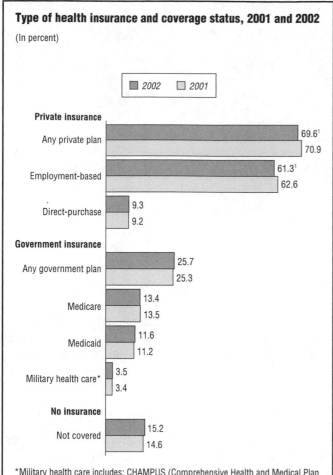

Type of health insurance and coverage status, 2001 and 2002

(In percent)

Legend: ■ 2002 □ 2001

Private insurance

Any private plan
- 69.6[1]
- 70.9

Employment-based
- 61.3[1]
- 62.6

Direct-purchase
- 9.3
- 9.2

Government insurance

Any government plan
- 25.7
- 25.3

Medicare
- 13.4
- 13.5

Medicaid
- 11.6
- 11.2

Military health care*
- 3.5
- 3.4

No insurance

Not covered
- 15.2
- 14.6

*Military health care includes: CHAMPUS (Comprehensive Health and Medical Plan for Uniformed Services)/Tricare and CHAMPVA (Civilian Health and Medical Program of the Department of Veterans Affairs), as well as care provided by the Veterans Administration and the military.
Note: The estimates by type of coverage are not mutually exclusive; people can be covered by more than one type of health insurance during the year.

SOURCE: Robert J. Mills and Shailesh Bhanderi, "Figure 1. Type of Health Insurance and Coverage Status: 2001 and 2002," in *Health Insurance Coverage in the United States: 2002,* U.S. Census Bureau, September 2003, http://www.census.gov/prod/2003pubs/p60-223.pdf (accessed July 10, 2004)

FIGURE 6.2

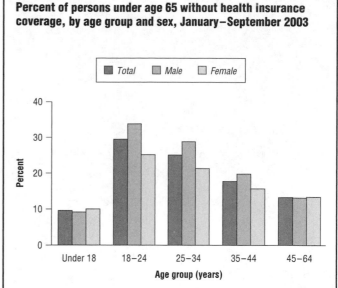

Percent of persons under age 65 without health insurance coverage, by age group and sex, January–September 2003

Legend: ■ Total ■ Male □ Female

Notes: A person was defined as uninsured if he or she did not have any private health insurance, Medicare, Medicaid, State Children's Health Insurance Program (SCHIP), State-sponsored or other government-sponsored health plan, or military plan at the time of the interview. A person was also defined as uninsured if he or she had only Indian Health Service coverage or had only a private plan that paid for one type of service such as accidents or dental care. The analyses excluded 793 persons (1.3%) with unknown health insurance status. The data on health insurance status were edited using an automated system based on logic checks and keyword searches.

SOURCE: "Percent of Persons under Age 65 Years without Health Insurance Coverage, by Age Group and Sex: United States, January–September 2003," in *Early Release of Selected Estimates Based on Data From the January–September 2003 National Health Interview Survey,* Centers for Disease Control and Prevention, March 2004, http://www.cdc.gov/nhis/200403_01.pdf (accessed July 6, 2004)

females. (See Table 6.1.) As would be expected, those age sixty-five and over were most likely to be covered by insurance, since almost all of them qualified for Medicare. (Some older adults also qualified for Medicaid.) Less than 1% of those over sixty-five went without health insurance in 2002. Persons eighteen to twenty-four years of age were the least likely to have insurance coverage—29.6% of Americans in that age group lacked health insurance in 2002. Persons who were foreign-born were more likely than those born in the United States to be uninsured (33.4 versus 12.8%), and among persons who were foreign-born, those who were not citizens were most likely to be uninsured (43.3%).

Effects of Education Level, Income, and Employment

Education levels and health coverage are closely related. Generally, the better educated a person, the more likely he or she is to have a job that offers health insurance and other benefits. In 2002 those who had not completed high school were more than three times as likely to be uninsured as those who held a bachelor's or higher degree (28% versus 8.4%). (See Table 6.1.)

As household income increases, the chances of being uninsured drop dramatically. Table 6.1 shows the 2002 percentages of uninsured persons according to income level and other selected characteristics. While only 8.2% of individuals with an income of $75,000 or more lacked insurance, 23.5% of those with incomes under $25,000 were uninsured. The same was true in 1999—only 7% of high-income individuals were uninsured, while 23.2% of Americans in the lowest income bracket went without insurance.

Not surprisingly, persons who worked full-time were most likely to have health insurance. In 2002 about 17% of full-time workers were uninsured, compared to 23.5% of part-time workers and 25.7% of those who did not work. (See Table 6.1.)

About 55.2% of workers age eighteen to sixty-four had insurance coverage through their employers. Large companies were more likely to provide health insurance

TABLE 6.1

People without health insurance for the entire year, by selected characteristics, 2001 and 2002

(Numbers in thousands)

Characteristic	2001 Total	2001 Uninsured Number	2001 Uninsured Percent*	2002 Total	2002 Uninsured Number	2002 Uninsured Percent	Change 2002 less 2001* Uninsured Number	Change 2002 less 2001* Uninsured Percent
People								
Total	282,082	41,207	14.6	28,593	43,574	15.2	2,367	0.6
Sex								
Male	137,871	21,722	15.8	139,876	23,327	16.7	1,606	0.9
Female	144,211	19,485	13.5	146,057	20,246	13.9	761	0.4
Age								
Under 18 years	72,628	8,509	11.7	73,312	8,531	11.6	22	−0.1
18 to 24 years	27,312	7,673	28.1	27,438	8,128	29.6	456	1.5
25 to 34 years	38,670	9,051	23.4	39,243	9,769	24.9	718	1.5
35 to 44 years	44,284	7,131	16.1	44,074	7,781	17.7	650	1.6
45 to 64 years	65,419	8,571	13.1	67,633	9,106	13.5	535	0.4
65 years and over	33,769	272	0.8	34,234	258	0.8	−14	−0.1
Nativity								
Native	249,629	30,364	12.2	252,463	32,388	12.8	2,023	0.7
Foreign born	32,453	10,843	33.4	33,471	11,186	33.4	343	—
Naturalized citizen	11,962	2,060	17.2	12,837	2,251	17.5	191	0.3
Not a citizen	20,491	8,782	42.9	20,634	8,935	43.3	153	0.4
Region								
Northeast	53,300	6,399	12.0	54,139	7,057	13.0	658	1.0
Midwest	63,779	6,840	10.7	64,581	7,533	11.7	694	0.9
South	100,652	16,712	16.6	101,800	17,773	17.5	1,061	0.9
West	64,351	11,257	17.5	65,413	11,210	17.1	46	−0.4
Household income								
Less than $25,000	62,209	14,474	23.3	62,979	14,776	23.5	302	0.2
$25,000 to $49,999	76,226	13,516	17.7	75,927	14,638	19.3	1,122	1.5
$50,000 to $74,999	58,114	6,595	11.3	58,622	6,904	11.8	309	0.4
$75,000 or more	85,532	6,623	7.7	88,406	7,256	8.2	633	0.5
Education (18 years and older)								
Total	209,454	32,698	15.6	0.2	212,622	35,042	2,344	0.9
No high school diploma	35,423	9,776	27.6	0.7	34,829	9,768	−8	0.4
High school graduate only	66,682	11,618	17.4	0.3	67,512	12,671	1,053	1.3
Some college, no degree	40,282	5,815	14.4	0.5	41,319	6,214	398	0.6
Associate degree	16,183	1,754	10.8	0.7	16,350	1,981	226	1.3
Bachelor's degree or higher	50,884	3,734	7.3	0.3	52,612	4,408	674	1.0
Work experience (18 to 64 years old)								
Total	175,685	32,426	18.5	0.3	178,388	34,785	2,359	1.0
Worked during year	142,474	24,230	17.0	0.3	142,918	25,679	1,449	1.0
Worked full-time	118,776	19,014	16.0	0.3	118,411	19,911	897	0.8
Worked part-time	23,698	5,216	22.0	0.7	24,506	5,767	552	1.5
Did not work	33,211	8,197	24.7	0.7	35,470	9,106	909	1.0

— Represents zero or rounds to zero.
*Details may not sum to totals because of rounding.

SOURCE: Robert J. Mills and Shailes Bhanderi, "Table 1. People without Health Insurance for the Entire Year by Selected Characteristics: 2001 and 2002," in *Health Insurance Coverage in the United States: 2002,* U.S. Census Bureau, September 2003, http://www.census.gov/prod/2003pubs/p60-223.pdf (accessed July 10, 2004)

coverage than were smaller firms. Employees of firms with one thousand or more workers were more than twice as likely to receive health insurance benefits as those in firms with twenty-five or fewer employees (68.7 and 30.8%, respectively). (See Figure 6.3.) Many small firms cannot afford health insurance for their employees. Insurers charge higher premiums for small firms because of the higher per person administrative costs of small groups.

The Consequences and Impact of Uninsured Americans

A report prepared for the Kaiser Commission on Medicaid and the Uninsured, "Sicker and Poorer: The Consequences of Being Uninsured" (Jack Hadley, *The*

TABLE 6.2

People in poverty without health insurance for the entire year, by selected characteristics, 2001 and 2002

(Numbers in thousands.)

Characteristic	2001			2002			Change 2002 less 2001*	
		Uninsured			Uninsured			Uninsured	
	Total	Number	Percent*	Total	Number	Percent	Number	Percent
People								
Total	32,907	10,093	30.7	34,570	10,492	30.4	399	−0.3
Sex								
Male	14,327	4,854	33.9	15,162	5,042	33.3	188	−0.6
Female	18,580	5,239	28.2	19,408	5,450	28.1	211	−0.1
Age								
Under 18 years	11,733	2,497	21.3	12,133	2,434	20.1	−62	−1.2
18 to 24 years	4,449	2,025	45.5	4,536	1,991	43.9	−34	−1.6
25 to 34 years	4,255	2,108	49.5	4,674	2,273	48.6	165	−0.9
35 to 44 years	3,822	1,703	44.6	4,087	1,882	46.0	178	1.5
45 to 64 years	5,234	1,669	31.9	5,564	1,844	33.1	175	1.2
65 years and over	3,414	91	2.7	3,576	67	1.9	−23	−0.8
Nativity								
Native	27,698	7,223	26.1	29,012	7,418	25.6	196	−0.5
Foreign born	5,209	2,870	55.1	5,558	3,074	55.3	204	0.2
Naturalized citizen	1,186	377	31.8	1,285	449	35.0	72	3.2
Not a citizen	4,023	2,493	62.0	4,273	2,625	61.4	132	−0.5
Region								
Northeast	5,687	1,504	26.4	5,871	1,394	23.7	−110	−2.7
Midwest	5,966	1,546	25.9	6,616	1,798	27.2	252	1.3
South	13,515	4,366	32.3	14,019	4,617	32.9	252	0.6
West	7,739	2,677	34.6	8,064	2,682	33.3	5	−1.3
Education (18 years and older)								
Total	21,174	7,596	35.9	22,437	8,058	35.9	461	—
No high school diploma	8,033	2,992	37.2	8,221	3,113	37.9	122	0.6
High school graduate only	7,029	2,523	35.9	7,487	2,728	36.4	205	0.5
Some college, no degree	3,392	1,194	35.2	3,678	1,231	33.5	37	−1.7
Associate degree	886	314	35.4	929	301	32.3	−13	−3.1
Bachelor's degree or higher	1,832	574	31.3	2,122	684	32.3	−13	−3.1
Work experience (18 to 64 years old)								
Total	17,760	7,506	42.3	18,861	7,990	42.4	485	0.1
Worked during year	8,172	3,978	48.7	8,608	4,080	47.4	102	−1.3
Worked full-time	5,121	2,575	50.3	5,277	2,603	49.3	28	−1.0
Worked part-time	3,051	1,403	46.0	3,331	1,477	44.4	74	−1.6
Did not work	9,588	3,528	36.8	10,253	3,910	38.1	382	1.3

— Represents zero or rounds to zero.
*Details may not sum to totals because of rounding.

SOURCE: Robert J. Mills and Shailesh Bhanderi, "Table 2. People in Poverty without Health Insurance for the Entire Year by Selected Characteristics: 2001 and 2002," in *Health Insurance Coverage in the United States: 2002*, U.S. Census Bureau, September 2003, http://www.census.gov/prod/2003pubs/p60-223.pdf (accessed July 10, 2004)

Cost of Not Covering the Uninsured Project, Washington, DC: The Urban Institute, May 2002, updated May 2003), contained an exhaustive review of the literature detailing the major findings of more than twenty-five years of health services research on the effects of health insurance. The report found that the uninsured receive less preventive care, are diagnosed at more advanced stages of disease, and receive less treatment as measured in terms of pharmaceutical and surgical interventions.

In addition to receiving less medical care and treatment, uninsured persons often pay more for medical care. In a June 25, 2004, article, "Uninsured Patients Pay Far More for Care," (Associated Press, http//www.CNN.com), Lara Jakes Jordan reported that hospitals routinely overcharge persons without health insurance—as much as four times more than insured hospital patients are charged. The overcharging is attributed to hospitals' efforts to recoup the costs of providing care to persons who are indigent.

The Kaiser Commission report also concluded that if the uninsured were provided with health insurance, their mortality rates would be reduced by between 10 and 15%. The reduction in mortality would largely result from improved access to timely and appropriate care. This finding supports the Institute of Medicine (IOM) estimate that eighteen thou-

FIGURE 6.3

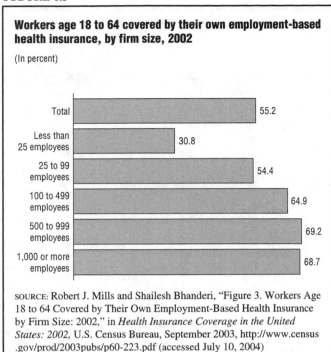

Workers age 18 to 64 covered by their own employment-based health insurance, by firm size, 2002

(In percent)

SOURCE: Robert J. Mills and Shailesh Bhanderi, "Figure 3. Workers Age 18 to 64 Covered by Their Own Employment-Based Health Insurance by Firm Size: 2002," in *Health Insurance Coverage in the United States: 2002*, U.S. Census Bureau, September 2003, http://www.census.gov/prod/2003pubs/p60-223.pdf (accessed July 10, 2004)

sand Americans die each year because they lack health insurance. Further, better health would enable uninsured persons to improve their annual earnings by 10 to 30% and would also act to increase their educational attainment.

SOURCES OF HEALTH INSURANCE

Persons under Age Sixty-five

For persons under age sixty-five, there are two principal sources of health insurance coverage: private insurance (from employers or private policies) and Medicaid (the government program for low-income or disabled persons). From 1989 to 1999 the proportion of those covered by private insurance declined from 75.9 to 72.8%. (See Table 6.3.) During this time the percentage covered by Medicaid increased (from 7.2% in 1989 to 9.1% in 1999) and the proportion of uninsured increased (from 15.6% in 1989 to 16.1% in 1999). (See Table 6.4 and Table 6.5.) The percentage of those privately insured remained between 70.7 and 71.5% in the years from 1997 to 2001, while those on Medicaid increased (from 9.7% in 1997 to 10.4% in 2001). Persons under age sixty-five without health insurance accounted for 16.1% of the population in 2001, down from 17.5% in 1997. (See Table 6.5.)

In 2001 the National Center for Health Statistics estimated that about 71.5% of the under-sixty-five population had private health insurance policies, with 67% covered through the workplace, a decrease from the 68% covered by employers in 1999. (See Table 6.3.) Although the percentage of persons who received health insurance coverage through the workplace rose slowly from 1995 to

1999, it did not rise to levels observed during the 1980s when close to 70% of workers obtained private insurance through their employers. Considerable variation by geographic region persists, with workers in the Northeast (73%) more likely to receive private insurance at the workplace than those in the South (61.8%) in 2001.

Three major factors contributed to the long-term decline in private health insurance. The first is the rising cost of health care, which frequently leads to greater cost sharing between employers and employees. Some workers simply cannot afford the higher premiums and co-payments (the share of medical bills the employee pays for each health service). A second factor is the shift in American commerce from the goods-producing sector, where health benefits have traditionally been provided, to the service sector, where many employers do not offer health insurance.

A third factor is the changing nature of the relationship between employers and employees. In the past many companies took a paternalistic (fatherly) approach to employee welfare to promote a healthy workforce and foster employee loyalty. Since the mid-1990s many companies have assumed less responsibility for their workers' health and have found that measures to cut health care costs effectively reduce business expenditures ("Sources of Health Insurance and Characteristics of the Uninsured," *EBRI Issue Brief*, no. 170, February 1996).

RACE AND ETHNICITY. In the under-sixty-five age group, more than three-fourths of non-Hispanic whites (79.2%) had private health insurance in 2001, down from 82.4% in 1984. More than half (57.6%) of non-Hispanic African-Americans had private health insurance policies in 2001, while 59.4% were insured in 1984. In 2001 more than two-thirds (72.1%) of Asians had private policies, an increase from the 70.9% covered in 1984.

The most dramatic drop in private coverage was among Hispanics. In 2001 less than half (47.6%) of Hispanic-Americans had private health insurance coverage, down from 57.1% in 1984. (See Table 6.3.)

INCOME AND LOCATION. Persons under sixty-five with higher incomes in 2001 were more likely to have private health insurance. All income levels, however, were less likely to have private insurance than in 1984. In 1984 more than half (61.8%) of individuals living at 100–149% of the poverty level had private insurance; by 2001 the proportion sank to 39.6%. For people earning 200% or more above the poverty line, 92.3% were covered by private insurance in 1984, compared to 88.4% in 2001. (See Table 6.3.)

From 1984 to 2001 all geographic regions showed overall decreases in the percentage of persons under sixty-five covered by private health insurance, along with corresponding increases in the percentages of unin-

TABLE 6.3

Private health insurance coverage among persons under 65 years of age, by selected characteristics, selected years 1984–2001

[Data are based on household interviews of a sample of the civilian noninstitutionalized population]

Characteristic	1984	1989	1995	1996	1997[1]	1998	1999	2000	2001
					Number in millions				
Total[2]	157.5	162.7	164.2	165.6	165.8	170.8	174.3	173.0	174.1
					Percent of population				
Total, age adjusted[2,3]	77.1	76.2	71.6	71.5	70.9	72.3	72.9	71.7	71.5
Total, crude[2]	76.8	75.9	71.3	71.2	70.7	72.1	72.8	71.7	71.5
Age									
Under 18 years	72.6	71.8	65.2	66.2	66.1	68.4	68.8	67.0	66.7
Under 6 years	68.1	67.9	59.5	60.8	61.3	64.7	64.7	63.1	63.4
6–17 years	74.9	74.0	68.3	68.9	68.5	70.2	70.9	68.9	68.3
18–44 years	76.5	75.5	70.9	70.5	69.4	71.1	72.0	70.9	70.6
18–24 years	67.4	64.5	60.8	60.3	59.3	61.5	63.2	60.9	60.9
25–34 years	77.4	75.9	70.1	69.4	68.1	70.6	71.2	70.6	70.8
35–44 years	83.9	82.7	77.7	77.4	76.4	76.9	77.9	77.1	76.3
45–64 years	83.3	82.5	80.1	79.4	79.0	79.0	79.3	78.7	78.6
45–54 years	83.3	83.4	80.9	80.4	80.4	80.0	80.4	80.0	79.4
55–64 years	83.3	81.6	79.0	78.0	76.9	77.3	77.7	76.6	77.3
Sex[3]									
Male	77.7	76.5	72.1	71.9	71.2	72.5	73.0	72.1	71.7
Female	76.5	75.9	71.1	71.1	70.6	72.1	72.8	71.4	71.3
Race[3,4]									
White only	80.1	79.3	74.7	74.5	74.3	75.9	76.8	75.8	75.2
Black or African American only	59.2	58.7	54.9	55.9	56.1	55.9	58.1	56.9	57.4
American Indian and Alaska Native only	#	#	#	#	#	#	41.3	44.2	49.4
Asian only	70.9	71.6	68.4	68.3	68.2	72.2	73.2	71.9	72.1
Native Hawaiian and other Pacific Islander only	—	—	—	—	—	—	*	*	*
2 or more races	—	—	—	—	—	—	63.5	63.1	62.6
Hispanic origin and race[3,4]									
Hispanic or Latino	57.1	53.2	48.0	48.2	47.9	49.9	50.3	49.0	47.6
Mexican	54.9	48.5	44.3	44.3	43.9	45.6	48.0	46.6	45.0
Puerto Rican	51.0	46.8	48.9	52.4	48.2	52.7	51.4	52.6	51.5
Cuban	72.1	70.0	63.4	65.6	70.7	71.7	71.4	63.6	66.1
Other Hispanic or Latino	62.0	62.4	52.9	53.2	51.2	52.8	53.4	51.6	50.5
Not Hispanic or Latino	78.9	78.6	74.6	74.6	74.1	75.5	76.3	75.1	75.2
White only	82.4	82.5	78.6	78.6	78.0	79.6	80.3	79.3	79.2
Black or African American only	59.4	58.8	55.3	56.3	56.3	56.1	58.2	57.0	57.6
Age and percent of poverty level[5]									
All ages:[3]									
Below 100 percent	33.0	27.5	23.0	21.8	23.4	24.1	26.1	25.8	25.6
100–149 percent	61.8	54.2	47.9	46.6	42.0	43.3	40.1	39.5	39.6
150–199 percent	77.2	70.6	65.2	65.8	63.6	61.4	59.4	58.4	57.0
200 percent or more	91.6	91.0	88.4	88.4	87.6	88.3	88.7	87.2	87.1
Under 18 years									
Below 100 percent	28.7	22.3	16.9	17.0	17.3	18.9	19.5	18.9	16.7
100–149 percent	66.2	59.6	48.5	48.5	42.5	45.8	40.4	37.9	39.4
150–199 percent	80.9	75.9	67.4	72.1	66.8	66.5	61.6	59.8	56.9
200 percent or more	92.3	92.7	89.5	89.8	88.9	89.9	90.4	88.0	88.4
Geographic region[3]									
Northeast	80.7	82.1	75.5	75.4	74.3	76.4	77.1	76.5	76.5
Midwest	80.9	81.7	77.5	78.7	77.3	79.1	80.2	78.9	78.1
South	74.5	71.7	67.1	66.5	67.5	67.8	68.0	67.0	66.3
West	72.3	71.8	68.1	67.7	65.8	67.8	68.9	67.1	68.6
Location of residence[3]									
Within MSA[6]	77.8	76.8	72.5	72.9	71.5	73.2	74.3	72.7	72.6
Outside MSA[6]	75.5	74.0	68.1	66.3	68.5	68.9	67.8	67.7	66.9

sured and Medicaid recipients. In 2001 persons in the South and West were least likely to have private insurance and the most likely to be uninsured. In 1984 and in 2001 more people living within metropolitan statistical areas (large cities and their surrounding suburbs) had private insurance than did those living in rural areas. (See Table 6.3.)

Accompanying the declines in private health insurance for those under sixty-five from 1984 to 2001 was the significant increase in the proportion of individuals receiving Medicaid health benefits at all income levels. Most surprising was the sharp increase in Medicaid participation by people living above the poverty level—persons who qualify for the federal program as a result of their disabilities. (See Table 6.4.)

TABLE 6.3

Private health insurance coverage among persons under 65 years of age, by selected characteristics, selected years 1984–2001 [CONTINUED]

[Data are based on household interviews of a sample of the civilian noninstitutionalized population]

Characteristic	Private insurance obtained through workplace[7]								
	1984	1989	1995	1996	1997[1]	1998	1999	2000	2001
	Number in millions								
Total[2]	141.8	146.3	150.7	151.1	155.6	159.3	162.6	161.6	163.1
	Percent of population								
Total, age adjusted[2,3]	69.2	68.4	65.6	65.2	66.5	67.4	68.1	67.0	67.0
Total, crude[2]	69.1	68.3	65.4	65.0	66.3	67.3	68.0	67.0	67.0
Age									
Under 18 years	66.5	65.8	60.4	60.8	62.7	64.1	64.6	63.1	63.2
Under 6 years	62.1	62.3	55.1	56.2	58.2	60.9	60.8	59.2	59.6
6–17 years	68.7	67.7	63.3	63.2	64.9	65.7	66.5	65.0	64.9
18–44 years	69.6	68.4	65.3	64.6	65.5	66.5	67.7	66.5	66.3
18–24 years	58.7	55.3	53.5	52.2	54.7	55.7	57.8	55.5	55.8
25–34 years	71.2	69.5	65.0	64.3	64.5	66.7	67.2	66.6	66.7
35–44 years	77.4	76.2	72.7	71.9	72.6	72.5	73.8	72.8	72.2
45–64 years	71.8	71.6	72.2	71.4	72.6	72.7	72.7	72.5	72.5
45–54 years	74.6	74.4	74.7	73.9	75.4	75.1	75.1	75.3	74.5
55–64 years	69.0	68.3	68.4	67.5	68.3	69.1	69.2	68.1	69.4
Sex[3]									
Male	70.1	68.9	66.3	65.7	66.9	67.6	68.1	67.4	67.1
Female	68.4	67.9	65.0	64.7	66.1	67.2	67.2	66.6	66.8
Race[3,4]									
White only	72.0	71.2	68.5	67.8	69.6	70.8	71.6	70.8	70.3
Black or African American only	53.3	53.6	51.1	52.7	53.9	53.2	55.4	54.1	55.1
American Indian and Alaska Native only	#	#	#	#	#	#	38.4	42.0	47.3
Asian only	64.4	60.2	59.8	59.4	61.7	63.8	65.3	64.9	65.7
Native Hawaiian and other Pacific Islander only	—	—	—	—	—	—	*	*	*
2 or more races	—	—	—	—	—	—	59.9	61.2	58.6
Hispanic origin and race[3,4]									
Hispanic or Latino	52.9	48.6	44.6	44.4	45.1	46.8	47.3	46.1	45.0
Mexican	51.7	45.6	42.3	41.3	42.1	43.4	45.4	44.3	43.1
Puerto Rican	48.3	43.4	45.6	49.8	46.1	50.2	48.3	50.6	48.4
Cuban	57.6	56.3	53.8	54.7	58.1	60.3	63.7	53.5	56.7
Other Hispanic or Latino	57.7	55.7	47.7	48.2	48.2	49.4	50.0	48.0	48.0
Not Hispanic or Latino	70.7	70.5	68.3	67.9	69.4	70.3	71.1	70.1	70.4
White only	74.0	74.0	72.1	71.5	73.1	74.2	74.8	73.9	74.0
Black or African American only	53.4	53.7	51.5	53.1	54.1	53.4	55.5	54.2	55.3
Age and percent of poverty level[5]									
All ages:[3]									
Below 100 percent	23.8	19.7	17.6	16.7	19.9	19.8	22.2	21.2	22.0
100–149 percent	51.1	45.0	41.7	40.4	37.3	38.5	35.9	35.0	35.0
150–199 percent	68.6	61.9	58.6	58.9	59.0	55.7	53.9	53.6	52.3
200 percent or more	85.0	83.9	82.4	81.8	83.6	83.7	84.5	83.1	82.9
Under 18 years									
Below 100 percent	23.2	17.5	13.6	13.9	15.5	16.5	16.7	15.9	14.8
100–149 percent	58.3	52.5	43.6	43.0	38.9	41.8	37.4	34.8	35.9
150–199 percent	75.8	70.1	61.8	66.8	63.8	62.1	57.2	56.4	53.9
200 percent or more	86.9	86.7	84.4	83.6	85.5	85.3	86.5	84.3	84.7

Persons Age Sixty-five and Over

There are three sources of health insurance for persons age sixty-five and over: private insurance, Medicare, and Medicaid. Medicare is the federal government's primary health program for those sixty-five years old and older, and all persons in this age group are eligible for certain basic benefits under Medicare. Medicaid is the government's program for the poor and persons with disabilities. In 2002 a scant 0.8% of adults age sixty-five or older went without some type of health insurance. (See Table 6.1.)

Older adults may be covered by a combination of private health insurance and Medicare, or Medicare and Medicaid, depending on their incomes and levels of disability. Almost all of those over sixty-five are covered by Medicare. Thus, in 2001, the 62.7% of all adults age sixty-five or older who had private insurance were covered by a combination of their private insurance and Medicare. Nearly 13% were enrolled in a Medicare health maintenance organization (HMO), 8.1% had Medicaid, and 17.9% had Medicare only. (See Table 6.6.)

Whites were far more likely to have both Medicare and private insurance (66.4%) than any other ethnic or racial group. Only 24% of Hispanics and 37.6% of African-Americans had both Medicare and private coverage. (See Table 6.6.)

TABLE 6.3

Private health insurance coverage among persons under 65 years of age, by selected characteristics, selected years 1984–2001 [CONTINUED]

[Data are based on household interviews of a sample of the civilian noninstitutionalized population]

Characteristic	Private insurance obtained through workplace[7]								
	1984	1989	1995	1996	1997[1]	1998	1999	2000	2001
Geographic region[3]									
Northeast	74.1	75.1	69.9	69.1	71.0	73.0	73.5	72.2	73.0
Midwest	72.1	73.4	71.4	72.5	72.6	73.7	75.4	74.7	73.7
South	66.2	63.8	62.0	60.8	63.0	63.3	63.7	62.4	61.8
West	64.9	64.2	60.8	60.1	60.9	61.6	61.9	61.1	62.8
Location of residence[3]									
Within MSA[6]	71.0	69.8	66.9	66.9	67.4	68.5	69.6	68.1	68.3
Outside MSA[6]	65.3	63.5	60.8	58.9	62.8	63.0	62.0	62.3	61.6

#Estimates calculated upon request.
*Estimates are considered unreliable.
— Data not available.
[1]In 1997 the National Health Interview Survey (NHIS) was redesigned, including changes to the questions on health insurance coverage.
[2]Includes all other races not shown separately and unknown poverty level.
[3]Estimates are for persons under 65 years of age and are age adjusted to the year 2000 standard using three age groups: under 18 years, 18–44 years, and 45–64 years.
[4]The race groups, white, black, American Indian and Alaska Native (AI/AN), Asian, Native Hawaiian and Other Pacific Islander, and 2 or more races, include persons of Hispanic and non-Hispanic origin. Persons of Hispanic origin may be of any race. Starting with data year 1999 race-specific estimates are tabulated according to 1997 Standards for Federal data on Race and Ethnicity and are not strictly comparable with estimates for earlier years. The five single race categories plus multiple race categories shown in the table conform to 1997 Standards. The 1999 and later race-specific estimates are for persons who reported only one racial group; the category "2 or more races" includes persons who reported more than one racial group. Prior to data year 1999, data were tabulated according to 1977 Standards with four racial groups, and the category "Asian only" included Native Hawaiian and Other Pacific Islander. Estimates for single race categories prior to 1999 included persons who reported one race or, if they reported more than one race, identified one race as best representing their race. The effect of the 1997 Standard on the 1999 estimates can be seen by comparing 1999 data tabulated according to the two standards: Age-adjusted estimates based on the 1977 Standards of the percent with private health insurance are: 0.1 percentage points lower for the white group; 0.1 percentage points higher for the black group; 0.9 percentage points lower for the Asian and Pacific Islander group; and 0.2 percentage points higher for the AI/AN group than estimates based on the 1997 Standards.
[5]Missing family income data were imputed for 15–17 percent of the sample under 65 years of age in 1994–96. Percent of poverty level was unknown for 19 percent of sample persons under 65 in 1997, 24 percent in 1998, 27 percent in 1999, and 26 percent in 2000 and 2001.
[6]MSA is metropolitan statistical area.
[7]Private insurance originally obtained through a present or former employer or union. Starting in 1997 also includes private insurance obtained through workplace, self-employment, or professional association.

SOURCE: "Table 127. Private Health Insurance Coverage among Persons under 65 years of Age, according to Selected Characteristics: United States, Selected Years 1984–2001," in *Health, United States, 2003*, National Center for Health Statistics, 2003, http://www.cdc.gov/nchs/data/hus/tables/2003/03hus127.pdf (accessed July 10, 2004)

CHILDREN

In 2002 8.5 million children, or 11.6% of children under the age of eighteen, were uninsured. Among poor children under the age of eighteen, 20.1% had no health insurance. Hispanic children were the most likely to be uninsured—22.7% in 2002, followed by 13.9% of African-American children and 11.5% of Asian children. (See Figure 6.4.) Just 7.8% of non-Hispanic white children had no health care coverage, making them the least likely children to be uninsured in 2002. Older children, age twelve through seventeen, were more likely to be uninsured (12.9%) than children under twelve (10.9% of children under six and 11% of those six to eleven were uninsured).

In 2002 67.5% of American children were insured under private health insurance plans, either privately purchased or obtained through the parents' workplace (Robert J. Mills and Shailesh Bhandari, "Health Insurance Coverage in the United States: 2002," in *Current Population Reports,* U.S. Census Bureau, September 2003). Nearly one-quarter of American children (23.9%) were covered by Medicaid. (See Figure 6.5.) Medicaid covered a higher percentage of African-American children (41.2%) and Hispanic children (37.3%) than Asian (18.1%) or non-Hispanic white children (15.5%). (See Figure 6.4.)

Some health care industry observers believed that the 1996 welfare reform law, the Personal Responsibility and Work Opportunity Reconciliation Act (PL 104-193), would reduce enrollment in Medicaid. Under the 1996 law, federal money once dispensed through the Aid to Families with Dependent Children (AFDC) program was now given as a block grant (a lump sum of money) to states. In addition, the law no longer required that children who received cash assistance automatically enroll in the Medicaid program. The law gave states greater leeway in defining their requirements for aid, and in some states some families were no longer eligible for Medicaid.

Although it did not prove to reduce Medicaid enrollment dramatically, after three previous years of fairly steady enrollment, the percentage of children under eighteen enrolled in Medicaid dropped from 20.7% in 1996, when the welfare reform legislation was enacted, to 18.1% in 1999. For the same years, Medicaid enrollment dropped from 11.1% to 9.1% among the general population, but in 2000 Medicaid had risen to 9.5%. By 2002, 11.6% of the general population was covered by this entitlement program.

Some industry analysts attributed the declining proportion of uninsured children and children covered by Medicaid in the late 1990s to expansion of the State

TABLE 6.4

Medicaid coverage among persons under 65 years of age, by selected characteristics, selected years 1984–2001

[Data are based on household interviews of a sample of the civilian noninstitutionalized population]

Characteristic	1984	1989	1995	1996	1997[1]	1998	1999	2000	2001
					Number in millions				
Total[2]	14.0	15.4	26.6	25.8	22.9	21.1	21.9	22.9	25.2
					Percent of population				
Total, age adjusted[2,3]	6.7	7.1	11.3	10.9	9.6	8.8	9.0	9.4	10.3
Total, crude[2]	6.8	7.2	11.5	11.1	9.7	8.9	9.1	9.5	10.4
Age									
Under 18 years	11.9	12.6	21.5	20.7	18.4	17.1	18.1	19.4	21.2
Under 6 years	15.5	15.7	29.3	28.2	24.7	22.4	23.5	24.3	25.8
6–17 years	10.1	10.9	17.4	16.9	15.2	14.5	15.5	17.0	19.0
18–44 years	5.1	5.2	7.8	7.6	6.6	5.8	5.7	5.6	6.3
18–24 years	6.4	6.8	10.4	9.7	8.8	8.0	8.1	8.1	8.4
25–34 years	5.3	5.2	8.2	7.8	6.8	5.7	5.7	5.5	6.2
35–44 years	3.5	4.0	5.9	6.2	5.2	4.6	4.3	4.3	5.1
45–64 years	3.4	4.3	5.6	5.3	4.6	4.5	4.4	4.5	4.7
45–54 years	3.2	3.8	5.1	4.9	4.0	4.1	3.9	4.2	4.4
55–64 years	3.6	4.9	6.4	5.9	5.6	5.0	5.3	4.9	5.2
Sex[3]									
Male	5.2	5.6	9.2	8.9	8.1	7.5	7.7	8.0	8.9
Female	8.0	8.6	13.3	12.8	11.0	10.1	10.4	10.8	11.6
Race[3,4]									
White only	4.6	5.1	8.8	8.7	7.5	6.7	6.9	7.2	8.1
Black or African American only	18.9	17.8	26.0	23.0	20.5	19.6	18.7	19.4	20.4
American Indian and Alaska Native only	#	#	#	#	#	#	41.3	44.2	15.5
Asian only	9.1	11.3	10.7	*11.5	9.4	6.7	8.4	7.8	8.8
Native Hawaiian and other Pacific Islander only	—	—	—	—	—	—	*	*	*
2 or more races	—	—	—	—	—	—	15.8	15.6	14.6
Hispanic origin and race[3,4]									
Hispanic or Latino	12.2	12.7	19.8	18.5	16.0	14.1	14.1	14.2	16.0
Mexican	11.1	11.5	18.8	17.6	15.3	12.6	12.4	12.5	14.6
Puerto Rican	28.6	26.9	31.1	31.3	28.9	24.5	27.0	27.6	28.5
Cuban	4.8	7.8	13.8	*13.1	8.2	*9.1	8.3	9.7	12.2
Other Hispanic or Latino	7.4	10.4	16.9	15.0	13.9	13.9	13.8	14.1	15.0
Not Hispanic or Latino	6.2	6.6	10.2	9.7	8.7	8.0	8.2	8.6	9.3
White only	3.7	4.2	7.1	7.0	6.2	5.7	6.0	6.3	7.0
Black or African American only	19.1	17.8	25.6	22.7	20.3	19.4	18.7	19.3	20.3
Age and percent of poverty level[5]									
All ages:[3]									
Below 100 percent	30.5	35.3	44.7	42.9	38.8	37.9	36.8	37.2	39.0
100–149 percent	7.5	11.0	18.0	17.4	17.5	16.0	18.6	20.3	23.5
150–199 percent	3.1	5.0	7.9	8.0	7.4	7.2	9.8	10.8	13.3
200 percent or more	0.6	1.1	1.8	1.7	1.7	1.8	2.0	2.3	2.6
Under 18 years:									
Below 100 percent	43.1	47.8	66.0	65.2	59.7	58.7	59.9	60.9	64.3
100–149 percent	9.0	12.3	27.2	26.6	30.2	25.9	33.5	37.1	41.4
150–199 percent	4.4	6.1	13.1	12.2	12.2	12.8	18.0	21.5	26.5
200 percent or more	0.8	1.6	3.3	2.8	2.9	3.2	3.7	4.7	5.3
Geographic region[3]									
Northeast	8.5	6.8	11.7	11.5	11.2	9.8	10.1	10.5	10.8
Midwest	7.2	7.5	10.3	8.7	8.2	7.5	7.3	7.9	9.0
South	5.0	6.4	11.1	11.1	8.6	8.6	8.9	9.4	10.7
West	6.9	8.2	12.4	12.4	11.4	9.7	10.3	10.2	10.6

Children's Health Insurance Program (SCHIP) that targeted children from low-income families and was instituted during the late 1990s. Others feel that the economic boom of the late 1990s may have played a role in preventing enrollment growth in Medicaid, and accurately predicted that the economic downturn and uncertainty of the early years of the twenty-first century would reverse the downward trend in both the share of the population without health insurance and Medicaid enrollment.

In 2004 many health care advocacy groups including the American Academy of Pediatrics (AAP), which represents fifty-seven thousand primary care pediatricians, pediatric medical subspecialists, and pediatric surgical specialists, continued to agitate for federal legislation such as the MediKids Health Insurance Act (S.588/HR1205) to insure every infant, child, teenager, and young adult through age twenty-two. One of many supporters of the May 10–16, 2004, "Cover the Uninsured Week," the AAP also sought to protect Medicaid and

TABLE 6.4

Medicaid coverage among persons under 65 years of age, by selected characteristics, selected years 1984–2001 [CONTINUED]

[Data are based on household interviews of a sample of the civilian noninstitutionalized population]

Characteristic	1984	1989	1995	1996	1997[1]	1998	1999	2000	2001
					Percent of population				
Location of residence[3]									
Within MSA[6]	7.1	7.0	11.1	10.4	9.5	8.5	8.4	8.8	9.8
Outside MSA[6]	5.9	7.8	12.0	12.7	9.9	9.8	11.5	11.9	12.4

#Estimates calculated upon request.
*Estimates are considered unreliable.
— Data not available.
Notes: Medicaid includes other public assistance through 1996. Starting in 1997 includes state-sponsored health plans. Starting in 1999 includes State Children's Health Insurance Program (SCHIP). In 2001, 7.9 percent were covered by Medicaid, 1.2 percent by state-sponsored health plans, and 1.2 percent by SCHIP.
[1]In 1997 the National Health Interview Survey (NHIS) was redesigned, including changes to the questions on health insurance coverage.
[2]Includes all other races not shown separately and unknown poverty level.
[3]Estimates are for persons under 65 years of age and are age adjusted to the year 2000 standard using three age groups: under 18 years, 18–44 years, and 45–64 years.
[4]The race groups, white, black, American Indian and Alaska Native (AI/AN), Asian, Native Hawaiian and Other Pacific Islander, and 2 or more races, include persons of Hispanic and non-Hispanic origin. Persons of Hispanic origin may be of any race. Starting with data year 1999 race-specific estimates are tabulated according to 1997 Standards for Federal data on Race and Ethnicity and are not strictly comparable with estimates for earlier years. The five single race categories plus multiple race categories shown in the table conform to 1997 Standards. The 1999 and later race-specific estimates are for persons who reported only one racial group; the category "2 or more races" includes persons who reported more than one racial group. Prior to data year 1999, data were tabulated according to 1977 Standards with four racial groups, and the category "Asian only" included Native Hawaiian and other Pacific Islander. Estimates for single race categories prior to 1999 included persons who reported one race or, if they reported more than one race, identified one race as best representing their race. The effect of the 1997 Standard on the 1999 estimates can be seen by comparing 1999 data tabulated according to the two Standards: Age-adjusted estimates based on the 1977 Standards of the percent with Medicaid are; 0.1 percentage points higher for the white group; 0.1 percentage points lower for the black group; 0.8 percentage points higher for the Asian and Pacific Islander group; and 0.8 percentage points higher for the AI/AN group than estimates based on the 1997 Standards.
[5]Missing family income data were inputed for 15–17 percent of the sample under 65 years of age in 1994–96. Percent of poverty level was unknown for 19 percent of sample persons under 65 in 1997, 24 percent in 1998, 27 percent in 1999, and 26 percent in 2000 and 2001.
[6]MSA is metropolitan statistical area.

SOURCE: "Table 128. Medicaid Coverage among Persons under 65 Years of Age, according to Selected Characteristics: United States, Selected Years 1984–2001," in *Health, United States, 2003,* National Center for Health Statistics, 2003, http://www.cdc.gov/nchs/data/hus/tables/2003/03hus128.pdf (accessed July 10, 2004)

SCHIP, which together provide coverage to more than twenty-eight million children. Both programs have seen cuts in funding, services, and enrollment.

HEALTH INSURANCE PORTABILITY AND ACCOUNTABILITY ACT OF 1996

On August 21, 1996, President Bill Clinton signed the Health Insurance Portability and Accountability Act (PL 104-191). Also known as the Kennedy-Kassebaum Act (after its sponsors, Senators Edward Kennedy and Nancy Kassebaum) or HIPAA, this legislation aimed to provide better portability (transfer) of employer-sponsored insurance from one job to another. By preventing "job lock"—the need to remain in the same position or with the same employer or risk losing health care coverage—it hoped to afford American workers greater career mobility and the freedom to pursue job opportunities. Industry observers and policymakers viewed HIPAA as an important first step in the federal initiative to significantly reduce the number of uninsured people in the United States.

HIPAA stipulated that American workers who had previous insurance coverage were immediately eligible for new coverage. The law prohibited group health plans from denying new coverage based on past or present poor health and guaranteed that employees could retain their health care coverage even after they left their jobs. New employers could still require a routine waiting period (usually no more than three months) before paying for

health benefits, but the new employee who applied for insurance coverage could be continuously covered during the waiting period.

The following sections describe some of the major provisions of HIPAA. In addition to these provisions discussed, the act clarified current law and stiffened penalties for fraud and abuse. The law applies to both group and individual health insurance policies.

Preexisting Medical Conditions

In the past insurers could refuse to cover treatment for a preexisting disease or medical condition—an illness or condition that had been diagnosed or treated before a person enrolled in the health insurance program. Under the new law, if the preexisting condition had been diagnosed or treated within six months of the patient's enrollment in the insurance program, the insurance company could withhold coverage for that condition for no longer than twelve months. If the preexisting condition had not been diagnosed or treated within six months of changing insurance, there was no waiting period beyond the short time an employer may require before providing benefits to a new employee.

This provision, along with the portability provision, means that insured employees are no longer trapped by the fear of losing their health insurance coverage if they lose or leave their jobs. In the past many workers stayed in unsatisfactory jobs because they

TABLE 6.5

No health insurance coverage among persons under 65 years of age, by selected characteristics, selected years 1984–2001

[Data are based on household interviews of a sample of the civilian noninstitutionalized population]

Characteristic	1984	1989	1995	1996	1997[1]	1998	1999	2000	2001
					Number in millions				
Total[2]	29.8	33.4	37.1	38.6	41.0	39.2	38.5	40.5	39.2
					Percent of population				
Total, age adjusted[2,3]	14.3	15.3	15.9	16.5	17.4	16.5	16.1	16.8	16.2
Total, crude[2]	14.5	15.6	16.1	16.6	17.5	16.6	16.1	16.8	16.1
Age									
Under 18 years	13.9	14.7	13.4	13.2	14.0	12.7	11.9	12.4	11.0
Under 6 years	14.9	15.1	11.8	11.7	12.5	11.5	11.0	11.7	9.7
6–17 years	13.4	14.5	14.3	13.9	14.7	13.3	12.3	12.8	11.7
18–44 years	17.1	18.4	20.4	21.1	22.4	21.4	21.0	22.0	21.7
18–24 years	25.0	27.1	28.0	29.3	30.1	29.0	27.4	29.7	29.3
25–34 years	16.2	18.3	21.1	22.4	23.8	22.2	22.1	22.7	22.3
35–44 years	11.2	12.3	15.1	15.2	16.7	16.4	16.3	16.8	16.7
45–64 years	9.6	10.5	10.9	12.1	12.4	12.2	12.2	12.7	12.3
45–54 years	10.5	11.0	11.6	12.4	12.8	12.6	12.8	12.8	13.0
55–64 years	8.7	10.0	9.9	11.6	11.8	11.4	11.4	12.5	11.0
Sex[3]									
Male	15.0	16.4	17.2	17.8	18.5	17.5	17.2	17.8	17.2
Female	13.6	14.3	14.6	15.2	16.2	15.5	15.0	15.8	15.1
Race[3,4]									
White only	13.4	14.2	15.3	15.8	16.3	15.2	14.6	15.2	14.7
Black or African American only	20.0	21.4	18.2	19.6	20.2	20.7	19.5	20.0	19.3
American Indian and Alaska Native only	#	#	#	#	#	#	38.3	38.2	33.4
Asian only	18.0	18.5	18.2	19.0	19.3	18.1	16.4	17.3	17.1
Native Hawaiian and other Pacific Islander only	—	—	—	—	—	—	*	*	*
2 or more races	—	—	—	—	—	—	16.8	18.4	18.6
Hispanic origin and race[3,4]									
Hispanic or Latino	29.1	32.4	31.5	32.4	34.3	34.0	33.9	35.4	34.8
Mexican	33.2	38.8	36.2	37.5	39.2	40.0	38.0	39.9	39.0
Puerto Rican	18.1	23.3	18.3	15.1	19.4	19.4	19.8	16.4	16.0
Cuban	21.6	20.9	22.1	18.8	20.5	18.4	19.7	25.2	19.2
Other Hispanic or Latino	27.5	25.2	29.7	30.5	32.9	31.1	30.8	32.7	33.1
Not Hispanic or Latino	13.0	13.5	14.0	14.5	15.1	14.1	13.5	14.1	13.4
White only	11.8	11.9	12.9	13.3	13.7	12.5	12.1	12.5	11.9
Black or African American only	19.7	21.3	18.1	19.5	20.1	20.7	19.4	20.0	19.2
Age and percent of poverty level[5]									
All ages:[3]									
Below 100 percent	34.7	35.8	31.7	34.5	34.4	34.6	34.4	34.2	33.3
100–149 percent	27.0	31.3	31.7	33.3	36.1	36.5	35.8	36.5	32.4
150–199 percent	17.4	21.8	24.0	24.3	25.9	26.7	27.7	27.3	26.4
200 percent or more	5.8	6.8	8.6	8.6	8.8	8.0	7.7	8.7	8.4
Under 18 years:									
Below 100 percent	28.9	31.6	20.0	21.0	22.4	21.5	21.6	20.4	19.8
100–149 percent	22.8	26.1	24.8	25.0	26.1	28.0	24.9	25.6	18.5
150–199 percent	12.7	15.8	18.0	16.0	19.7	17.3	18.8	16.8	16.1
200 percent or more	4.2	4.4	6.4	6.1	6.1	5.0	4.4	5.5	4.5
Geographic region[3]									
Northeast	10.1	10.7	13.1	13.5	13.4	12.3	12.2	12.1	11.6
Midwest	11.1	10.5	12.1	12.2	13.1	11.9	11.5	12.3	11.7
South	17.4	19.4	19.2	20.0	20.7	20.0	19.8	20.4	20.0
West	17.8	18.4	17.7	18.6	20.4	19.9	18.6	20.2	18.6

were ill or had dependents with existing medical conditions. They were afraid to change jobs for fear of losing coverage or having to wait a long time before obtaining new coverage.

Pregnancies are exempt from the twelve-month waiting period and are covered within thirty days. Newborns and adopted children are also covered within thirty days. This provision aimed to better accommodate the needs of working mothers and ensure access to, and availability of, uninterrupted prenatal care for expectant mothers.

Medical Savings Accounts

The 1996 law also authorized a pilot program—a five-year demonstration project designed to test the concept of medical savings accounts (MSAs). Beginning January 1, 1997, about 750,000 people with high-deductible health plans (high-deductible plans were defined as those that carried a deductible of $1,600 to $2,400 for an individual or $3,200 to $4,800 for families) could make tax-deductible contributions into interest-bearing savings accounts. The funds deposited into these accounts may be

TABLE 6.5

No health insurance coverage among persons under 65 years of age, by selected characteristics, selected years 1984–2001 [CONTINUED]

[Data are based on household interviews of a sample of the civilian noninstitutionalized population]

Characteristic	1984	1989	1995	1996	1997[1]	1998	1999	2000	2001
					Percent of population				
Location of residence[3]									
Within MSA[6]	13.3	14.9	15.2	15.6	16.7	15.8	15.3	16.3	15.6
Outside MSA[6]	16.4	16.9	18.7	19.7	19.9	19.2	18.9	18.8	18.5

#Estimates calculated upon request.
*Estimates are considered unreliable.
— Data not available.
Notes: Persons not covered by private insurance, Medicaid, State Children's Health Insurance Program (SCHIP), public assistance (though 1996), state-sponsored or other government-sponsored health plans (starting in 1997), Medicare, or military plans are included.
[1]In 1997 the National Health Interview Survey (NHIS) was redesigned, including changes to the questions on health insurance coverage.
[2]Includes all other races not shown separately and unknown poverty level.
[3]Estimates are for persons under 65 years of age and are age adjusted to the year 2000 standard using three age groups: under 18 years, 18–44 years, and 45–64 years.
[4]The race groups, white, black, American Indian and Alaska Native (AI/AN), Asian, Native Hawaiian and Other Pacific Islander, and 2 or more races, include persons of Hispanic and non-Hispanic origin. Persons of Hispanic origin may be of any race. Starting with data year 1999 race-specific estimates are tabulated according to 1997 Standards for Federal data on Race and Ethnicity and are not strictly comparable with estimates for earlier years. The five single race categories plus multiple race categories shown in the table conform to 1997 Standards. The 1999 and later race-specific estimates are for persons who reported only on racial group; the category "2 or more races" includes persons who reported more than one racial group. Prior to data year 1999, data were tabulated according to 1977 Standards with four racial groups, and the category "Asian only" included Native Hawaiian and other Pacific Islander. Estimates for single race categories prior to 1999 included persons who reported one race or, if they reported more than one race, identified one race as best representing their race. The effect of the 1997 Standard on the 1999 estimates can be seen by comparing 1999 data tabulated according to the two Standards: Age-adjusted estimates based on the 1977 Standards of the percent with no health insurance coverage are: 0.1 percentage points higher for the white group; identical for the black group; 0.1 percentage points lower for the Asian and Pacific Islander group; and 1.5 percentage points higher for the AI/AN group than estimates based on the 1997 Standards.
[5]Missing family income data were imputed for 15–17 percent of the sample under 65 years of age in 1994–96. Percent of poverty level was unknown for 19 percent of sample persons under 65 in 1997, 24 percent in 1998, 27 percent in 1999, and 26 percent in 2000 and 2001.
[6]MSA is metropolitan statistical area.

SOURCE: "Table 129. No Health Insurance Coverage among Persons under 65 Years of Age, according to Selected Characteristics: United States, Selected Years 1984–2001," in *Health, United States 2003,* National Center for Health Statistics, 2003, http://www.cdc.gov/nchs/data/hus/tables/2003/03hus129.pdf (accessed July 10, 2004)

used to purchase health insurance policies, and pay co-payments and deductibles. Persons using MSAs also may deduct any employer contributions into the accounts as tax-deductible income. Any unspent money remaining in the MSA at the end of the year is carried over to the next year, allowing the account to grow.

MSAs are similar to individual retirement accounts (IRAs). To be eligible to create a MSA, individuals must be less than sixty-five years old, self-employed and uninsured, or must work in a firm with fifty or fewer employees that does not offer health care coverage. Withdrawals to cover out-of-pocket medical expenses are tax-free and the money invested grows on a tax-deferred basis. Using MSA funds for any purpose unrelated to medical care or disability results in a 15% penalty. However, when MSA users reach age sixty-five, the money may be withdrawn for any purpose and is taxed at the same rate as ordinary income.

Supporters of MSAs believed that consumers would be less likely to seek unnecessary or duplicative medical care if they knew they could keep the money left in their accounts for themselves at the end of the year. Experience has demonstrated that MSAs can simultaneously help to contain health care costs, allow consumers greater control and freedom of choice of health care providers, enable consumers to save for future medical and long-term care expenses, and improve access to medical care.

Critics felt that the HIPAA legislation created unnecessarily complicated MSAs. They blamed Congress for simply renaming MSAs (they are now known as "Archer MSAs" to honor Bill Archer, the Texas legislator who advocated their enactment) and failing to simplify MSAs when in December 2000 it renewed the MSA program through December 31, 2002.

In February 2001 President George W. Bush advocated more liberal rules governing MSAs and proposed making them available to all eligible Americans permanently. Congress reviewed the president's proposed reforms and during its 2001–02 session lowered the minimum annual deductible to increase the number of eligible Americans, allowed annual MSA contributions up to 65% of the maximum deductible for individuals and 75% for families, and extended the availability of the Archer MSA through December 31, 2003.

The Medicare Modernization Act of 2003 included provisions to establish Health Savings Accounts (HSAs) for the general population. Like their MSA predecessors, these accounts offer a variety of benefits, including more choice, greater control, and individual ownership. Specific features of HSAs include:

• permanence and portability

• availability to all individuals with a qualified high-deductible plan

• minimum deductible of $1,000 per individual plan and $2,000 per family plan

• allowing annual contributions to equal 100% of the deductible

FIGURE 6.4

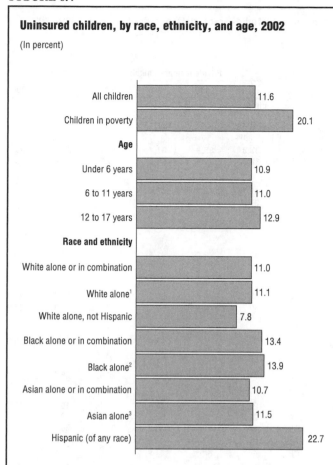

Uninsured children, by race, ethnicity, and age, 2002

(In percent)

All children	11.6
Children in poverty	20.1
Age	
Under 6 years	10.9
6 to 11 years	11.0
12 to 17 years	12.9
Race and ethnicity	
White alone or in combination	11.0
White alone[1]	11.1
White alone, not Hispanic	7.8
Black alone or in combination	13.4
Black alone[2]	13.9
Asian alone or in combination	10.7
Asian alone[3]	11.5
Hispanic (of any race)	22.7

[1]The 2003 Current Population Survey asked respondents to choose one or more races. White alone refers to people who reported White and did not report any other race category. The use of this single-race population does not imply that it is the preferred method of presenting or analyzing data. The Census Bureau uses a variety of approaches. Information on people who reported more than one race, such as "White and American Indian and Alaska Native" or "Asian and Black or African American," is available from Census 2000 through American FactFinder. About 2.6% of people reported more than one race in 2000.
[2]Black alone refers to people who reported Black or African American and did not report any other race category.
[3]Asian alone refers to people who reported Asian and did not report any other race category.

SOURCE: Robert J. Mills and Shailesh Bhanderi, "Figure 4. Uninsured Children by Race, Ethnicity, and Age: 2002," in *Health Insurance Coverage in the United States: 2002,* U.S. Census Bureau, September 2003, http://www.census.gov/prod/2003pubs/p60-223.pdf (accessed July 10, 2004)

FIGURE 6.5

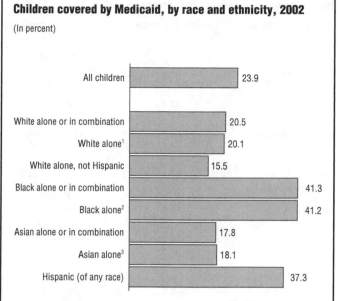

Children covered by Medicaid, by race and ethnicity, 2002

(In percent)

All children	23.9
White alone or in combination	20.5
White alone[1]	20.1
White alone, not Hispanic	15.5
Black alone or in combination	41.3
Black alone[2]	41.2
Asian alone or in combination	17.8
Asian alone[3]	18.1
Hispanic (of any race)	37.3

[1]The 2003 CPS asked respondents to choose one or more races. White alone refers to people who reported White and did not report any other race category. The use of this single-race population does not imply that it is the preferred method of presenting or analyzing data. The Census Bureau uses a variety of approaches. Information on people who reported more than one race, such as "White and American Indian and Alaska Native" or "Asian and Black or African American," is available from Census 2000 through American FactFinder. About 2.6 percent of people reported more than one race in 2000.
[2]Black alone refers to people who reported Black or African American and did not report any other race category.
[3]Asian alone refers to people who reported Asian and did not report any other race category.
Note: For discussion of statistically significant differences between groups, see text.

SOURCE: Robert J. Mills and Shailesh Bhanderi, "Figure 5. Children Covered by Medicaid by Race and Ethnicity: 2002," in *Health Insurance Coverage in the United States: 2002,* U.S. Census Bureau, September 2003, http://www.census.gov/prod/2003pubs/p60-223.pdf (accessed July 10, 2004)

- allowing both employer and employee contributions

- not placing a cap on taxpayer participation

- allowing tax-free rollover of up to $500 in unspent Flexible Spending Accounts. These balances are currently forfeited at the end of each year.

Tax Benefits of HIPAA

HIPAA also changed several tax provisions involving health expenses:

- The allowable tax deductions of health-insurance premiums for the self-employed increased. Formerly, self-employed persons could deduct only 30% of their premiums from their taxes. The new law set up a graduated increasing scale of deductions—45% in 1998, 60% in 1999–2001, 70% in 2002, and 100% thereafter.

- Long-term care plan contributions. When an employer contributes to a long-term health care plan for a worker, a spouse, and dependents, those contributions will not be counted as taxable employee income. Long-term care includes rehabilitative care and personal care, such as feeding, bathing, and dressing, for a chronically ill person, defined as a person who has been unable for twelve months to perform the activities of daily living, such as eating and bathing.

- Individual retirement account (IRA) withdrawals. Ordinarily, withdrawals from an IRA before age fifty-nine carry a 10% penalty. If medical expenses, however, exceed 7.5% of a person's annual income, he or she may withdraw funds from an IRA without penalty. This provision also allows persons who have collected federal or state unemployment benefits for at least twelve weeks to withdraw money from their IRAs without penalty.

TABLE 6.6

Health insurance coverage for persons age 65 and older, by type of coverage and selected characteristics, selected years 1989–2001

(Data are based on household interviews of a sample of the civilian noninstitutionalized population)

Characteristic	Private insurance[1]						Private insurance obtained through workplace[1,2]					
	1989	1995	1998	1999	2000	2001	1989	1995	1998	1999	2000	2001
	Number in millions											
Total[3]	22.4	23.5	21.5	20.8	20.6	20.6	11.2	12.4	12.0	11.3	11.7	11.9
	Percent of population											
Total, age adjusted[3,4]	76.1	74.5	66.7	64.0	63.1	62.7	37.3	38.9	37.1	34.6	35.6	36.0
Total, crude[3]	76.5	74.6	66.7	64.1	63.1	62.7	38.4	39.5	37.3	34.9	35.8	36.1
Age												
65–74 years	78.2	75.1	66.6	64.5	62.7	63.0	43.7	43.3	40.4	38.6	39.4	39.7
75 years and over	73.9	73.9	66.8	63.5	63.6	62.4	30.2	34.1	33.5	30.3	31.4	31.9
75–84 years	75.9	75.7	68.1	64.6	64.6	63.9	32.0	36.0	35.7	32.3	33.1	33.3
85 years and over	65.5	67.3	61.8	59.6	59.5	57.0	22.8	27.3	25.3	23.2	24.7	26.7
Sex[4]												
Male	77.4	76.6	68.5	64.5	64.3	63.8	42.1	43.3	41.4	38.6	39.7	40.1
Female	75.4	73.2	65.5	63.8	62.2	61.9	34.0	35.8	34.0	31.8	32.5	33.0
Race[4,5]												
White only	79.8	78.3	70.3	67.6	66.9	66.4	38.7	40.4	38.5	35.8	37.2	37.4
Black or African American only	42.3	40.3	40.3	39.9	35.6	37.6	23.7	24.6	27.4	27.5	25.0	27.9
American Indian and Alaska Native only			37.9	35.2		31.8				33.3		
Asian only			40.8	33.1	43.3	40.9			28.3	21.4	23.2	23.5
Native Hawaiian and Other Pacific Islander only	—	—	—				—	—	—			
2 or more races	—	—	—	56.0	63.1	50.0	—	—	—	26.9	48.4	32.3
Hispanic origin and race[4,5]												
Hispanic or Latino	42.3	39.8	29.1	26.9	23.4	24.0	22.2	18.4	17.9	17.4	15.1	16.2
Mexican	33.5	31.8	26.5	27.4	20.3	24.8	20.2	15.9	17.5	16.9	12.8	16.8
Not Hispanic or Latino	77.2	76.2	68.7	66.2	65.5	65.2	37.7	39.9	38.2	35.7	36.8	37.2
White only	81.0	80.3	72.3	69.7	69.1	68.8	39.3	41.7	39.5	36.8	38.3	38.6
Black or African American only	42.4	40.1	40.5	40.1	35.6	37.6	23.7	24.4	27.6	27.6	25.0	28.0
Percent of poverty level[4,6]												
Below 100 percent	46.1	40.0	32.8	28.3	29.9	27.8	11.6	13.8	10.2	8.8	10.8	11.9
100–149 percent	67.7	67.6	48.7	44.6	44.2	45.7	22.2	26.7	19.3	14.7	16.1	20.6
150–199 percent	81.1	76.0	65.6	62.0	63.1	63.1	39.0	38.7	31.4	27.2	29.8	28.1
200 percent or more	85.5	85.3	78.6	75.5	74.4	74.2	49.4	49.3	49.8	45.4	47.3	46.8
Geographic region[4]												
Northeast	76.1	76.2	72.0	66.0	66.7	66.1	42.2	44.6	43.9	39.7	38.7	38.8
Midwest	81.9	82.3	78.3	77.0	75.9	72.4	40.0	44.7	41.6	38.5	41.2	40.5
South	73.0	70.7	62.0	60.2	58.4	60.2	32.0	33.7	33.3	31.0	31.9	34.1
West	74.7	68.8	54.9	51.5	51.5	51.7	37.1	33.6	30.9	30.6	31.7	30.6
Location of residence[4]												
Within MSA[7]	76.6	74.7	65.5	62.8	61.4	61.2	39.9	40.9	38.7	36.0	36.9	36.5
Outside MSA[7]	74.8	73.9	70.6	68.2	68.5	68.1	30.2	32.2	31.8	30.0	31.5	34.1

MEDICARE C

Medicare C, also known as "Medicare+Choice," became available to Medicare recipients on January 1, 1999. Medicare C came about as a result of the Balanced Budget Act of 1997 and was designed to supplement Medicare Parts A and B. Medicare C offers beneficiaries a wider variety of health plan options than previously available. These options include traditional (fee-for-service) Medicare, Medicare health maintenance organizations (HMOs), preferred provider organizations (PPOs), provider-sponsored organizations (PSOs), and medical savings accounts (MSAs).

Medicare provider-sponsored organizations are organized and operate the same way that HMOs do. They are administered, however, by providers—physicians and hospitals. Medicare preferred provider organizations are similar to HMOs but permit patients to see providers outside the network and do not require their members to choose a network primary care physician to coordinate their care. Patients in PPOs may seek care from any physician associated with the plan. Medicare private fee-for-service plans are more like traditional Medicare, except patients may pay more out-of-pocket expenses. Medical savings accounts (MSAs) have two parts—an insurance policy and a savings account. Medicare will pay the insurance premium and deposit a fixed amount in an MSA each year to pay for an individual's health care.

CHANGING MEDICARE REIMBURSEMENT

Medicare reimbursement varies in different parts of the country, despite the fact that everyone pays the same amount to Medicare through taxes. As a result, older

TABLE 6.6

Health insurance coverage for persons age 65 and older, by type of coverage and selected characteristics, selected years 1989–2001 [CONTINUED]

(Data are based on household interviews of a sample of the civilian noninstitutionalized population)

Characteristic	Medicare fee-for-service only[1,8]						Medicare health maintenance organization[1,9]					
	1989	1995	1998	1999	2000	2001	1989	1995	1998	1999	2000	2001
						Number in millions						
Total[3]	4.5	4.6	4.7	5.1	5.5	5.9	—	—	4.7	5.2	5.0	4.2
						Percent of population						
Total, age adjusted[3,4]	15.7	14.8	14.5	15.8	16.8	17.9	—	—	14.4	16.0	15.2	12.9
Total, crude[3]	15.4	14.7	14.5	15.8	16.8	17.9	—	—	14.5	16.0	15.2	12.9
Age												
65–74 years	13.8	14.4	13.7	15.6	16.4	17.4	—	—	15.3	16.1	15.8	12.8
75 years and over	17.8	15.2	15.4	15.9	17.4	18.4	—	—	13.5	15.9	14.6	13.1
75–84 years	16.2	14.1	14.2	15.2	16.0	17.0	—	—	13.7	16.5	15.5	13.4
85 years and over	24.9	19.2	19.7	18.4	22.7	23.7	—	—	12.8	13.7	11.1	11.9
Sex[4]												
Male	14.9	14.3	13.2	15.4	16.1	17.4	—	—	14.7	16.5	15.6	12.5
Female	16.2	15.0	15.4	16.0	17.4	18.2	—	—	14.2	15.6	15.0	13.3
Race[4,5]												
White only	13.9	13.5	13.3	14.4	15.5	16.5	—	—	14.0	15.8	15.2	13.0
Black or African American only	34.9	29.0	26.7	28.0	29.6	30.5	—	—	17.6	16.5	14.7	11.2
American Indian and Alaska Native only			26.6	39.1		37.9	—	—				
Asian only			12.6	22.0	21.4	19.8	—	—	17.0	18.9	16.0	13.4
Native Hawaiian and Other Pacific Islander only	—	—	—				—	—	—			
2 or more races	—	—	—	19.1		21.7	—	—	—	21.8	29.8	16.3
Hispanic origin and race[4,5]												
Hispanic or Latino	22.7	23.6	20.6	22.8	20.8	23.9	—	—	24.4	25.7	25.0	20.1
Mexican		21.5	26.3	22.7	29.3		—	—	23.3	26.0	24.5	18.9
Not Hispanic or Latino	15.5	14.3	14.2	15.3	16.6	17.5	—	—	13.9	15.4	14.6	12.5
White only	13.6	12.9	12.9	13.9	15.3	16.1	—	—	13.5	15.2	14.5	12.5
Black or African American only	34.9	29.1	26.7	28.0	29.6	30.5	—	—	17.5	16.5	14.7	11.2
Percent of poverty level[4,6]												
Below 100 percent	26.4	23.4	21.9	24.8	23.6	23.3	—	—	11.0	13.8	14.4	8.6
100–149 percent	20.7	18.6	22.2	23.1	22.0	24.5	—	—	16.6	17.7	17.0	12.5
150–199 percent	13.6	16.8	14.3	17.1	16.6	16.6	—	—	18.6	20.4	16.0	15.0
200 percent or more	11.0	10.8	8.0	10.3	11.4	11.5	—	—	15.2	15.7	16.7	14.5
Geographic region[4]												
Northeast	17.4	15.3	12.3	13.8	17.1	17.6	—	—	12.7	17.5	12.5	13.5
Midwest	13.8	11.0	12.9	11.7	13.5	16.1	—	—	7.7	9.0	8.4	7.5
South	16.6	15.9	17.5	20.3	19.6	19.7	—	—	12.5	12.2	13.2	10.2
West	14.4	17.2	13.7	14.9	15.7	17.3	—	—	28.2	31.0	30.6	23.8
Location of residence[4]												
Within MSA[7]	15.9	14.9	13.4	14.9	16.4	17.6	—	—	17.7	19.7	18.7	15.8
Outside MSA[7]	15.5	14.2	18.2	18.7	18.2	19.0	—	—	3.5	3.4	4.4	3.1

adults in some geographic regions have access to a more comprehensive range of services such as prescription drug coverage and coverage for eyeglasses, while those in other areas do not receive these benefits.

Describing this practice as "unfair and outdated," legislators called for more equitable reimbursement formulas in August 2002. U.S. Representative Leonard Boswell, a Democrat from Idaho, and Republican Congressman Tom Osborne from Nebraska introduced bipartisan legislation to ensure that no state receives Medicare reimbursement greater than five percentage points above or below the national average. In 2003 thirty-five states, including Iowa, received less than average reimbursement while states with higher health care costs received above average reimbursement.

THE MEDICARE PERSCRIPTION DRUG, IMPROVEMENT, AND MODERNIZATION ACT OF 2003

On December 8, 2003, President George W. Bush signed the Medicare Prescription Drug, Improvement, and Modernization Act of 2003 (PL 108-173) into law. Heralded as landmark legislation, the act provides older adults and persons with disabilities with a prescription drug benefit, more choices, and improved benefits under Medicare. On June 1, 2004, seniors and people with disabilities began using their Medicare-approved drug discount cards to obtain savings on prescription medicines. Low-income beneficiaries qualified for $600 credit to help pay for their prescriptions. In addition to providing coverage for prescription drugs, this legislation offers

TABLE 6.6

Health insurance coverage for persons age 65 and older, by type of coverage and selected characteristics, selected years 1989–2001 [CONTINUED]

(Data are based on household interviews of a sample of the civilian noninstitutionalized population)

Characteristic	Medicaid[1,10]						Characteristic	Medicaid[1,10]					
	1989	1995	1998	1999	2000	2001		1989	1995	1998	1999	2000	2001
	Number in millions						Hispanic origin and race[4,5]						
Total[3]	2.0	3.0	2.6	2.4	2.5	2.7	Hispanic or Latino	26.4	32.7	27.2	24.0	29.6	30.1
	Percent of population						Mexican			29.0	17.5	28.1	25.6
Total, age adjusted[3,4]	7.2	9.6	8.1	7.4	7.6	8.1	Not Hispanic or Latino	6.6	8.5	7.1	6.4	6.3	6.8
Total, crude[3]	7.0	9.4	8.1	7.3	7.6	8.1	White only	4.9	6.1	5.4	4.7	4.6	4.9
Age							Black or African American only	21.1	28.5	18.0	18.1	19.5	20.0
65–74 years	6.3	8.4	7.8	6.6	7.7	7.8	Percent of poverty level[4,6]						
75 years and over	8.2	10.9	8.4	8.1	7.5	8.5	Below 100 percent	28.2	36.4	36.7	35.7	35.0	38.8
75–84 years	7.9	9.9	7.8	7.2	7.2	8.1	100–149 percent	9.0	12.8	14.1	15.3	16.2	18.6
85 years and over	9.7	14.3	10.5	11.4	8.6	10.3	150–199 percent	4.7	5.9	6.1	4.2	4.7	7.1
Sex[4]							200 percent or more	2.4	2.4	3.5	2.9	2.8	3.1
Male	5.2	5.8	6.2	5.3	5.5	6.1	Geographic region[4]						
Female	8.6	12.2	9.5	8.8	9.2	9.7	Northeast	5.4	8.9	7.5	7.3	7.4	7.9
Race[4,5]							Midwest	3.7	5.8	4.9	5.7	4.5	5.1
White only	5.6	7.4	6.4	5.6	5.6	6.2	South	9.7	11.8	9.6	8.2	9.4	9.3
Black or African American only	21.2	28.4	18.0	18.2	19.6	20.0	West	9.4	11.5	10.2	8.2	8.6	10.0
American Indian and Alaska Native only					35.8		Location of residence[4]						
Asian only			33.4	28.2	21.3	23.7	Within MSA[7]	6.5	8.9	8.0	6.9	7.2	8.1
Native Hawaiian and Other Pacific Islander only	—	—	—				Outside MSA[7]	8.8	11.7	8.4	8.8	9.0	8.3
2 or more races	—	—	—			19.9							

— Data not available.

[1] Almost all persons 65 years of age and over are covered by Medicare also. In 2001, 90 percent of older persons with private insurance also had Medicare.

[2] Private insurance originally obtained through a present or former employer or union. Starting in 1997 also includes private insurance obtained through workplace self-employed, or professional association.

[3] Includes all other races not shown separately and unknown poverty level.

[4] Estimates are for persons 65 years of age and older and are age adjusted to the year 2000 standard using two age groups; 65–74 years and 75 years and over.

[5] The race groups, white, black, American Indian and Alaska Native (AI/AN), Asian, Native Hawaiian and other Pacific Islander, and 2 or more races, include persons of Hispanic and non-Hispanic origin. Persons of Hispanic origin may be of any race. Starting with data year 1999 race-specific estimates are tabulated according to 1997 Standards for Federal data on Race and Ethnicity and are not strictly comparable with estimates for earlier years. The five single race categories plus multiple race categories shown in the table conform to 1997 Standards. The 1999 and later race-specific estimates are for persons who reported only one racial group; the category "2 or more races" includes persons who reported more than one racial group. Prior to data year 1999, data were tabulated according to 1977 Standards with four racial groups and the category "Asian only" included Native Hawaiian and other Pacific Islander. Estimates for single race categories prior to 1999 included persons who reported one race or, if they reported more than one race, identified one race as best representing their race. The effect of the 1997 Standard on the 1999 estimates can be seen by comparing 1999 data tabulated according to the two Standards: Age-adjusted estimates based on the 1977 Standards of the percent with private health insurance are: 0.1 percentage points lower for the white group; 0.3 percentage points higher for the black group; and 1 percentage point higher for the Asian and Pacific Islander group than estimates based on the 1997 Standards.

[6] Missing family income data were imputed for 22–25 percent of the sample 65 years of age and over in 1994–96. Percent of poverty level was unknown for 29 percent of sample persons 65 or older in 1997, 34 percent in 1998, 38 percent in 1999, 39 percent in 2000, and 40 percent in 2001.

[7] MSA is metropolitan statistical area.

[8] Medicare fee-for-service only includes persons who are not covered by private health insurance, Medicaid, or a Medicare health maintenance organization.

[9] Persons reporting Medicare coverage are considered to have HMO coverage if they responded yes when asked if they were under a Medicare managed care arrangement such as an HMO.

[10] Includes public assistance through 1996. Starting in 1997 includes State-sponsored health plans. In 2001 the age-adjusted percent of the population 65 years of age and over covered by Medicaid was 7.6 percent, and 0.5 percent were covered by State-sponsored health plans.

Note: Percents do not add to 100 because elderly persons with more than one type of insurance in addition to Medicare appear in more than one column, and because the percent of elderly persons without health insurance (1.3 percent in 2001) is not shown.

SOURCE: "Table 130. Health Insurance Coverage for Persons 65 Years of Age and Over, According to Type of Coverage and Selected Characteristics: United States, Selected Years 1989–2001," in *National Health Interview Survey,* Centers for Diesease Control and Prevention, National Center for Health Statistics, 2003, http://www.cdc.gov/nchs/data/hus/tables/2003/03hus130.pdf (accessed November 16, 2004)

---

seniors the opportunity to choose the coverage and care that best meets their needs. For example, some older adults may opt for traditional Medicare coverage along with the new prescription benefit. Others may wish to obtain dental or eyeglass coverage, or to enroll in managed care plans that reduce out-of-pocket costs.

The legislation stipulated that beginning in 2005, all newly enrolled Medicare beneficiaries will be covered for a complete physical examination and other preventive services such as blood tests to screen for diabetes. The new law also aimed to assist all Americans in paying out-of-pocket health costs by enabling creation of health savings accounts (HSAs). HSAs allow Americans to set aside up to $4,500 every year, tax free, to save for medical expenses.

Will New Medicare Law Erode Retiree Benefits?

Some health care industry observers and older adults fear that full implementation of Medicare prescription drug coverage in 2006 will prompt employers to sharply reduce or even entirely eliminate prescription drug benefits for as many as one third of the nation's retirees with employer-sponsored drug coverage—about 3.8 million older adults. In the July 14, 2004, article "Medicare Law Is Seen Leading to Cuts in Drug Benefits for Retirees," *New York Times* journalist Robert Pear reported that the new law, which from 2006 to 2013 will provide federal subsidies to encourage more employers to continue providing drug benefits, may actually further erode the level of benefits offered to retirees.

According to the U.S. Department of Health and Human Services, the new law will provide 7.6 million retirees with drug benefits through employer plans subsidized by the government, and 3.8 million will continue to receive their primary drug coverage from Medicare. This number is expected to swell to 4.1 million by 2010. Supporters of the new law and many employers contend that it will help stabilize retiree health benefits and support employers to continue providing drug coverage—satisfying the wishes of retirees, labor unions, and members of Congress from both parties.

To qualify for federal subsidies, equal to 28% of drug costs from $250 to $5,000 a year per retiree, employers must demonstrate that their retiree drug benefits are as generous as those provided by Medicare. The subsidies will be tax-free to employers, who can still take tax deductions for the cost of retiree health benefits. Detractors fear that if criteria for participation and compliance with federal rules and administrative regulations become too burdensome for employers, they will likely drop their retiree coverage, forcing retirees to rely on conventional Medicare including its standard prescription drug benefit, which is valued at about $1,200 per year.

HEALTH INSURANCE COSTS CONTINUE TO SKYROCKET

According to a survey conducted by the Kaiser Family Foundation and the Health Research and Educational Trust, 2003 was the seventh straight year of increases and third consecutive year of double-digit increases in insurance costs (*Annual Employer Health Benefit Survey*, Sep-

tember 2003). Private health insurance premiums rose 13.9%, the largest annual increase since 1990. Premiums averaged $3,383 for individual coverage and $9,068 for family coverage. Employee contributions remained stable for individual coverage but contributions for family coverage increased by 13%. Workers paid an average of $508 per year toward the premium for individual coverage and $2,412 per year toward the premium for family coverage.

The survey found that two in five workers incur a separate deductible, co-payment, or co-insurance for each hospital admission. Deductibles and co-payments averaged about $200 per admission. Workers enrolled in preferred provider organizations (PPOs) faced higher deductibles for out-of-network services, HMO members had higher co-payments for office visits, and across all plans, enrollees faced higher co-payments for prescription drugs.

The increase was attributed to larger insurance claims resulting from higher prices for hospital care and prescription drugs coupled with increasing consumer demand for, and utilization of, health care services. The researchers reported many employers, particularly large employers with two hundred or more workers, said they would likely have to increase the amounts their employees must pay for heath care coverage in 2004, and some employers said they would very likely offer workers a high deductible plan (a plan with a deductible of at least $1,000 for individual coverage) next year. As reported in surveys from prior years, employers remain extremely concerned about continuing increases in health care costs, with more than half of those surveyed identifying health insurance the "greatest concern for the company."

The researchers and other industry analysts observe that if there is no relief from premium increases in the near future, despite employers' stated reluctance to drop employee health care coverage, some may stop offering health benefits to their employees and some workers may be forced to drop their coverage because they are unable to contribute their share of the cost. Industry observers and policymakers fear that rising insurance premiums will swell the ranks of Americans without insurance coverage.

CHAPTER 7

INTERNATIONAL COMPARISONS OF HEALTH CARE

International comparisons are often difficult to interpret, because definitions of terms and reliability of data as well as cultures and values differ. What is important in one society may be unimportant or even nonexistent in another. A political or human right that is important in one nation may be meaningless in a neighboring state. Evaluating the quality of health care systems is an example of the difficulties involved in comparing one culture to another.

Even within the United States, there are cultural and regional variations in health care delivery. A visit to a busy urban urgent care center might begin with the patient completing a brief medical history, five or ten minutes with a nurse who measures and records the patient's vital signs (pulse, respiration, temperature), and conclude with a fifteen-minute visit during which the physician diagnoses the problem and prescribes treatment. In contrast, on the islands of Hawaii, a visit with a healer may last several hours and culminate with a prayer, song, or an embrace. Hawaiian healers, called "kahunas," are unhurried and offer an array of herbal remedies, bodywork (massage, touch, and manipulative therapies), and talk therapies (counseling and guidance) because they believe that the healing quality of the encounter, independent of any treatment offered, improves health and well-being.

While comparing the performance of health care systems and health outcomes (how people fare as a result of receiving health care services) is of benefit to health care planners, administrators, and policymakers, the subjective nature of such assessments should be duly considered.

A COMPARISON OF HEALTH CARE SPENDING, RESOURCES, AND UTILIZATION

The Organisation for Economic Co-operation and Development (OECD) provides information about, and to, thirty member countries that are governed democratically and participate in the global market economy. It collects and publishes data about a wide range of economic and social issues including health and health care policy. The OECD member nations are generally considered the wealthier, more developed nations in the world. The OECD includes the Western European nations, Canada, the United States, Japan, Australia, New Zealand, Mexico, the Czech Republic, South Korea, Poland, Hungary, and the Slovak Republic.

Percentage of Gross Domestic Product Spent on Health Care

Although health has always been a concern for Americans, the growth in the health care industry since the mid-1970s has made it a major factor in the American economy. For many years the United States has spent a larger proportion of its gross domestic product (GDP) on health care than have other nations with similar economic development. From 1990 to 2000 U.S. health expenditures grew 2.3 times faster than GDP, rising from 13% in 1997 to 14.6% in 2002, the highest rate in the OECD. (See Figure 7.1.) Other nations that spent large percentages of GDP on health care in 2002 included Switzerland (11.2%), Germany (10.9%), Iceland (9.9%) France (9.7%), Canada (9.6%), and Greece (9.5%). Of the member nations that reported health care expenditure data in 2002, Mexico (6.1%), Poland (6.1%), South Korea (5.9%), and the Slovak Republic (5.7%) spent the least in the OECD.

While the growth in health care spending (as expressed by an increase in health expenditures as a percentage of GDP) in the United States from 1997 to 2002 (1.6%) was not a universal trend, several other countries also experienced significant increases in the percentage of their GDP spent on health care during this period. These included Iceland (up 1.8%), South Korea (1.2%), New Zealand (from 1.1%), Sweden (1%), and Switzerland (1%). (See Figure 7.2.) These countries, however, were spending a relatively small percentage of their GDP on health care in 1990. Only the Slovak Republic saw a slight decline—a scant 0.1%

FIGURE 7.1

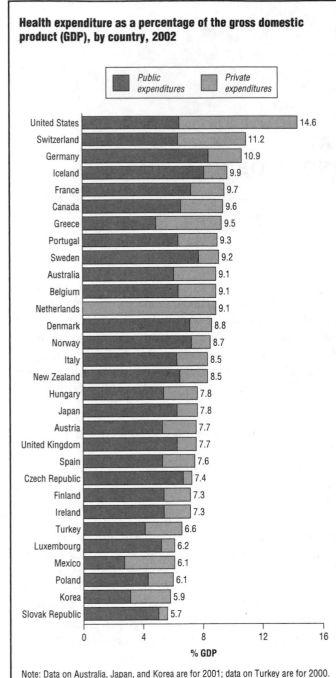

Health expenditure as a percentage of the gross domestic product (GDP), by country, 2002

Note: Data on Australia, Japan, and Korea are for 2001; data on Turkey are for 2000.

SOURCE: "Chart 1. Health Expenditure as a Percentage of GDP, 2002," in *OECD Health Data 2004, 1st edition,* Organisation for Economic Co-operation and Development (France), 2004, http://www.oecd.org/document/16/0,2340,en_2649_37407_2085200_1_1_1_37407,00.html (accessed July 13, 2004). Copyright OECD. Reproduced by permission of the OECD.

FIGURE 7.2

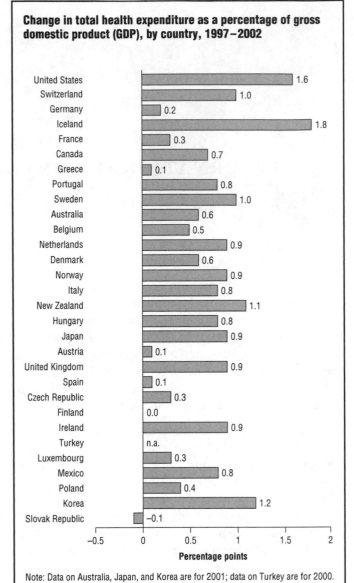

Change in total health expenditure as a percentage of gross domestic product (GDP), by country, 1997–2002

Note: Data on Australia, Japan, and Korea are for 2001; data on Turkey are for 2000.

SOURCE: "Chart 2. Change in Total Health Expenditure as a Percentage of GDP, 1997–2002," in *OECD Health Data 2004, 1st edition,* Organisation for Economic Co-operation and Development (France), 2004, http://www.oecd.org/document/16/0,2340,en_2649_37407_2085200_1_1_1_37407,00.html (accessed July 13, 2004). Copyright OECD. Reproduced by permission of the OECD.

drop in total health spending as a percentage of GDP between 1997 and 2002. The majority of other countries experienced small increases. (See Figure 7.2.)

Per Capita Spending on Health Care

In 2002 the United States also experienced the highest per capita spending for health care services, spending an average of $5,267 per citizen. (See Figure 7.3.) No other country came close to spending that amount per capita in 2002: Switzerland spent $3,445 per citizen; Norway, $3,083; Luxembourg, $3,065; Canada, $2,931; Germany, $2,817; Iceland, $2,807; and France, $2,736. In 2002 Turkey spent the least per capita of any OECD nation on health care ($446) followed by Mexico ($553), Poland ($654), the Slovak Republic ($698), and South Korea ($931).

Who Pays for Health Care?

Public expenditures for health care services, as a percentage of GDP, vary widely between the OECD member

FIGURE 7.3

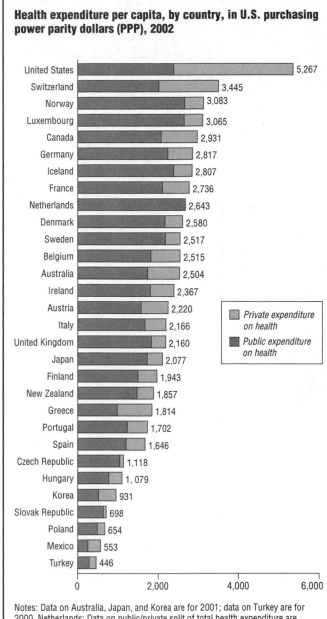

Health expenditure per capita, by country, in U.S. purchasing power parity dollars (PPP), 2002

Country	Value
United States	5,267
Switzerland	3,445
Norway	3,083
Luxembourg	3,065
Canada	2,931
Germany	2,817
Iceland	2,807
France	2,736
Netherlands	2,643
Denmark	2,580
Sweden	2,517
Belgium	2,515
Australia	2,504
Ireland	2,367
Austria	2,220
Italy	2,166
United Kingdom	2,160
Japan	2,077
Finland	1,943
New Zealand	1,857
Greece	1,814
Portugal	1,702
Spain	1,646
Czech Republic	1,118
Hungary	1,079
Korea	931
Slovak Republic	698
Poland	654
Mexico	553
Turkey	446

■ Private expenditure on health
■ Public expenditure on health

Notes: Data on Australia, Japan, and Korea are for 2001; data on Turkey are for 2000. Netherlands: Data on public/private split of total health expenditure are unavailable. Purchasing power parities (PPPs) provide a means of comparing spending between countries on a common base. PPPs are the rates of currency conversion that equalize the cost of a given 'basket' of goods and services in different countries.

SOURCE: "Chart 3. Health Expenditure Per Capita, US$PPP, 2002," in *OECD Health Data 2004, 1st edition*, Organisation for Economic Co-operation and Development (France), 2004, http://www.oecd.org /document/16/0,2340,en_2649_37407_2085200_1_1_1_37407,00.html (accessed July 13, 2004). Copyright OECD. Reproduced by permission of the OECD.

nations. Public spending on health accounted for nearly 75% of total health spending on average across OECD countries in 2002, virtually unchanged from its share in 1995. The remaining 25% of spending was paid by private sources, mainly private insurance and individuals. In the United States public funding accounted for 45% of total health spending. In contrast, in the Czech Republic 91.4% of total health spending was publicly funded, and in the

Slovak Republic public funding accounted for 89.1% of the total health expenditure. Other nations with above-average contributions of public funding to health expenditures included Denmark (83.1%), Iceland (84%), Luxembourg (85.4%), Norway (85.3%), Sweden (85.3%), and the United Kingdom (83.4%). (See Table 7.1.)

Of the nineteen OECD nations that reported out-of-pocket, per capita payments in 2002, the United States and Switzerland far exceeded other countries. Swiss citizens spent the equivalent of $1,085 out-of-pocket and U.S. citizens spent an average of $737 out-of-pocket for health care, about 60% more than the per capita amount of Italy ($439) and nearly ten times the per capita amount spent by citizens of the Slovak Republic ($76). (See Table 7.2.)

Private health insurance fills the gap between public expenditures and out-of-pocket costs. Only sixteen OECD member nations reported private insurance expenditures for health care in 2002. However, among the countries declaring private insurance as a percentage of total expenditures for health, the United States far exceeded the others. At 36.2%, the U.S. private insurance expenditure was twice that of the Netherlands (17.1%) and far outstripped the other countries—France (13.2%), Canada (12.7%), Switzerland (9.6%), Austria (7.4%), and New Zealand (5.7%). (See Table 7.3.) Since the United States is the only developed country without a national health care program, U.S. private insurance expenditures cover the costs generally assumed by government programs that finance health care delivery in comparable OECD member nations.

Spending for Hospitalization and Pharmaceutical Drugs

Interestingly, though the United States spends more on health care than other OECD nations, it devoted a smaller percentage of total health expenditures (27.6%) to inpatient hospitalization than all the other countries (except Spain, which spent the same percentage on inpatient hospitalization) that reported inpatient expenditures in 2002. (See Table 7.4.) This finding is attributable to lower rates of hospitalization, shorter average lengths of stay, and a rise in outpatient hospital and other ambulatory care services in the United States.

In 2002 the United States spent 12.8% of its health care dollars on pharmaceutical drugs and durable medical supplies and equipment. (See Table 7.5.) This number was comparable to the percent of total expenditures that Denmark, Italy, Luxembourg, the Netherlands, and Switzerland spent on pharmaceuticals. Other countries reporting pharmaceutical expenditures spent considerably more— the Czech Republic 22.6%; France 20.8%; Hungary 27.6%; Italy 22.4%; Mexico 21.6%; the Slovak Republic 37.3%; and Spain 21.5%.

TABLE 7.1

Public funding on health as a percentage of total health expenditure, by country, selected years 1960–2003

Country	1960	1970	1980	1985	1990	1991	1992	1993	1994	1995	1996	1997	1998	1999	2000	2001	2002	2003
Australia	50.4	63	63	71.4	62.5	66.8	66.4	65.9	65.8	66.7	66.1	67.8	68.2	69.4	68.7	68.2	69.9	
Austria	69.4	63	68.8	76.1	73.5	73.4	73.5	74.2	74.4	70.9	69.7	70	69.7	69.6	69.6	68.5	71.2	
Belgium										69.5	71.1	69.8	70.2	70.6	70.5	71.4		69.8
Canada	42.6	69.9	75.6	75.5	74.5	74.6	74.1	72.7	72	71.4	70.9	70.1	70.6	70.3	70.4	70.1	69.9	
Czech Republic		96.6	96.8	92.2	97.4	96.8	95.5	94.8	93.9	92.7	92.5	91.7	91.9	91.5	91.4	91.4	91.4	
Denmark			87.8	85.6	82.7	83.5	83.2	82.7	82.2	82.5	82.4	82.3	82	82.2	82.5	82.6	83.1	
Finland	54.1	73.8	79	78.6	80.9	81.1	79.6	76.1	75.5	75.6	75.8	76.1	76.3	75.3	75.1	75.5	75.7	
France	62.4	75.5	80.1	78.5	76.6	76.3	76.6	76.5	76	76.3	76.1	76.2	76	76	75.8	75.9	76	
Germany		72.8	78.7	77.4	76.2		80.9	80.2	80.2	80.5	80.6	79.1	78.6	78.6	78.8	78.6	78.5	
Greece		42.6	55.6		53.7	53.4	54.6	54.5	50.2	52	53	52.8	52.1	53.4	53.9	53.1	52.9	
Hungary						89.1	88	87.4	87.3	84	81.6	81.3		72.4	70.7	69	70.2	
Iceland	66.7	66.2	88.2	87	86.6	86.7	84.8	83.3	83.6	83.9	83.3	83.7	83	83.9	83.6	83.2	84	
Ireland	76	81.7	81.6	75.7	71.9	73	71.5	73.3	71.9	71.6	71.4	74.6	76.5	72.8	73.3	75.6	75.2	
Italy	60.4	69.8	71.3	70.7	79.3	79.2	77.1	76.7	74.9	72.2	71.8	72.2	71.8	72.3	73.7	76	75.6	75.3
Japan					77.6	78.3	78.1	79.2	78.6	83	82.8	81.5	80.8	81.1	81.3	81.7		
Korea				28.1	37.4	34.1	35.1	35.1	35.4	38.1	40.9	43.4	48.5	45.9	47.6	54.4		
Luxembourg		88.9	92.8	89.2	93.1	93	92.8	92.9	91.7	92.4	92.8	92.5	92.4	89.8	89.7	89.8	85.4	
Mexico					40.4	43.9	43.1	43.2	45	42.1	41.4	44.7	46	47.8	46.5	44.8	44.9	
Netherlands			69.4	70.8	67.1	69	72.8	73.6	72.9	71	66.2	67.8						
New Zealand	77.8	80.3	88	87	82.4	82.2	79	76.6	77.5	77.2	76.7	77.3	77	77.5	78	76.4	77.9	
Norway		91.6	85.1	85.8	82.8	84.5	84.8	84.6	84.6	84.2	84.2	84.3	84.7	85.2	85	85.2	85.3	85.5
Poland					91.7	75.6	76.4	73.8	72.8	72.9	73.4	72	65.4	71.1	70	71.9	72.4	
Portugal		59	64.3	54.6	65.5	62.8	59.6	63	63.4	62.6	65.3	65.7	67.1	67.6	69.5	70.6	70.5	
Slovak Republic												91.7	91.6	89.6	89.4	89.3	89.1	
Spain	58.7	65.4	79.9	81.1	78.7	77.5	77.4	76.6	75.5	72.2	72.4	72.5	72.2	72	71.5	71.3	71.4	
Sweden		86	92.5	90.4	89.9	88.2	87.2	87.4	87.1	86.6	86.9	85.8	85.8	85.7	84.9	84.9	85.3	
Switzerland				50.3	52.4	52.8	53.8	54.3	54.2	53.8	54.7	55.2	54.9	55.3	55.6	57.1	57.9	
Turkey		37.3	27.3	50.2	61	62.9	67	66.4	68.9	70.3	69.2	71.6	71.9	61.1	62.9			
United Kingdom	85.2	87	89.4	85.8	83.6	83.3	84.6	85.1	83.9	83.9	82.9	80.4	80.4	80.6	80.9	83	83.4	
United States	23.3	36.4	41.5	39.9	39.6	41.2	42.4	43.1	44.8	45.3	45.6	45.3	44.5	44.3	44.4	44.9	44.9	

SOURCE: Public Funding on Health as a Percentage of Total Health Expenditure, in *OECD Health Data 2004*, 1st edition, Organisation for Economic Co-operation and Development (France), 2004, http://www.oecd.org/document/16/0,2340,en_2649_37407_2085200_1_1_1_37407,00.html (accessed July 13, 2004). Copyright OECD. Reproduced by permission of the OECD.

The Health Care System

TABLE 7.2

Out-of-pocket payments for health care, per capita, by country, in U.S. purchasing power parity dollars (PPP), selected years 1960–2002

	1960	1970	1980	1985	1990	1991	1992	1993	1994	1995	1996	1997	1998	1999	2000	2001	2002
Australia	34	—	110	142	216	237	252	269	286	287	317	337	381	403	450	483	—
Austria	—	—	—	—	—	—	—	—	—	277	309	325	349	377	400	397	388
Belgium	—	—	—	—	—	—	—	—	—	—	—	—	—	—	—	—	—
Canada	—	—	—	—	247	264	279	299	314	324	329	358	373	392	404	419	445
Czech Republic	—	—	—	—	14	17	25	39	50	64	68	76	75	80	84	94	96
Denmark	—	55	107	173	249	245	259	286	306	300	316	331	354	369	373	399	396
Finland	27	45	107	175	220	242	255	285	285	293	307	311	312	333	346	371	389
France	21	36	89	159	177	196	202	211	214	218	220	223	231	238	254	263	268
Germany	—	37	99	154	192	—	193	201	213	225	242	262	277	279	278	290	292
Greece	—	—	—	—	—	—	—	—	—	—	—	—	—	—	—	—	—
Hungary	—	—	—	—	—	63	75	80	91	108	125	129	173	204	223	266	283
Iceland	21	55	82	146	214	223	254	289	293	298	329	329	382	410	419	451	450
Ireland	—	—	—	95	131	145	154	157	167	188	185	191	159	227	240	245	311
Italy	—	—	86	145	214	232	271	303	343	372	388	411	440	446	454	425	439
Japan	—	—	—	—	—	—	—	—	—	—	—	—	—	—	330	342	—
Korea	—	—	—	102	177	199	221	235	243	261	288	292	305	313	335	347	364
Luxembourg	—	—	46	84	84	90	98	104	130	127	153	159	174	201	200	219	288
Mexico	—	—	—	—	169	181	205	217	220	213	206	213	221	232	252	281	266
Netherlands	—	—	—	—	—	—	—	—	—	—	—	—	206	222	233	253	298
New Zealand	—	—	51	67	143	144	174	198	190	200	205	212	234	243	247	290	298
Norway	—	—	—	—	202	231	240	251	263	288	315	331	342	367	399	421	439
Poland	—	—	—	—	25	87	89	101	104	115	131	142	195	165	173	177	180
Portugal	—	—	—	—	—	—	—	—	—	—	—	—	—	—	—	—	—
Slovak Republic	—	—	—	—	—	—	—	—	—	—	—	45	47	60	63	68	76
Spain	—	—	—	—	—	177	194	210	225	281	290	297	319	342	353	372	388
Switzerland	—	—	—	554	728	789	804	791	813	843	833	908	972	993	1023	1042	1085
Turkey	—	—	—	—	—	—	59	63	55	55	71	—	—	114	123	—	—
United Kingdom	—	—	41	—	104	121	131	133	148	152	161	—	—	—	—	—	—
United States	71	122	256	401	550	562	569	565	546	550	564	594	635	661	682	703	737

— Data unavailable

SOURCE: "Out-of-Pocket Payments—Per Capita US$ PPP," in *OECD Health Data 2004, 1st edition*, Organisation for Economic Co-operation and Development (France), 2004, http://www.oecd.org/document/16/0,2340, en_2649_37407_2085200_1_1_1_37407,00.html (accessed July 13, 2004). Copyright OECD. Reproduced by permission of the OECD.

TABLE 7.3

Private insurance as a percent of total expenditure on health, by country, selected years 1960–2002

	1960	1970	1980	1985	1990	1991	1992	1993	1994	1995	1996	1997	1998	1999	2000	2001	2002
Australia	10.3	—	15.7	9.6	11.4	11.6	11.5	11.2	10.9	10.7	10.5	9	7.6	6.6	6.9	7.6	—
Austria	6.8	8.1	7.6	9.8	9	9	8.9	8.8	8.6	8.3	7.7	8.1	7.6	7.3	7.3	7.4	7.4
Belgium	—	—	—	—	—	—	—	—	—	—	—	—	—	—	—	—	—
Canada	—	—	—	—	8.1	8.4	8.9	9.5	9.8	10.3	10.7	10.9	11.2	11.2	11.5	12.4	12.7
Czech Republic	—	—	—	—	—	—	—	—	—	—	—	—	—	—	—	—	—
Denmark	—	—	0.8	0.8	1.3	1.2	1.2	1	1.1	1.2	1.4	1.4	1.4	1.7	1.6	1.6	1.6
Finland	2.4	1.7	1.4	1.8	2.1	1.9	2.4	2.5	2.5	2.4	2.4	2.6	2.6	2.7	2.6	2.5	2.4
France	5.7	5.1	5.7	5.9	11	11	11	11.2	12	11.9	12.4	12.4	12.6	12.6	12.6	12.9	13.2
Germany	—	7.5	5.9	6.5	7.2	—	7.5	7.8	7.8	7.6	7.4	7.9	8	8.2	8.3	8.4	8.6
Greece	—	—	—	—	—	—	—	—	—	—	—	—	—	—	—	—	—
Hungary	—	—	—	—	—	—	—	—	—	—	—	—	0	0.1	0.2	0.3	0.4
Iceland	—	—	—	—	—	—	—	—	—	—	—	—	—	—	—	—	—
Ireland	—	—	—	—	9.1	9	8.6	8.9	9.2	9.1	9.2	8.7	8.9	8	7.6	6.3	5.4
Italy	—	—	—	—	0.6	0.7	0.8	0.9	0.9	1	1	1	0.9	0.9	0.9	0.9	0.9
Japan	—	—	—	—	—	—	—	—	—	0.4	0.3	0.3	0.3	0.3	0.3	0.3	—
Korea	—	—	—	2.8	2.6	2.8	2.6	2.9	2.8	2.6	2.6	2.5	2.6	2.7	2.9	2.2	—
Luxembourg	—	—	—	—	—	—	—	—	—	—	—	—	—	1.4	1.4	1.4	1.4
Mexico	—	—	—	—	1.2	1.7	1.7	1.8	1.8	1.7	2	2.2	2.2	2.2	2.5	2.8	3
Netherlands	—	—	—	—	—	—	—	—	—	—	—	16.9	16.6	16.9	16.1	16.5	17.1
New Zealand	—	—	1.1	1.8	2.8	3.6	4.8	5.2	6.1	6.4	6.7	6.8	6.4	6.2	6.3	6.3	5.7
Norway	—	—	—	—	—	—	—	—	—	—	—	—	—	—	—	—	—
Poland	—	—	—	—	—	—	—	—	—	—	—	—	—	—	—	—	—
Portugal	—	—	—	0.2	0.8	0.9	1.2	1.3	1.4	1.3	1.4	1.5	—	—	—	—	—
Slovak Republic	—	—	—	—	—	—	—	—	—	—	—	0	0	—	—	—	—
Spain	—	3.3	3.2	3.7	3.7	2.9	3	3.2	3.4	3.4	3.5	3.5	3.7	3.8	3.9	4	4.1
Sweden	—	—	—	—	—	—	—	—	—	—	—	—	—	4.2	4.4	—	—
Switzerland	—	—	—	11.1	11	10.7	10.9	11.5	11.7	12.2	12.9	11.5	11.4	10.4	10.5	10.2	9.6
Turkey	—	—	—	1.2	—	0.1	—	—	0.7	—	—	—	—	—	—	—	—
United Kingdom	—	0.9	1.3	2.5	3.3	3.4	3.4	3.4	3.3	3.2	3.3	—	—	—	—	—	—
United States	22.5	21.9	28.4	31.1	34.2	33.9	33.7	34.2	33.8	33.9	33.7	33.5	33.9	34.4	35.1	35.7	36.2

— Data unavailable

SOURCE: "Private Insurance—% Total Expenditure on Health," in *OECD Health Data 2004*, *1st edition*, Organisation for Economic Co-operation and Development (France), 2004, http://www.oecd.org/document/16/0,2340,en_2649_37407_2085200_1_1_1_37407,00.html (accessed July 13, 2004). Copyright OECD. Reproduced by permission of the OECD.

TABLE 7.4

Total expenditure on in-patient care as a percent of total expenditure on health, by country, selected years 1960–2003

	1960	1970	1980	1985	1990	1991	1992	1993	1994	1995	1996	1997	1998	1999	2000	2001	2002	2003
Australia	43	—	51.6	48.8	46.5	46.1	44.5	43.2	43.1	43.1	42.9	43.3	43.1	41.9	40.7	40.2	—	—
Austria	—	—	—	—	—	—	—	—	—	44.7	43.6	39.6	38.6	38.5	38.3	38	38.2	—
Belgium	—	25.7	33.1	34	32.8	33.6	34	35.1	35.7	33.5	34.5	34.6	—	—	—	—	—	—
Canada	43.7	52.6	53.8	51.6	49.1	48.9	48.5	47.4	45.8	44.6	44	43.2	42.5	—	30	29.1	28.8	28.8
Czech Republic	—	—	—	—	—	—	—	—	—	29.6	33.8	35.6	35.4	33.9	34.6	36.6	37.8	—
Denmark	39.9	—	61.6	60.4	56.7	56.4	55.9	55.3	55.4	55	55.3	54.7	54.5	54.4	53.2	51.9	51.1	—
Finland	38.6	46.4	46.3	46	44.7	44.4	43.9	43.1	42.2	42	41.7	41.3	41.1	40.5	39.9	39.3	39.2	—
France	—	40.6	50.2	48.7	45.7	44.9	44.7	44.6	45	45.1	45.2	45	44.3	43.2	42.3	41.7	41.3	—
Germany	—	30.8	33.2	34.1	34.7	—	35.8	37.4	37.6	36.9	36.3	36.4	36.7	36.5	36.6	36.1	36.1	—
Greece	—	—	—	—	—	—	—	—	—	—	—	—	—	—	—	—	—	—
Hungary	—	—	—	—	—	65.2	62.6	59.1	55.8	54.8	52.4	—	29.3	29.3	29.3	28.1	29	—
Iceland	37	50.9	59.1	56.5	54.7	54.8	53.6	54.1	54	54.4	54.7	54.8	54.9	53.6	55.2	54.6	—	—
Ireland	—	—	58.8	—	—	—	—	—	—	—	—	—	—	—	—	—	—	41.8
Italy	34.1	—	—	—	42.7	43.9	44	45.2	45.9	44.8	41.7	42.5	41.4	41.8	41.4	41.5	41.5	—
Japan	—	26.4	30.9	32.8	33	32.1	32.8	32.2	31	36.8	37	37.7	38.3	38.5	39	38.9	—	—
Korea	—	—	31.3	19.2	23.3	23.5	24.1	23.6	22.9	23.4	24.3	25.3	25.8	27	25.5	22.9	—	—
Luxembourg	—	—	—	27.4	26.4	26.7	26.9	28	27.7	31.3	32.4	36	30.7	40.2	41.2	39.5	40.3	—
Mexico	—	—	—	—	—	—	—	—	—	—	—	—	—	36	37.3	41.6	33	—
Netherlands	—	—	54.6	54.1	49.2	49.8	49.7	49.8	49.7	49.1	49.6	49.9	40.1	39.9	39.8	40.5	40.8	—
New Zealand	—	—	72.2	76.2	60.4	59.1	56.5	59.1	—	—	—	—	—	—	—	—	—	—
Norway	38.1	68.2	63.9	64.8	61.7	—	—	—	—	—	—	—	—	—	—	—	—	—
Poland	—	—	—	—	—	33	35	36.5	36.8	33.9	—	—	—	—	—	—	—	—
Portugal	—	—	28.7	26.4	32.3	—	—	—	—	—	—	—	—	30.7	26.4	28.7	35	—
Slovak Republic	—	—	—	—	—	—	—	—	—	—	—	—	—	—	—	—	—	—
Spain	—	—	—	—	—	—	—	—	—	31	30.8	30	29.3	28.8	28.2	27.9	27.6	—
Sweden	—	—	54.1	55.7	44.1	47.3	47.6	48.1	47.5	49	47.7	47.2	42.6	40.8	46.3	31.6	31.2	—
Switzerland	35.7	44.4	47.5	46.7	47.9	49.9	49.8	49.9	49.1	47.9	48	47.8	47.2	46.8	46.8	47.3	48.1	—
Turkey	—	—	—	—	33.4	35.1	25.3	25.9	26.9	28.7	28.2	28.8	29.3	21.3	19.9	—	—	—
United Kingdom	—	—	—	—	—	—	—	—	—	—	—	—	—	—	—	—	—	—
United States	35.6	41.1	44.1	40.4	36.1	35.7	35	34.1	33.1	32.2	31.6	30.9	30.2	29.1	28.4	28	27.6	—

— Data unavailable

SOURCE: "Total Expenditure on In-Patient Care, % Total Expenditure on Health," in *OECD Health Data 2004, 1st edition*, Organisation for Economic Co-operation and Development (France), 2004, http://www.oecd.org/document/16/0,2340,en_2649_37407_2085200_1_1_1_37407,00.html (accessed July 13, 2004). Copyright OECD. Reproduced by permission of the OECD.

TABLE 7.5

Expenditure on pharmaceuticals as a percentage of total expenditure on health care, by country, selected years 1960–85 and 1990–2003

% total expenditure on health

	1960	1970	1980	1985	1990	1991	1992	1993	1994	1995	1996	1997	1998	1999	2000	2001	2002	2003
Australia	22.6		8	8.1	9	9.5	9.9	10.4	11	11.2	11.5	11.7	11.9	12.4	13.4	13.8		
Austria										11.1	11.2	13.1	14	14.6	15.4	15.8	16.1	
Belgium		28.1	17.4	15.7	15.5	15.6	16.3	17.4	17.5	16.3	15.5	16.2						
Canada	12.9	11.3	8.5	9.6	11.5	11.8	12.4	13	13.1	13.8	14	14.8	15.2	15.5	16	16.3	16.6	16.7
Czech Republic						21	18.4	21.1	19.4	24.7	25.6	25.5	25.3	23.2	22.7	22	21.9	22.6
Denmark			6	6.6	7.5	8	7.9	8.5	8.8	9.1	8.9	9	9	8.7	8.7	8.8	9.2	
Finland	17.1	12.6	10.7	9.7	9.4	9.9	10.8	12.3	13.4	14.1	14.4	14.8	14.6	15.1	15.5	15.7	15.9	
France	23.5	23.8	16	16.2	16.9	17.2	17.1	17.5	17.4	17.6	17.6	18	18.6	19.5	20.3	20.9	20.8	
Germany		16.2	13.4	13.8	14.3		14.7	13.2	12.9	12.7	12.8	12.9	13.4	13.5	13.6	14.3	14.5	
Greece		25.5	18.8	14.3	16.3	17	16.6	16.1	15.7	16.1	16.2	13.9	14.4	15.4	15.6	15.3		
Hungary						27.6	26.5	28.4	28	25	26	25.9				28.5	27.6	
Iceland	18.5	17.1	15.9	16.6	13.5	12.3	13	12.4	13.1	13.4	14	13.6	13.6	14.1	14.1	14		
Ireland		22.2	10.9	9.9	12.2	11.6	11.1	10.7	10.6	10.4	10.5	10.2	10.4	10.5	10.6	10.3	11	
Italy				21.2	20.4	20.4	19.9	19.9	20.9	21.1	21.3	21.8	22.3	22.3	22.4	22.4		21.9
Japan			21.2	18	21.4	22.9	22	22.3	21.1	22.3	21.6	20.6	18.9	18.4	18.7	18.8		
Korea				27.1	24.5	25.6	23.5	22.9	21.4	21	19	16.3	13.4	13.5	16	22.4		
Luxembourg		19.7	14.5	14.7	14.9	15			12.2	12	11.5	12.6	12.3	11.9	12	12	11.6	
Mexico														18.6	19.5	19.9	21.6	
Netherlands			8	9.3	9.6	9.6	10.5	11	10.9	11	11	11	10.2	10.6	10.8	10.6	10.4	
New Zealand			11.9	13.3	13.8	14.1	14.2	14.9	15.8	14.8	14.5	14.4						
Norway		7.8	8.7	9.1	7.2	7.3	7.5	9.6	8.8	9	9.1	9.2						
Poland																		
Portugal		13.4	19.9	25.4	24.9	24.3	24.7	25.6	25.2	23.6	23.8	23.8	23.4					
Slovak Republic														34	34	34	37.3	
Spain			21	20.3	17.8					19.2	19.8	20.8	21	21.5	21.3	21.2	21.5	
Sweden		6.6	6.5	7	8	8.7	9.7	10.9	11.9	12.5	13.7	12.5	13.8	14	13.9	13.3	13.1	
Switzerland				11.3	10.2	9.8	9.4	9.7	9.8	10	10	10.3	10.2	10.5	10.7	10.6	10.3	
Turkey				13.2	20.5				31.6					24.3	24.8			
Unitek Kingdom		14.7	12.8	14.1	13.5	13.8	14.2	14.8	15.1	15.3	15.6	15.8						
United States	16.6	12.4	9.1	9	9.2	9.1	8.8	8.6	8.6	8.9	9.2	9.6	10.3	11.2	11.9	12.4	12.8	

SOURCE: "Total Expenditure on Pharmaceuticals, Percent Total Expenditure on Health," in *OECD Health Data 2004, 1st edition*, Organisation for Economic Co-operation and Development (France), 2004, www.oecd.org/dataoecd/13/9/31963517.xls (accessed November 16, 2004). Copyright OECD. Reproduced by permission of the OECD.

Hospital Utilization Statistics

Of the fifteen OECD countries reporting acute care hospital utilization data, the Czech Republic and Austria had the highest number of acute care beds in 2002 (6.5 and 6.1 beds per one thousand population, respectively). (See Table 7.6.) Hungary had the next-highest number of beds, at 5.9 per one thousand population in 2002. The United States was among the lowest, 2.9 in 2002, trailed only by Finland, Turkey, and Mexico with 2.3, 2.1, and 1 beds, respectively, per one thousand population.

Hospital lengths of stay have consistently declined since 1960, in part because increasing numbers of illnesses could be treated as effectively in outpatient settings and because many countries have reduced inpatient hospitalization rates and average length of stay (ALOS) to control health care costs. In 2002 South Korea had the longest acute-care ALOS of the OECD nations reporting (11.0 days), followed by and Switzerland and the Czech Republic with ALOS of 9.2 and 8.3 days, respectively. (See Table 7.7.) The shortest hospital stays in 2002 occurred in Mexico, Denmark, and Finland, where ALOS was 3.5, 3.7, and 4.3 days, respectively. The United States ALOS was 5.7 days in 2002, on par with Norway, also at 5.7.

Medical practice, particularly the types and frequency of procedures performed, also varies from one country to another. The OECD looked at rates of Caesarian section (also known as C-section; delivery of a baby through an incision in the abdomen as opposed to vaginal delivery) per one thousand births and found considerable variation in the rates for this surgical procedure. Among the fifteen countries reporting in 2002, the highest rates for Caesarian section were reported in the United Kingdom (427), South Korea (392.1), Italy (361.9), Mexico (336), the United States (261), and Luxembourg (258). (See Table 7.8.) Since Caesarian section is performed in the hospital and generally involves at least an overnight stay, the frequency with which it and other surgical procedures are performed contributes to hospitalization rates and expenditures.

Physicians' Numbers Are Increasing

Since 1960, the OECD member nations have all enjoyed growing physician populations. In 2002, of those countries reporting, Italy reported the highest ratio of practicing physicians, 4.4 per one thousand population, with most countries ranging between two and four physicians per one thousand population. (See Table 7.9.) In 2002 the fewest practicing physicians were found in Turkey (1.3 per one thousand population), followed by South Korea (1.5 physicians per one thousand population) Mexico (1.5), and Japan (2). Canada, New Zealand, and the United Kingdom all reported data showing 2.1 physicians per one thousand

TABLE 7.6

Acute care beds, per 1,000 population, by country, selected years 1960–2002

	1960	1970	1980	1985	1990	1995	2000	2001	2002
Australia	6.5	6	6.4	5.3	—	4.2	3.8	3.7	—
Austria	—	—	—	7.5	7.1	6.6	6.3	6.2	6.1
Belgium	—	4.7	5.5	5.9	4.9	4.7	—	—	—
Canada	—	—	4.6	4.4	4	4.3	3.3	3.2	—
Czech Republic	—	—	8.6	8.6	8.5	7.2	6.6	6.5	6.5
Denmark	—	—	5.3	4.7	4.1	3.9	3.5	3.4	—
Finland	3.9	4.8	4.9	4.8	4.3	4	2.4	2.4	2.3
France	—	—	6.2	5.7	5.2	4.6	4.1	4	—
Germany	—	—	—	—	—	9.7	9.1	9	—
Greece	—	—	4.7	4.2	4	4	4	—	—
Hungary	4.6	5.6	6.6	6.8	7.1	7	6.3	6	5.9
Iceland	—	—	—	—	4.3	3.7	—	—	—
Ireland	—	—	4.3	4.2	3.3	3.2	3	3	3
Italy	—	—	7.9	7	6.2	5.5	4.3	4.6	—
Japan	—	—	—	—	—	—	—	—	—
Korea	—	—	—	—	2.7	3.8	5.2	5.2	5.7
Luxembourg	—	—	7.4	7.5	6.8	6.2	5.9	5.9	5.8
Mexico	—	—	—	—	—	1.1	1.1	1	1
Netherlands	5.1	5.5	5.2	4.7	4.3	3.8	3.5	3.3	—
New Zealand	—	—	—	—	8	—	—	—	—
Norway	—	—	5.2	4.7	3.8	3.3	3.1	3.1	3.1
Poland	4.6	5.1	5.6	5.7	6.3	5.8	5.1	5	4.6
Portugal	3.6	4.2	4.2	3.5	3.4	3.3	3.3	3.2	—
Slovak Republic	—	—	—	—	—	—	5.9	5.6	5.5
Spain	—	—	—	3.5	3.3	3	2.8	—	—
Sweden	—	—	5.1	4.6	4.1	3	2.4	—	—
Switzerland	8.2	7.1	7.2	6.8	6.5	5.5	4.1	4	3.9
Turkey	—	1.3	1.5	1.6	2	2.1	2.2	2.1	2.1
United Kingdom	—	—	3.5	3.3	2.8	4	3.9	3.9	3.9
United States	3.5	4.1	4.4	4.2	3.7	3.3	2.9	2.9	2.9

— Data unavailable

SOURCE: "Acute Care Beds, per 1,000 Population," in *OECD Health Data 2004, 1st edition,* 2004, Organisation for Economic Co-operation and Development (France), 2004, http://www.oecd.org/document/16/0,2340,en_2649_37407_2085200_1_1_1_37407,00.html (accessed July 13, 2004). Copyright OECD. Reproduced by permission of the OECD.

population. Though figures for 2002 were not reported from the United States, the number from 2001 was 2.4 physicians for one thousand people.

The ratio of physicians to population is a limited measure of health care quality, because many other factors, such as the availability of other health care providers as well as accessibility and affordability of health care services, also influence the quality of health care systems. Furthermore, during the last two decades research has shown that more medical care, in terms of numbers and concentration of health care providers, is not necessarily linked to better health status for the population. Researchers in the United States have found that an oversupply of providers may result in unnecessary treatment, procedures, and health care costs.

OVERVIEWS OF SELECTED HEALTH CARE SYSTEMS

The OECD international health data enable researchers to compare health systems to one another in terms of health care costs and quality. In May 2004 Peter Hussey, Gerard Anderson, Robin Osborn, Colin Feek, Vivienne McLaughlin, John Millar, and Arnold Epstein published "How Does the Quality of Care Compare in Five Countries?" (*Health Affairs,* vol. 23, Issue 3, 2004). The investigators considered how well five countries—Australia, Canada, England, New Zealand, and the United States—performed on twenty-one measures of health care quality developed by the Commonwealth Fund International Working Group on Quality Indicators. The measures included survival rates for selected cancers, kidney and liver transplant, acute myocardial infarction (heart attack), and ischemic stroke; avoidable outcomes such as suicide, asthma mortality, and the incidence of pertussis (whooping cough) and hepatitis B; and process measures such as rates of screening for breast and cervical cancer as well as influenza and polio vaccination rates. The measures were selected by the group of health care quality experts as key indicators of health system performance, and also because they identify opportunities for improving health and health care.

The investigators concluded that no one country delivers the best or worst medical care and observed that there was room for improvement in health care delivery in every nation. For example, while the United states spends the most money on health care and boasts the highest five-year survival rates for breast cancer, it had higher mortality rates for asthma than Australia or England and the

TABLE 7.7

Average length of stay for acute care, in days, by country, selected years 1960–2002

	1960	1970	1980	1985	1990	1991	1992	1993	1994	1995	1996	1997	1998	1999	2000	2001	2002
Australia	11.5	8.7	7.7	7.4	—	6.5	6.6	6.4	6.4	6.5	6.4	6.2	6.1	6.2	6.1	6.1	—
Austria	—	—	14.5	10.8	9.3	8.8	8.5	8.2	8	7.9	7.6	7.1	6.8	6.5	6.3	6.2	6
Belgium	—	—	—	—	—	—	—	9.8	9.6	9.4	9.2	8.8	8.7	8	—	—	—
Canada	—	—	10	10.4	10.3	10.2	10	9.9	7.4	7.2	7.1	7	7	7.1	7.2	7.3	—
Czech Republic	15	15	13.6	13.1	12	11.9	11.6	11.2	10.8	10.2	9.6	9.1	8.8	8.6	8.7	8.5	8.3
Denmark	—	12.5	8.5	7.8	6.4	6.3	6.1	6	4.1	4.1	4.1	4	3.9	3.9	3.8	3.8	3.7
Finland	12.5	12.8	8.8	8	7	7	6.1	5.7	5.6	5.5	5.3	5	4.7	4.5	4.4	4.4	4.3
France	—	—	10.2	8.6	7	6.7	6.5	6.4	6.4	6.2	6.1	5.9	5.8	5.5	5.6	5.7	—
Germany	—	24.6	19.6	18	16.7	16.2	15.6	15	14.7	14.2	13.5	12.5	12.3	12	11.9	11.6	—
Greece	—	—	10.2	8.9	7.5	7.2	7.1	6.6	6.7	6.4	6.5	6.3	6.3	6.3	—	—	—
Hungary	11.3	11.2	11.2	10.6	9.9	9.7	9.5	—	9.8	9.2	8.6	8.2	7.8	7.5	7.1	7	6.9
Iceland	—	—	—	—	7	6.6	6.4	6.4	6.3	5.9	—	—	5.7	—	—	—	—
Ireland	—	—	8.5	7.4	6.7	6.7	6.8	6.7	6.7	6.6	6.5	6.5	6.5	6.5	6.4	6.4	6.5
Italy	—	—	—	—	—	9.5	9.3	9.2	9	8.4	8	7.3	7.2	7.1	7	6.9	—
Japan	—	—	—	—	—	—	—	—	—	—	—	—	—	—	—	—	—
Korea	—	—	10	11	12	11	11	11	11	11	11	11	11	10	11	11	11
Luxembourg	—	—	13	11.9	11	10.8	10.3	10.2	9.9	9.8	9.8	—	8	7.9	7.7	7.6	7.6
Mexico	—	—	—	—	4.2	4.3	4.3	4.2	3.8	3.7	3.6	3.5	3.7	3.7	3.6	3.5	3.5
Netherlands	20.1	18.8	14	12.5	11.2	10.9	10.6	10.4	10.1	9.9	9.8	9.6	9.5	9.2	9	8.6	—
New Zealand	—	—	—	—	—	—	—	—	—	—	—	5.5	4.9	—	—	—	—
Norway	—	14.8	10.9	9.6	7.8	7.4	6.9	6.8	6.6	6.5	6.3	6.4	6.2	6.1	6	5.8	5.7
Poland	—	—	—	—	—	—	—	—	—	—	—	—	—	—	—	—	—
Portugal	—	15.3	11.4	11.1	8.4	8.3	7.9	7.7	7.7	7.9	7.9	7.5	7.3	7.3	7.7	7.3	7.8
Slovak Republic	—	—	—	—	—	—	—	—	—	—	10.6	10.2	9.4	8.7	8.6	8.3	—
Spain	—	—	—	10.1	9.6	9.3	9.2	9.1	9	8.8	8	7.6	7.5	5	7.1	—	—
Sweden	—	11	8.5	7.5	6.5	6.2	5.8	5.5	5.3	5.2	5	5.1	5.1	5	5	5	4.8
Switzerland	—	—	15.5	14.7	13.4	13	12.1	12.1	12	12	12	10.5	9.9	9.8	9.3	9.2	9.2
Turkey	—	—	6.3	6.2	6	6	6	5.9	5.8	5.7	5.6	5.5	5.4	5.4	5.4	5.4	5.2
United Kingdom	—	—	8.7	8.1	5.9	5.9	5.7	5.6	5.4	7	7.1	7.1	6.8	6.8	6.9	6.9	6.9
United States	7.6	8.2	7.6	7.1	7.3	7.2	7.1	7	6.8	6.5	6.2	6.1	6	5.9	5.8	5.8	5.7

— Data unavailable

SOURCE: "ALOS: Acute Care, Days," in *OECD Health Data 2004, 1st edition*, Organisation for Economic Co-operation and Development (France), 2004, http://www.oecd.org/document/16/0,2340,en_2649_37407_2085200_1_1_1_37407,00.html (accessed July 13, 2004). Copyright OECD. Reproduced by permission of the OECD.

TABLE 7.8

Caesarean section surgical procedures per 1,000 live births, by country, selected years 1960–2002

	1960	1970	1980	1985	1990	1991	1992	1993	1994	1995	1996	1997	1998	1999	2000	2001	2002
Australia	—	42	128	150	175	179	182	188	192	192	193	201	209	217	231	261	—
Austria	—	—	—	—	—	—	—	—	—	123.9	130.9	139.5	145.8	164.2	172	188.6	206.1
Belgium	—	—	74	94.2	104.5	116.1	119.7	129.4	129.4	134.5	139.6	145.4	144.1	159.2	—	—	—
Canada	—	—	—	—	—	—	—	—	174.8	174.8	178.7	183.8	187.6	195.9	209.2	222.3	—
Czech Republic	—	21.9	44.1	62.7	76.1	83.5	—	91	100.9	112	115.6	117.9	122.7	123.4	128.9	132.5	140.7
Denmark	—	57	104	128.9	124	122.6	122.2	125.2	125.2	124.8	125.5	125.6	133.1	136.7	144.5	160.6	176.2
Finland	—	60	—	148	142	142.3	143.5	144.9	152.4	155.1	155.2	154.4	152.8	154.7	157.3	164.1	161.4
France	—	—	—	—	139.4	127.5	145.1	152	—	—	—	155.7	162.3	166.9	171.2	177.2	—
Germany	—	—	—	—	—	157	152.2	159.4	165.7	170.7	172.4	176.1	181.4	190.7	198	208.9	220
Greece	—	—	—	—	—	—	—	—	—	—	—	—	—	—	—	—	—
Hungary	—	—	—	—	—	—	—	—	125.6	136.1	145.5	156.8	170.1	189	201	219	235
Iceland	—	31	74	112.3	118.1	114.3	134.3	129.8	137.6	141.1	151.5	162.6	159.2	173.2	176.8	167.7	—
Ireland	—	—	—	77.1	105.4	115.6	120.4	128.7	—	—	—	—	—	204.2	—	—	—
Italy	—	—	112	158	207.9	226	232.4	241.3	247.6	260.7	268.8	268.9	307.4	323.9	332.7	347.6	361.9
Japan	—	—	—	—	—	—	—	—	—	—	—	—	—	—	—	—	—
Korea	—	—	386	—	—	—	—	—	—	—	—	—	—	—	—	395.7	392.1
Luxembourg	—	—	132	167	165	170	174	—	168	164	164	169	181	209	218	242	258
Mexico	—	—	—	—	—	—	—	—	—	—	—	—	—	—	—	323	336
Netherlands	—	21.4	46.8	64.1	74.1	77.4	79.5	84.4	91.8	96.5	100.6	103.9	110.6	113.4	118.7	136.4	135.2
New Zealand	—	—	—	—	121	129.9	124.7	138.1	144.3	151.2	156.8	164.5	181.6	183.7	201.7	212.1	222.4
Norway	—	—	83.8	119.7	127.5	124.8	125.6	124.8	126	126.4	127.3	128.8	136.7	134.5	136.6	156	—
Poland	—	—	—	—	—	—	—	—	137.8	151.8	155.6	161.2	—	—	—	—	—
Portugal	—	—	—	—	—	—	—	222.3	230.7	232.8	237	250.5	256	261.8	263.3	282.4	—
Slovak Republic	—	—	—	62.7	87.1	91.2	99.2	105.9	111.7	115	122.3	129.9	133.1	138.6	147	166.3	178.3
Spain	—	—	—	104.5	142.2	150.3	162	173.3	177.8	188	192.9	198	205.4	—	—	—	—
Sweden	—	—	118.4	120.6	107.9	112.3	112	116	117.3	120	117.3	131.6	137.6	144.1	152.4	164.5	—
Switzerland	—	—	—	198	186	177	—	—	—	—	—	—	—	—	—	—	242
Turkey	—	—	—	—	—	—	—	—	—	—	—	—	—	136	—	—	—
United Kingdom	28	43	88	106	—	—	—	—	417	459	483	—	—	403	408	440	427
United States	—	—	—	—	227	226	223	218	212	208	207	208	212	220	229	244	261

— Data unavailable

SOURCE: "Surgical Procedures: Caesarean Section, per 1,000 Live Births," in *OECD Health Data 2004, 1st edition,* Organisation for Economic Co-operation and Development (France), 2004, http://www.irdes.fr/ecosante/OCDE/362000.html (accessed July 13, 2004). Copyright OECD. Reproduced by permission of the OECD.

lowest five-year survival rates for kidney transplants. Australia had higher rates of breast cancer screening than other countries and the lowest mortality rates for persons suffering from acute myocardial infarction but also the lowest five-year survival rates for childhood leukemia and a higher incidence of pertussis than other nations.

Canada had the highest five-year survival rates for childhood leukemia and the highest polio vaccination rate; however, it also reported the second-highest incidence of pertussis and the highest rates for ischemic stroke. England had the lowest five-year survival rates for breast cancer and lower survival rates for colorectal cancer than other countries but boasts the highest polio vaccination rates and among the lowest rates for suicide. New Zealand reported the highest five-year survival rates for colorectal cancer and non-Hodgkins lymphoma but also suffered the highest suicide rates, particularly among young people aged fifteen to nineteen, as well as the highest mortality rates for ischemic stroke.

Another article in the May 2004 issue of *Health Affairs,* "U.S. Health Care Spending in an International Context" by renowned political economist Uwe Reinhardt and his public health colleagues Peter Hussey and Gerard Anderson, found that the United States spent $4,887 per capita on health care in 2001, far outstripping other OECD countries, and averaging $2,000 more per capita than Canada, the next-highest spending country of the five quality indicator nations, which spent $2,792. Australia spent $2,513 per capita, the U.K. $1,992, and New Zealand $1,710.

The authors cited several factors contributing to higher U.S. health costs—a fragmented financing system that generates higher administrative costs; and health care providers with greater market power than health care purchasers, which allows prices to rise above levels of other countries where the government intervenes to control prices. They also noted that the U.S. health system provides a more specialized, intensive form of care and observed that although U.S. prices for drugs are high by international standards, there is widespread speculation that foreign governments keep drug prices artificially low, while simultaneously forcing the United States to assume the significant economic burden of drug research and development. The authors also wondered whether the growth of health care spending as a component of the U.S. GDP is economically or politically sustainable. Like other industry observers, they predicted that increasing health insurance premiums might prompt some firms to drop coverage for low-wage workers, adding to the ranks of the uninsured.

TABLE 7.9

Practicing physicians, density per 1,000 population, by country, selected years 1960–2002

	1960	1970	1980	1985	1990	1995	2000	2001	2002
Australia	—	—	—	1.9	2.2	2.4	2.5	2.5	—
Austria	1.4	1.4	1.6	1.9	2.2	2.7	3.2	3.3	3.3
Belgium	1.3	—	2.3	2.8	3.3	3.5	3.9	3.9	3.9
Canada	—	1.4	1.8	2	2.1	2.1	2.1	2.1	2.1
Czech Republic	—	1.8	2.3	2.6	2.7	3	3.4	3.4	3.5
Denmark	1.2	1.4	2.2	2.5	2.9	3	3.2	3.3	3.3
Finland	0.6	0.9	1.7	2.1	2.4	2.8	3.1	3.1	3.1
France	—	1.2	1.9	2.7	3.1	3.2	3.3	3.3	3.3
Germany	—	—	—	—	—	3.1	3.3	3.3	3.3
Greece	1.3	1.6	2.4	2.9	3.4	3.9	4.5	4.5	—
Hungary	1.5	2	2.3	2.5	2.8	3	—	—	3.2
Iceland	1.2	1.4	2.1	2.6	2.8	3	3.4	3.5	3.6
Ireland	.	—	—	—	—	2.1	2.2	2.4	2.4
Italy	—	—	—	—	—	3.9	4.1	4.3	4.4
Japan	1	1.1	1.3	1.5	1.7	—	1.9	—	2
Korea	—	—	—	0.6	0.8	1.1	1.3	1.4	1.5
Luxembourg	1	1.1	1.7	1.8	2	2.2	2.5	2.5	2.6
Mexico	—	—	—	—	—	1.6	1.4	1.5	1.5
Netherlands	1.1	1.2	1.9	2.2	2.5	—	3.2	3.3	3.1
New Zealand	—	—	1.6	1.7	1.9	2	2.2	2.2	2.1
Norway	1.2	1.4	2	2.2	—	2.8	2.9	3	3.4
Poland	1	1.4	1.8	2	2.1	2.3	2.2	2.2	2.3
Portugal	0.8	0.9	2	2.5	2.8	2.9	3.2	3.2	—
Slovak Republic	—	—	—	—	—	—	3.7	3.6	3.6
Spain	—	—	—	—	—	2.5	3.1	3	2.9
Sweden	1	1.3	2.2	2.6	2.9	2.8	3	—	—
Switzerland	1.4	1.5	2.5	2.7	3	3.2	3.5	3.5	3.6
Turkey	0.3	0.4	0.6	0.7	0.9	1.1	1.3	1.3	1.3
United Kingdom	0.8	0.9	1.3	1.4	1.5	1.8	2	2	2.1
United States	1.1	1.2	1.5	1.7	1.8	2	2.2	2.4	—

— Data unavailable

SOURCE: "Practising Physicians, Density/1.000," in *OECD Health Data 2004, 1st edition,* Organisation for Economic Co-operation and Development (France), 2004, http://www.irdes.fr/ecosante/OCDE/2100300.html (accessed July 13, 2004). Copyright OECD. Reproduced by permission of the OECD.

In 2001 Reinhardt, Hussey, and Anderson analyzed OECD data describing the health care systems in the thirty member countries. The researchers studied the economic development, spending, supply, population health status, service utilization, and technology, and issued a paper detailing key differences between the systems, "Cross-National Comparisons of Health Systems Using OECD Data, 1999" (*Health Affairs,* May/June 2002). An earlier report by Anderson of the Center for Hospital Finance and Management of Johns Hopkins University ("Multinational Comparisons of Health Care," Commonwealth Fund, October 1998) provided a comprehensive examination of health care expenditures, coverage, and outcomes in eight OECD member countries. These overviews draw upon these researchers' and industry observers' assessments of the strengths, weaknesses, and challenges faced by the various models of health service delivery.

United States

The U.S. health care financing system is based on the consumer sovereignty, or private insurance, model. There are more than one thousand private insurance companies in the United States. Employer-based health insurance is tax-subsidized: health insurance premiums are a tax-deductible business expense and are not generally taxed as employee compensation. The premiums for individually purchased policies purchased by self-employed Americans became fully tax-deductible in 2003. Benefits, premiums, and provider reimbursement methods differ among private insurance plans and among public programs as well.

Most physicians who provide both ambulatory care—hospital outpatient service and office visits—and inpatient hospital care are generally reimbursed on either a fee-for-service basis, per capita (literally, per head, but in managed care frequently per member per month, or PMPM) and payment rates vary among insurers. Increasing numbers of physicians are salaried; they are employees of the government, hospital and health care delivery systems, universities, and private industry.

The nation's more than sixty-five hundred hospitals are paid on the basis of charges, costs, negotiated rates, or diagnosis-related groups (DRGs), depending on the patient's insurer. There are no overall global budgets or expenditure limits. Nevertheless, managed care (oversight by some group or authority to verify the medical necessity of treatments and to control the cost of health care) has assumed an expanding role. Health maintenance organizations (HMOs), preferred provider organizations (PPOs), and other managed care plans and payers (government and private health insurance) now exert greater control over the practices of individual health care providers in an effort to control costs. To the extent that they govern reimbursement, managed care organizations are viewed by many physicians and other industry observers as dictating the methods, terms, and quality of health care delivery.

IS THE UNITED STATES SPENDING MORE AND GETTING LESS? A primary indicator of the quality of health care delivery in any nation is the health status of its people. Many factors can affect the health of individuals and populations: heredity, race/ethnicity, gender, income, education, geography, violent crime, environmental agents, and exposure to infectious diseases, as well as access to, and availability of, health care services.

Still, in the nation that spends the most on the health of its citizens, it seems reasonable to expect to see tangible benefits of expenditures for health care—measurable gains in health status. This section considers three health outcomes—measures used to assess the health of a population—including life expectancy at birth, infant mortality, and the incidence of cancer, to determine the extent to which Americans citizens derive health benefits from record-high outlays for medical care.

Overall life expectancy at birth consistently increased in all thirty OECD member nations between 1960 and 2002; however, in every year including 2001, U.S. life

TABLE 7.10

Life expectancy in years, males and females at birth, by country, selected years 1960–2002

	1960		1970		1980		1990		1995		2000		2001		2002	
	Females at birth	Males at birth	Females at birth	Males at birth	Females at birth	Males at birth	Females at birth	Males at birth	Females at birth	Males at birth	Females at birth	Males at birth	Females at birth	Males at birth	Females at birth	Males at birth
Australia	73.9	67.9	74.2	67.4	78.1	71	80.1	73.9	80.8	75	82	76.6	82.4	77	82.6	77.4
Austria	71.9	65.4	73.4	66.5	76.1	69	78.8	72.2	79.9	73.3	81.1	75.1	81.5	75.6	81.7	75.8
Belgium	73.5	67.7	74.2	67.8	76.8	70	79.4	72.7	80.2	73.4	80.8	74.6	81.1	74.9	81.1	75.1
Canada	*	*	*	*	78.9	71.7	80.8	74.4	81.1	75.1	82	76.7	82.2	77.1	*	*
Czech Republic	73.4	67.9	73	66.1	73.9	66.8	75.4	67.6	76.6	69.7	78.4	71.7	78.5	72.1	78.7	72.1
Denmark	74.4	70.4	75.9	70.7	77.3	71.2	77.7	72	77.8	72.7	79.3	74.5	79.3	74.7	79.5	74.8
Finland	72.5	65.5	75	66.5	77.6	69.2	78.9	70.9	80.2	72.8	81	74.2	81.5	74.6	81.5	74.9
France	73.6	67	75.9	68.4	78.4	70.2	80.9	72.8	81.8	73.9	82.7	75.3	82.9	75.5	82.9	75.6
Germany	72.4	66.9	73.6	67.2	76.1	69.6	78.4	72	79.7	73.3	81	75	81.3	75.6	*	*
Greece	72.4	67.3	73.8	70.1	76.8	72.2	79.5	74.6	80.3	75	80.6	75.5	80.7	75.4	80.7	75.4
Hungary	70.1	65.9	72.1	66.3	72.7	65.5	73.7	65.1	74.5	65.3	75.9	67.4	76.4	68.1	76.7	68.4
Iceland	75	70.7	77.3	71.2	79.7	73.7	80.5	75.4	80	75.9	81.4	78	82.2	78.3	82.3	78.5
Ireland	71.9	68.1	73.5	68.8	75.6	70.1	77.6	72.1	78.4	72.9	79.1	73.9	79.7	74.7	80.3	75.2
Italy	*	*	*	*	77.4	70.6	80.1	73.6	81.3	74.9	82.5	76.6	82.8	76.7	82.9	76.8
Japan	70.2	65.3	74.7	69.3	78.8	73.4	81.9	75.9	82.9	76.4	84.6	77.7	84.9	78.1	85.2	78.3
Korea	53.7	51.1	*	*	*	*	*	*	77.4	69.6	*	*	80	72.8	*	*
Luxembourg	72.2	66.5	73.4	67.1	75.9	69.1	78.5	72.3	80.2	73	81.1	74.8	80.7	75.2	81.5	74.9
Mexico	59.2	55.8	63.2	58.5	70.2	64.1	74.1	68.3	75.3	70	76.5	71.6	76.8	71.9	77.1	72.1
Netherlands	75.4	71.5	76.5	70.8	79.2	72.5	80.9	73.8	80.4	74.6	80.5	75.5	80.7	75.8	80.7	76
New Zealand	73.9	68.7	74.6	68.3	76.3	70	78.3	72.4	79.5	74.2	80.9	76	80.9	76	*	*
Norway	75.8	71.3	77.3	71	79.2	72.3	79.8	73.4	80.8	74.8	81.4	76	81.5	76.2	81.5	76.4
Poland	70.6	64.9	73.3	66.6	74.4	66	76.3	66.7	76.4	67.6	77.9	69.7	78.3	70.2	78.7	70.4
Portugal	66.8	61.2	70.8	64.2	75.2	67.7	77.4	70.4	78.7	71.6	80	73.2	80.3	73.5	80.5	73.8
Slovak Republic	72.7	68.4	72.9	66.7	74.3	66.8	75.4	66.6	76.3	68.4	77.4	69.2	77.7	69.6	77.8	69.9
Spain	72.2	67.4	74.8	69.2	78.6	72.5	80.3	73.3	81.5	74.3	82.5	75.7	82.9	75.6	83.1	75.7
Sweden	74.9	71.2	77.1	72.2	78.8	72.8	80.4	74.8	81.4	76.2	82	77.4	82.1	77.6	82.1	77.7
Switzerland	74.5	68.7	76.9	70.7	79.6	72.8	80.7	74	81.7	75.3	82.6	76.9	83	77.4	83	77.8
Turkey	50.3	46.3	56.3	52	60.3	55.8	68.7	64.2	69.4	64.9	70.4	65.8	70.6	66	70.9	66.2
United Kingdom	73.7	67.9	75	68.7	76.2	70.2	78.5	72.9	79.2	74	80.2	75.5	80.4	75.7	*	*
United States	73.1	66.6	74.7	67.1	77.4	70	78.8	71.8	78.9	72.5	79.5	74.1	79.8	74.4	*	*

*Data not available

SOURCE: "Life Expectancy, Males and Females at Birth (Years)," in *OECD Health Data 2004, 1st edition,* Organisation for Economic Co-operation and Development (France), 2004, http://www.irdes.fr/ecosante/OCDE/2100300.html (accessed July 13, 2004). Copyright OECD. Reproduced by permission of the OECD.

expectancy was slightly below the OECD median (half were higher and half were lower) for males and females. (See Table 7.10.) Infant mortality also declined sharply during the same period but the United States fared far worse than the majority of OECD countries—in 2001 the United States had the sixth-highest infant mortality rate. (See Table 7.11.) Finally, despite the well-funded U.S. battle against cancer, in 2000 the incidence rates of cancer per one hundred thousand were higher than seven of the sixteen OECD nations reporting (321.9 per one hundred thousand). (See Table 7.12.)

Reinhardt and his colleagues suggest that part of the explanation of why exceedingly high U.S. health care expenditures do not produce better health outcomes is excessive spending on health care administration. The researchers note that financing a less complex and less costly administrative bureaucracy might enable the United States to focus more resources on direct provision of health care services.

Germany

The German health care system is based on the social insurance model. Statutory sickness funds and private insurance cover the entire population. Approximately twelve hundred sickness funds cover about 92% of the population. Employees and employers finance these sickness funds through payroll contributions. Nearly all employers, including small businesses and low-wage industries, must participate.

During the late 1990s Germany had the second-highest per capita health care expenditures, but by 2002 Germany ranked sixth in health expenditures per capita. (See Figure 7.3.) Contributions to sickness funds averaged about 13% of a worker's salary, and about 10% of sickness fund members purchased complementary private insurance. Another 8% of the population chose not to participate in the public system and were fully covered by private insurance. Nearly three quarters of all health expenditures were public, and about 11% were direct, out-of-pocket payments. Less than 1% of the population does not have health insurance.

Unlike U.S. health insurance, which is not always "portable," losing or changing jobs does not affect health insurance protection in Germany among the sickness fund members. The German government does not require its

TABLE 7.11

Infant mortality, deaths per 1,000 live births, by country, selected years 1960–2002

	1960	1970	1980	1985	1990	1995	2000	2001	2002	2003
Australia	20.2	17.9	10.7	9.9	8.2	5.7	5.2	5.3	5	*
Austria	37.5	25.9	14.3	11.2	7.8	5.4	4.8	4.8	4.1	*
Belgium	31.2	21.1	12.1	9.8	8	6.1	4.8	4.5	4.9	*
Canada	27.3	18.8	10.4	8	6.8	6	5.3	5.2	*	*
Czech Republic	20	20.2	16.9	12.5	10.8	7.7	4.1	4	4.2	*
Denmark	21.5	14.2	8.4	7.9	7.5	5.1	5.3	4.9	4.4	*
Finland	21	13.2	7.6	6.3	5.6	3.9	3.8	3.2	3	*
France	27.5	18.2	10	8.3	7.3	4.9	4.6	4.5	4.2	*
Germany	35	22.5	12.4	9.1	7	5.3	4.4	4.3	4.3	*
Greece	40.1	29.6	17.9	14.1	9.7	8.1	6.1	5.1	5.9	*
Hungary	47.6	35.9	23.2	20.4	14.8	10.7	9.2	8.1	7.2	*
Iceland	13	13.2	7.7	5.7	5.9	6.1	3	2.7	2.2	*
Ireland	29.3	19.5	11.1	8.8	8.2	6.4	6.2	5.7	5.1	*
Italy	43.9	29.6	14.6	10.5	8.2	6.2	4.5	4.7	4.7	*
Japan	30.7	13.1	7.5	5.5	4.6	4.3	3.2	3.1	3	*
Korea		45	*	13	*	*	*	*	*	*
Luxembourg	31.5	24.9	11.5	9	7.3	5.5	5.1	5.9	5.1	*
Mexico		79.3	50.9	41.1	36.1	27.5	23.3	22.4	21.4	20.1
Netherlands	17.9	12.7	8.6	8	7.1	5.5	5.1	5.4	5	*
New Zealand	22.6	16.7	13	10.9	8.4	6.7	6.3		*	*
Norway	18.9	12.7	8.1	8.5	7	4	3.8	3.9	*	*
Poland	54.8	36.7	25.5	22	19.3	13.6	8.1	7.7	7.5	*
Portugal	77.5	55.5	24.3	17.8	11	7.5	5.5	5	5	*
Slovak Republic	28.6	25.7	20.9	16.3	12	11	8.6	6.2	7.6	*
Spain	43.7	28.1	12.3	8.9	7.6	5.5	3.9	3.5	3.4	*
Sweden	16.6	11	6.9	6.8	6	4.1	3.4	3.7	2.8	*
Switzerland	21.1	15.1	9.1	6.9	6.8	5	4.9	5	4.5	*
Turkey	189.5	145	117.5	88	57.6	45.6	41.9	40.6	39.4	38.3
United Kingdom	22.5	18.5	12.1	9.3	7.9	6.2	5.6	5.5	5.3	*
United States	26	20	12.6	10.6	9.2	7.6	6.9	6.8	*	*

*Data unavailable

SOURCE: "Infant Mortality, Deaths per 1,000 Live Births," in *OECD Health Data 2004, 1st edition,* Organisation for Economic Co-operation and Development (France), 2004, http://www.irdes.fr/ecosante/OCDE/113010.html (accessed July 13, 2004). Copyright OECD. Reproduced by permission of the OECD.

wealthiest citizens to purchase health insurance, but almost all of them do so voluntarily.

Ambulatory (outpatient) and inpatient care operate in completely separate spheres in the German health care system. German hospitals are public and private, operate for profit and not-for-profit, and generally do not have outpatient departments. Ambulatory care physicians are paid on the basis of fee schedules negotiated between the organizations of sickness funds and organizations of physicians. A separate fee schedule for private patients uses a similar scale.

Public (federal, state, and local) hospitals account for about 50% of hospital beds; private voluntary hospitals, often run by religious organizations, account for 35% of beds; and private for-profit hospitals, generally owned by physicians, account for 15%. Ambulatory care physicians are generally self-employed professionals paid on a fee-for-service basis, while most hospital-based physicians are salaried employees of the hospital.

On January 1, 1993, Germany's Health Care Reform law went into effect. Among its many provisions, the law tied increases in physician, dental, and hospital expenditures to the income growth rate of members of the sickness funds. It also limited the licensing of new ambulatory

care physicians (based on the number of physicians already in an area) and set a cap for overall pharmaceutical outlays. Still, in 2002 Germany boasted 3.3 practicing physicians per one thousand population, a higher ratio than well over half of the OECD countries reporting. (See Table 7.9.) The 1993 legislation also changed the hospital compensation system from per diem payments to specific fees for individual procedures and conditions.

Other German health-care reform measures instituted in the 1990s also served to stimulate competition between sickness funds, and improved coordination of inpatient and ambulatory care. During the mid-1990s, the government also attempted to control health care costs by reducing health benefits, such as limiting how often patients could visit health spas to recuperate.

The health care reforms were not, however, successful at containing health care costs. In 2002 total health care spending accounted for 10.9% of the GDP, with only Switzerland and the United States allocating more of their GDP to health. (See Figure 7.1.) Growth in health care spending was attributed to the comparatively high level of health care activity and resources along with rising pharmaceutical expenditures and efforts to meet the health care needs of an aging population. Discharge rates and selected surgical procedures are higher in Germany than

TABLE 7.12

Malignant neoplasms (cancer), by total number and incidence per 100,000 population, by country, selected years 1960–2001

	1960		1970		1980		1985		1990		1995		2000		2001	
	Total cases	Inc./100,000 p.	Total cases	Inc./100,000 p.	Total cases	Inc./100,000 p.	Total cases	Inc./100,000 p.	Total cases	Inc./100,000 p.	Total cases	Inc./100,000 p.	Total cases	Inc./100,000 p.	Total cases	Inc./100,000 p.
Australia	*	—	—	—	—	—	51,913	258.9	61,993	274	78,767	312.4	85,231	298.9	—	—
Austria	—	—	—	—	—	—	29,609	261.6	31,426	270.4	33,635	280.6	35,152	280	—	—
Belgium	—	—	—	—	—	—	—	—	32,095	—	30,828	178.6	—	—	—	—
Canada	—	—	—	—	—	—	—	—	—	—	—	324.5	—	—	—	—
Czech Republic	24,761	—	29,774	—	36,805	243.9	40,093	267.9	43,809	286.9	52,126	326.2	57,044	335.4	—	—
Denmark	9,118	197.9	—	—	23,645	288.3	25,833	303.5	27,541	318.9	28,295	322.2	31,758	—	32,862	250.8
Finland	—	—	11,417	213	14,875	229.4	16,371	231.8	17,739	232.8	20,332	248.7	22,380	255.4	22,430	—
France	—	—	—	—	170,177	223.1	187,837	234.3	211,073	247.9	241,989	264.3	278,253	286.1	—	—
Germany	—	—	—	—	—	—	—	—	318,882	—	341,501	—	—	—	—	—
Greece	—	—	—	—	—	—	—	—	—	—	—	—	—	—	—	—
Hungary	—	—	—	—	—	—	—	—	—	—	—	—	68,370	411	65,419	386.4
Iceland	352	—	475	—	676	—	787	—	893	—	1,100	—	1,154	—	1,193	—
Ireland	—	—	—	—	—	—	—	—	—	—	16,655	337.4	18,719	357.6	19,763	368.9
Italy	—	—	143,000	266	178,000	315	—	—	214,000	377	—	—	239,000	418	—	—
Japan	—	—	—	—	251,041	—	331,485	—	386,668	—	453,564	205.4	—	—	—	—
Korea	—	—	—	—	—	—	—	—	—	—	—	—	—	—	—	—
Luxembourg	—	—	—	—	—	—	1,191	324.4	1,409	366.6	1,664	403.1	1,808	409.7	1,886	424.7
Mexico	—	—	—	—	—	—	—	—	—	—	—	—	—	—	—	—
Netherlands	—	—	—	—	45,282	320	51,433	354.9	57,549	384.9	64,779	419	68,964	433	—	—
New Zealand	4,087	155.4	6,292	203.1	9,360	253.9	10,434	255.5	11,941	272.4	15,865	329.6	17,700	327.3	—	—
Norway	8,479	167.7	11,439	193.7	15,073	225.6	16,811	237.5	18,386	250.4	20,192	267.2	22,346	289.4	22,432	288.4
Poland	—	—	—	—	—	182.6	—	206.8	—	219	—	—	—	—	—	—
Portugal	—	—	—	—	—	—	—	—	—	—	—	—	—	—	—	—
Slovak Republic	—	—	12,297	271.6	14,128	281.4	16,252	313.8	17,926	340.8	20,253	377.6	21,887	405.3	—	—
Spain	—	—	—	—	—	—	—	—	—	—	—	—	—	—	—	—
Sweden	20,249	183.6	28,518	217.8	35,011	234.7	38,111	243.7	40,608	252.2	42,003	255.3	45,482	268.2	46,380	272.4
Switzerland	—	—	—	—	—	—	—	—	—	—	—	—	28,933	—	—	—
Turkey	—	—	—	—	—	—	—	—	—	—	—	—	—	—	—	—
United Kingdom	—	—	—	—	197,902	216.8	222,322	233.8	233,096	239.3	250,500	241.9	270,443	253.5	—	—
United States	—	—	—	—	—	278.5	—	300.5	—	321.5	—	322.6	—	321.9	—	—

— Data unavailable

SOURCE: "Cancer: Malignant Neoplasms (Number of Total Cases and Incidence per 100,000 Population)," in *OECD Health Data 2004, 1st edition*, Organisation for Economic Co-operation and Development (France), 2004, http://www.irdes.fr/ecosante/OCDE/127000.html (accessed July 13, 2004). Copyright OECD. Reproduced by permission of the OECD.

in relation to other OECD countries, and Germany has above average levels of resources.

In a January 20, 2004, address, "Health Systems—Approaching the Future," Dr. Berglind Ásgeirsdóttir, the Deputy Secretary-General of OECD, observed that improved quality of care was not necessarily linked to higher spending and identified multiple opportunities to improve the efficiency of all health care systems, including Germany's. For example, the Deputy Secretary-General cited adopting the U.S. hospital reimbursement schema based on diagnosis-related groups (DRGs) as a strategy that would enable Germany to better respond to health care needs without increasing costs.

Canada

The Canadian system has been characterized as a provincial government health insurance model, in which each of the ten provinces operates its own health system under general federal rules and with a fixed federal contribution. All provinces are required to offer insurance coverage for "all medically necessary services," including hospital care and physician services. Additional services and benefits, however, may be offered at the discretion of each province. Most provinces cover preventive services, routine dental care for children, and outpatient drugs for the elderly (with a co-payment) and the poor. No restrictions are placed on a patient's choice of physicians.

Canadian citizens have equal access to medical care, regardless of their ability to pay. Entitlement to benefits is linked to residency, and the system is financed through general taxation. Private insurance is prohibited from covering the same benefits covered by the public system, yet more than 60% of Canadians are covered by private supplemental insurance policies. These policies generally cover services such as adult dental care, cosmetic surgery, and private or semiprivate hospital rooms. Seventy percent of all health expenditures are public, and consumers pay about 30% of health care expenditures out-of-pocket. (See Table 7.1 and Table 7.2.)

The majority of hospitals are not-for-profit and are funded on the basis of global institution-specific or regional budgets. (A global budget allocates a lump sum of money to a large department or area. Then all the groups in that department or area must negotiate to see how much of the total money each group receives.) Physicians in both inpatient and outpatient settings are paid on a negotiated, fee-for-service basis. The systems vary somewhat from province to province, and certain provinces, such as Quebec, have also established global budgets for physician services. The federal government's contribution to Canada's health care bill has progressively declined in the past two decades. During the early 1980s the federal government paid for a historic high of 50% of the total health care bill. This dropped in subsequent

years, to 38% in 1990, 30% in 1993, and less than 20% in 1998. The resulting shift in costs has increased expenditures by the provinces and territories as well as out-of-pocket expenses paid by Canadians. The delivery system is composed largely of community hospitals and self-employed physicians. About 95% of Canadian hospital beds are public; private hospitals do not participate in the public insurance program.

FINANCIAL PROBLEMS. During the 1990s public revenues did not increase rapidly enough in Canada to cover rising health care costs. The Canadian government attributed many of the financial problems to lower revenue from taxes, higher prices for biomedical technology, and relatively lengthy hospital stays. In 1993, for the first time since Canada instituted universal health insurance twenty-seven years earlier, Canadians were required to pay for common services such as throat cultures to test for streptococcal infections (the bacterial cause of strep throat).

As a result of cutbacks and inadequate equipment, waiting times for nonemergency surgery, such as hip replacement, and high-technology diagnostic tools, such as computerized tomography (CT scans), could amount to months, or even years. Although Canadians generally still support their present system, physicians and consumers have expressed growing dissatisfaction with the rising costs and long waiting periods for diagnostic tests and nonemergency treatment.

THE SAFETY VALVE TO THE SOUTH. Some Canadians cross the border to the United States to avoid the waiting lines in their hospitals, clinics, and physicians' offices. Canadian physicians have been known to refer seriously ill patients in need of immediate medical attention to U.S. hospitals in such nearby cities as Buffalo, New York; Cleveland, Ohio; and Detroit, Michigan. In fact, many American hospitals market medical services, most notably cardiac care and addiction treatment, to Canadians. Overall, however, there has been very little border-crossing to seek health care services. Canadians accounted for less than 1% of total admissions in the nine border hospitals surveyed by the American Medical Association.

CONTROLLING COSTS. The general consensus is that no one wants to disassemble what has become Canada's most popular social program, but most agree that change is inevitable. The Ontario Health Insurance Plan insures ten million people, or almost 40% of all Canadians. They have managed to cut costs in several ways, such as:

• Reducing fees to commercial laboratories and allowing them to bill patients directly for tests performed

• Stopping payment for certain services connected with employment. For example, many Canadians must pay out of pocket for pre-employment physical examinations.

- Ending coverage of electrolysis (removal of unwanted hair) and reviewing coverage of services and procedures such as psychoanalysis, vasectomies, newborn circumcision, in vitro fertilization, as well as chiropractic, podiatric, and osteopathic services

- Increasing co-payments—the amounts patients must pay for prescriptions covered under the Ontario Drug Benefit Plan, which is used mainly by persons over age sixty-five

Similarly, in an effort to cut hospital costs, British Columbia has moved to shift some services away from hospitals to outpatient clinics, public health programs, and home care. Canadian officials hoped that cutbacks in covered services, caps on physicians' fees and hospital budgets, and controlling the use of expensive medical technology could keep the popular health care system afloat.

United Kingdom

The United Kingdom employs the National Health Service (NHS), or Beveridge, model to finance and deliver health care. The entire population is covered under a system that is financed mainly from general taxation. There is minimal cost sharing. About 12% of the population also purchases private insurance as a supplement to the public system. Slightly more than 83% of all health spending is from public funds, and in 2002 about 8% of health expenditures were out-of-pocket payments. (See Table 7.1.)

Services are organized and managed by regional and local public authorities. General practitioners serve as primary care physicians and are reimbursed on the basis of a combination of capitation payments (payments for each person served), fee-for-service, and other allowances. Hospitals receive overall budget allotments from district health authorities, and hospital-based physicians are salaried. Private insurance reimburses both physicians and hospitals on a fee-for-service basis.

Self-employed general practitioners are considered independent contractors, and salaried hospital-based physicians are public employees. The United Kingdom continues to face acute physician shortages: there are fewer physicians per capita (2.1 per one thousand population in 2002) than in most other OECD countries. (See Table 7.9.) Of the United Kingdom's hospital beds, 90% are public and generally owned by the National Health Service. As of 1991 it became possible for large physician practices to become "budget holders" and receive larger capitation payments. Similarly, individual hospitals may become "self-governing trust hospitals," enabling them to compete for patients and market their services. While emergency health service is immediate, persons requiring elective surgery, such as hip replacement, may end up on a waiting list for years.

The NHS pioneered many cost-containment measures that are currently used by the United States and other countries seeking to slow escalating health care expenditures. These approaches to evaluating and managing health care costs include:

- Cost-effective analysis: Calculated as a ratio, and often expressed as the cost per year per life saved, the cost-effectiveness analysis of a drug or procedure relates the cost of the drug or procedure to the health benefits it produces. This analysis enables delivery of clinically efficient, cost-effective care.

- Cost-minimization analysis: Primarily applied to the pharmaceutical industry, this technique identifies the lowest cost among pharmaceuticals alternatives that provide clinically comparable health outcomes.

- Cost-utility analysis: This measures the costs of therapy or treatment. Economists use the term "utility" to describe the amount of satisfaction a consumer receives from a given product or service. This analysis measures outcomes in terms of patient preference and is generally expressed as quality-adjusted life years. For example, an analysis of cancer chemotherapy drugs considers the various adverse side effects of these drugs because some patients may prefer a shorter duration of symptom-free survival rather than a longer life span marked by pain, suffering, and dependence on others for care.

France

The French health care system is based on the social insurance, or Bismarck, model. Virtually the entire population is covered by a legislated, compulsory health insurance plan that is financed through the social security system. Three major programs, and several smaller ones, are quasi-autonomous, nongovernmental bodies. The system is financed through employee and employer payroll tax contributions. More than 80% of the population supplements their public benefits by purchasing insurance from private, nonprofit *mutuels,* and about 2% of the population has private commercial insurance. Among OECD countries, the share of health care financed by private insurance is the third highest behind the United States and the Netherlands, two countries where private coverage is the primary source of payment for a large percentage of the citizenry.

The public share of total health spending is 76%, and about 19% of expenditures represent direct, out-of-pocket payments. (See Table 7.1.) Physicians practicing in municipal health centers and public hospitals are salaried, but physicians in private hospitals and in ambulatory care settings are typically paid on a negotiated, fee-for-service basis. Public hospitals are granted lump-sum budgets, and private hospitals are paid on the basis of negotiated per diem payment rates. About 65% of hospital beds are public, while the remaining 35% are private (and equally divided between profit and nonprofit).

In April 1996 the French government announced major reforms aimed at containing rising costs in the national health care system. The new system monitored each patient's total health costs and penalized physicians if they overran their budgets for specific types of care and prescriptions. In addition, French citizens were required to consult general practitioners before going to specialists. Initially, physicians—specialists, in particular—denounced the reforms and warned that they could lead to rationing and compromise the quality of health care. Over time, however, these cost-containment efforts met with less resistance from physicians and consumers. By 2004 physicians and hospitals were generally accepting of moderate fee schedules, cost-sharing arrangements, and global budgeting to control costs.

Japan

Japan's health care financing is also based on the social insurance model and, in particular, on the German health care system. Three general programs cover the entire population: Employee Health Insurance, Community Health Insurance, and Health and Medical Services for the Aged. About 62% of the population obtains coverage through some nineteen hundred not-for-profit, nongovernmental, employer-sponsored plans. Small businesses, the self-employed, and farmers are covered through Community Health Insurance, which is administered by a conglomeration of local governmental and private bodies. The elderly are covered by a separate plan that largely pools funds from the other plans. The Japanese health expenditure is below the expected level for a country with Japan's standard of living, and its emphasis is on the government, as opposed to business, bearing the major financial burden for the nation's health care.

The health system is financed through employer and employee income-related premiums. There are different levels of public subsidization of the three different programs. Limited private insurance exists for supplemental coverage, which is purchased by about one-third of the population and accounts for 7% of health expenditures. In 2003 public expenditures accounted for about 75% of total health spending, while out-of-pocket expenses account for about 20%. (See Table 7.1.)

Physicians and hospitals are paid on the basis of national, negotiated fee schedules. Japan manages with fewer physicians per capita than most OECD countries—less than two per one thousand population. (See Table

7.9.) Physicians practicing in public hospitals are salaried, while those practicing in physician-owned clinics and private hospitals are reimbursed on a fee-for-service basis. The amount paid for each medical procedure is rigidly controlled. Physicians not only diagnose, treat, and manage illnesses, they also prescribe and dispense pharmaceuticals, and a considerable portion of a physician's income is derived from dispensing prescription drugs.

A close physician-patient relationship is unusual in Japan; the typical physician endeavors to see as many patients as possible in a day in order to earn a living. A patient going to a clinic for treatment may have to wait many hours in a very crowded facility. As a result, health care is rarely a joint physician-patient effort. Instead, physicians tend to dictate treatment without fully informing patients about their conditions or the tests, drugs, and therapy that have been ordered or prescribed.

About 80% of Japan's hospitals are privately operated (and often physician-owned) and the remaining 20% are public. Hospitals are paid according to a uniform fee schedule, and for-profit hospitals are prohibited. Although hospital admissions are less frequent, hospital stays are typically far longer than in the United States or any other developed member nation of OECD, allowing hospitals and physicians to overcome the limitations of the fee schedules.

The health status of the Japanese is one of the best in the world. Japanese men and women are among the longest-living in the world. In 2002 life expectancy was 85.2 years for women and 78.3 years for men. (See Table 7.10.) The Japanese infant mortality rate in 2002, at three per one thousand live births, was tied with Finland and remained almost the lowest in the world, bested only by Iceland at 2.2 and Sweden at 2.8 per one thousand live births. (See Table 7.11.) These two statistics are usually considered reliable indicators of a successful health care system. It should be noted, though, that Japan does not have a large impoverished class, as the United States does, and its diet is considered to be among the healthiest in the world.

While Japan's health care system has no doubt contributed to this preeminent health status, the current state of research in health economics does not permit the determination of the extent of its contribution. The Japanese system, based on social insurance, has provided both basic care and free choice of doctors to every citizen at affordable costs. It has, however, become increasingly clear that the system has not succeeded in its efforts to allocate resources properly, ensure financial equity, and adapt to changing patterns of demand.

CHAPTER 8
CHANGE, CHALLENGES, AND INNOVATION IN HEALTH CARE DELIVERY

Since the 1970s the U.S. health care system has experienced rapid and unprecedented change. The sites where health care is delivered have shifted from acute inpatient hospitals to outpatient settings such as ambulatory care and surgical centers, clinics, and physicians' offices as well as long-term care and rehabilitation facilities. Patterns of disease have changed from acute infectious diseases that require episodic care to chronic conditions that require ongoing care. Even threats to U.S. public health have changed—epidemics of infectious diseases have been replaced by epidemics of health risks such as obesity, mental illness, substance abuse, and physical inactivity. At the end of 2001 the threat of bioterrorism became an urgent concern of health care planners, providers, policymakers, and the American public.

There are new health care providers—mid-level practitioners (advance practice nurses, certified nurse midwives, physician assistants, medical technologists) and new equipment for diagnosis such as magnetic resonance imaging (MRI) and genetic testing. Furthermore, the rise of managed care, explosion of biotechnology, and availability of information on the Internet have dramatically changed how health care is delivered.

Some health care industry observers suggest that the speed at which these changes have occurred has further harmed an already complicated and uncoordinated health care system. There is concern that the present health care system cannot keep pace with scientific and technological advances. Many worry that the health care system is already unable to deliver quality care to all Americans and that it is so disorganized that it will be unable to meet the needs of the growing population of older Americans.

This chapter considers several of the most pressing challenges and opportunities faced by the U.S. health care system. These include:

• Safety: Ensuring safety by protecting patients from harm or injury inflicted by the health care system—

preventing medical errors, reducing hospital infections, and safeguarding consumers from medical fraud. In addition to actions to reduce problems caused by the health care system, safety and quality may be ensured by providers' use of clinical practice guidelines—standardized plans for diagnosis and treatment of disease and the effective application of technology to information and communication systems.

• Information Management: Information technology, including the Internet, has the potential to provide health care providers and consumers with timely access to medical data, patient information, and the clinical expertise of specialists. Reliable public sources of consumer and provider health information on the Internet include the National Institutes of Health (NIH), Centers for Disease Control and Prevention (CDC), and *MEDLINE*. Using this technology effectively is a health system challenge, especially in terms of protecting patient privacy and confidentiality and ensuring that consumers have access to accurate and reliable health information.

• Innovation: Widespread use of innovations in health care delivery should be recommended only after objective analysis has demonstrated that the innovation will measurably benefit the safety, effectiveness, efficiency, or timeliness of health service delivery. Innovations should also be considered if they have the potential to reduce waste of equipment, supplies, or personnel time or if they have the capacity to allocate or distribute health care more equitably. Equitable distribution refers to care that does not vary in quality based on the characteristics, such as race, gender, ethnicity, or socioeconomic status, of the population served.

SAFETY

Although the United States is generally viewed as providing quality health care services to its citizens, a 1999 report issued by the Institute of Medicine (IOM) *To Err Is Human: Building a Safer Health System* (Washington, DC: Academy Press) estimated that as many as ninety-eight thousand American deaths per year are the result of preventable medical errors. More than seven thousand of these deaths were estimated to be due to preventable medication errors.

The IOM calculated the cost of medical errors, in terms of lost income, disability, and health care costs, at about $29 billion per year. Other costs, such as pain, loss of loved ones, and human suffering are incalculable. However, they are important because unlike errors in other industries, medical errors often do more than merely inconvenience consumers—they may cause disability and death. According to the CDC, adverse events (bad outcomes) affecting medical care occur in about 3 to 4% of all patients. The IOM report found that most medical errors occurred as a result of system problems rather than mistakes made by individual health care providers.

In 2004 HealthGrades, Inc., an independent health-care quality research organization that grades hospitals based on a range of criteria and provides hospital ratings to health plans and other payers, updated the 1999 IOM study. The study, *Patient Safety in American Hospitals* (Lakewood, CO: HealthGrades, July 2004), revealed that the IOM report may have underestimated the number of deaths attributable to medical errors and also concluded that little progress to reduce the frequency of medical error has been made in the five years since the IOM report was issued.

The HealthGrades hospital patient safety study looked at thirty-seven million Medicare patient records to assess the mortality and economic impact of medical errors and injuries that occurred during hospital admissions nationwide from 2000 to 2002. The study found that an average of 195,000 people in the United States died as a result of potentially preventable, in-hospital medical errors in each of the years 2000, 2001, and 2002—nearly twice the number of deaths from medical errors found by the 1999 IOM report.

Some of the most significant patient safety findings were:

- From 2000 to 2002 approximately 1.14 million patient-safety incidents occurred in the Medicare population considered by the study.

- One in every four Medicare patients hospitalized from 2000 to 2002 who experienced a patient-safety incident died.

- The selected patient-safety incidents studies accounted for $8.54 billion in excess inpatient costs to the Medicare system over three years. Applying these results to the entire United States, an extra $19 billion was spent and more than 575,000 preventable deaths occurred from 2000 to 2002.

- Patient-safety incidents with the highest rates per one thousand hospitalizations were failure to rescue, decubi-

tus ulcer (bedsores), and postoperative sepsis (infection following surgical procedures), which accounted for nearly 60% of all documented patient-safety incidents.

- The best performing hospitals (hospitals that had the lowest overall patient safety incident rates of all hospitals studied, defined as the top 7.5% of all hospitals studied) had five fewer deaths per one thousand hospitalizations. This significant mortality difference is attributable to fewer patient-safety incidents at the best performing hospitals.

- Fewer patient safety incidents in the best performing hospitals resulted in a lower cost of $740,337 per one thousand hospitalizations.

Strengthening Safety Measures

In response to a request from the U.S. Department of Health and Human Services (HHS), the Committee on Data Standards for Patient Safety of the IOM created a detailed plan to develop standards for the collection, coding, and classification of patient safety information. The 550-page plan, *Patient Safety: Achieving a New Standard for Care* (Washington, DC: Academy Press, 2004), called upon the HHS to assume the lead in establishing a national health information infrastructure that would provide immediate access to complete patient information and decision support tools, such as clinical practice guidelines, and capture patient safety data for use in designing ever-improving and safer health care delivery systems.

The IOM plan exhorted all health care settings to develop and implement comprehensive patient safety programs and recommended that the federal government launch patient safety research initiatives aimed at increasing knowledge, developing tools, and disseminating results to maximize the effectiveness of patient safety systems. The plan also advised the designation of a standardized format and terminology for identifying and reporting data related to medical errors.

Who Is Responsible for Patient Safety?

Many federal, state, and private sector organizations work together to reduce medical errors and improve patient safety. The CDC and Food and Drug Administration (FDA) are the leading federal agencies that conduct surveillance and collect information about adverse events resulting from treatment or the use of medical devices, drugs, or other products. The CDC directs the National Nosocomial Infections Surveillance (NNIS) system to track the hospital-acquired infections estimated to affect about two million patients and claim more than ninety thousand lives per year. (Nosocomial infections are defined as infections that are not present or incubating at the time of admission to the hospital and as such are considered hospital-acquired.) The sixth-leading cause of death in the United States, hospital-acquired infections

TABLE 8.1

TABLE 8.2

Decrease in hospital-acquired infection rates in National Nosocomial Infections Surveillance (NNIS) hospitals, 1990–99

Type of ICU	Bloodstream infection rate[1] (%)	Ventilator-associated pneumonia rate (%)	Urinary tract infection rate[2] (%)
Coronary	43	42	40
Medical	44	56	46
Surgical	31	38	30
Pediatric	32	26	59

[1]Central line associated.
[2]Catheter associated.

SOURCE: Robert Gaynes, et al, "Table 2. Decrease in Hospital-Acquired Infection Rates, NNIS, 1990–1999," in "Feeding Back Surveillance Data To Prevent Hospital-Acquired Infections," in *Emerging Infectious Diseases*, Centers for Disease Control and Prevention, vol. 7, no. 2, March–April 2001, http://www.cdc.gov/ncidod/eid/vol7no2/gaynes.htm (accessed September 13, 2004)

Public opinion on personal experience with medical errors, 2002

HAVE YOU EVER BEEN PERSONALLY INVOLVED IN A SITUATION WHERE A PREVENTABLE MEDICAL ERROR WAS MADE IN *YOUR OWN* MEDICAL CARE OR THAT OF A *FAMILY* MEMBER?

	Public	Physicians
Yes	42%	35%
No	57%	65%
Don't know	1%	—

SOURCE: "April 2002 Medical Errors Survey," in *Kaiser Health Poll Report 2003*, #3373, The Henry J. Kaiser Family Foundation, August 2003, http://www.kff.org/healthpollreport (accessed July 15, 2004). This information was reprinted with permission of the Henry J. Kaiser Family Foundation. The Kaiser Family Foundation, based in Menlo Park, California, is a nonprofit, independent national health care philanthropy and is not associated with Kaiser Permanente or Kaiser Industries.

were estimated by the CDC during 2003 to have added $5 billion annually to direct patient care costs.

Table 8.1 shows the decline in hospital-acquired infection rates in hospitals participating in the NNIS system. In the March 3, 2001, issue of *Morbidity and Mortality Weekly Report* (MMWR), the CDC reported that the voluntary infection monitoring performed by NNIS hospitals produced significant reductions in hospital-acquired infections, including a 31–43% drop in bloodstream infections in the intensive care units (ICUs). The CDC collaborates with state and local health departments, private sector groups, academic medical centers, and health care providers to develop and implement other programs to reduce errors and adverse (bad) outcomes of care.

The Centers for Medicare and Medicaid Services (CMS; formerly known as the Health Care Financing Administration) acts to reduce medical errors for the approximately seventy-five million Medicare, Medicaid, and State Children's Health Insurance Program (SCHIP) beneficiaries through its peer review organizations (PROs). The PROs concentrate on preventing delays in diagnosis and treatment that have adverse effects on health.

The Department of Defense (DoD) and Department of Veterans Affairs (VA), responsible for health care services for U.S. military personnel, their families, and veterans, have instituted computerized systems that have demonstrably reduced medical errors. The VA established Centers of Inquiry for Patient Safety, and its hospitals also use barcode technology and computerized medical records to prevent medical errors.

Safe medical care is also a top priority of the states and the private sector. In 2000 some of the nation's largest corporations, including General Motors and General Electric, joined together to address health care safety and efficacy and

to help direct their workers to health care providers—hospitals and physicians—with the best performance records. Called "The Leapfrog Group," this business coalition was founded by the Business Roundtable, a national association of Fortune 500 CEOs, to leverage employer purchasing power to initiate innovation to improve the safety of health care.

The Leapfrog Group publishes hospital quality and safety data to assist consumers in making informed hospital choices. Hospitals provide information to The Leapfrog Group through a voluntary survey that requests information about hospital performance across four quality and safety practices with the potential to reduce preventable medical mistakes and improve health care quality. As of 2004 The Leapfrog Group was composed of more than 150 Fortune 500 companies and other large private and public sector purchasers of health care benefits. Its mission was to promote health care safety programs and advocate innovative solutions to existing problems, such as equipping physicians with handheld devices to record patient information and perform electronic prescribing.

HEALTH CARE PROVIDERS SEEK TO PREVENT MEDICAL ERRORS AND IMPROVE PATIENT SAFETY. Because medical errors occur with alarming frequency, it is not surprising that nearly all physicians (95%) and the overwhelming majority of nurses (89%) and health care executives (82%) surveyed reported having seen serious medical errors ("Proportion of Medical Professionals Who Have Witnessed Serious Medical Errors, 2001," in *Trends and Indicators in the Changing Health Care Marketplace,* Menlo Park, CA: Henry J. Kaiser Family Foundation, 2002). Furthermore, another poll of physicians found that more than one third said they had been in a situation where a preventable error was made in their own care or that of a family member. (See Table 8.2.) ("Medical Errors Survey," conducted by Henry J. Kaiser Foundation, Harvard School of Public Health, April 24–July 22, 2002, in *Kaiser Health Poll Report,* Menlo Park, CA: Henry J. Kaiser Family Foundation, July/August 2003.)

Professional societies also are concerned with patient safety. More than 50% of all Joint Commission on Accreditation of Healthcare Organizations (JCAHO) hospital standards pertain to patient safety. As of July 1, 2002, hospitals seeking accreditation from the JCAHO were required to adhere to stringent patient safety standards to prevent medical errors. The JCAHO standards also require hospitals and individual health care providers to inform patients when they have been harmed in the course of treatment. The aim of these standards is to prevent medical errors by identifying actions and systems likely to produce problems before they occur. An example of this type of preventive measure, which is called "prospective review," is close scrutiny of hospital pharmacies to be certain that ordering, preparation, and dispensing of medications is accurate. Similar standards have been developed for JCAHO-accredited nursing homes, outpatient clinics, laboratories, and managed care organizations.

On January 1, 2004, the JCAHO began surveying and evaluating health care organizations using new medication management standards. The new standards revise and consolidate existing standards and place even greater emphasis on medication safety. The revised standards increase the role of pharmacists in managing appropriate and safe medication use and strengthen their authority to implement organization-wide improvements in medication safety.

Chief among the safety measures that concern professional societies are programs to prevent and report medication errors. Researchers estimate that about half of all medication errors are preventable. They suggest that when a medication error occurs, it is not the result of a single mistake, but rather a series of breakdowns in the health care delivery system. Research also supports the idea that the underreporting of medication errors stems from practitioners' concern that individuals will be punished rather than health system failures corrected. These researchers and many professional societies such as the Oncology (cancer) Nursing Society take the position that confidential voluntary reporting of medical errors will increase the frequency with which errors are reported and fully described and thereby will better identify health system deficiencies that lead to errors.

Professional organizations for nurses have also expressed concern about the effects of understaffed health care facilities on patient safety. On July 9, 2001, the CDC Division of Healthcare Quality Promotion and National Center for Infectious Diseases held a meeting to discuss the impact of the nation's nursing shortage on quality of care and patient safety with particular emphasis on health care-associated infections. Studies cited at the meeting showed a relationship between nursing staffing patterns and adverse patient outcomes such as infection rates. The participants observed, however, that staffing problems were not problems with nurses that could be solved by actions targeting nurses, but rather system problems that could only be resolved by actions to change the system.

WORKING OVERTIME INCREASES THE LIKELIHOOD OF MEDICAL ERRORS. The chance of a hospital nurse making a mistake was three times higher once a shift exceeded 12.5 hours, according to researchers from the University of Pennsylvania. Ann Rogers and her colleagues published the findings of their study of 393 hospital nurses ("The Working Hours of Hospital Staff Nurses and Patient Safety," *Health Affairs,* vol. 23, issue 4, July 2004), which revealed that about 40% of the nurses' shifts exceeded 12.5 hours over a four-week period. The risks of making an error were significantly increased when work shifts were longer than twelve hours, when nurses worked overtime, or when they worked more than forty hours per week.

During the 5,317 shifts the researchers scrutinized, there were 199 medical errors. Most were medication errors such as administering the wrong drug or the wrong dose, or delays—giving medication later than scheduled. The IOM, along with professional associations and patient advocacy groups has recommended limiting nurses' workdays to twelve hours.

Additional Actions to Improve Safety

The landmark 1999 IOM report called for aggressive national action to reduce the number of medical errors by 50% over five years. Representatives from eleven federal departments and agencies (the departments of Commerce, Defense, Health and Human Services, Labor, Veterans Affairs, the Federal Bureau of Prisons, Federal Trade Commission, National Highway Transportation and Safety Administration, Office of Personnel Management, Office of Management and Budget, and United States Coast Guard) formed the Quality Interagency Coordination Taskforce (QuIC). In February 2000 QuIC issued recommendations to the president for improving patient safety and a blueprint for implementing them.

The recommendations focused on education and technology and included:

• Enhancing public awareness of medical errors—A survey conducted during 2002 found that despite a wave of news media reports about the frequency and prevalence of medical errors, health care consumers are more likely to believe that medical errors are a frequent occurrence in general than they are to believe that errors occur frequently in their own medical care. Although nearly half of survey respondents believed that medical errors occurred "very often" (10%) or "somewhat often" (39%), when it comes to their own health care, just a third feel mistakes are made "often" (8%) or "sometimes" (26%) and nearly two-thirds feel mistakes occur "rarely" (42%) or "never" (22%). (See

TABLE 8.3

Public opinion on the frequency of preventable medical errors, 2000

GENERALLY SPEAKING, HOW OFTEN WOULD YOU SAY THAT THE DOCTORS, HOSPITALS AND OTHER COMPONENTS OF THE MEDICAL SYSTEM YOU COME IN CONTACT WITH MAKE MISTAKES IN DIAGNOSING AND TREATING YOUR MEDICAL PROBLEMS?

Often	8%
Sometimes	26%
Rarely	42%
Never	22%
No opinion	2%

SOURCE: "Perceived Frequency of Preventable Medical Errors," in *Kaiser Health Poll Report 2003*, #3373, The Henry J. Kaiser Family Foundation, August 2003, http://www.kff.org/insurance/upload/14100_1.pdf (accessed July 15, 2004). This information was reprinted with permission of the Henry J. Kaiser Family Foundation. The Kaiser Family Foundation, based in Menlo Park, California, is a nonprofit, independent national health care philanthropy and is not associated with Kaiser Permanente or Kaiser Industries.

Table 8.3.) The QuIC taskforce asserted that alert, well-informed consumers could act to avert at least some medical errors by questioning providers, rather than assuming their actions are always correct. Improving the public's understanding of patient safety and the risks involved in obtaining medical care would also enable consumers to be more vigilant about the care they receive.

- Building purchasers' awareness of medical errors—To assist employers in offering quality health care plans and providers to their workers, it is vital that they be informed about quality, as well as cost, of competing plans and practitioners. In December 1998 the U.S. Department of Labor launched a Health Benefits Education Campaign to teach employers how to make informed choices about health care plans and benefits.

- Intensifying provider education—QuIC agencies resolved to work with professional societies and credentialing and accrediting organizations as well as with health care facilities to upgrade their overall safety knowledge with special emphasis on how to prevent medical errors.

- Applying information technology to health care delivery systems—Computerized medical records, computer reminder systems for laboratory testing, electronic prescribing, and test ordering should be widely adopted to reduce errors and enhance quality. Electronic patient records give health care providers immediate access to patient data such as recent diagnostic test results. Interactive decision-support tools can alert providers to allergies and potential drug interactions, thereby preventing medication errors. An example of a decision support system's capacity to improve care is its ability to recommend the most appropriate antibiotic for a patient's diagnosed infection. Barcodes on medications and mechanical or robotic dispensing can help to ensure that the right patient receives the right prescription at the right time.

- Incorporating standardized procedures and checklists in medical devices—QuIC called for the FDA to intensify its premarket analyses of medical devices since some have been found to be substandard or defective after they have gone to market. This analysis also applied to human factors associated with misuse of medical devices—stringent testing of operating, maintenance, and user instructions, and labels with instructions intended to prevent errors.

The member agencies of QuIC resolved to seek documentation from independent accrediting organizations to find out how they are working to strengthen patient safety standards. QuIC also identified its ability to gather data from various member agencies to improve research and practice related to patient safety. For example, the FDA could use hospital and pharmaceutical company databases to identify the frequency of specific medication or prescribing errors.

PROPOSED LEGISLATION TO IMPROVE SAFETY. On June 5, 2002, the "Patient Safety and Quality Improvement Act (S. 2590)," a legislative response to the IOM report, was introduced by U.S. Senators Jim Jeffords of Vermont, Bill Frist of Tennessee, John Breaux of Louisiana, and Judd Gregg of New Hampshire. The following day a comparable bill, H.R. 4889, sponsored by Nancy Johnson of Connecticut, was introduced in the U.S. House of Representatives. In addition to bipartisan support in the Senate, the legislation was widely hailed by hospital and health care practitioners' professional societies.

The legislation promotes the reporting, analysis, and prevention of medical errors by giving legal protection to health care providers who report patient safety data. The act protects this confidential information from being subpoenaed, disclosed under the Freedom of Information Act, or admitted as evidence in civil, criminal, or administrative proceedings. It also ensures that information reported may not be used to enforce personnel actions such as denying practitioners certain privileges (such as the ability to admit patients to the hospital) or credentials, such as licensure or recertification. Unlawful disclosure of patient safety data would be punishable by fines as high as $10,000 per violation.

The Act does not change existing remedies available to injured patients or limit patient access to medical records. It does stipulate that medical errors will be reported to "patient safety organizations," which may voluntarily submit the data they obtain to a national, non-identifiable patient safety database linked to the Agency for Healthcare Research and Quality. "Patient safety data" is an inclusive term and covers all reports, statements, and quality improvement information that are collected, developed, or reported by providers to patient safety organizations.

The Act was read twice during June 2002 and was referred to the Senate Committee on Health, Education, Labor, and Pensions. In March 2003 it was reintroduced in the 108th Congress as S. 720 with a related bill, H.R. 663, which passed by more than four hundred votes in the House of Representatives on March 12, 2003. On November 17, 2003, S. 720 was placed on the Senate legislative calendar. In June 2004 the American Medical Association (AMA), Medical Group Management Association (MGMA), and JCAHO along with other professional societies called upon the Senate to act on this legislation.

On July 23, 2004, the bill was easily approved by the Senate. It may be signed into law once it is reconciled with similar legislation passed by the House of Representatives in 2003.

PROTECTING CONSUMERS FROM HEALTH CARE FRAUD

According to the FDA and the Federal Trade Commission (FTC), the lead agencies charged with protecting health care consumers from fraud, common health fraud targets are persons who are battling serious diseases, conditions with no known cure, and persons who are overweight. People who feel frightened or hopeless or those suffering from chronic pain may be especially vulnerable. Officials at these federal agencies cite persons with diagnoses of cancer, diabetes, multiple sclerosis, Alzheimer's disease, HIV/AIDS, and arthritis as examples of consumers who may become victims of fraudulently marketed, frequently useless health care products, devices, and treatments.

Unproven and fraudulently marketed "miracle cures" are nearly always entirely ineffective, although most are harmless. They are dangerous, however, when consumers use them instead of seeking more effective, conventional medical care and treatment. Most victims of health fraud simply lose time and money, but some lose their health, either by delaying needed treatment or by using a product or device that is harmful to their health.

The FTC and FDA urge consumers to exercise caution when purchasing medical or health care devices, products, and treatment. They encourage consumers to view claims of immediate cures or relief of chronic health problems with appropriate skepticism. Basically, the adage "if it sounds too good to be true, it probably is" holds true when evaluating the claims of health care products or services. Examples of such unbelievable and misleading claims are those for dietary supplements that promise, "eat all you like and still lose weight," or devices promising "instant relief from arthritis pain."

The Internet has provided a new arena for unscrupulous purveyors of prescription drugs as well as marketers of unproven health care products and services. It is often difficult for consumers to distinguish between legitimate Web sites that offer pharmaceutical drugs and irresponsible, unsafe sellers of prescription drugs. The FDA warns consumers that Web site purchases are risky—drugs may be counterfeit, doses may be incorrect, or the wrong drug may be delivered. The FDA also advises against filling prescriptions through a Web site that allows consumers to order prescription drugs after simply completing a health questionnaire. Both the FDA and AMA consider a completed health questionnaire as an insufficient, and potentially dangerous, basis for prescribing drugs. Additional FDA warnings include:

- Consumers should not purchase prescription drugs for the first time from sites that sell drugs without a prescription or a physical examination, or sites that sell drugs that are not FDA approved.

- It is unwise to purchase drugs from sites that do not have a registered pharmacist available to respond to questions.

- It is not advisable to order from sites that do not offer a U.S. address and phone number to contact in the event of problems with the drug, product, or device purchased.

- Purchases from foreign Web sites are especially risky because the U.S government cannot take any action if consumers are victims of fraud or receive otherwise unsatisfactory service.

CLINICAL PRACTICE GUIDELINES

Clinical practice guidelines (CPGs) are evidence-based protocols—documents that advise health care providers about how to diagnose and treat specific medical conditions and diseases. CPGs offer physicians, nurses, other health care practitioners, health plans, and institutions objective, detailed, condition- or disease-specific action plans.

Widespread dissemination and use of CPGs began during the 1990s in an effort to improve the quality of health care delivery by giving health care professionals access to current scientific information on which to base clinical decisions. The use of guidelines also aimed to enhance quality by standardizing care and treatment throughout a health care delivery system such as a managed care plan or hospital, and throughout the nation.

Early attempts to encourage physicians and other health professionals to use practice guidelines was met with resistance because many physicians rejected CPGs as formulaic "cookbook medicine" and believed that they interfered with physician-patient relationships. Over time physicians were educated about the quality problems resulting from variations in medical practice, and opinions about CPGs gradually changed. Physician willingness to use practice guidelines also increased when they learned that adherence to CPGs offered some protection from medical malpractice and other liability. Nurses and other health professionals more readily adopted CPGs, presumably because their training and practice was oriented more toward following instructions than physicians' practices had been.

The National Guideline Clearinghouse (NGC) is a database of CPGs produced by the Agency for Healthcare Research and Quality in conjunction with the American Medical Association (AMA) and American Association of Health Plans. The NGC offers guideline summaries and comparisons of guidelines covering the same disease or condition prepared by different sources and serves as a resource for the exchange of guidelines between practitioners and health care organizations.

Clinical practice guidelines vary depending on their source. All detail recovery and treatment plans, however, are intended to generate the most favorable health outcomes. Federal agencies such as the U.S. Public Health Service and CDC, as well as professional societies, managed care plans, hospitals, academic medical centers, and health care consulting firms, have produced their own versions of clinical practice guidelines.

Practically all guidelines assume that treatment and healing will occur without complications. Since CPGs represent an optimistic approach to treatment, they are not used as the sole resource for development or evaluation of treatment plans for specific patients. CPGs are intended for use in conjunction with evaluation by qualified health professionals able to determine the applicability of a specific CPG to the specific circumstances involved. Modification of the CPGs is often required and advisable to meet specific, organizational objectives of health care providers and payers.

It is unrealistic to expect that all patients will obtain ideal health outcomes as a result of health care providers' use of CPGs. Guidelines may have greater utility as quality indicators. Evaluating health care delivery against CPGs enables providers, payers, and policymakers to identify and evaluate care that deviates from CPGs as part of a concerted program of continuous improvement of health care quality.

INFORMATION AND COMMUNICATION TECHNOLOGY

The explosion of communication and information management technologies has already revolutionized health care delivery and holds great promise for the future. Health care data can be easily and securely collected, shared, stored, and used to promote research and development over great geographic distances and across traditionally isolated industries. Online distance learning programs for health professionals and the widespread availability of reliable consumer health information on the Internet have increased understanding and awareness of the causes and treatment of illness. This section describes several recent applications of technology to the health care system.

Telemedicine

Telemedicine is the term used to describe a variety of interactions that occur via telephone lines. Telemedicine may be as simple and commonplace as a conversation between a patient and a health professional in the same town or as sophisticated as surgery directed via satellite and video technology from one continent to another.

According to the Telemedicine Research Center (TRC), a non-profit public research organization based in Portland, Oregon, there are two types of technology used in most telemedicine applications. The first type stores and sends digital images taken with a digital camera from one location to another. The most common application of this kind of telemedicine is teleradiology—sending X-rays, computerized tomography (CT) scans, or MRIs from one facility to another. The same technology may be used to send slides or images from the pathology laboratory to another physician or laboratory for a second opinion. Another example of the use of digital image transfer is the rural primary care physician who, miles from the nearest dermatologist (physician specialist in skin diseases), can send a photograph of a patient's rash or lesion and receive an immediate, long-distance consultation from the dermatologist.

Another application of telemedicine that uses only the standard telephone line in a patient's home is transtelephonic pacemaker monitoring. (Cardiac pacemakers are battery-operated implanted devices that maintain normal heart rhythm.) Cardiac technicians at the other end of the telephone are able to check the implanted cardiac pacemaker's functions, including the status of its battery. Transtelephonic pacemaker monitoring is able to identify early signs of possible pacemaker failure and detect potential pacemaker system abnormalities, thereby reducing the number of emergency replacements. It can also send an ECG (electrocardiogram) rhythm strip to the patient's cardiologist.

The other type of technology described by the TRC is two-way interactive television (IATV), which uses video-teleconferencing equipment to create a "meeting" between a patient and primary care physician in one location and a physician specialist elsewhere when a face-to-face consultation is not feasible because of time or distance. Peripheral equipment even enables the consulting physician specialist to perform a "virtual physical examination" and hear the patient's heart sounds through a stethoscope. The availability of desktop videoconferencing has expanded this form of telemedicine from a novelty found exclusively in urban, university teaching hospitals to a valuable tool for patients and physicians in rural areas who were previously underserved and unable to access specialists readily.

Despite the promise of telemedicine, there are several obstacles that prevent Americans from realizing all of its potential benefits. As of July 2004, many states did not permit physicians who are not licensed in their states to practice telemedicine, and the Centers for Medicare and Medicaid Services will reimburse for interactive teleconference services but will not pay for digital image transfer. Many private insurers are reluctant to pay for telemedicine, and some physicians fear additional liability (medical malpractice suits or other litigation) arising from telemedicine. Finally, some of the communities that would benefit most from telemedicine do not have the telecommunications equipment necessary to deliver the bandwidth for telemedicine.

Wireless Technology in the Hospital.

In *Hospitals Unplugged: The Wireless Revolution Reaches Healthcare* (California HealthCare Foundation, April 3, 2001), Glenn Wachter describes a hospital where nurses enter patient data at wireless mobile workstations, pagers deliver patients' ECGs and vital signs, a wireless scanning device verifies the correct medication and dosage for a patient, and physicians access instantly updated medical records on their wireless personal digital assistants (PDAs). Wachter asserts that mounting pressure to increase hospital and health service delivery efficiencies is driving interest and use of wireless technology, but observes that its advocates maintain that along with saving money, it also will improve quality.

By improving communication of medical information, wireless technology can increase the accuracy of patient data, increase the efficiency of health care workers, deliver immediate access to medical and administrative information, and sharply reduce paperwork. Furthermore, by linking wireless technology to pharmacy management systems, it can reduce prescribing and dispensing errors. Wachter also observed the application of wireless technology in pre-hospital care. Ambulances equipped with wireless devices can transmit video, audio, ECG, vital signs, and other images to the emergency department team awaiting arrival of the critically ill patient.

Online Patient-Physician Consultations

In November 2001 a separate report issued by the California Health Care Foundation called online exchanges between patients and health professionals "e-encounters" and defined them as "a two-way Web-based exchange of clinical information between a patient and his or her care-giver that involves a closed loop conversation around a particular clinical question or problem specific to the patient. It may be initiated by either the patient or the caregiver."

Although no one is certain about the frequency with which e-encounters occur, by 2004 an estimated five million Americans had communicated with their physicians via electronic mail (e-mail). Hence, with more than two-thirds of U.S. physicians and more than half of American adults online, the popularity of this practice is believed to be increasing. Some industry observers consider e-encounters simply as alternatives to telephone consultations, while others think they may ultimately prove to be more time-efficient, affordable, and convenient than the "telephone tag" and frequent call-backs that commonly occur when physicians and patients attempt to speak by phone.

One advantage of e-encounters over telephone conversations is the patient's ability to communicate home monitoring results such as blood pressure or blood glucose levels in a format that is easily included as documentation in the patient's permanent (paper or electronic) medical record. Another advantage is that less time devoted to telephone calls improves the efficiency of the physician's office, boosting productivity, and potentially reducing practice expenses. Other electronic communications between patients and physicians' offices include appointment scheduling, reminders of follow-up visits, prescription renewal requests, and administrative functions such as billing, insurance verification, and changes of address.

Concerns about e-encounters center on privacy and security of patient information exchanged and physician reimbursement for the time spent in electronic correspondence with patients. In addition to legal and privacy issues, some industry observers suggest that guidelines should be developed for e-encounters to ensure that they are clinically appropriate and are not used as substitutes for needed, but more costly, face-to-face office visits.

Is Applied Technology the Solution to the Nursing Shortage?

According to surveys conducted in 2001 and 2002, most U.S. hospitals, where nurses comprise up to 25% of the workforce, are facing a nursing shortage with estimates of between 10 to 15% vacancy rates for registered nurses, licensed practical nurses, and nursing assistants. The shortage is expected to increase. One study speculates that the nation will be short by half a million nurses needed to care for patients by 2020. Many industry observers attribute the shortage to the profession's diminished appeal since a wider range of career opportunities for women became available. Nurses themselves insist that working conditions such as caring for older, sicker patients, mounting paperwork, and reduced nursing personnel and other workers are causing the exodus from hospitals. (Howard

Berliner and Eli Ginzberg, "Why This Hospital Nursing Shortage Is Different," *Journal of the American Medical Association,* vol. 288, no. 21, December 4, 2002).

While hospitals are intensifying recruitment efforts in order to fill nursing vacancies, they are also looking at ways to improve working conditions for nurses. One approach to improving working conditions is the application of technology systems to increase patient safety and clinical quality—key factors that contribute to nurses' job satisfaction. Automated workflow and clinical systems do not always increase nurses' efficiency. However, a report prepared by First Consulting Group for the California HealthCare Foundation in June 2002 found widespread support for a variety of technologies designed to safeguard patients and support nurses, including:

- Scheduling nurses to shifts via the Internet

- Messaging, and automated documentation

- Mobile communication

- Patient education

- Medication administration systems—dispensing devices, bar-code technology, and "smart" IV (intravenous) pumps that check orders against a database to prevent errors

- Clinical decision support

- Computerized physician order entry and computerized patient record/data repository

The authors concluded that increasing adoption of technology, the urgent need for hospital nurses, and a generation of graduating nursing students that has been computer-literate since childhood should spur hospitals to consider integrating computer technology into nursing practices.

The Promise of Robotics

One technological advance that promises to reduce hospital operating costs and enable hospital workers to spend more time caring for patients is the use of robots. Once relegated to the realm of science fiction, the twenty-first century has seen a resurgence of interest in automated machines such as self-guided robots to perform many routine hospital functions.

A July 6, 2004, Associated Press technology feature, "Courier Robots Get Traction in Hospitals"(http://www.cnn.com/2004/TECH/07/06/hospital.robots.ap/index.htm), described the "RoboCart," a motorized table that transports linens, medical supplies, X-rays, food, and other materials throughout the hospital. Another automated robot courier, a four-foot tall cabinet with flashing lights and turn signals called "HelpMate," speaks in Spanish and English. The robots use wireless radio to call elevators and open automatic doors, and they communicate respectfully, saying "thank you" upon entering an elevator and inviting hospital employees to "please examine my

contents when making deliveries." About 120 robotic couriers were in use at hospitals throughout the country during 2004 and their ranks are expected to increase.

Some robots are involved in more than simply routine, menial tasks. In July 2004 the FDA approved the marketing of a robotic system to assist in heart surgery to open clogged arteries or reroute the blood supply around the blocked vessels. The robotic system allows a cardiovascular surgeon to perform heart surgery without touching the patient. Seated at a console with a computer and video monitor, the surgeon uses handgrips and foot pedals to manipulate three robotic arms that hold surgical instruments and actually perform the operation. The robotic system has also been approved by the FDA for use in other surgeries such as laparoscopic gall bladder surgery and procedures to treat acid reflux disease (Michael Smith, "Robotic-Like Device Cleared for Heart Surgery," WebMD Medical News, http://webcenter.health.webmd.netscape.com/content/article/90/100690.htm, July 9, 2004).

INNOVATION SUPPORTS QUALITY HEALTH CARE DELIVERY

The health care industry is awash in wave after wave of new technologies, models of service delivery, reimbursement formulae, legislative and regulatory changes, and increasingly specialized personnel ranks. Creating change in hospitals and other health care organizations requires an understanding of diffusion—the process and channels by which new ideas are communicated, spread, and adopted throughout institutions or organizations.

Diffusion of technology involves all of the stakeholders in the health care system. Policymakers and regulatory agencies establish safety and efficacy; government and private payers determine reimbursement; vendors of the technology are compared and one is selected; hospitals and health professionals adopt the technology and are trained in its use; and consumers are informed about the benefits of the new technology.

The decision to adopt new technology involves a five-stage process beginning with knowledge about the innovation. The second stage is persuasion, the period when decision makers form opinions based on experience and knowledge. Decision is the third phase, when commitment is made to a trial or pilot program, and is followed by implementation, the stage during which the new technology is put in place. The process concludes with the confirmation stage, the period during which the decision makers seek reinforcement for their decision to adopt and implement the new technology.

Communicating Quality

The IOM report on health care quality (*Crossing the Quality Chasm: A New Health System for the 21st Centu-*

ry, Washington DC: Academy Press, 2001) set forth six aims for improvement and ten rules for redesign of the U.S. health care system. These ten rules are:

1) Care is based on continuous healing relationships.

2) Care is customized according to patient needs and values.

3) The patient is the source of control.

4) Knowledge is shared and information flows freely.

5) Decision-making is evidence-based.

6) Safety is a system priority.

7) Transparency is necessary.

8) Needs are anticipated.

9) Waste is continuously decreased.

10) Cooperation among clinicians is a priority.

This chapter has described some of the efforts currently underway to address and comply with these rules within the existing health care system, and concludes with a discussion of rule number seven, the need for transparency. Transparency refers to the need for public accountability for the quality of the health care system. Health care consumers should be given information that allows them to make thoughtful, informed choices and decisions about health insurance plans and providers. Although family, friends, and health care providers remain consumers' primary sources of information about quality of health services, a Kaiser Family Foundation and Agency for Healthcare Research and Quality survey, *National Survey on Americans as Health Care Consumers: An Update on the Role of Quality Information* (Washington, DC: December 2000), found 37% of consumers willing to contact a health plan representative or read materials to obtain quality information; 28% wanted to access information online. The information provided must be understandable and should focus on performance measures of the plan or provider that show its commitment to safety, evidence-based practice, and patient satisfaction.

The requirement for transparency requires health care providers and plans to disclose information they previously did not share among themselves or with consumers. Furthermore, many health care plans and providers have found that in order to compete successfully for health care consumers, they not only must demonstrate the ability to deliver health care services effectively but also to docu

ment and communicate measures of clinical quality and fiscal accountability.

Publication of medical outcomes report cards and disease and procedure-specific morbidity and mortality rates has attracted widespread media attention and sparked controversy. Advocates of the public release of clinical outcomes and other performance measures contend that despite some essential limitations, these studies offer consumers, employers, and payers the means for comparing health care providers.

Some skeptics question the clinical credibility of scales such as surgical mortality as incomplete indicators of quality. Others cite problems with data collection or speculate that the data is readily manipulated by providers to enhance marketing opportunities sufficient to compromise the utility and validity of published reports. Long-term, the effect of published comparative evaluation of health care providers on network establishment, contracting, and exclusion from existing health plans is uncertain and in many instances may be punitive. Hospitals and medical groups may be forced to compete for network inclusion on the basis of standardized performance measures.

Despite legitimate concern about the reliability, validity, and interpretation of data, there is consensus that scrutiny and dissemination of quality data will escalate. To date, consumer interest has focused on individual providers—local hospitals and physicians. Employers, choosing between health plans involving the same group of participating hospitals and physicians, are requesting plan-specific information to guide their decisions. Companies and employer-driven health care coalitions seeking to assemble their own provider networks rely on physician and hospital-specific data, such as the quality data provided by Healthgrades, Inc., during the selection process. By July 2004, the Leapfrog Group, an employer-based coalition with strong interest in health care quality, was composed of more than 150 member companies that purchase coverage for about thirty-four million people.

The most beneficial use of the data is not punitive, but as inspiration and incentive to improve health care delivery systematically. When evidence of quality problems is identified, health plans and providers must be prepared to launch a variety of interventions to address and promptly resolve problems.

CHAPTER 9

PUBLIC OPINION ABOUT HEALTH CARE

As with many other social issues, public opinion about health care systems, providers, plans, coverage, and benefits varies in response to a variety of personal, political, and economic forces. Personal experience, and the experience of friends, family, and community opinion leaders—trusted sources of information such as members of the clergy, prominent physicians, and local business and civic leaders—exert powerful influences on public opinion. Health care marketing executives have known for years that the most potent advertising any hospital, medical group, or managed care plan can have is not a full-page newspaper advertisement or primetime television ad campaign. It is positive word-of-mouth publicity.

Political events and election campaigns can focus public attention on a particular health care concern, supplant one health-related issue with another, or eclipse health care from public view altogether. Health care reform and a strong push for national health insurance were hallmarks of former U.S. President Bill Clinton's campaigns in the 1990s but by 2000 were all but forgotten in favor of debates about Medicare reform, prescription drug benefits, and passage of a patients' bill of rights. The events of September 11, 2001, also realigned health concerns as much as they affected other national priorities. In the final months of 2001, several public opinion surveys reported preventing bioterrorism as Americans' number-one health concern. During September 2002 the media were focused on U.S. preparations to take military action in Iraq. As a result, there were far fewer news stories about the upcoming open-enrollment period (when employees can switch health plans) than usual.

By 2004, economists, political observers, and pollsters opined that after concern about the U.S. economy and Iraq, health care costs would be a prominent issue in the election year. A record 9.5% increase in health care spending in 2002—the largest annual increase in more than a decade, followed by a 7.4% increase in 2003—coupled with consumer and media attention to issues such as prescription drug costs combined to intensify Americans' concerns about their ability to afford health care services.

The national economy and the rate of increase of health care costs, especially out-of-pocket expenses, play important roles in shaping public opinion. When unemployment rates are high, the proportion of persons without insurance increases, workers fear losing their jobs and their health care coverage, and dissatisfaction with the present health care system grows. Multiple surveys have shown a direct relationship between rising out-of-pocket expenses and dissatisfaction with the health care system. The recent spike in health care costs coupled with survey findings that employers intend to pass off some of the increasing costs to their employees will likely inspire renewed interest in health care reform.

There also is evidence that Americans do not anticipate that reform will substantially improve health care access, availability, or quality in the foreseeable future. A 2004 Gallup Poll revealed that Americans anticipate that health care will continue to be a problem twenty-five years from now (Raksha Arora, "Future Imperfect: Americans Predict Woes of 2029," *The Gallup Poll Tuesday Briefing,* February 2004). Survey respondents named healthcare as likely to be the fifth most pressing problem, and concern about Social Security and Medicare was considered the second most pressing problem, following concern about the economy in general. (See Figure 9.1.)

Demographic changes, particularly the aging of the "baby boomer" generation (people born between 1943 and 1960) into Medicare eligibility, may also fuel dissatisfaction with the health care system. If the health care futurists who have projected glaring deficiencies in the current system's capacity to meet the needs of the aging population are correct, this generation may become the largest and most vocal advocates for health care reform.

FIGURE 9.1

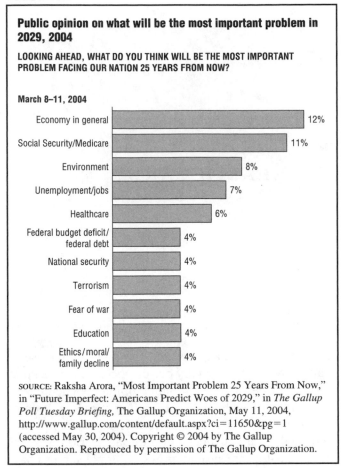

Public opinion on what will be the most important problem in 2029, 2004

LOOKING AHEAD, WHAT DO YOU THINK WILL BE THE MOST IMPORTANT PROBLEM FACING OUR NATION 25 YEARS FROM NOW?

March 8–11, 2004

Economy in general	12%
Social Security/Medicare	11%
Environment	8%
Unemployment/jobs	7%
Healthcare	6%
Federal budget deficit/federal debt	4%
National security	4%
Terrorism	4%
Fear of war	4%
Education	4%
Ethics/moral/family decline	4%

SOURCE: Raksha Arora, "Most Important Problem 25 Years From Now," in "Future Imperfect: Americans Predict Woes of 2029," in *The Gallup Poll Tuesday Briefing,* The Gallup Organization, May 11, 2004, http://www.gallup.com/content/default.aspx?ci=11650&pg=1 (accessed May 30, 2004). Copyright © 2004 by The Gallup Organization. Reproduced by permission of The Gallup Organization.

Finally, the influence of the news media, advertising, and other attempts to sway health care consumers' attitudes and purchasing behaviors cannot be overlooked. A single story about a miraculous medical breakthrough or lifesaving procedure can reflect favorably on an entire hospital or health care delivery system. Similarly, a lone mistake or misstep by a single health care practitioner can impugn a hospital or managed care plan for months or even years, prompting intense media scrutiny of every action taken by the facility or organization.

Some industry observers believe that health care providers, policymakers, biomedical technology and research firms, and academic medical centers have fanned the flames of consumer dissatisfaction with the health care system by "overselling" the promise and the progress of modern medicine and the U.S. health care system. They fear that overzealous promotion of every scientific discovery with a potential clinical application has created unrealistic expectations of modern medicine. Health care consumers who believe there should be "one pill for every ill" or feel that all technology should be made widely available even before its efficacy has been demonstrated are more likely to be dissatisfied with the present health care system.

MOST AMERICANS BELIEVE THAT ACCESS TO HEALTH CARE IS A RIGHT

A January 2004 Kaiser Family Foundation poll reconfirmed Americans' belief that everyone should have equal access to health care ("Health Care Should Be Provided Equally to Everyone," *Kaiser Health Poll Report,* Washington, DC: Henry J. Kaiser Family Foundation, February 2004). Since 1993, eight in ten survey respondents resolved that health care should be provided equally to all, and more than half agreed "completely" that access to health care should be provided independent of age, income, health status, or employment. In 2004 more than three-quarters of survey respondents (76%) affirmed "strongly" or "somewhat" that access to health care should be a right. (See Figure 9.2.)

In addition to agreeing that everyone should have access to health care, about two-thirds of Americans feel that the federal government should guarantee medical care for the uninsured. There is, however, little consensus about the extent to which the government should intervene to solve this problem. A May 2003 poll, "Major Versus Limited Effort to Help the Uninsured" (*Kaiser Health Poll Report,* Washington, DC: Henry J. Kaiser Family Foundation, February 2004), found Americans divided about whether the government should commit to a major initiative or a limited effort to provide health insurance to the uninsured. When offered a range of policy options to extend health insurance coverage to more people, Americans voiced majority support for every option except a national health plan financed by taxpayers, but when asked to select the best course of action, no single plan won widespread support. (See Figure 9.3.)

Public Opinion about Health Care Costs, Access, and the Uninsured

A Kaiser Family Foundation *Health Poll Report Survey* conducted in February 2004 revealed persistent widespread concern about a number of key health care issues. Some 82% of Americans said it was very important for the President and Congress to act to lower the costs of health insurance and prescription drugs. More than three-quarters of survey respondents felt it was vital to increase the number of Americans covered by health insurance, and 75% thought that families should receive financial assistance to help pay for long-term care for older adults or persons with disabilities. (See Figure 9.4.)

When forced to choose the most important health priority from a list, increasing the number of Americans covered by health insurance was named by about one-fifth (21%) of the respondents, behind reducing the cost of health insurance (25%), but ahead of other pressing issues such as lowering the cost of prescription drugs (15%) and helping families finance long-term care (11%). (See Figure 9.4.) While health care costs were clearly the priority

FIGURE 9.2

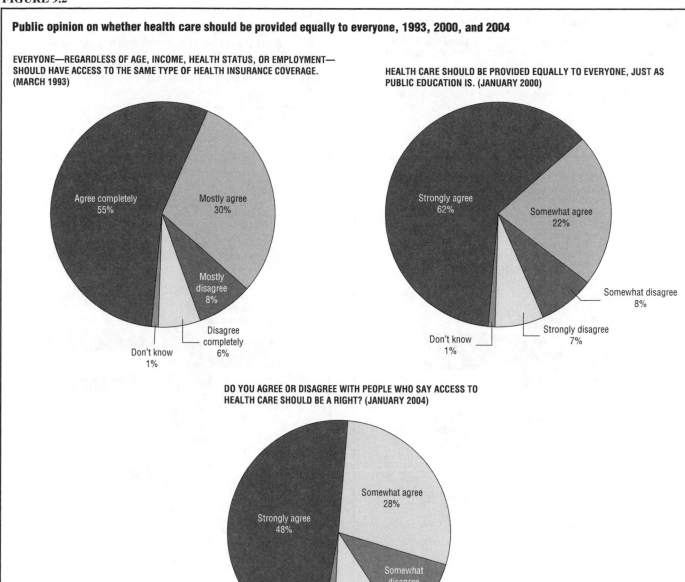

Public opinion on whether health care should be provided equally to everyone, 1993, 2000, and 2004

EVERYONE—REGARDLESS OF AGE, INCOME, HEALTH STATUS, OR EMPLOYMENT—
SHOULD HAVE ACCESS TO THE SAME TYPE OF HEALTH INSURANCE COVERAGE.
(MARCH 1993)

Agree completely 55%
Mostly agree 30%
Mostly disagree 8%
Disagree completely 6%
Don't know 1%

HEALTH CARE SHOULD BE PROVIDED EQUALLY TO EVERYONE, JUST AS
PUBLIC EDUCATION IS. (JANUARY 2000)

Strongly agree 62%
Somewhat agree 22%
Somewhat disagree 8%
Strongly disagree 7%
Don't know 1%

DO YOU AGREE OR DISAGREE WITH PEOPLE WHO SAY ACCESS TO
HEALTH CARE SHOULD BE A RIGHT? (JANUARY 2004)

Somewhat agree 28%
Strongly agree 48%
Somewhat disagree 11%
Strongly disagree 10%
Don't know 2%

SOURCE: "Health Care Should Be Provided Equally to Everyone," in *Kaiser Health Poll Report 2004,* #7034, The Henry J. Kaiser Family Foundation, February 2004, http://www.kff.org/healthpollreport/archive_April2004/6.cfm (accessed September 13, 2004). This information was reprinted with permission of the Henry J. Kaiser Family Foundation. The Kaiser Family Foundation, based in Menlo Park, California, is a nonprofit, independent national health care philanthropy and is not associated with Kaiser Permanente or Kaiser Industries.

for survey respondents, nearly one-quarter expressed concern about access including universal health coverage and access to health care for the poor. (See Figure 9.5.)

A Kaiser Family Foundation *Health Poll Report Survey* conducted in April 2004 confirmed that one-third of insured Americans are deeply concerned about the prospect of losing their health insurance, and nearly half (47%) of all survey respondents (insured and uninsured) were worried about having to pay more for their health insurance.

MANY AMERICANS ARE CONCERNED ABOUT THEIR ABILITY TO PAY FOR HEALTH CARE

Although a Gallup Organization poll conducted in April 2004 named retirement planning—Americans' fears that they will be unprepared to retire from the workforce because they will not have enough money—as number one in terms of urgent concerns, anxiety about health care costs was a close second (Lydia Said, "Retirement Planning Leads Americans' Financial List," *Gallup Poll News Service,* The Gallup Organization, May 18, 2004). Nearly

FIGURE 9.3

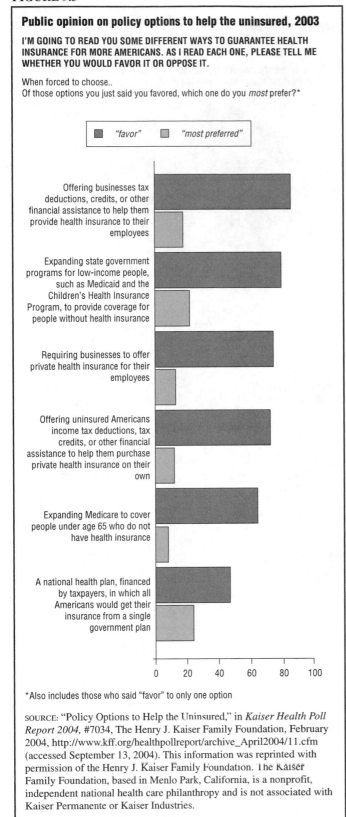

Public opinion on policy options to help the uninsured, 2003

I'M GOING TO READ YOU SOME DIFFERENT WAYS TO GUARANTEE HEALTH INSURANCE FOR MORE AMERICANS. AS I READ EACH ONE, PLEASE TELL ME WHETHER YOU WOULD FAVOR IT OR OPPOSE IT.

When forced to choose..
Of those options you just said you favored, which one do you *most* prefer?*

■ "favor" □ "most preferred"

Offering businesses tax deductions, credits, or other financial assistance to help them provide health insurance to their employees

Expanding state government programs for low-income people, such as Medicaid and the Children's Health Insurance Program, to provide coverage for people without health insurance

Requiring businesses to offer private health insurance for their employees

Offering uninsured Americans income tax deductions, tax credits, or other financial assistance to help them purchase private health insurance on their own

Expanding Medicare to cover people under age 65 who do not have health insurance

A national health plan, financed by taxpayers, in which all Americans would get their insurance from a single government plan

*Also includes those who said "favor" to only one option

SOURCE: "Policy Options to Help the Uninsured," in *Kaiser Health Poll Report 2004*, #7034, The Henry J. Kaiser Family Foundation, February 2004, http://www.kff.org/healthpollreport/archive_April2004/11.cfm (accessed September 13, 2004). This information was reprinted with permission of the Henry J. Kaiser Family Foundation. The Kaiser Family Foundation, based in Menlo Park, California, is a nonprofit, independent national health care philanthropy and is not associated with Kaiser Permanente or Kaiser Industries.

FIGURE 9.4

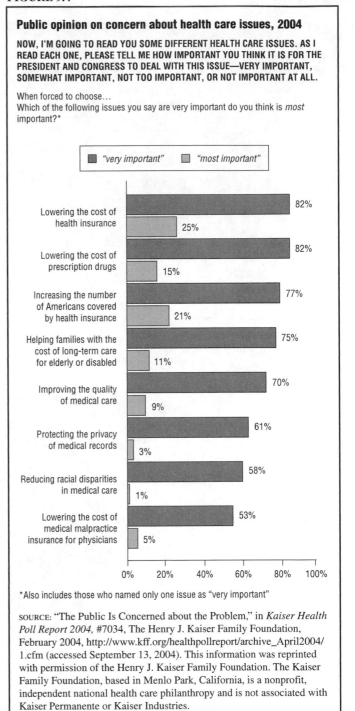

Public opinion on concern about health care issues, 2004

NOW, I'M GOING TO READ YOU SOME DIFFERENT HEALTH CARE ISSUES. AS I READ EACH ONE, PLEASE TELL ME HOW IMPORTANT YOU THINK IT IS FOR THE PRESIDENT AND CONGRESS TO DEAL WITH THIS ISSUE—VERY IMPORTANT, SOMEWHAT IMPORTANT, NOT TOO IMPORTANT, OR NOT IMPORTANT AT ALL.

When forced to choose...
Which of the following issues you say are very important do you think is *most* important?*

■ "very important" □ "most important"

Issue	very important	most important
Lowering the cost of health insurance	82%	25%
Lowering the cost of prescription drugs	82%	15%
Increasing the number of Americans covered by health insurance	77%	21%
Helping families with the cost of long-term care for elderly or disabled	75%	11%
Improving the quality of medical care	70%	9%
Protecting the privacy of medical records	61%	3%
Reducing racial disparities in medical care	58%	1%
Lowering the cost of medical malpractice insurance for physicians	53%	5%

*Also includes those who named only one issue as "very important"

SOURCE: "The Public Is Concerned about the Problem," in *Kaiser Health Poll Report 2004*, #7034, The Henry J. Kaiser Family Foundation, February 2004, http://www.kff.org/healthpollreport/archive_April2004/1.cfm (accessed September 13, 2004). This information was reprinted with permission of the Henry J. Kaiser Family Foundation. The Kaiser Family Foundation, based in Menlo Park, California, is a nonprofit, independent national health care philanthropy and is not associated with Kaiser Permanente or Kaiser Industries.

half of the adults surveyed (47%) said they were worried about their ability to pay for the costs associated with a serious illness or accident, and 37% were worried about paying for normal or routine health care services. Two of the top five financial concerns expressed by the survey respondents centered on fears about health care costs. (See Figure 9.6.)

The Gallup Poll also revealed that the proportion of Americans that is fearful—very worried or moderately worried—about the ability to pay for routine or serious medical care costs has not significantly changed in recent years. For example, the proportion of Americans who were very worried about being unable to pay for normal health care was comparable in 2001 (22%) and 2004 (21%). Similarly, in 2001 27% of survey respondents

FIGURE 9.5

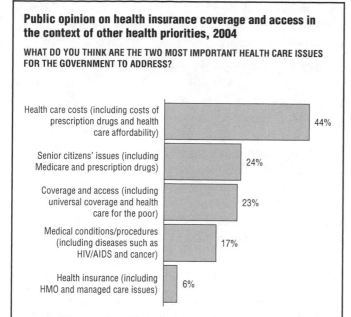

Public opinion on health insurance coverage and access in the context of other health priorities, 2004

WHAT DO YOU THINK ARE THE TWO MOST IMPORTANT HEALTH CARE ISSUES FOR THE GOVERNMENT TO ADDRESS?

Health care costs (including costs of prescription drugs and health care affordability) — 44%

Senior citizens' issues (including Medicare and prescription drugs) — 24%

Coverage and access (including universal coverage and health care for the poor) — 23%

Medical conditions/procedures (including diseases such as HIV/AIDS and cancer) — 17%

Health insurance (including HMO and managed care issues) — 6%

SOURCE: "Concern about Coverage and Access in Context with Other Health Priorities," in *Kaiser Health Poll Report 2004,* #7034, The Henry J. Kaiser Family Foundation, February 2004, http://www.kff.org/healthpollreport/archive_April2004/2.cfm (accessed September 13, 2004). This information was reprinted with permission of the Henry J. Kaiser Family Foundation. The Kaiser Family Foundation, based in Menlo Park, California, is a nonprofit, independent national health care philanthropy and is not associated with Kaiser Permanente or Kaiser Industries.

FIGURE 9.6

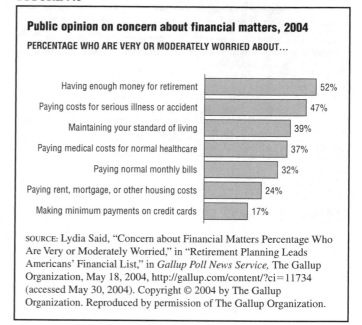

Public opinion on concern about financial matters, 2004

PERCENTAGE WHO ARE VERY OR MODERATELY WORRIED ABOUT...

Having enough money for retirement — 52%

Paying costs for serious illness or accident — 47%

Maintaining your standard of living — 39%

Paying medical costs for normal healthcare — 37%

Paying normal monthly bills — 32%

Paying rent, mortgage, or other housing costs — 24%

Making minimum payments on credit cards — 17%

SOURCE: Lydia Said, "Concern about Financial Matters Percentage Who Are Very or Moderately Worried," in "Retirement Planning Leads Americans' Financial List," in *Gallup Poll News Service,* The Gallup Organization, May 18, 2004, http://gallup.com/content/?ci=11734 (accessed May 30, 2004). Copyright © 2004 by The Gallup Organization. Reproduced by permission of The Gallup Organization.

worried about being unable to pay medical care costs in the event of a serious illness, and in 2004 26% expressed this concern. More than one-third of Americans worry about how to pay for routine medical expenses, according to the 2004 data, and nearly half are concerned about their ability to pay the costs associated with a serious illness or accident. (See Table 9.1.)

While the percentage of Americans who worry about their ability to pay for health care has remained relatively constant in recent years, the percentage of Americans who are very dissatisfied with the availability of affordable health care steadily increased from 37% in January 2001 to 45% in January 2004. (See Figure 9.7.)

Who Is Most Concerned about Health Care Costs?

The January 2004 Gallup Poll found significant differences among adults who said they were worried about their ability to pay for medical care in the coming months. More women (38%) than men (25%) expressed concern about paying for health care. Not surprisingly, more than half of respondents with annual household incomes under $30,000 worried that they would be unable to pay medical bills in the coming year, compared to only 12% of those with household incomes in excess of $75,000. Interestingly, concern about paying health care costs varied based on political party affiliation. Just 15% of Republicans said

they worried about paying for health care compared to 37% of Democrats and 43% of Independents.

CONSUMER SATISFACTION WITH HEALTH CARE FACILITIES

Despite the problems that continue to plague hospitals such as shortages of nurses and other key personnel, diminished reimbursement, shorter inpatient lengths-of-stay, sicker patients, and excessively long waiting times for patients in emergency and other hospital departments, consumer satisfaction with hospital services has remained relatively constant since 2000. Gallup data revealed that satisfaction with inpatient hospital care dropped slightly between 2000 and 2001 (from a mean score of 3.51 in 2000 to 3.49 in 2001), yet since 2001 it has improved slightly each year, rising to 3.50 in 2002 and 3.51 in 2003. (Rick Blizzard, "Patient Satisfaction Stable among Unstable Conditions," *The Gallup Poll Tuesday Briefing,* The Gallup Organization, May 18, 2004.)

In view of the challenges faced by emergency departments, it is not surprising that these hospital departments received the lowest overall satisfaction scores. Still, in terms of consumer satisfaction, emergency departments did not lose ground during the four-year period. (See Figure 9.8.)

Outpatient services received the highest scores for consumer satisfaction. According to Blizzard in *The Gallup Poll Tuesday Briefing,* outpatient surgery was the highest-rated area in terms of patient satisfaction, earning 3.68 and 3.69 out of a possible four across the four years of the survey. Outpatient testing and treatment also earned high marks. Since these services are often consumers' first encounters with hospitals, these high levels of satisfaction may have a favorable impact on consumers' overall perceptions of hospitals.

TABLE 9.1

Public opinion on concern about paying for health care, 2001–04

PLEASE TELL ME HOW CONCERNED YOU ARE RIGHT NOW ABOUT EACH OF THE
FOLLOWING FINANCIAL MATTERS, BASED ON YOUR CURRENT FINANCIAL SITUATION?

A. Not being able to pay medical costs for normal health care

	Very worried %	Moderately worried %	Not too worried %	Not worried at all %	Doesn't apply (vol.) %	No opinion %
2004 Apr 5–8	21	16	24	36	3	*
2003 Apr 7–9	17	20	24	36	3	*
2002 Apr 8–11	18	17	26	36	2	1
2001 Apr 6–8	22	22	24	31	1	0

B. Not being able to pay medical costs in the event of a serious illness or accident

	Very worried %	Moderately worried %	Not too worried %	Not worried at all %	Doesn't apply (vol.) %	No opinion %
2004 Apr 5–8	26	21	24	27	2	*
2003 Apr 7–9	24	22	23	29	2	—
2002 Apr 8–11	21	24	25	28	1	1
2001 Apr 6–8	27	23	24	25	1	*

*Less than 0.5%
(vol.) Volunteered response

SOURCE: Lydia Said, "Next, Please Tell Me How Concerned You Are Right
Now about Each of the Following Financial Matters, Based on Your Current
Financial Situation," in *Gallup Poll News Service,* The Gallup Organization,
May 18, 2004, http://gallup.com/content/default.aspx?ci=11734&pg=2
(accessed May 30, 2004). Copyright © 2004 by The Gallup Organization.
Reproduced by permission of The Gallup Organization.

Interestingly, patient satisfaction with hospital care was also linked to the hospital's success in meeting patients' spiritual and emotional needs. (See Figure 9.9.) This finding, that satisfaction is associated with intangible qualities of the hospital experience such as sensitivity, attention, and responsiveness to emotional and spiritual needs, underscores the fact that many health care consumers assess the quality of service they receive in terms of the care and compassion displayed by hospital personnel.

Americans Still Trust Hospitals and Physicians but Pharmaceutical Companies Have Lost Ground

An April 2003 Harris Poll survey, in which Americans maligned health insurance companies and managed care plans for failing to adequately meet their needs, nevertheless found hospitals high on the list of companies that consumers credited with good performance records (Humphrey Taylor, "Supermarkets, Food Companies, Hospitals, and Banks Top the List of Industries Doing Good Job for Their Consumers," *The Harris Poll,* Harris Interactive, May 28, 2003). Nearly three-quarters (73%) of survey respondents said they felt hospitals were doing a good job of serving consumers.

In contrast, pharmaceutical companies are no longer held in high esteem. At the top of the list of companies Americans admired in 1997, pharmaceutical companies dropped from fourth place to eleventh place by 2003. Pharmaceutical companies' positive ratings have declined steadily from 79% in 1997, to 73% in 1998, 66% in 1999, 59% in 2000, to 49% in 2003. Industry observers attribute the sharp decline to adverse media publicity about prescription drug costs.

While physicians may not enjoy the preeminence and reputations for infallibility they held in the past, most Americans still have confidence in their personal physicians. More than 80% of respondents to a 2002 survey conducted by the Kaiser Family Foundation, Harvard University's Kennedy School of Government, and National Public Radio said they trusted their doctor to take correct action "just about always" (48%) or "most of the time" (33%). The majority of respondents (77%) even expressed confidence that their physicians would inform them if a mistake were made in their care.

EMPLOYER-SPONSORED HEALTH PLANS

The *Employer Health Benefits 2003 Annual Survey*, conducted since 1999 by the Henry J. Kaiser Family Foundation and the Health Research and Educational Trust (Washington, DC, 2003), found that despite escalating premiums and increases in worker cost sharing, overall levels of coverage have not declined. In 2003 more than two-thirds of all firms offered health coverage to their workers. The decision to offer health benefits varies by company size—nearly all firms with fifty or more workers offer health benefits. Benefits are offered by 84% of firms with twenty-five to forty-nine employees, 76% of firms with ten to twenty-four workers, and 55% of companies with three to nine employees. More than 90% of companies that employ union workers offer health benefits.

The survey revealed that as employers endeavor to rein in the rising cost of health insurance, the vast majority of workers pay for premiums and encounter substantial cost sharing (deductibles, coinsurance, and co-payments) for services such as office visits, prescription drugs, and hospital admissions. Nearly four in five workers pay a deductible before health care expenses are covered by their plans. More than two in five employees pay a separate deductible, co-payment, or coinsurance when they are admitted to a hospital, and almost all workers pay a co-payment or coinsurance for physician office visits. The majority of workers also are in plans with cost-sharing arrangements for prescription drugs.

Rising Premiums and Reduced Benefits May Reduce Satisfaction with Employer-Sponsored Plans

Between May 2002 and May 2003, employer health insurance premiums rose 13.9%, which was the third consecutive year of double-digit insurance premium increases and the sharpest increase since 1990, according to the *Employer Health Benefits 2003 Annual Survey.* Average annual premiums rose to $3,383 for individual coverage and $9,068 for family coverage for employer-sponsored

FIGURE 9.7

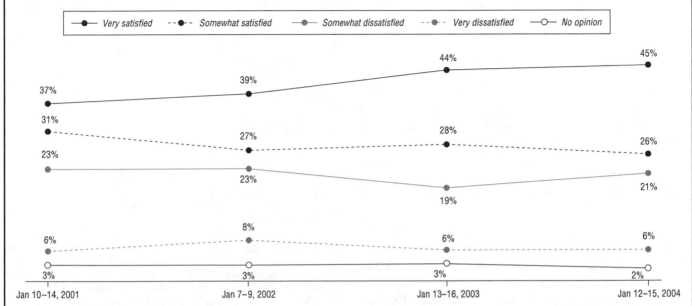

Public opinion on availability of affordable healthcare, 2001–04

NEXT, WE'D LIKE TO KNOW HOW YOU FEEL ABOUT THE STATE OF THE NATION IN EACH OF THE FOLLOWING AREAS. FOR EACH ONE, PLEASE SAY WHETHER YOU ARE VERY SATISFIED, SOMEWHAT SATISFIED, SOMEWHAT DISSATISFIED, OR VERY DISSATISFIED. IF YOU DON'T HAVE ENOUGH INFORMATION ABOUT A PARTICULAR SUBJECT TO RATE IT, JUST SAY SO. HOW ABOUT...THE AVAILABILITY OF AFFORDABLE HEALTHCARE?

SOURCE: Coleen McMurray, "Satisfaction with Availability of Affordable Healthcare," in "Healthcare Costs Dominate Americans' Health Concerns," in *The Gallup Poll Tuesday Briefing,* The Gallup Organization, February 3, 2004, http://www.gallup.com/content/default.aspx?ci=10486 (accessed May 30, 2004). Copyright © 2004 by The Gallup Organization. Reproduced by permission of The Gallup Organization.

plans. The percentage of premiums paid by workers was essentially unchanged over the last two years, at 16% for single coverage and 27% for family coverage. Health maintenance organizations (HMOs), which enrolled 24% of covered workers in 2003, remain the least costly, and preferred provider organizations (PPO plans), which enrolled more than half of all employees with health coverage, continue to offer the most expensive family coverage. Indemnity insurance, which provides reimbursement for medical expenses regardless of who provided the service, enrolled only 5% of employees.

The survey attributed the high rate of premium growth in 2003 to the combined effects of rapid inflation in the costs of health care services and insurers' intensified efforts to assure profitability. Employers attributed increases in health insurance premiums to higher spending for prescription drugs (61%) and higher spending for hospital services (55%). Skyrocketing premiums have prompted many employers to consider alternatives to their current health plans. More than 60% claimed that they shopped for a different arrangement, and 33% reported that they either changed carriers or plan type. Despite their enthusiasm for less costly alternatives, a scant 5% of employers opted to offer high deductible health plans (defined as plans with a deductible of $1,000 or more for single coverage), which have been extolled by insurers and benefit experts as effective methods to reduce health spending.

The survey also found retiree benefits dwindling—just 38% of large employers (two hundred or more workers) offer retiree benefits compared to 66% in 1988. Health care benefits administrators and industry observers contend that reduced benefits, higher costs, and fewer small employers offering coverage may combine to sharply reduce employee satisfaction with employer-sponsored health plans.

SATISFACTION WITH HEALTH INSURANCE PLANS

Harris Interactive and other researchers report increasingly negative public attitudes about managed care. In fact, the April 2003 Harris Poll that asked Americans how well they thought different industries were serving their customers found the health insurance industry and managed care plans at the bottom of the list. Just 40% of respondents felt health insurance companies were doing a good job, and 30% credited managed care plans with a job well done. The Harris Poll researchers distinguish the growing dissatisfaction with the concept of managed care from how consumers feel personally about their own plans. The researchers contend that the personal experiences of most Americans are not as awful as the accounts described in the media (Humphrey Taylor, "Supermarkets, Food Companies, Hospitals, and Banks Top the List of Industries Doing Good Job for Their Consumers," *The Harris Poll,* Harris Interactive, May 28, 2003).

FIGURE 9.8

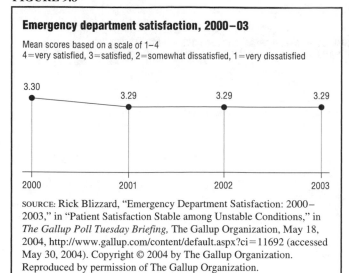

Emergency department satisfaction, 2000–03

Mean scores based on a scale of 1–4
4=very satisfied, 3=satisfied, 2=somewhat dissatisfied, 1=very dissatisfied

3.30   3.29   3.29   3.29

2000   2001   2002   2003

SOURCE: Rick Blizzard, "Emergency Department Satisfaction: 2000–2003," in "Patient Satisfaction Stable among Unstable Conditions," in *The Gallup Poll Tuesday Briefing,* The Gallup Organization, May 18, 2004, http://www.gallup.com/content/default.aspx?ci=11692 (accessed May 30, 2004). Copyright © 2004 by The Gallup Organization. Reproduced by permission of The Gallup Organization.

FIGURE 9.9

Correlation* between meeting spiritual needs, patient satisfaction, and patient loyalty, 2004

	Overall, how satisfied were you with the hospital stay?	How likely would you be to return to this same hospital if you ever needed to be hospitalized again?
How satisfied were you with how well the staff was able to meet your spiritual needs?	.45	.32
How satisfied were you with how well the staff was able to meet your spiritual and emotional needs?	.60	.40

*A correlation of 1.0 means that variables always change in the same direction and to the same degree. A correlation of 0 indicates there is no relationship at all between the variables.

SOURCE: Rick Blizzard, "Correlation between Meeting Spiritual Needs, Patient Satisfaction, and Patient Loyalty," in "Praying for Patient Satisfaction," in *The Gallup Poll Tuesday Briefing,* The Gallup Organization, March 30, 2004, http://www.gallup.com/content/default .aspx?ci=11116 (accessed May 30, 2004). Copyright © 2004 by The Gallup Organization. Reproduced by permission of The Gallup Organization.

In contrast to public opinion and many media reports, many people are quite satisfied with their health plans. In "Satisfaction with Own Health Insurance Remarkably Stable"(*Health Care News, Harris Interactive,* vol. 4, issue 5, March 29, 2004), Humphrey Taylor and Robert Leitman observed that for the fifth consecutive year the majority of the insured public continues to report high levels of satisfaction with their health plans. In 2004 about two-thirds of health plan members gave their plans high marks—As and Bs.

In 2004 more than three-quarters of adults with health insurance (76%) said they would "probably" or "definitely" recommend their plan to a family member or friend who was healthy, and more than two-thirds (68%) said they would likely recommend their plan to a family member or friend suffering from a serious or chronic illness. (See Table 9.2 and Table 9.3.) Persons insured by employers or unions were even more likely to recommend their health plans. Nearly 80% would "probably" or "definitely" recommend their plan to a healthy family member or friend, and 70% would likely recommend their plan to a family member or friend suffering from a serious or chronic illness. (See Table 9.4 and Table 9.5.)

According to Taylor and Leitman in the Harris Interactive survey, overall consumer dissatisfaction with health plans has not substantially changed from 2001 to 2004. Slightly more Medicare recipients (29%) gave their health plan low grades in 2004 than in 2001 (24%), and there was a comparable increase in the percentage of Medicare recipients who would not recommend their plans to their healthy friends.

More Medicaid beneficiaries are dissatisfied than persons enrolled in Medicare or employer-sponsored health plans. According to Taylor and Leitman, some 18% of Medicaid recipients awarded their health plan a failing grade (D or F) compared to 12% of persons with employer-provided plans, 15% of Medicare beneficiaries, and 11% of persons who purchased private insurance. Dissatisfaction with Medicaid has also increased in recent years—33% of recipients reported in 2004 that they would not recommend it to friends or family members who have serious or chronic illnesses, compared to 24% in 2001.

Are Members of For-Profit HMOs Less Satisfied with Care Than Members of Nonprofit HMOs?

During the 1980s just one-quarter of all HMO members were enrolled in for-profit HMOs. However, conversion of many not-for-profit plans resulted in a dramatic shift, and by the late 1990s nearly two-thirds of HMO members were enrolled in for-profit plans. Some industry observers worried that large, for-profit health plan owners might jeopardize the quality of care delivered by denying members needed services to save money. Investigators Ha Tu and James Reschovsky at the Center for Studying Health System Change in Washington, D.C., looked at the relationship between members' assessments of their care and the profit status of their HMOs to find out if profit status affected members' perceptions of the quality of health care they received.

The investigators examined data from more than thirteen thousand HMO members and published the results of their analysis in the *New England Journal of Medicine* (vol. 346, no. 17, April 25, 2002). They found that slightly

TABLE 9.2

Public opinion on recommending a health plan to a healthy relative or friend, 1998–2004

WOULD YOU DEFINITELY, PROBABLY, PROBABLY NOT OR DEFINITELY NOT RECOMMEND YOUR HEALTH CARE PLAN TO A FAMILY MEMBER OR FRIEND WHO IS BASICALLY HEALTHY?

Base: Insured adults

	1998 %	1999 %	2000 %	2001 %	2002 %	2004 %
Definitely recommend	39	31	41	34	40	41
Probably recommend	40	44	37	39	36	35
Probably not recommend	12	13	11	16	10	11
Definitely not recommend	7	8	6	7	8	7
Not sure/refused	3	5	4	4	5	6

SOURCE: "Table 2-A. Recommending Health Plan to a Healthy Relative or Friend: 1998–2004," in *Health Care News: Satisfaction with Own Health Insurance Remarkably Stable,* vol. 4, no. 5, Harris Interactive, March 29, 2004, http://www.harrisinteractive.com/news/newsletters/healthnews/HI_HealthCareNews2004Vol4_Iss05.pdf (accessed September 13, 2004). © 2004, Harris Interactive Inc. All rights reserved. Reproduced with permission in 2004.

TABLE 9.3

Public opinion on recommending a health plan to a sick relative or friend, 1998–2004

WOULD YOU DEFINITELY, PROBABLY, PROBABLY NOT OR DEFINITELY NOT RECOMMEND YOUR HEALTH CARE PLAN TO A FAMILY MEMBER OR FRIEND WHO HAS A SERIOUS OR CHRONIC ILLNESS?

Base: Insured adults

	1998 %	1999 %	2000 %	2001 %	2002 %	2004 %
Definitely recommend	34	28	38	34	38	37
Probably recommend	34	38	30	33	29	31
Probably not recommend	16	13	13	14	15	14
Definitely not recommend	13	14	12	11	11	10
Not sure/refused	3	7	6	6	7	8

SOURCE: "Table 3-A. Recommending Health Plan to a Sick Relative or Friend: 1998–2004," in *Health Care News: Satisfaction with Own Health Insurance Remarkably Stable,* vol. 4, no. 5, Harris Interactive, March 29, 2004, http://www.harrisinteractive.com/news/newsletters/healthnews/HI_HealthCareNews2004Vol4_Iss05.pdf (accessed September 13, 2004). © 2004, Harris Interactive Inc. All rights reserved. Reproduced with permission in 2004.

TABLE 9.4

Public opinion on recommending an employer-provided health plan to a healthy relative or friend, 1998–2004

WOULD YOU DEFINITELY, PROBABLY, PROBABLY NOT OR DEFINITELY NOT RECOMMEND YOUR HEALTH CARE PLAN TO A FAMILY MEMBER OR FRIEND WHO IS BASICALLY HEALTHY?

Base: Adults insured by employers or unions

	Currently insured through work, union				
	1999 %	2000 %	2001 %	2002 %	2004 %
Definitely recommend	26	42	33	40	40
Probably recommend	53	40	42	37	39
Probably not recommend	12	9	17	11	11
Definitely not recommend	8	6	6	7	6
Not sure/refused	2	3	3	4	4

SOURCE: "Table 2-B. Recommending Health Plan to a Healthy Relative or Friend: 1998–2004 Employer-Provided Plans," in *Health Care News: Satisfaction with Own Health Insurance Remarkably Stable,* vol. 4, no. 5, Harris Interactive, March 29, 2004, http://www.harrisinteractive.com/news/newsletters/healthnews/HI_HealthCareNews2004Vol4_Iss05.pdf (accessed September 13, 2004). © 2004, Harris Interactive Inc. All rights reserved. Reproduced with permission in 2004.

TABLE 9.5

Public opinion on recommending an employer-provided health plan to a sick relative or friend, 1998–2004

WOULD YOU DEFINITELY, PROBABLY, PROBABLY NOT OR DEFINITELY NOT RECOMMEND YOUR HEALTH CARE PLAN TO A FAMILY MEMBER OR FRIEND WHO HAS A SERIOUS OR CHRONIC ILLNESS?

Base: Adults insured by employers or unions

	Currently insured through work, union				
	1999 %	2000 %	2001 %	2002 %	2004 %
Definitely recommend	24	36	32	38	36
Probably recommend	44	33	35	30	34
Probably not recommend	14	13	15	15	14
Definitely not recommend	14	12	11	11	9
Not sure/refused	4	6	6	6	6

SOURCE: "Table 3-B. Recommending Health Plan to a Sick Relative or Friend: 1998–2004 Employer-Provided Plans," in *Health Care News: Satisfaction with Own Health Insurance Remarkably Stable,* vol. 4, no. 5, Harris Interactive, March 29, 2004, http://www.harrisinteractive.com/news/newsletters/healthnews/HI_HealthCareNews2004Vol4_Iss05.pdf (accessed September 13, 2004). © 2004, Harris Interactive Inc. All rights reserved. Reproduced with permission in 2004.

more members of nonprofit HMOs were very satisfied with their care (64%) than members of for-profit plans (58.1%). In the for-profit HMOs, sick members reported greater dissatisfaction than healthy members, with sick members reporting more delays in receiving care, unmet needs, organizational or administrative obstacles to receiving treatment, and higher out-of-pocket expenses. In nonprofit HMOs, the only difference between sick and healthy members was that sick members expressed greater confidence that they would be referred for care when necessary.

The investigators speculated that while there may have been significant differences in the operation of for-profit and nonprofit plans in the past, in recent years all plans have been subjected to comparable market pressures and economic constraints, rendering the plans nearly indistinguishable from one another in terms of quality and health service delivery.

REPORT CARDS MAY HELP CONSUMERS MAKE INFORMED CHOICES

Report cards that grade health plans, hospitals, and other providers offer consumers a way to make accurate comparisons and informed choices. Since the early 1990s the number of agencies, organizations, and employer coalitions issuing report cards has grown. In 1995 the federal government initiated the Consumer Assessment of Health Plans Study (CAHPS) to develop a consumer information project. By 1999, nine million federal employees had access to CAHPS data about available health plans. In 2002 Medicare beneficiaries also gained access to CAHPS data about Medicare managed care plans. CAHPS data are available to the public in print and on the Internet.

Many federal and state employees as well as workers employed in large corporations have become accustomed to comparing health plans using report cards, but report cards examining the quality of health care systems are relatively new additions to quality improvement and consumer education programs. Researchers from the Health Research Center, Park Nicollet Institute, and Minnesota Health Data Institute studied consumer response to report cards that compared health care systems that deliver care rather than health plans that provide insurance coverage. Barbara Braun and her colleagues published their findings in *American Journal of Managed Care* (vol. 8, no. 6, June 2002).

The report cards that the study participants were given measured seven aspects of care:

- Obtaining care without long waits
- Physician-patient communication
- Courtesy of office staff
- Ease of obtaining needed medical care
- Overall rating of the clinic experience
- Rating of health care provided
- Rating of the health care provider

The investigators found that most study participants had been unaware of the widespread use of report cards to compare health plans and the more recent use of them to measure and compare health service delivery. Nonetheless, the survey participants were very interested in quality measurement and considered report cards to be most valuable in two different circumstances—when they were faced with the personal choice of health care delivery system, and as a way to direct system-wide quality improvement efforts. Participants felt they would be most likely to consider report card data if they were dissatisfied with their current providers of medical care. Many said their own personal experiences and the opinions of friends and family would remain their primary and most trusted means of evaluating health care quality.

A GROWING NUMBER LOOK FOR HEALTH INFORMATION ONLINE

Although trust in hospitals and personal physicians remains high, and many people receive health education from physicians, nurses, and other health professionals, a growing number of Americans are seeking health infor-

TABLE 9.6

Adults who use the Internet to search for health care information, 1998–2004

	1998	1999	2001	2002	2003	Feb. 2004
	%	%	%	%	%	%
Percent of all adults who are online*	38	46	63	66	67	69
Percent of all those online who have ever looked for health information online	71	74	75	80	78	74
Percent of all adults who have ever looked for health information online	27	34	47	53	52	51
Percent of all adults who have looked for health information online in last month	N/A	N/A	N/A	N/A	N/A	35
Numbers of adults who have ever looked for health information online	54 million	69 million	97 million	110 million	109 million	111 million

*Includes those online from home, office, school, library or other location
Note: 2004 figures calculated based on number of U.S. adults online (146 million) which is based on U.S. Census estimate of 218 million adults overall in the U.S.

SOURCE: "Table 1. Cyberchondriacs: Trends," in *Health Care News: No Significant Change in the Number of 'Cyberchondriacs'—Those Who Go Online for Health Care Information*, vol. 4, no. 7, Harris Interactive, April 12, 2004, http://www.harrisinteractive.com/news/newsletters/healthnews/HI_HealthCareNews2004Vol4_Iss07.pdf (accessed September 13, 2004). © 2004, Harris Interactive Inc. All rights reserved. Reproduced with permission in 2004.

mation online. Harris Poll researchers have dubbed the more than 110 million adults who seek information about specific diseases or tips about how to maintain health on the Internet "cyberchondriacs."

When the nationwide survey was updated in February 2004, Harris Poll researchers found a relatively stable percentage of adults seeking health information online between 1998 and 2004 (Humphrey Taylor and Robert Leitman, "No Significant Change in the Number of Cyberchondriacs," *Health Care News, Harris Interactive*, vol. 4, issue 7, April 12, 2004). From mid-1998 to February 2004, the number of adults who had ever looked for health information online more than doubled from 54 million to 111 million. As of 2004, 69% of all adults who were online said they had sought health care information on the Internet. (See Table 9.6.)

The 2002 Harris Poll found that like the most frequent users of the Internet, cyberchondriacs tended to be young adults—82% of those between the ages of eighteen and twenty-nine had looked for health information online. Cyberchondriacs also were more likely to have had postgraduate education (84% of those adults looking for information online) and were more likely to be wealthier (77% of those reporting incomes in excess of $75,000 had looked for information online).

Table 9.7 shows that when cyberchondriacs go online in search of health information, they are more likely to use a portal or search engine (51%) to search multiple sites rather than look for information at a specific health Web site (23%). Despite the proliferation of sites devoted to health and medical care, the proportions of cyberchondriacs that visit them first when seeking health information has not changed from 2001 to 2004.

MARKETING PRESCRIPTION DRUGS TO CONSUMERS

Although health care consumers continue to receive much of their information from physicians, nurses, other health professionals, and the Internet, many also learn about health care services and products from reports in the news media and from advertising. Media advertising—promotion of hospitals, health insurance, managed care plans, medical groups, and related health services and products—has been a mainstay of health care marketing efforts since the 1970s. During the early 1990s pharmaceutical companies made their first forays into advertising of prescription drugs directly to consumers. Prior to the 1990s pharmaceutical companies' promotion efforts had focused almost exclusively on physicians, the health professionals who prescribe their products.

Since the mid-1990s, spending on prescription drugs has escalated and has become the fastest-growing segment of U.S. health care expenditures. In 1997 the Food and Drug Administration (FDA) released guidelines governing direct-to-consumer advertising and seemingly opened a floodgate of print, radio, and television advertisements promoting prescription drugs. Industry observers wondered if this upsurge of direct-to-consumer advertising had resulted in more, and possibly inappropriate, prescribing and higher costs.

Researchers from the Harvard School of Public Health and the Sloan School of Management at the Massachusetts Institute of Technology (MIT) examined the relationship between spending for promotional purposes and prescription drug sales and published their findings in the *New England Journal of Medicine* (vol. 346, no. 7, February 14, 2002). The researchers observed that pharmaceutical companies' budgets for promotion increased from $266 million in 1994 to almost $2.5 billion in 2000, and that television advertising, which accounted for 13% of direct-to-consumer promotions in 1994 and 64% in 2000, contributed to this growth. They found that direct-to-consumer advertising was generally used to promote long-term-use drugs prescribed for chronic conditions such as allergies, elevated blood cholesterol, and ulcers.

Is Direct-to-Consumer Advertising Effective?

It stands to reason that pharmaceutical companies must be receiving significant returns on their direct-to-consumer advertising investments in order to justify increasing budgets for consumer advertising, but it is difficult to measure the precise impact of consumer advertising on drug sales. The Harvard and MIT researchers observed that consumer awareness of prescription drug ads, in terms of adults surveyed who reported having seen drug ads, has more than doubled from nearly 40% in 1993 to more than 90% of consumers surveyed in 2000.

Mollyann Brodie evaluated consumers' reactions to drug ads by showing research participants actual prescription drug ads and recording their responses. In *Understanding the Effects of Direct-to-Consumer Prescription Drug Advertising* (Washington, DC: Henry J. Kaiser Family Foundation, November 2001), Brodie reported that one in three adults said they talked with their doctor after seeing an ad for a prescription drug and nearly half of those who spoke with their physicians about the drug (44%) received a prescription for that drug. Brodie also found that two-thirds of consumers who viewed prescription drug ads trusted the information they received in the ads, and 84% said the ads did an excellent or good job informing them about the condition that the advertised drug was intended to treat. Despite the ad viewers' perception that they were well informed, Brodie found that recall about potential drug side effects, and viewer knowledge about where they could find more information about the advertised medication, varied widely. In view of the speed with which some television drug ads announce potential side effects and adverse reactions, it was not surprising that as many as 75% of viewers could not accurately identify many of the advertised drug's side effects.

TABLE 9.7

Public opinion on where people look for health information online, 2004

"THE LAST TIME YOU LOOKED FOR INFORMATION ONLINE ABOUT A HEALTH TOPIC WHERE DID YOU *FIRST* GO TO GET THE INFORMATION YOU WERE INTERESTED IN? DID YOU *FIRST* GO TO A ...?"

Base: All "cyberchondriacs"

	2001	2002	2003	2004
	%	%	%	%
Site that focuses only on health-related topics OR	24	26	20	23
A site that focuses on many subjects that may have a section devoted to health issues, OR	16	12	17	14
A portal or search engine which will allow you to search for health information across many different sites	52	53	54	51
Not sure/refused	7	8	8	12

Note: Numbers may not add up due to rounding.

SOURCE: "Table 4. Where People Go to Look for Health Topics Online," in *Health Care News: No Significant Change in the Number of 'Cyberchondriacs'—Those Who Go Online for Health Care Information*, vol. 4, no. 7, Harris Interactive, April 12, 2004, http://www.harrisinteractive.com/ news/newsletters/healthnews/HI_HealthCareNews2004Vol4_Iss07.pdf (accessed September 13, 2004). © 2004, Harris Interactive Inc. All rights reserved. Reproduced with permission in 2004.

FIGURE 9.10

Most common new diagnoses to result from physician visits prompted by "direct-to-consumer advertising" (DCTA) of prescription drugs, 2001–02

Base: The 35% of adults who were prompted by DTCA to have a discussion with a doctor.

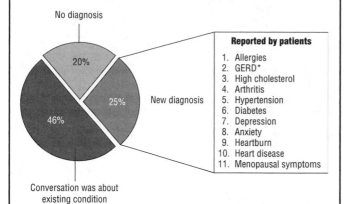

No diagnosis

20%

25% New diagnosis

46%

Conversation was about existing condition

Reported by patients
1. Allergies
2. GERD*
3. High cholesterol
4. Arthritis
5. Hypertension
6. Diabetes
7. Depression
8. Anxiety
9. Heartburn
10. Heart disease
11. Menopausal symptoms

Note: 9% could not/would not name the condition.
*Gastroesophageal reflux disease

SOURCE: "Table 2. Most Common New Diagnoses From DCTA Visits," in *Health Care News: The Impact of Direct-To-Consumer Advertising of Prescription Drugs on Consumer Behavior, Diagnosis and Treatment,* vol. 3, no. 11, Harris Interactive, June 23, 2003, http://www.harrisinteractive.com/news/newsletters/healthnews/HI_HealthCareNews2003Vol3_Iss11.pdf (accessed September 13, 2004). © 2004, Harris Interactive Inc. All rights reserved. Reproduced with permission in 2004.

TABLE 9.8

Actions taken by physicians on behalf of patients having recent office visits prompted by "direct-to-consumer advertising" (DCTA) of prescription drugs, 2001–02

"AS A RESULT OF THE VISIT AND ANY FOLLOW-UP VISITS YOU HAD WITH YOUR DOCTOR, DID YOUR DOCTOR DO ANY OF THE FOLLOWING?"

Base: The 35% of adults who were promoted by DTCA to have a discussion with a doctor.

	Patient reports %
Prescribed DTCA drug	43
Prescribed a drug for you	72
Prescribed any drug (and patient was not receiving treatment for condition priority to visit)	23
Referred you to a specialist	32
Suggest a change in your diet or how much you should exercise	52
Recommended OTC drug	19
Order a laboratory or diagnostic test	57
Suggest that you quit smoking or drinking	33

SOURCE: "Table 3. Actions Taken by Physicians on Behalf of Patients Having Recent DCTA Visits," in *Health Care News: The Impact of Direct-to-Consumer Advertising of Prescription Drugs on Consumer Behavior, Diagnosis and Treatment,* vol. 3, no. 11, Harris Interactive, June 23, 2003, http://www.harrisinteractive.com/news/newsletters/healthnews/HI_HealthCareNews2003Vol3_Iss11.pdf (accessed September 13, 2004). © 2004, Harris Interactive Inc. All rights reserved. Reproduced with permission in 2004.

TABLE 9.9

Overall health and results of lab tests following office visits prompted by "direct-to-consumer advertising" (DCTA) of prescription drugs, 2001–02

Base: The 21% of the adults taking prescription drugs following a DTCA visit

	Type of drug			Switched drugs	
	All	DTCA	Other	To DTCA	To other
Overall health					
Much/some better	81	81	81	86	78
About the same	13	11	15	10	18
Some/much worse	5	6	4	4	3
Lab tests (where done before and after) showed:					
Change for better	84	86	82	94	87
No change/not sure	3	4	2	6	3
Change for worse	13	10	16	0	10

SOURCE: "Table 4. Overall Health and Results of Lab Tests," in *Health Care News: The Impact of Direct-to-Consumer Advertising of Prescription Drugs on Consumer Behavior, Diagnosis and Treatment,* vol. 3, no. 11, Harris Interactive, June 23, 2003, http://www.harrisinteractive.com/news/newsletters/healthnews/HI_HealthCareNews2003Vol3_Iss11.pdf (accessed September 13, 2004). © 2004, Harris Interactive Inc. All rights reserved. Reproduced with permission in 2004.

A nationwide survey of adults conducted by Harris Interactive between July 2001 and January 2002 reconfirmed the marketing impact of direct-to-consumer advertising. The overwhelming majority of survey respondents (86%) recalled seeing or hearing the direct-to-consumer advertising of prescription drugs, and more than one-third (35%) discussed an advertised drug with a physician (Humphrey Taylor and Robert Leitman, "The Impact of Direct-to-Consumer Advertising of Prescription Drugs on Consumer Behavior, Diagnosis and Treatment," *Health Care News, Harris Interactive,* vol. 3, issue 11, June 23, 2003). Further, the survey aimed to determine the specific conditions that were diagnosed as a result of physician visits prompted by direct-to-consumer advertising, the actions taken during such visits, and the outcomes that resulted from taking prescription medication prescribed during these visits.

The researchers found that at one-quarter of the physician visits prompted by advertising, the physician diagnosed new conditions—identifying previously undiagnosed conditions. The most common new diagnoses were allergies, GERD (gastroesophageal reflux disease), high cholesterol, arthritis, hypertension, diabetes, depression, anxiety, heartburn, heart disease, and the effects of menopause. (See Figure 9.10.) Nearly three-quarters of physician visits prompted by advertising resulted in a prescription being written, and in 43% of visits the prescription was for the drug the patient had seen advertised. (See Table 9.8.)

The majority (81%) of patients who received prescriptions at their advertising-induced physician visits reported overall improvement in their health. Interestingly, patients who were prescribed the advertised drug were more likely to report favorable health outcomes than those who received prescriptions for drugs other than the advertised drug. (See Table 9.9.)

IMPORTANT NAMES AND ADDRESSES

Accreditation Association for Ambulatory Health Care, Inc.
3201 Old Glenview Rd.
Suite 300
Wilmette, IL 60091-2992
(847) 853-6060
FAX: (847) 853-9028
E-mail: info@aaahc.org
URL: http://www.aaahc.org

Administration on Aging
Washington, DC 20201
(202) 619-0724
Toll-free: 1-800-677-1116
FAX: (202) 357-3555
E-mail: AoAInfo@aoa.gov
URL: http://www.aoa.gov

Agency for Healthcare Research and Quality
540 Gaither Rd.
Rockville, MD 20850
(301) 427-1364
E-mail: info@ahrq.gov
URL: http://www.ahrq.gov

American Academy of Family Physicians
11400 Tomahawk Creek Pkwy.
Leawood, KS 66211-2672
(913) 906-6000
Toll-free: 1-800-274-2237
FAX: (913) 906-6077
E-mail: fp@aafp.org
URL: http://www.aafp.org

American Academy of Physician Assistants
950 North Washington St.
Alexandria, VA 22314-1552
(703) 836-2272
FAX: (703) 684-1924
E-mail: aapa@aapa.org
URL: http://www.aapa.org

American Cancer Society
2200 Century Pkwy.
Suite 950
Atlanta, GA 30345
(404) 816-4994
Toll-free: 1-800-ACS-2345
FAX: (404) 315-9348
URL: http://www.cancer.org

American Chiropractic Association
1701 Clarendon Blvd.
Arlington, VA 22209
(703) 276-8800
Toll-free: 1-800-986-4636
FAX: (703) 243-2593
E-mail: memberinfo@amerchiro.org
URL: http://www.amerchiro.org

American College of Nurse Practitioners
1111 19th Street NW
Suite 404
Washington, DC 20002
(202) 659-2190
FAX: (202) 659-2191
E-mail: acnp@nurse.org
URL: http://www.nurse.org

American Dental Association
211 East Chicago Ave.
Chicago, IL 60611
(312) 440-2500
FAX: (312) 440-2800
E-mail: publicinfo@ada.org
URL: http://www.ada.org

American Diabetes Association
1701 North Beauregard St.
Alexandria, VA 22311
(703) 549-1500
Toll-free: 1-800-DIABETES
FAX: (703) 549-6995
E-mail: askada@diabetes.org
URL: http://www.diabetes.org

American Geriatrics Society
The Empire State Building
350 Fifth Ave.
Suite 801
New York, NY 10118
(212) 308-1414
Toll-free: 1-800-247-4779
FAX: (212) 832-8646
E-mail: info@americangeriatrics.org
URL: http://www.americangeriatrics.org

American Heart Association
7272 Greenville Ave.
Dallas, TX 75231-4596
(301) 223-2307
Toll-free: 1-800-AHA-USA1
URL: http://www.americanheart.org

American Hospital Association
1 North Franklin
Chicago, IL 60606-3421
(312) 422-3000
Toll-free: 1-800-424-4301
FAX: (312) 422-4796
URL: http://www.aha.org

American Medical Association
515 North State St.
Chicago, IL 60610
(312) 464-5000
Toll-free: 1-800-621-8335
FAX: (312) 464-4184
URL: http://www.ama-assn.org

American Osteopathic Association
142 East Ontario St.
Chicago, IL 60611
(312) 202-8000
Toll-free: 1-800-621-1773
FAX: (312) 202-8200
E-mail: info@aoa-net.org
URL: http://www.aoa-net.org

American Pharmacists Association
2215 Constitution Ave. NW

Washington, DC 20037-2985
(202) 628-4410
Toll-free: 1-800-237-APHA
FAX: (202) 783-2351
E-mail: apha-appm@aphanet.org
URL: http://www.aphanet.org

American Physical Therapy Association
1111 North Fairfax St.
Alexandria, VA 22314-1488
(703) 684-2782
Toll-free: 1-800-999-2782
FAX: (703) 684-7343
E-mail: kathygiancoli@apta.org
URL: http://www.apta.org

Association of American
Medical Colleges
2450 N St. NW
Washington, DC 20037-1136
(202) 828-0400
FAX: (202) 828-1125
E-mail: amcas@aamc.org
URL: http://www.aamc.org

Center for Studying Health
System Change
600 Maryland Ave. SW
Suite 550
Washington, DC 20024
(202) 484-5261
FAX: (202) 484-9258
E-mail: hscinfo@hschange.org
URL: http://www.hschange.org

Centers for Disease Control
and Prevention
1600 Clifton Rd.
Atlanta, GA 30333
(404) 639-3311
Toll-free: 1-800-311-3435
URL: http://www.cdc.gov

Centers for Medicare & Medicaid
Services (CMS)
7500 Security Blvd.
Baltimore, MD 21244-1850
(410) 786-3000
Toll-free: 1-877-267-2323
URL: http://www.cms.gov

Children's Defense Fund
25 E St. NW
Washington, DC 20001
(202) 628-8787
FAX: (202) 662-3510
E-mail: cdfinfo@childrensdefense.org
URL: http://www.childrensdefense.org

Families USA
1334 G St. NW
Washington, DC 20005
(202) 628-3030
FAX: (202) 347-2417
E-mail: info@familiesusa.org
URL: http://www.familiesusa.org

Hospice Association of America
228 7th St. SE
Washington, DC 20003
(202) 546-4759
FAX: (202) 547-9559
E-mail: exec@nahc.org
URL: http://www.nahc.org/HAA

Joint Commission on Accreditation of
Healthcare Organizations (JCAHO)
1 Renaissance Blvd.
Oakbrook Terrace, IL 60181
(630) 792-5000
Toll-free: 1-800-994-6610
FAX: (630) 792-5005
E-mail: complaint@jcaho.org
URL: http://www.jcaho.org

March of Dimes Birth Defects
Foundation, National Office
1275 Mamaroneck Ave.
White Plains, NY 10605
(914) 428-7100
Toll-free: 1-800-996-2724
FAX: (914) 997-4537
URL: http://www.marchofdimes.com

Medical Group Management Association
104 Inverness Terrace E.
Englewood, CO 80112-5306
(303) 799-1111
Toll-free: 1-877-ASKMGMA
FAX: (303) 643-4439
E-mail: infocenter@mgma.com
URL: http://www.mgma.com

National Association of Community
Health Centers
7200 Wisconsin Ave.
Suite 210
Bethesda, MD 20814
(301) 347-0400
FAX: (301) 347-0459
E-mail: contact@nachc.com
URL: http://www.nachc.com

National Association of Public Hospitals
and Health Systems
1301 Pennsylvania Ave. NW
Suite 950
Washington, DC 20004
(202) 585-0100
FAX: (202) 585-0101
E-mail: naph@naph.org
URL: http://www.naph.org

National Center for Health Statistics
U.S. Department of Health and
Human Services
3311 Toledo Rd.
Hyattsville, MD 20782
(301) 458-4000
Toll-free: 1-866-441-NCHS
FAX: (301) 436-4258
URL: http://www.cdc.gov/nchs

National Committee for
Quality Assurance
2000 L Street NW
Suite 500
Washington, DC 20036
(202) 955-3500
Toll-free: 1-888-275-7585
FAX: (202) 955-3599
E-mail: customersupport@ncqa.org
URL: http://www.ncqa.org

United Network for Organ Sharing
P.O. Box 2484
Richmond, VA 23218
(804) 782-4800
Toll-free: 1-888-TXINFO1
FAX: (804) 782-4817
URL: http://www.unos.org

RESOURCES

Agencies of the U.S. Department of Health and Human Services (HHS) collect, analyze, and publish a wide variety of health statistics that describe and measure the operation and effectiveness of the American health care system. The Centers for Disease Control and Prevention (CDC) in Atlanta, Georgia, tracks nationwide health trends and reports its findings in several periodicals, especially its *Advance Data* series, *National Ambulatory Medical Care Survey, HIV/AIDS Surveillance Reports,* and *Morbidity and Mortality Weekly Reports.* The National Center for Health Statistics (NCHS) provides a complete statistical overview of the nation's health in its annual *Health, United States.*

The National Institutes of Health (NIH) provide definitions, epidemiological data, and research findings about a comprehensive range of medical and public health subjects. The Centers for Medicare and Medicaid (CMS) monitors the nation's health spending. The agency's quarterly *Health Care Financing Review* and annual *Data Compendium* provide complete information on health care spending, particularly allocations for Medicare and Medicaid. The Administration on Aging (AoA) provides information about the health, welfare, and services available for older Americans.

The Agency for Healthcare Research and Quality (AHRQ) researches and documents access to health care, quality of care, and efforts to control health care costs. It also examines the safety of health care services and ways to prevent medical errors. The Joint Commission on Accreditation of Healthcare Organizations (JCAHO) and the National Committee for Quality Assurance (NCQA) are accrediting organizations that focus attention on institutional health care providers including the managed care industry.

The Bureau of the Census, in its *Current Population Reports* series, details the status of insurance among selected American households.

Medical, public health, and nursing journals offer a wealth of health care system information and research findings. The studies cited in this edition are drawn from a range of professional publications including the *Journal of the American Medical Association, Annals of Internal Medicine, New England Journal of Medicine, Health Affairs, American Journal of Managed Care,* and *Journal of Nursing Administration.*

Thomson Gale thanks the Gallup Organization and Harris Interactive/The Harris Poll for the use of its public opinion research about employer-sponsored health plans and accessing health information online. We also express appreciation to the Organisation for Economic Cooperation and Development for permission to use information from its *OECD Health Data 2004* (Paris, France, 2004). We are grateful to the Henry J. Kaiser Family Foundation for permission to use information from its many fine reports, including *2001 Kaiser Women's Health Survey—Women's Health in the United States: Health Coverage and Access to Care* (Menlo Park, CA: 2004), *Kaiser Health Poll Report 2004,* and *Kaiser Health Poll Report 2003.* Our thanks also go to the many professional associations, voluntary medical organizations, and foundations dedicated to research, education, and advocacy about efforts to reform and improve the health care system that were included in this edition.

INDEX

HIV/AIDS treatment costs, 93–94
HMOs. *See* Health maintenance organizations (HMOs)
Home health care
  expenditures, 87
  overview, 55–58
  patients by age, sex and diagnosis, 57*t*
Homeopathic medicine, 31–32
Hospice care, 58, 60, 61*t*, 73
Hospital-acquired infections, 138–139, 139(*t*8.1)
Hospitals
  acute care beds, by country, 127*t*
  American Hospital Association (AHA), 75
  Caesarean sections, by country, 129*t*
  closings, 42
  consumer satisfaction surveys, 151–152
  cost trends, 83
  emergency department satisfaction, 154(*f*9.8)
  emergency department visits, 41*t*–42*t*, 43*t*–44*t*
  hospital-acquired infections, 138–139, 139(*t*8.1)
  hospitalization reasons, 42–44
  inpatients by age, 45(*f*3.2)
  international utilization rates, 126, 127*t*, 128*t*
  Joint Commission on Accreditation of Healthcare Organizations (JCAHO), 73–74
  malpractice insurance costs, 80–81
  medical error studies, 137
  organ transplants, 45–49
  overview, 1
  procedures, 50*t*
  public opinion, 151–152
  stay lengths, 45(*f*3.1), 49(*f*3.3), 128*t*
  types, 39–42
Hospitals Unplugged: The Wireless Revolution Reaches Healthcare (Wachter), 144
"How Does the Quality of Care Compare in Five Countries?" (Hussey et al.), 127, 129
HRSA (Health Resource and Service Administration), 66

I

IHS (Indian Health Service), 66–67
"The Impact of Direct-to-Consumer Advertising of Prescription Drugs on Consumer Behavior, Diagnosis and Treatment" (Taylor and Leitman), 158
Inpatient care expenditures, by country, 121, 125*t*
Income and insurance coverage, 102, 105–106
Independent practice association model HMOs, 62
Indian Health Service (IHS), 66–67
Infant mortality, by country, 132*t*
Information dissemination, 141–142, 146
Information technology, 143–145
Innovation, 52, 143–146
Institute of Medicine, 138

Insurance, health
  barriers to health care, 4–5
  children's coverage, 108–110
  consumer satisfaction, 153–155, 155*t*
  cost trends, 117
  coverage status, 101–105, 102(*f*6.1)
  elderly persons, 107, 114*t*–116*t*
  geographic regions and, 105–106
  Health Insurance Portability and Accountability Act (HIPAA), 110–114
  health maintenance organizations (HMOs), 60–64
  HIV/AIDS treatment costs, 93
  Medicaid coverage by selected characteristics, 109*t*–110*t*
  Medicaid covered children by race/ethnicity, 113(*f*6.5)
  medical savings accounts, 111–113
  Medigap policies, 93
  preferred provider organizations (PPOs), 64
  private coverage, 106*t*–108*t*, 124*t*
  public opinion on concern over, 151(*f*9.5)
  public opinion on employer-sponsored health plans, 152–153
  report cards, 155–156
  sources, 105–107
  uninsured children by race/ethnicity and age, 113(*f*6.4)
  uninsured persons and poverty, 104*t*
  uninsured persons by age group and sex, 102(*f*6.2)
  uninsured persons by selected characteristics, 103*t*, 111*t*–112*t*
  workers with employment-based insurance, 105*f*
Insurance, malpractice, 80–81
Intensivists, 16
Interactive television, 143–144
Intermediate care facilities (ICFs), 51
International comparisons
  Caesarian sections, 129*t*
  Canadian health care system, 134–135
  cancer rates, 133*t*
  difficulties in, 119
  expenditures as a percentage of gross domestic product, 119–120, 120(*f*7.1)
  French health care system, 135–136
  German health care system, 131–132, 134
  health care costs and quality, 127, 129–132, 134–136
  health expenditure changes as a percentage of gross domestic product, 119–120, 120(*f*7.2)
  hospital utilization, 126, 127*t*, 128*t*
  inpatient care expenditures, 121, 125*t*
  infant mortality, 132*t*
  Japanese health care system, 136
  life expectancy, 131*t*
  out-of-pocket payments for health care by country, 121, 123*t*
  per capita health expenditures, 120, 121*f*
  pharmaceuticals expenditures, 121, 126*t*
  physician/population ratio, 126–127, 130*t*
  private insurance, by country, 121, 124*t*

  public funding, 120–121, 122*t*
  United Kingdom health care system, 135
  United States health care system, 130–131
Internet
  fraud, 142
  health care information, 156–157, 156*t*
  patient-physician consultations, 144

J

Japanese health care system, 136
Jaroff, Leon, 34
Joint Commission on Accreditation of Healthcare Organizations (JCAHO), 73–74, 140

K

Kaiser Health Poll Survey, 9–11
Kennedy-Kassebaum Act. *See* Health Insurance Portability and Accountability Act (HIPAA)

L

Lawsuits
  HMOs, 62–64
  malpractice, 80–81
Leapfrog Group, 139
Legislation
  Balanced Budget Act of 1997, 58, 92
  Health Insurance Portability and Accountability Act (HIPAA), 110–114
  Medicare Modernization Act, 112–113
  Medicare Prescription Drug, Improvement, and Modernization Act, 115–117
  Patient Safety and Quality Improvement Act (pending), 141–142
  Patients' Bill of Rights, 63–64
  Personal Responsibility and Work Opportunity Reconciliation Act, 92, 108
  Tax Equity and Fiscal Responsibility Act, 90
Liability of HMOs, 62–64
Life expectancy, by country, 131*t*
Long-term care
  costs, 92–94
  facilities, 51–55

M

"Major Versus Limited Effort to Help the Uninsured" (Kaiser Family Foundation), 148
Malignant neoplasms. *See* Cancer
Malpractice insurance costs, 80–81
Managed care
  cost control, 82
  disparities, 12–13
  health maintenance organizations (HMOs), 60–64
  National Committee for Quality Assurance (NCQA), 74–75
  See also Health maintenance organizations (HMOs)
March of Dimes, 76
Marine Hospital Service, 67–68